DEMOCRACY, CULTURE, CATHOLICISM

Democracy, Culture, Catholicism

VOICES FROM FOUR CONTINENTS

MICHAEL J. SCHUCK AND JOHN CROWLEY-BUCK

Editors

FORDHAM UNIVERSITY PRESS

New York *2016*

Fordham University Press has no responsibility for the
persistence or accuracy of URLs for external or third-party
Internet websites referred to in this publication and does
not guarantee that any content on such websites is, or will
remain, accurate or appropriate.

Fordham University Press also publishes its books in a
variety of electronic formats. Some content that appears in
print may not be available in electronic books.

Visit us online at www.fordhampress.com.

Library of Congress Cataloging-in-Publication Data

Democracy, culture, Catholicism : voices from four continents /
edited by Michael J. Schuck and John Crowley-Buck. —
First edition.
pages   cm
Includes bibliographical references and index.
ISBN 978-0-8232-6730-9 (cloth : alk. paper) —
ISBN 978-0-8232-6885-6 (pbk. : alk. paper)
1. Democracy—Religious aspects—Catholic Church.
2. Christianity and culture.   I. Schuck, Michael Joseph, 1953– editor.
BX1793.D38   2016
261.7088'282—dc23
2015017363

Printed in the United States of America

18 17 16   5 4 3 2 1

First edition

In loving memory of our colleagues
Christina Handayani, PhD
Jeffrey L. Klaiber, SJ

CONTENTS

Introduction

Michael J. Schuck

This volume is the result of the Democracy, Culture, and Catholicism International Research Project (DCCIRP), a three-year project led by the Joan and Bill Hank Center for the Catholic Intellectual Heritage at Loyola University Chicago. The twenty-three chapters in this volume explore dynamic relationships between democracy, culture, and Catholicism in the modern world. The volume pays special attention to the shifting interplay between these features of life in four diverse countries: Lithuania, Indonesia, Peru, and the United States. Why explore these three features and why focus on these four countries?

As part of its mission to encourage new scholarship in Catholic studies, the Joan and Bill Hank Center invited scholars in 2010 to participate in research on the relationship between Catholicism and politics. The widespread discussion of Samuel Huntington's book, *The Third Wave: Democratization in the Late Twentieth Century*, as well as the Occupy Wall Street movement and the Arab Spring, further suggested the value of narrowing the project's political focus to the phenomenon of democracy. At the same time, Pope Benedict XVI's 2009 encyclical *Caritas in veritate* redoubled the Catholic Church's longstanding critique of consumer culture and its toxic effect on the practice of citizenship in civic life. This development suggested adding culture to the project's mix of research foci.

As the DCCIRP's vision was being refined, Jesuit institutions of higher education were encouraged by the superior general of the Society of Jesus, Adolfo Nicolás, to collaborate in creating international research projects. In response to this request, the DCCIRP solicited participation from scholars working at Jesuit universities around the world. Existing collaborations between Loyola University Chicago and Universitas Sanata Dharma in Yogyakarta, Indonesia, and Universidad Antonio Ruiz de Montoya in Lima, Peru, helped engage faculty at those institutions. Lithuanian Catholic scholars were connected with the project through encouragement from the Jesuit Curia in Rome and the Jesuit community in Vilnius.

It soon became apparent that the four countries of Indonesia, Lithuania, Peru, and the United States offered a rich and instructive comparison regarding the relationship between democracy, culture, and Catholicism. Since the nineteenth century, each nation had experienced episodes of political, social, and religious oppression, oscillating between periods of liberation, tolerance, and religious freedom. Yet, each country's experience of this oscillation was unique. With four societies of such unique histories and ethnographies, the project organizers felt the variable intersections of democracy, culture, and Catholicism offered here would bear fruit for anyone interested in the relationship between politics, society, and religion in the contemporary world.

The DCCIRP Process

Once the research focus was sufficiently identified, the Joan and Bill Hank Center issued an interdisciplinary call for papers to scholars interested in conducting new research concerning democracy, culture, and Catholicism. Specific research topics were not suggested in the call for papers; rather, an open approach was taken in order to cast a wide net and encourage scholars who might be approaching research in this area for the first time. Project applications were received and evaluated. From them, thirty-one proposals were accepted. The approved projects represented scholars from four countries, fourteen academic disciplines, and four religious traditions. A truly multicultural, interdisciplinary, and interreligious group of scholars was assembled.

Project members first met in 2010 at a three-day workshop held at Loyola University Chicago. Most participants admitted knowing little about the political and cultural history of their colleagues' home countries. For example, many in the group learned for the first time about the impact of Peru's Sendero Luminoso, the exact boundaries of Indonesia, what Soviet rule had meant for day-to-day life in Lithuania, and why North American religious women could be so outspoken. The connections created at this workshop initiated professional and personal relationships that would grow throughout the project.

In the DCCIRP's second year, participants gathered for regional colloquia at Universitas Sanata Dharma in Yogyakarta, Indonesia, Vilnius University in Vilnius, Lithuania, and Universidad Antonio Ruiz de Montoya in Lima, Peru. These meetings were invaluable. Here, project scholars presented and discussed first drafts of their research among themselves, with students, and before visitors from the general public. The colloquia also gave participants an opportunity to experience practical intersections of democracy, culture, and Catholicism in each country. In the Indonesian jungle village of Samigaluh, participants shared a sacred meal with local farmers and participated in musyawarah, Indonesia's indigenous form of democratic discussion. In Peru, participants walked the steep and narrow street leading to the El Agustino childcare center. Here, on the outskirts of Lima, barrio women bravely maintained an island of hope for children living in a sea of stark poverty and gang violence. In an unforgettable evening at the Lietuvių Katalikų Mokslo Akademija in Vilnius, Lithuania, project members heard first-hand narratives from their Lithuanian colleagues on what it meant to defend faith and culture during the long nightmare of Soviet occupation.

In year three, DCCIRP members met for a final time at the Pontificia Università Gregoriana in Rome. For three days, participants delivered abstracts of their completed research projects and responded to questions from students, visiting scholars, and their DCCIRP partners. When asked for an exemplary intersection of democracy, culture, and Catholicism in the world today, one participant pointed to the group itself. In the interdisciplinary, multicultural, interfaith, and personal bonds formed among DCCIRP participants, a small but powerful witness was given to what is possible for the interplay between Catholicism and politics in the future.

Organization

Twenty-two of the thirty-one DCCIRP research projects appear in this volume, with the addition of an epilogue by co-editor Michael Schuck. The nine projects that do not appear here can be found on the DCCIRP website: http://luc.edu/dccirp/.

The volume is divided into five sections: Lithuanian Voices, Indonesian Voices, Peruvian Voices, US Voices, and Global Interpretations. Each section has an introductory overview by co-editor John Crowley-Buck. With the exception of the concluding section, each section ends with a note by Crowley-Buck introducing each section's final chapter or chapters, as in the case of the Lithuanian Voices.

Readers can approach the chapters in this volume in several ways. Some readers may wish to focus on one or more of the featured countries, others may wish to follow themes that emerge through the sequence of chapters, and still others may prefer to concentrate on chapters written from the perspective of a particular academic discipline. As noted above, introductory remarks are given in the volume for each set of chapters grouped by country. Therefore, the remainder of this introduction will suggest themes that can be followed across the entire volume. It will conclude with brief remarks about reading the chapters with particular academic disciplines in mind.

Themes

From the several themes that arise within these twenty-three chapters, eight are offered here in order to open up the volume. The eight themes highlight different directions of influence between the features under study: from democracy to culture and Catholicism, from culture to Catholicism and democracy, from Catholicism to democracy and culture.

From Democracy to Culture and Catholicism

While the story of Catholicism's gradual acceptance of democracy from the nineteenth to the twentieth century is a central thread in this volume, a much-cited theme throughout several of the chapters is the impact this acceptance has had on Catholicism itself. Here, a seemingly contrary reality surfaces. Despite acceptance of democracy in official Catholic social teaching, old divisions continue to exist within the Church over the merits of democracy.

Arūnas Streikus notes these divisions in the history of Lithuanian Catholicism. The European legacy of "hard" secularism that accompanied democracy in the manner of French laïcité is no doubt part of the wariness that some Lithuanian Catholics have held against democratization. Russell Powell's chapter offers a fascinating parallel between this and a similar experience in Islam, where the same wariness is felt among some Turkish

Muslims. Nevertheless, Powell imagines an opportunity for the future of the relationship between Islam and democracy based on a comparison with the Catholic experience, where most Catholics have come to see the possibility of retaining their faith tradition within democracies of "soft" secularism. In this case, religions need to restrict religious speech and action in the public sphere that contradict the principles of democracy, while states need to ensure that citizens may expressly draw from their religious traditions in speech and actions that accept the principles of democracy. David Ingram's chapter offers an excellent analysis of this delicate issue across each country included in this volume.

Catholic division over democracy manifests somewhat differently for the Peruvian authors. As María Soledad Escalante, Gonzalo Gamio, and Oscar Espinosa reveal, the Spanish colonial legacy continues to echo through Peru's stubborn class divisions. For Peruvian Catholics in possession of political power, democratization can threaten the social status quo. For Peruvians without political power, democratization is a sign of hope. Endorsement of democracy in official Catholic teaching has not completely erased this class division inside or outside the Church.

Class division may not seem a likely tool for an analysis of democracy and American Catholicism. Yet, in his provocative chapter on racism and incarceration rates in the United States, William O'Neill points to a serious divide within the American Roman Catholic community over the meaning of criminal justice in a democratic society. From a different angle, Bren Ortega Murphy and Barry Sullivan suggest how the issues of the status of women in the Church and the clerical sexual abuse scandal disclose Catholic divisions over the merits of democracy in America. In these cases, the issues raise the contentious question of democratization within the Church itself.

A second theme concerning the influence of democracy on culture and Catholicism is the motivation its ideals have provided for the formation of cultural and Catholic social movements. The Lithuanian youth movement Ateitis is an outstanding example cited by Streikus. Paulus Wiryono Priyotamtama details a similar case for the Ikatan Petani Pancasila movement in Indonesia. Jorge Aragón also makes this point for the relationship between politics and religion in South America, while Jeffrey Klaiber highlights how the ideal of democracy found expression in the peasant comunidades de base movement. Murphy's chapter also contributes to this theme as it describes the impact of democratic values on the contribution of religious women in the fight for gender equity during the second wave feminist movement in the United States.

From Culture to Catholicism and Democracy

Democracies incubate within what cultural anthropologist Clifford Geertz called the ensemble of "symbolic forms by means of which [people] communicate, perpetuate, and develop their knowledge about and attitudes toward life,"[1] or, put more concisely, within culture. For Geertz, religion is a fundamental dimension of culture, and he famously defined it as "a (1) system of symbols which acts to (2) establish powerful, pervasive, and long-lasting moods and motivations in [people] by (3) formulating conceptions of a general order of existence and (4) clothing these conceptions with such an aura of factuality that (5) the moods and motivations seem uniquely realistic."[2] Religions sustain culture by mediating a people's beliefs about their connection to the universe (their cosmology), the nature of the domain they inhabit (their worldview), and their rules for living in both (their norms). From this perspective, an enculturated democracy always assimilates a measure of religion. A people's cosmology, worldview, and norms cannot be utterly sealed off from their political ideas, desires, and practices.

Geertz's understandings of culture and religion and their implications for democracy are mentioned here to contextualize three more interesting themes in these chapters. The first theme is the function that social trust plays in culture and the impact this has on Catholicism and democracy. The second theme concerns the opposite: the effect of social trauma on a nation's religious and political life. A third theme concerns the cultural role of memory for both religion and politics.

Several authors allude to the necessity of a culture of trust for a functioning democracy and the degree to which a Catholic religious worldview can facilitate that trust. Paulus Wiryono's chapter explains how trust works for village farmer collectives and nonprofit organizations in Indonesia. Klaiber cites the need for a democratically inspired cultural mediator between governments and the people in South America and the new non-patronizing role the Church could play in this regard. He imagines an increase in this Church function if citizen support for the new populist regimes (e.g., Venezuela, Ecuador, and Bolivia) weakens. In her fascinating chapter about Catholic religious women in the United States, Murphy shows how religious women understood their role as cultural mediators between democratic government and the Catholic immigrant population.

From the opposite direction, Danutė Gailienė raises the second theme by detailing the psychological trauma in Lithuanian society that resulted from fifty years of systematic Soviet oppression and torture. Nerija Putinaitė argues that even after the collapse of the Soviet Union and the recovery of freedom in Lithuania, the cultural trust necessary for a functioning democracy remains deeply broken. Marcia Hermansen points out how the social trauma occasioned by the 9/11 attacks in the United States and the subsequent "war on terror" affected the democratic treatment of Muslims in the United States and Europe. These events "[exacerbated] the fear of Muslims as outsiders and their treatment as unequal citizens" in the United States and Europe.

Memory is vital for a people to tell its cultural narrative, the storied form of a society's cosmology, worldview, and norms. In his chapter, Gonzalo Gamio analyzes the religious and cultural destruction that comes from perverse attempts by individuals and groups seeking to preserve or gain political power to erase or distort a society's memory. From a completely different angle, Albertus Budi Susanto describes kethoprak theater in Indonesia. Among its many social functions, kethoprak draws on traditional cultural stories of ancient kings and royal families to criticize contemporary injustices in Indonesian politics. As a "subversive" art, kethoprak "gives democratic voice to the social and political frustrations of the Indonesian people."

From Catholicism to Democracy and Culture

At least three important themes surface in the chapters regarding the impact of Catholicism on democracy and culture. The first concerns Catholic political participation, the second highlights the role of Catholic social teaching on democratization, and the third notes the important political role played by Catholic leaders in all three countries.

On the matter of Catholic political participation, Streikus's chapter shows the social tenacity with which Lithuanian Catholics worked for democratization in the twentieth century, contrasted with the weakening of this energy by the beginning of the twenty-first century. Putinaitė reiterates this observation; Baskara Wardaya identifies this trend in Indonesia, and Klaiber sees it across the whole of South America.

These authors locate the causes of this weakening within a combination of complex cultural factors. These factors include both a lack of effective Church leadership and increased privatization of the faith. To this last point, Vidmantas Šimkunas makes the important and nuanced claim that the illegality of publicly expressed religious faith in Lithuania during the Soviet era necessitated privatization. According to Šimkunas, privatization both strengthened and weakened faith in Lithuania, complicating the religious and cultural picture even further.

In his discussion of Soviet repression, Streikus touches on a second theme related to the influence of Catholicism on democracy and culture. Streikus points out the important role documents of Catholic social teaching played in keeping democratic hopes alive in Lithuania. Streikus writes, "Catholic social teaching constituted a large obstacle for the Sovietization of society at large," in the "circumstances of totalitarian dictatorship, such letters were one of the few sources of alternative information that carried moral authority and a worldview not distorted by Soviet propaganda."

The crucial impact of Catholic social teaching in Peru is discussed by Espinosa and Jorge Aragón. Robert John Araujo notes the role of Church social teaching in the formation of the United Nations. Peter Schraeder also cites the impact of Catholic social teaching on the Third Wave of Democracy during the 1970s and 1980s, as does Francisca Ninik Yudianti in terms of Indonesian corporate social responsibility. It is a commonplace among North American Catholics to refer to the documents of Catholic social teaching as the Church's "best kept secret" (so named by Peter Henriot in his 1985 book of the same title). The broader scope of Church experience conveyed in this volume suggests, however, that Catholic social teaching has not been as secret as once imagined.

A third theme is the critical role of courageous Catholic leaders in advancing democracy in many national cultures. Sister Nijole Sadunaite in Lithuania (Šimkunas), Bishop Soegijapranata (Wardaya) and John Dijkstra, SJ (Wiryono) in Indonesia, Brother Paul McAuley and Monsignor Paco Gonzales (Espinosa) in Peru, and Sister Anita Caspary (Murphy) in the United States are but a few of the individuals discussed throughout the volume. David Posner draws this topic back four hundred years, to the thought of Michel de Montaigne. Though not a Catholic leader in the formal sense, Montaigne's position on religious tolerance was certainly a courageous one for its time. Posner's ingenious analysis of Montaigne's "De la liberté de conscience" is a compelling discussion that bears on contemporary debates over tolerance and inclusiveness in democratic societies.

The several themes under each of the above categories do not exhaust the multiplicity of issues that move across the chapters in this volume. Nor do they identify the specific theses argued within each chapter. Rather, they provide an initial introduction to the authors in this volume and to some of the large issues raised by the interplay between democracy, culture, and Catholicism in their chapters.

Missing Elements

Readers will also notice that some significant issues do not receive attention in this volume. For example, one-fifth of Lithuania's population has left the country since it gained independence from the Soviet Union in 1990. Most of the migrants have been between the ages of 20 and 29.[3] This demographic will surely have a powerful impact on the relative strengths and intersections of democracy, culture, and Catholicism in Lithuania.

Scientists estimate that Indonesia's vast rainforest—the third largest in the world—will be deforested in twenty years. Without a citizen vote or referendum, Indonesia's democratic government has given over the country's precious resources to global agribusiness and paper, pulp, and palm oil industries. Sensing disaster, the government has lately issued moratoria on deforestation, but most analysts consider this too late.[4] Today's environmental challenges in Indonesia and around the world are forcing not only a deep rethinking of democracy's functionality in times of ecological crisis but also the response (and responsibility) of culture and Catholicism.

Economic analysts estimate that Peru's booming economy will grow between 4 and 5 percent over the next five years. If true, this will be better than most countries in South America. Yet, the chasm between rich and poor in Peru grows ever deeper. In rural areas, Peru's poverty rate is 54 percent; in Lima it is 15 percent. This is further complicated by the legacy of colonial racism. The poor are largely the dark-skinned indigenous people, while the rich are mostly white.[5]

This issue of racism especially haunts democracy in the United States. In this volume, O'Neill rightly identifies the racism at the heart of America's thirty-year system of mass incarceration. But much more could—and needs—to be said about America's structural racism in the overall culture and in the specific areas of health care, employment, housing, and electoral politics.

Reading with Academic Disciplines

The interdisciplinary nature of the DCCIRP means that these chapters can also be resources for scholars in specific fields. Historians will find the chapters by Streikus, Wardaya, Klaiber, and Murphy informative on the unique interplay of democracy, culture, and Catholicism in Lithuania, Indonesia, South America, and the United States. The chapters by Wiryono on Indonesian *musyawarah*, Susanto on kethoprak theater, Espinosa on the indigenous people of Amazonia, and Posner on the "Other" in Montaigne will be of interest to scholars in cultural anthropology and cultural studies.

For political scientists, rich insights on the questions of religious language and civic discourse in democratic societies occur in the chapters by Putinaitė, Powell, and Ingram. The chapters by Escalante, Aragón, Sullivan, Araujo, and Schraeder will be of interest to political scientists and political philosophers specializing in both the influence of religion on society and church-state relations.

Social psychologists and social philosophers will discover new resources in Gailienė's work on political trauma and Gamio's treatment of political memory. Theologians, Christian ethicists, and religious studies scholars have creative treatments of social martyrdom, Catholic social teaching, and Muslim-Christian relations in the chapters by Šimkunas, Yudianti, O'Neill, and Hermansen.

In whatever manner readers put this volume to use, it is the authors' and editors' hope that as they move through the chapters, readers will draw on the comparisons, contrasts, and themes in order to hone their own understandings of democracy, culture, and Catholicism—and their optimal interplay—in the contemporary world. Such work will be the real fruit of the DCCIRP.

The photograph on the cover is the Hill of Crosses near the city of Šiauliai, in northern Lithuania. Since the nineteenth century, the Hill of Crosses has symbolized the cultural endurance and democratic aspirations of Lithuanian Catholics across periods of great political oppression. During the years of Soviet control, Lithuanians risked their lives under cover of darkness to plant crosses in defiance of their political and religious oppression. Today, the Hill of Crosses attracts pilgrims from all over the world to view its estimated 100,000 crosses—an apt symbol for the intersection of democracy, culture, and Catholicism explored in this volume.

NOTES

1. Clifford Geertz, *The Interpretation of Cultures* (New York: Basic Books, 1973), 89. Geertz's now classic definitions of culture and religion have, of course, undergone intense academic criticism over the past forty years. An able summary of these debates is given in Kevin Schilbrack, "Religion, Models of, and Reality: Are We Through with Geertz," *Journal of the American Academy of Religion* 73, no. 2 (2005): 429–52.

2. Geertz, *Interpretation of Cultures*, 90.

3. Aiste Marija Augustinaite, "Lithuanian Youth Emigration" (master's thesis, Leiden University, 2013), https://openaccess.leidenuniv.nl/bitstream/handle/1887/21557/Augustinaitethesis.pdf?sequence=3.

4. John Vidal, "The Sumatran Rainforest Will Mostly Disappear in Twenty Years," *Observer*, May 26, 2013, http://www.theguardian.com/world/2013/may/26/sumatra-borneo-deforestation-tigers-palm-oil.

5. Maria Arana, "Peru's Poor," *New York Times*, Op. Ed., March 20, 2013, http://opinionator.blogs.nytimes.com/2013/03/20/perus-poor/?_r=0.

Lithuanian Voices

When looking at the relationships between democracy, culture, and Catholicism within the Lithuanian context, what immediately comes to the fore are interactions characterized by trauma, distrust, and tragedy. The origins of this bleak picture can be traced back to Lithuania's history, to the decades this nation and its people spent alternating under the rule of Soviet, Nazi, and (again) Soviet occupation. The themes of trauma and distrust come out clearly in the chapters included in this section. The concepts of democracy, culture, and Catholicism, so foundational to the objectives of this book, remain indeterminate in the Lithuanian context. This is because each of these concepts, along with myriad others, have been repeatedly manipulated by both Nazi and Soviet propaganda, on the one hand, and different interest groups within and outside of Lithuania, on the other. The fallout from such indeterminacy is widespread distrust between individuals and between persons and institutions. This widespread distrust results in a traumatized form of political and civil identity. The tragedy of the Lithuanian context is that there does not seem to be a belief, or even a consensus on the possibility of belief, that this situation will find a remedy any time soon.

Arūnas Streikus offers some key insights into the relationships between democracy, culture, and Catholicism in the pre-Soviet, Nazi, Soviet, and post-Soviet contexts. Streikus's insights into the Lithuanian experience, and the conditions that have given rise to these very volatile conditions, are illuminative. He suggests that even basic discussions about democracy, culture, and Catholicism in Lithuania are difficult to undertake since different oppressive powers have repeatedly used and abused these concepts. This inability to trust even basic linguistic concepts has had a ripple effect in contemporary Lithuania, creating an intersubjective paralysis that one can see explored by each author in this section.

Vidmantas Šimkunas offers a theological interpretation of the history and the contemporary situation identified by Streikus. While he acknowledges the difficult situation in which contemporary Lithuanians find themselves, he suggests that there may be resources available to Lithuanians within the traditions and beliefs of the Catholic Church for reclaiming and reanimating their individual and national identities. As a crucible of resistance against the occupying Nazi and Soviet forces, the underground Lithuanian Catholic Church became the place where Lithuanian history, culture, and religiosity were preserved. Through the Catholic categories of *martyria*, *koinonia*, *diakonia*, and *leiturgia*, Šimkunas re-narrates the history of the Lithuanian struggle in the twentieth century in a way that offers both a reinterpretation of the suffering of past generations and an attempt to re-imagine the possibility of Lithuanian religiosity for future ones.

Danutė Gailienė recounts the history of occupation in Lithuania and narrates a story of traumatization for the Lithuanian people. The occupying forces in Lithuania in the twentieth century ruled by fear and deception and thus conditioned the Lithuanian people to live an almost paranoid existence—a "double life." Faith and trust were impossible, because anyone could be a Soviet informant. The potential repercussions for overt signs of political, social, or religious engagement were economic sanctions, physical torture, and life-long deportation to worker camps in Siberia. Even in the short run, living conditions like these can have a lasting effect on both the individual and collective imagination; to live under these conditions for over half a century, as many Lithuanians did, is almost impossible to imagine. The future of Lithuania and the Lithuanian people depends on its ability to come to terms with its traumatic history, but that history has still not fully become known.

Nerija Putinaitė asks the question: Does post-Soviet democracy in Lithuania need Christianity? While it is her belief that post-Soviet nations would benefit from the common, normative standards for society, politics, and religion offered by Christianity, she thinks these benefits will not be reaped because the trauma and mistrust conditioned into the psyche of the Lithuanian people runs too deep. In line with Gailienė, Putinaitė fears that the traumatic history of the "double life" phenomenon in Lithuania cannot be undone, at least in the near future. There does remain a glimmer of hope for a renewal of Christianity in the Lithuanian public square, as the Christian churches did play a vital role in preserving Lithuanian identity during the Soviet occupation. Yet, in the end, Putinaitė remains skeptical that this hope can be brought to fruition in the near future.

Democracy and Catholicism in Twentieth-Century Lithuania

Arūnas Streikus

Lithuania, like many other countries of Eastern Europe, has a very complicated story of democratization during the twentieth century. It is the story of a people who underwent staggering shifts from national independence to German occupation to horrifying Soviet oppression to reacquired freedom in less than one hundred years. The following overview divides this stunning narrative into four periods: 1905–1926, 1927–1939, 1940–1969, and 1970–1990.

Between Catholic Action and Christian Democracy (1905–1926)

After the collapse of the Russian Empire in 1918, Lithuania began its first modern experiment in democratic governance. This involved efforts at free elections, proportional representation, a strong legislative branch, and a multiparty system. However, after only eight years of democratic effort, the Lithuanian state devolved into an authoritarian regime emphasizing nationalist values. To understand why Lithuania retreated so quickly from the path of democratic development, it is necessary to see how the ideals of Christian Democracy functioned between 1918 and 1926.

The end of the nineteenth century marked major changes in the attitude of the Roman Catholic Church toward the modern world. Statements in the encyclicals of Pope Leo XIII (especially *Immortale Dei* in 1885, *Rerum novarum* in 1891, and *Graves de communi* in 1901) indicated a gradual recognition of democratic values by the Catholic Church. The statements acknowledged the value of citizen freedom in the political sphere, the importance of group deliberation and decision-making in worker associations, the existence of human rights in society, and the modern movement of Christian Democracy. With some delay, this recognition reached Lithuania where public bans on printing in the Lithuanian alphabet and forming Lithuanian cultural organizations still existed. With the lifting of these bans the ideas of Christian Democracy found their first expression in Lithuanian periodicals and special courses organized to explore the social teaching of the Church.

Though not intended by Pope Leo XIII, the concept of Christian Democracy encouraged the development of specifically Catholic political parties in Lithuania. The first program of the Lithuanian Christian Democratic Party (LCDP) in 1918, for example, sought to implement the principles of Catholic social teaching in Lithuanian society through political activities. These principles included the mutual rights and duties of workers and employers in society and the responsibility of public authority to support the common good. Reflecting the atmosphere of the political upheavals that followed the crash of the Russian Empire and in order to counter communist propaganda, the LCDP proposed a progressive social program. At the core of the program was land reform with the distribution of large estates. The hope was that this reform would strengthen small- and medium-sized farms that would be a strong pillar of democratic culture. It is noteworthy that the social reforms proposed by the LCDP had strong opposition from conservative clergy and representatives of the Holy See. Only through the support of Vilnius bishop Jurgis Matulaitis (later Blessed) were these reforms supported by the majority of the Catholic community.

Confusion existed in many people's minds over the relationship between the Catholic Church, with its many pastoral, fraternal, and community organizations, and the political party that claimed association with Catholic teaching. If one were a Catholic, did this require allegiance with the so-called Catholic party? The strong inclination to treat all Catholic organizations as linked to a Catholic political party was characteristic of the LCDP in the first years of the independence.[1] Such an understanding was reinforced by the fact that clergy played the decisive role in Catholic political activity at this time. Catholic laypeople were not prepared to take on these roles. As a result, priests occupied influential positions in the party's local and national executive bodies and also used their access to Catholic people and organizations in parishes to recruit members to the LCDP. In the end, this strong clericalism strengthened neither the LCDP nor the authority of the Church in Lithuanian society. The initial support enjoyed by the LCDP dropped from election to election. In 1920, Catholics had 52 percent of the seats in the Constituent Seimas. By 1926 the percentage had shrunk to 35.[2]

There is no doubt that the first constitution adopted in 1922 by the Constituent Seimas under guidance of the LCDP was a democratic charter. It secured cultural autonomy for national minorities (especially the Jewish community), which contributed a great deal to minority group support of the state. The constitution also gave the National Diet a central place in governance. However, this strong parliamentary model lacked a counterweight in the executive power, a feature that would later cause frequent crises in the political system.

Another characteristic of interwar public life in Lithuanian was the passionate ideological battles over competing worldviews. The main opponents were Catholics, liberal nationalists, and socialists. On gaining political power, each group sought uncompromising reorganization of public affairs according to their worldview. Catholics in the first half of 1920s secured favorable conditions for the Church's domination in spiritual matters. Compulsory religious education was introduced into primary and secondary schools and the Church was entrusted with registry of births and marriages, with no separate civil registry. This gave evidence to the fact that while the Catholic Church was coming to support certain democratic principles in society, it still preferred governments that gave it the status of a state church.[3]

In the spring of 1926, parliamentary elections were held and a leftist government came to power. The regime quickly launched an anti-clerical campaign, refusing to acknowledge newly established Church dioceses, cutting off payments of salaries to priests, and proposing to close the theological-philosophical faculty in the Lithuanian university.[4] Fearing even more vigorous attacks on the Church, most Catholics did not resist the December 1926 coup d'état that replaced the leftist government with an authoritarian military regime. The ill-fated hope was that after the political situation stabilized, democracy would be restored and Christian Democrats would return to power.

These events reveal the limited ability of the LCDP to foster democracy across Lithuanian society during this period. It embraced social reforms but not the principles required for the creation of a truly democratic culture. It must also be recognized that even with Pope Leo XIII's rapprochement toward democracy, many in the Catholic community did not support democracy. Thus, even if the LCDP was a rare and brave exception among European Catholic parties to use the word "democratic" in its title, its commitment to democracy was tactical, not principled.

Catholics during the Years of Authoritarian Rule (1927–1939)

At first, the new authoritarian regime based on a nationalistic ideology was benevolent toward the Catholic Church. Trying to strengthen its position internally and abroad, the regime signed a concordat with the Holy See in 1927 confirming compulsory religious instruction in the schools, state funding for the Church, and freedom for lay Catholic organizations. The majority of Church leadership was satisfied with the new situation.

This harmony began to disintegrate in the early 1930s. Seeking to curtail political activities of the LCDP, the government extended its restrictions to activities of non-political Catholic organizations and pastoral ministries. There was still no clear understanding in Lithuania of the distinction between the political activities of Catholics and the pastoral and community work lay Catholics performed as part of Catholic Action.[5] Thus, when the public activities of the LCDP were restricted, this restriction extended to the activities of Catholic organizations belonging to Catholic Action. This restriction was a violation of the 1927 concordat. Nevertheless, the political authorities could not tolerate broad, autonomous Catholic activity because the state's ideal was a political community consolidated around and subordinate to the state.

Foremost among state concerns was the reduction of Church influence in the upbringing of young people. A key decision in this field was the decree forbidding activities of all Catholic youth organizations in secondary schools. This was interpreted by Catholics as an effort to end the activities of the Ateitis movement. The Ateitis was the strongest democratically oriented youth organization in Lithuania. It consisted of three sections: the union of schoolchildren, the union of university students, and the union of professionals. The authoritarian regime feared this organization as the main *formateur* of socially and politically active Catholic intellectuals.

In spite of persecution by police and school administrators, Ateitis members continued their activities clandestinely. Their resistance hindered the authoritarian regime in its efforts to monopolize the formation

of youth and also converted large sections of Catholic society to true fighters for democratic ideals of civil government.

Some Catholic intellectuals and activists pointed out the similarity
between the rhetoric of the authoritarian regime in Lithuania and that of
the totalitarian fascist regimes in Italy and Germany. These Catholics tried
to show that the official rhetoric of national unity actually concealed a dictatorship of one party and that such rhetoric often hid a complete neglect
for the rights of individuals and national minorities. Many Lithuanian
nationalists supported the model of society promoted by Italian fascists, so
Catholic critics in Lithuania had to work hard to show the incompatibility
of this model with Christian values.[6]

The economic and political crises of the 1930s gave impetus for the
further development of Catholic social teaching. Pope Pius XI addressed
the new challenges in his 1931 encyclical *Quadragesimo anno*. There, the
pope supported reforms leading to the emergence of the modern social
state and put forward the principle of subsidiarity, which stressed the role
of human organizations and communities as mediators between the individual and the state.[7] These new ideas of social Catholicism were further
developed by leading Catholic philosophers of the time, such as Jacques
Maritain, whose democratic principles were very influential among young
intellectuals in Lithuania.

The 1930s saw a vivid rise in Catholic intellectual life in Lithuania.
Genuinely new ideas were proposed for the sake of building democracy
and resisting totalitarianism. In 1936, for example, a declaration entitled
Towards the Creation of an Organic State was signed and published by sixteen
young Catholic intellectuals. Though the term "organic state" was part of
fascist rhetoric, the authors differentiated their use of the phrase from that
of the fascists. The declaration offered a corporative system as an important way to facilitate democratic institutions. It stated:

> this corporative order is opposite to the pseudo-corporatism, which
> serves as a tool or ruling of one group or as a cover to abolish public
> liberties. Corporatism offered here is based not on the state but on
> associations and is growing organically from conditions of life in our
> country.[8]

The central point of corporatism for these young Catholic intellectuals
was the notion of cultural autonomy. This notion was linked to the aforementioned principle of subsidiarity: as social beings, people are united in a
variety of religious, ethnic, civic, and professional communities whose
freedom must be respected. The state should not restrict the activities of

these communities and organizations, but should ensure their moral freedom to exist and thrive. Of special concern to the authors of the declaration was full liberty for confessional schools and schools of national minorities.

The declaration stood in contradiction to the general trend of Lithuania's political evolution at the time. Just a few weeks before the publication of the declaration a new law of associations was promulgated that strengthened state control over the activities of public organizations. The new constitution adopted in 1938 also moved further away from democratic principles. For example, political candidates could no longer emerge from political parties. Instead, candidates had to be selected by local authorities linked to the ruling government. However, the authoritarian regime was not yet strong enough to subdue the Catholic opposition.

The effort of Lithuanian Catholic intellectuals and organizations was to preserve a distinct and free Catholic milieu in a society where politics was growing increasingly authoritarian. This effort was not in terms of an appeal to universal human rights; such an appeal would not develop in Catholic social thought until the middle of the twentieth century. Rather, the effort was rooted in an appeal to the freedom of the Catholic Church and its members to engage in social activity for the common good. This pressure against the state did have the effect of strengthening the organizational abilities of the Catholic community and it did prepare the community to embrace democratic principles in the future.

The Challenges of Nazism and Sovietization (1940–1969)

Lithuanian society was shocked by the loss of statehood and rough introduction of the Soviet order in 1940. In the Catholic community, this shock was most quickly replaced by efforts to preserve the structure of their organizations and adjust them for the new tasks of resistance.[9] This resistance was greatly assisted by the ongoing Ateitis movement. Members of the movement played the decisive role in the 1941 Lithuanian uprising that occurred during the first days of Germany's declaration of war against the Soviet Union. Although most of the Lithuanian Catholic elite counted on help from Germany to restore independence from the Soviet Union, there were not few who were skeptical about this orientation toward Nazi Germany.

It soon became clear that Germany would neglect Lithuanian national interests. The Provisional Government raised by the uprising was in danger of being used as a tool of the Nazis, who started the massive extermination of Jews after invading territories of the Soviet Union. In the face of such developments, many Lithuanian Catholics refused to collaborate with the new occupants and joined anti-Nazi resistance. Already in September 1941, Juozas Brazaitis attempted to collect signatures of eminent persons in protest of the killings of Jews.[10] Brazaitis later became the central figure in the Catholic anti-Nazi resistance.

Nevertheless, the public position of the Catholic Church during the Nazi occupation of Lithuania was very cautious. Lithuanian bishops did not publicly question the ideology or legitimacy of German rule. By highlighting the dangers of communism and remaining silent on Nazi atrocities, the bishops indirectly backed German rule. In the spring of 1943, auxiliary bishop Vincentas Brizgys of Kaunas and other priests went so far as to sign appeals exhorting men not to escape conscription to the Wehrmacht. Such conciliatory attitudes and actions were occasionally criticized in the Catholic underground periodicals that pointed out the incompatibility between Nazism and Catholicism.

The most significant test for the democratic values of Lithuanian Catholics during the short period of Nazi occupation was their attitude toward the Holocaust. In the face of the extermination of the Lithuanian Jewish community and the ongoing anti-Semitic sentiments, some Catholics felt a duty to offer aid for the persecuted. Their Church leaders, however, never directly condemned the persecution of Jews.[11] There are only a few cases where public appeals of the bishops intimated concern for the Jews. For instance, a 1941 pastoral letter by bishop Justinas Staugaitis of Telšiai states:

> Let us also not forget that each individual, whether a fellow-
> countryman or a stranger, a friend or not a friend, is a child of the
> same God, and therefore our brother. If he suffers, it is our duty to
> help him. Naturally, the world cannot be ruled only by love, justice
> is also needed. If someone does wrong, they have to be precluded
> from that and punished. But the appropriate institutions of the public
> authorities will do that. Let God save you from revenge and licence.[12]

Much more evidence exists for individual cases where priests publicly condemned Lithuanians who participated in the killings of Jews. Also, many places in Catholic institutions and organizations (e.g., rectories, convents, and children's shelters) were used to hide Jews.[13]

Catholic underground activities organized during the Nazi occupation later transformed into the armed resistance movement against Soviet rule that began in 1944. New research shows the strength and importance of such resistance movements across Europe and the importance this had for the shaping of the postwar political and social order. Lithuanian guerrilla fighters were an important element within this broader European phenomenon. As stated by Bernardas Gailius, "The striving for peace, democracy, Western culture and good-living was no less familiar to the Lithuanian guerrilla fighters than it was to their counterparts in Western Europe."[14]

The discovery of an affinity between the Eastern and Western guerrilla fighters contradicts the view of some Western scholars who treat the partisan wars of Eastern Europe as a phenomenon of premodern, rural societies.[15] At the same time, the claim of Gailius that contemporary Europe emerged out of the spirit of "guerrilla Europe" is weak. Germany, one of the pillars of postwar Europe, did not emerge out of a guerrilla resistance movement. A more likely proposition is that Catholic social teaching inspired the designers of the new Europe and provided a uniting basis for their thought.

Networks of Catholic youth organizations were important tools for mobilizing guerrilla fighters in Lithuania. Among the leaders of the guerrilla fighters were people active in the Ateitis movement before the occupations. The surviving structures of Catholic youth organizations offered useful mechanisms for recruiting members into the guerrilla opposition. Ordinary priests also played a vital role in the first phase of the partisan war by defining the ideology of guerrilla fighters in terms of the principles of Catholic social teaching. For example, the Council of the Movement of the Struggle for Freedom of Lithuania declared on February 16, 1949:

> The Council, joining in the efforts of other nations to create universally a constant peace founded upon justice and freedom, drawing support from a full implementation of the true principles of democracy stemming from an understanding of Christian morality and declared in the Atlantic Charter, Four Freedoms, President Truman's 12 Points, the Declaration of Human Rights and other declarations of justice and freedom, appeal to all of democratic world for assistance in implementing its goals.[16]

Catholic social teaching constituted a large obstacle for the Sovietization of society at large.[17] Some bishops were quite bold in their pastoral letters in addressing the issues of the day from a Christian standpoint. In the circumstances of totalitarian dictatorship, such letters were one of the few sources of alternative information that carried moral authority and a worldview not distorted by Soviet propaganda. As such, the elimination of the Church's moral influence was a pivotal goal of the regime's early rule in Lithuania.

The influence of the Catholic Church in Lithuania was considerably reduced by harsh repression of bishops (one was executed, three were sentenced) and activist priests (almost a third of Lithuanian Catholic priests fell victim to Stalinist terror between 1944 and 1953). The flight and repression of the Lithuanian cultural elite at the beginning of Soviet rule also caused a decline in the Christian intellectual culture.

The Soviets sought to eliminate Church influence in society by undermining its existing state and by falsifying its past. Indeed, the effort to erase any memory of the Christian dimension of Lithuanian national identity was among the most important tasks of the Soviet regime. From the outset of Soviet occupation, the repeated idea was that the main reason for all previous misfortune in Lithuanian society was the Catholic Church. Negative influences of Catholicism for the national culture were publicly and continuously raised: that Catholicism destroyed the high pre-Christian culture of Lithuanians, that Catholicism was the most important channel of unwanted Polish cultural influence in Lithuania, that Catholicism was a bulwark of political reaction and cultural intolerance.

Catholic Attempts to Revive Democratic Values (1970–1990)

After the guerrilla resistance was suppressed in the mid-1950s, a two-decade period of civil passivity followed. It appeared by the beginning of the 1970s that the Soviets had managed to bring Lithuanian society into submission. Soviet propaganda and art seemed to have irreversibly deformed the collective memory of prewar Lithuania and the guerrilla war. Most of the younger generation had endured miserable childhoods and now seemed to rejoice in the fruits of Soviet-led industrialization and urbanization. The Catholic Church had been almost totally cut off from society and put under close surveillance.

In spite of all this, the Catholic Church remained the main social resource for preserving the memory of a Lithuania not altered by Soviet domination. Out of the narrow space that remained for religious life, a new Catholic-inspired wave of public protest against the Soviet system emerged after the 1970s. A believers' rights movement grew, supported by the Second Vatican Council's 1965 declaration on religious freedom, *Dignitatis Humanae*. Many analysts identify this document, along with Pope John XXIII's 1963 *Pacem in Terris*, as the start of the Catholic human rights revolution.[18]

When compared with other growing protest movements inside the Soviet system (e.g., ethno-cultural identity movements, youth subculture movements), the Catholic movement was more seasoned and politically articulate. First, Catholic protesters began speaking openly about the undemocratic character of the Soviet system. Solidarity among protestors was often expressed in the signing of collective petitions that demanded respect for the right to know and publicly profess one's religious faith. Signing such petitions demanded courage because this act was inevitably followed by either direct repression by the KGB or more indirect forms of harassment at one's job or school.[19] Nevertheless, some petitions were signed by over ten thousand people, many of whom were the elders of Lithuanian society who had long memories of Lithuania's struggle for democracy.

At the end of the 1950s, priests, nuns, and laypeople began writing and publishing underground religious literature. At first, these publications were copies of sermons and spiritual writings. By the 1970s, sophisticated discussions of faith and society were being written and published. An important publication of the time was the *Chronicle of the Catholic Church in Lithuania*. Here was a courageous journal that brought alternative opinions into public discussion.

The *Chronicle* rapidly became the protest movement's main tool. Avoiding ideological debates, the publication focused on facts of religious discrimination and incidents of forced atheization in schools. The fight for the right of parents to bring up children according to their beliefs was the only challenge to the Soviet demand that all education remain in the hands of state. It was also a practical manifestation of the Catholic principle of subsidiarity.

The *Chronicle* built a readership large enough to keep KGB persecution at arm's length for almost two decades.[20] With courageous persistence, the *Chronicle* was the beginning of a free public space. This was eventually augmented by the broadcasting of its content through foreign radio stations in the Lithuanian language. These activities are examples of the many forms of voluntary personal commitment that increasingly challenged official Soviet ideology during this period.

The Lithuanian Catholic challenge to totalitarianism included the defense of the believers' right to worship and the right to be educated in the Christian heritage. As will be treated at greater length in Nerija Putinaitė's chapter in this volume, the power of Sovietization was overwhelming and it created a generation of young people effectively ignorant of religious education and values. The situation of highly educated people without sound knowledge of religion or of the country's religious heritage damaged Lithuanian culture. At the same time, the sparse religious education that had been available during Soviet times was presented as an unquestioned tradition and was based on a very primitive, unexamined knowledge of the old Catholic catechism. This was not enough for educated people. Sadly, the updated presentation of Church teachings inspired by the Second Vatican Council was absent from Lithuania due to the years of Soviet censorship.

For the majority of Lithuanians, by 1990 Catholicism had come to represent a symbol of noncompliance to the Soviet regime and a historical chapter in the national heritage. However, Catholicism no longer represented a meaningful faith and set of values for life in the post-Soviet contemporary world. There was weak Catholic representation among the elites who restored state independence in 1991. Therefore, little continuity remained between the Catholic democratic movement that began the century and the post-Soviet democracy that ended it.

More research is needed to understand and analyze the relationship between Catholicism and democracy in twentieth-century Lithuania. This chapter offers only an outline of this complex story, a story of Lithuania's struggles in faith and morality, institutions and movements, suffering and courage.

NOTES

1. See Kęstutis Skrupskelis, *Ateities draugai: ateitininku istorija iki 1940* (Vilnius: Naujasis Židinys-Aidai, 2010), 79.

2. See Danutė Blažytė-Baužienė, Mindaugas Tamošaitis, and Liudas Truska, *Lietuvos Seimo istorija XX–XXI a. pradžia* (Vilnius: Baltos lankos, 2009), 51, 147.

3. See Edward Bell, "Catholicism and Democracy: A Reconsideration," *Journal of Religion and Society* 10 (2008): 12.

4. There was only one university in Lithuania at the time. It was located in the city of Kaunas and its official title was the University of Lithuania.

5. The term "Catholic Action" refers to a broad array of lay Catholic organizations under the guidance of Church authorities during this period.

6. See Skrupskelis, *Ateities draugai*, 564.

7. See Manfred Spieker, "Christentum und freiheitlicher Verfassungsstaat," in *Das Christentum und die totalitären Herausforderungen des 20. Jahrhunderts: Rußland, Deutschland, Italien und Polen im Vergleich*, ed. Leonid Luks (Cologne, Germany: Böhlau Verlag, 2002), 165–67.

8. "Į organiškos valstybės kūrybą," *Naujoji Romuva* 8 (1936): 169–75.

9. Ramūnas Labanauskas, "Jaunųjų katalikų sąjūdžio santykis su sovietų režimu 1940–1941," *Genocidas ir rezistencija* 28 (2010): 7–29.

10. Juozas Brazaitis was a Catholic public figure, philologist, and former head of the Provisional Government.

11. Until most recently, the lack of reliable sources did not permit an unequivocal answer to how Lithuanian bishops reacted to the Holocaust. See Regina Laukaitytė, *Lietuvos Bažnyčios vokiečių okupacijos metais (1941–1944)* (Vilnius: Lietuvos istorijos institutas, 2010), 106.

12. Lithuanian State Historical Archives, fund 1671, catalog 5, file 63, sheet 16 (author's translation).

13. See Dalia Kuodytė and Stankevičius Rimantas, eds., *Whoever Saves One Life* . . . (Vilnius: Lietuvos gyventojų genocido ir rezistencijos centras, 2006).

14. Bernardas Gailius, *The Guerrilla War of 1944–1953 in the Historical, Political and Legal Culture of Contemporary Lithuania* (Vilnius: Vilnius University Press, 2009), 22.

15. See Roger Petersen, *Resistance and Rebellion: Lessons from Eastern Europe* (Cambridge: Cambridge University Press, 2001).

16. *Lietuvos Laisvės Kovos Sąjūdžio 1949 m. vasario 16 d. Deklaracija* (February 16, 1949, Declaration of the Council of the Movement of the Struggle for Freedom in Lithuania) (Vilnius: Seimo l-kla "Valstybės žinios," 1999), 23.

17. The term "Sovietization" is used to indicate the wide range of measures that were used to implant the Soviet political, social, economic order in the newly occupied territories.

18. See George Weigel, *Catholicism and the Renewal of American Democracy* (New York: Paulist Press, 1989), and Samuel Huntington, *The Third Wave: Democratization in the Late Twentieth Century* (Norman: University of Oklahoma Press, 1991).

19. KGB is an abbreviation for Komitet gosudarstvennoj bezopasnosti (Committee for State Security)—the odious Soviet intelligence and counter-intelligence service.

20. See Vidas Spengla, *The Church, "Kronika" and the KGB Web* (Vilnius: Katalikų akademija, 2002).

A Theological Reading of the Lithuanian Church during the Soviet Period: Martyria, Koinonia, Diakonia, and Leiturgia

Vidmantas Šimkunas, SJ

One way to understand the Roman Catholic Church in Lithuania during the period of Soviet oppression is through a historical-theological lens. This approach begins with the position, restated in the Second Vatican Council document *Lumen Gentium*, that the Church is not just a social institution but also "a kind of sacrament or sign of intimate union with God, and of the unity of all humankind." Because the Church lives this sacramentality in history, a full interpretation of that life must be sensitive to both the historical and the theological dimensions of its existence.

This chapter interprets the historical life of the Lithuanian Catholic Church from the Second World War to the restoration of Lithuanian independence in 1990 through the theological lenses of *martyria* (witness of faith), *koinonia* (community and communication), *diakonia* (service of love to one's neighbor), and *leiturgia* (worship). This approach does not claim to uncover previously unknown events in Church history but offers a window into the possible meaning of these events from a Christian faith perspective.

The Four Theological Lenses

MARTYRIA

The term *martyria* came to Christianity from Greek civil law. The word is rich in meaning. While a martyr can signify a Christian who has suffered persecution for his faith, with or without losing his life, it need not refer only to a single event or person. Martyrdom can be a prolonged experience of an entire faith community.[1]

There are two important elements in martyria. One is the *id quod* content of faith given to the Church in both the Word of God and in the fact of Jesus Christ. The other is the *id quo* mode of witnessing, which is determined by many factors: time, place, situation, and even peculiarities of concrete witness. Here, martyria is seen as the experience of the entire Lithuanian Church, not simply the individuals therein. When the Second Vatican Council speaks of *martyria*, it stresses the authentic Christian witnessing of faith that cannot exist without love, wisdom, and creativity.[2]

KOINONIA

Koinonia, from ancient Greek law and similar to the Latin *commune*, means that one has a stake in common property. The word initially referred to common objects but was eventually applied to groups of people bound by geographic and proprietary ties. As people grow together by sharing land and exchanging goods, communities of free, interpersonal relationships form. In this way, a koinonia differs from a sect, a crowd, or a collective.[3]

In a collective, people are only outwardly related. At the center of a collective there is no togetherness and no being, there are only autonomous people in so-called side-by-side relationships. The life of a single person is unimportant; what matters is the life of the collective. The extremes of collectivism and individualism are foreign to koinonia, understood as a community of neighbors.

Already in early Christianity, the understanding of the Church as a koinonia was theologically interpreted. With the development of the New Testament (see Acts 2:42, 44–47), and especially the writings of the Apostle Paul (see 1 Cor. 10:16; 2 Cor. 2:13), the koinonia of the followers of Christ was linked to salvation through the sacraments, especially baptism and the Eucharist.[4] By patristic times, koinonia was considered the best term to capture the meaning of the church as having a two-fold nature as both the Body of Christ and the gathering of the baptized.[5]

A distinguishing feature of the developing Christian koinonia was its Christological and sacramental character. Further theological developments added a "perichoretical" character to the Church as a koinonia.[6] The perichoretical character of Christian koinonia refers to the analogy drawn between the relationship of people in the Church and the relationship of the unity of persons within the Blessed Trinity. As in the divine Godhead, the oneness of people in the Christian koinonia does not suppress the identity and freedom of the members.

Diakonia

In the broadest sense, *diakonia* means both physical services (see Acts 6:2) and an expression of faith through the services of "proclaiming the word" and reconciliation (see Acts 6:4; 2 Cor. 5:18). Diakonia is always a sacramental sign of God's love for humanity. The Roman Catholic Church proclaims the dawning reign of God and, by concrete acts of love and devoted service of all kinds, makes that new reign tangible, understandable, and authentic.

The active love of neighbor was a distinguishing feature of Christian society from the earliest days. The foundation for this love is the experienced love of God, as it is found in the letters of John (see 1 John 4:16). Love of neighbor can be understood as a person's participation in God's love.[7] A deeper theological reflection on the Church's call and mission shows that active and ongoing love for neighbor is at the heart of the Church's mission.[8]

Through diakonia, the Church excludes no one from its loving service, yet priority is given to the poor, oppressed, and marginalized. Diakonia supports human rights and the works of justice. Both are authentic signs of hope in the world today.[9] When the Church takes human life to heart its mission becomes a prophetic, critical, and even political diakonia.[10]

Leiturgia

From the very beginning of Christianity, leiturgia was the community's inseparable and essential identity marker. Rooted in the Old Testament, leiturgia underwent a qualitative change in understanding when taken up by the early Christians. In Christianity, Jesus Christ becomes the one true priest and *leiturgos* of the New Covenant. In the dialogical aspect of leiturgia, two dimensions become known: the *katabatic*, the initiative of God's grace, and the *anabatic*, the response of the person touched by this grace. God's grace initially addresses the person and invites them to respond. It is crucial that these aspects of leiturgia be reflected and preserved.

As hierarchical structures became more dominant within the Church, leiturgia began to be seen primarily as ceremonies overseen by priests. Clement of Rome considered leiturgia as an act undertaken by the entire Christian community, but even he emphasized the roles of service performed by the bishop and the priest. Because Clement spoke of leiturgia in this way, it began to be more widely identified with cultic ceremony.[11] This identification dominated the Roman Catholic Church until the Second Vatican Council. After the Council, leiturgia became more Eucharist-focused and, thus, the form of community worship in which the great works of God were celebrated.

Leiturgia never takes place in a vacuum but rather takes place in a cultural and sociopolitical environment. There are various processes, both inside and outside of the Church, that influence the development and understanding of leiturgia. For all this, the mandate to worship God and to sanctify people remains the same. In order to accomplish this task, leiturgia has always adapted itself to new situations.

The Catholic Church of Lithuania in the Context of Soviet Dictatorship

MARTYRIA

Strengths

The experiences of the Lithuanian Catholic Church during the Soviet period affirm that martyria was one of the most evident marks of its living faith. Albert Chapelle, founder of the Catholic Institute in Brussels, compares the Lithuanian witness of faith during this time with that of the Christian martyrs of the first centuries.[12]

As explained in Arūnas Streikus's opening chapter, during the first decade after the Second World War, facing threats of deportations to Siberia, the primary concern of both Lithuanian society and the Lithuanian Catholic Church was physical survival. After meeting this challenge, the Church sought a method of coexistence with the state. Later, in the 1980s, the Church began more directly to address the oppression rampant in the Soviet state.

Lithuanian Catholics in their homeland and in places of deportation practiced their faith under adverse conditions and strove to hand it down to their children. Women distinguished themselves in this regard. Secret nuns, such as Nijole Sadunaite, spread the underground Catholic press. Other women secretly catechized children in preparation for First Communion.[13] The symbol of martyria at this time became the prayer book *Mary Save Us*, written by Adelė Dirsytė. Dirsytė was a deported Lithuanian girl who wrote her prayer book while in a Siberian labor camp. The book was translated into several languages.[14]

The living faith of Lithuanian Catholics was also expressed in pilgrimages to local shrines, the design of sacred architecture, and the production of fine art. The wooden crosses of Lithuania are an example of such a witness. Special in this regard is the Hill of the Crosses, home to thousands of crosses that were four times destroyed during the Soviet occupation. Each time the Soviets destroyed the crosses, the faithful returned under cover of night and faced great risk to replace the crosses. This act became the national symbol of a professed and defended faith.[15] It also became a powerful symbol of peaceful resistance against totalitarianism.[16] As Danutė Gailinenė notes, the act of risking one's life for one's faith is a catalyst for a religious community's social and psychological balance during periods of great adversity.[17]

The more daring faithful also defied threats of imprisonment and death by secretly translating and disseminating books on Christian spirituality and current events.[18] The best example of the latter was the *Chronicle of the Catholic Church in Lithuania*.

When the Soviet government limited the number of seminarians and priests, certain male religious orders secretly agreed to open an underground seminary that eventually prepared fifty-two priests.[19] In their turn, these zealous priests defied the menace of imprisonment by preparing children for the sacraments and organizing youth retreats.[20] Many other Lithuanian priests were discovered and exiled but then went to work among displaced Polish, Ukrainian, and German Catholic colonies in Siberia, Kazakhstan, and elsewhere.[21] Commitment to Christian faith under threat of death was the experience of thousands of Lithuanian Catholics, whether clergy, religious women, or lay believers.[22]

Catholic priests were the first to organize a petition-writing campaign to the Soviet government concerning the persecuted Church and the violations of human rights. This began in 1968.[23] This action, like the underground press, the Hill of Crosses, and the illegal seminaries, can justly be interpreted as martyria.[24]

Weaknesses

Through the prewar and postwar repressions, Lithuanian society lost almost all of its Catholic intellectuals and grew more and more isolated from the democratic world.[25] This limited the resources available for theological reflection on faith. Consequently, the Church stressed the posture of defense and preservation during the Soviet occupation.[26] This explains why martyria was emphasized more than diakonia, koinonia, or leiturgia. It also explains the distance that grew between the few remaining Catholic intellectuals and the majority of so-called traditional Catholics.[27]

The tendency to retain older forms of faith expression can be interpreted as a natural reaction to the anti-religious propaganda and the systematic Soviet indoctrination of Lithuanian youth. The Church felt it had no alternative but to observe the more traditional forms of faith that brought a greater sense of orientation and stability to Christian life. Eventually these unchanging forms of faith became equated with the content of unchanging faith as such. On the one hand, adhering to traditions helped to preserve the faith. On the other hand, it led to stiffness and created tensions between the local and universal Church when communism collapsed and this relationship was re-established.[28] In an ecclesiological sense, martyria must exist within an open and non-exclusive koinonia, lest members drift apart over religious practices and points of view. When koinonia is damaged, danger arises for martyria as well.

Koinonia

Strengths

The Soviet government tolerated liturgy, so long as it was not publicly manifested. Koinonia, on the other hand, was severely restricted. Liturgy, therefore, did at least a partial service to koinonia. In Church services, practices of popular devotion, and pilgrimages, Lithuanian Catholics experienced vital aspects of koinonia.[29]

Other experiences of koinonia during Soviet occupation were the aforementioned writing of petitions to the government in defense of those persecuted for their faith and the maintenance of contact with Christians from other countries.[30] Thousands of the signatures on petitions to the government demanded the return of the nationalized church in Klaipėda to the Catholic community, while another petition demanded the release from prison of priests who had been sent there for organizing and partaking in religious activities.[31] Seventeen thousand Lithuanian Catholics signed a memorandum to Leonid Brezhnev in 1972 demanding the freedom to train and ordain priests, teach religion, and provide religious literature.

Relations between Lithuanian Catholics and Catholics from around the world also provided support. These relationships allowed Lithuanian Catholics to see that they were not alone but rather part of the universal Church. As noted above, the *Chronicle of the Lithuanian Catholic Church*, published in Lithuania and distributed to Christians in the West, was an important means of contact and witness. It informed the world about the true politics of the Soviet Union regarding religion and human rights.[32]

Weaknesses

Alongside the Soviet collectivization of agriculture, isolation from the universal Church had a devastating effect on people's physical and mental relationships within their parish communities. It destroyed both their sense of trust and confidence in each other as well as their sense of personal responsibility for the common good.[33] As a result, people were less motivated to work with and for one another in a voluntary way. A person could never be sure if their neighbor, or even a family member, would accept them or turn them in to authorities.[34]

While Soviet collectivization drew people together outwardly, it inwardly estranged them. This greatly affected the life of the Catholic Church. Most people moved away from the active core of the community. Gradually, the Church began to be considered more as a religious institution than as a community of believers. Eventually, thanks to the sustained efforts of the Soviet propagandists, more and more people subscribed to the view that religious belief must be restricted to private life and have no bearing on public life.[35]

The Soviets also sought to limit all contact among the clergy in Lithuania. Consequently, suspicion and distrust began to take root between the priests patronized by the government and the underground press editors who criticized them.[36] Distrust between the clergy within the borders of Lithuania and those who emigrated also became noticeable.[37]

To a strong degree, the Soviet government's actions succeeded in alienating the faithful.[38] The belief began to spread that the Church was just the hierarchy, the priests were their hired cult employees, and the faithful were the passive recipients of their dubious services. This attitude was actively informed by Soviet propaganda, but the hierarchy, too, passively contributed to it.[39] The ideas of Vatican II on the Church as koinonia had no responsive echo in Lithuania. All of these issues contributed to long-lasting, negative consequences in the life of the Church.[40]

DIAKONIA

Strengths

One of the positive expressions of diakonia during Soviet occupation was that the Catholic Church in Lithuania remained faithful to the Gospel and treated everyone equally. It neither ingratiated itself with influential persons nor depreciated ordinary people. Biographies written about Lithuanian Catholics at this time attest to this phenomenon. During the Second World War and after, Bishop Vincentas Borisevicius assisted people in their needs as far as possible without regard to their nationality or religion. Secret nuns worked as doctors and nurses and lovingly served everyone under their care, without discrimination. This showed that people with an active faith and deep spiritual life put their lives in service to their neighbor.[41] Even though all houses of religious orders in Lithuania were closed by the Soviet government in 1949, religious sisters kept serving the people.[42] They worked in churches and hospitals, secretly catechized children, and printed religious literature.

The examples of solidarity, compassion, and support for imprisoned priests and dissidents offered by ordinary Catholics show that diakonia was understood in a much broader sense than just mere material assistance. At the same time, the underground press stimulated diakonia in the form of "love of neighbor." Hospitality and helpfulness have always been valued in Lithuanian culture, but the circumstances of Soviet oppression elevated these virtues to extraordinary works of Christian diakonia.[43]

Weaknesses

The totalitarian and atheistic Soviet system contributed to the separation of faith and social life in Lithuanian. The Soviets considered the Christian churches solely as institutions for conducting religious rites. Activities such as charity and the founding of mutual-aid funds were prohibited by law.[44] It was asserted that these activities had nothing to do with religion. This position was justified by appealing to a 1918 decree that separated the Church from the state in Lithuania.[45]

This prohibition had serious consequences. People became more passive in the Catholic community. Charity and other social service works were greatly reduced. The assumption grew that these activities should be limited to one's personal life. The view that it was not the Church's business to speak on social issues became tantamount to law. All these actions lent themselves to both the privatization of faith and an exaggerated spiritualization of Catholic living.

The legal prohibition against diakonia has had a lasting effect on Lithuanian Catholics. A dualistic perception of the relationship between the human being and the world resulted, in contradiction to the Christian conception of the oneness of the love of God and the love of neighbor. A narrow conception of the Church emerged, which limited the Church's purpose to religious services, disjoined from social life.

LEITURGIA

Strengths

The Lithuanian experience shows that, in adverse conditions, the Christian faith is best preserved and most actively lived out where traditions of popular devotion are strongest. Because of these devotions, the Catholic faithful in Lithuania resisted the powerful atheistic propaganda of the Soviet Union and handed their faith down to new generations.

Leiturgia was celebrated in the liveliest manner where it was closest to the people's lives. In the places of exile, where no priests were available, laypeople sometimes presided over funeral and wedding liturgies.[46] The importance of leiturgia for the faithful manifested itself in the faithful's ardent efforts to oppose the closure of churches and pilgrimage places by the Soviets.[47] By 1988, a reverse effort was also underway: to reopen closed churches. The most famous of these efforts was the demand for the reopening of the only church built during Soviet occupation, the Church of Mary Queen of Peace in Klaipėda.[48]

Weaknesses

As previously indicated, leiturgia was tolerated by the Soviets as long as the religious ceremonies were for adult believers and took place inside the church building. If leiturgia was taken outside the church building, for outdoor masses or processions, it was treated either as a disturbance of public order or as religious propaganda. This was prohibited by law.[49]

The leiturgia of this period had strong traditionalist tendencies. Lithuanian priests were unable to take part in the processes of theological development that were occurring in the free countries outside the Soviet regime. Coming to the fore of the Catholic imagination at the Second Vatican Council, it was widely recognized that leiturgia, like the Church itself, should always be renewed: koinonia and leiturgia must be both intimately connected and constantly renewed. However, given its context, the more isolated Catholic Church of Lithuania believed it more important to preserve the Catholic faith by adhering to long-held and settled forms rather than the processes of renewal. The liturgical reforms of the Second Vatican Council were not welcomed with great enthusiasm in the Lithuanian Catholic Church and, as a result, were only slowly implemented.

If leiturgia is considered an expression of faith, as has been argued here, then we must acknowledge that the negative impact of Soviet rule on leiturgia eventually affected the conception and content of Lithuanian faith itself. The Church developed as a hierarchical structure and, consequently, leiturgia was conceived of as the strictly regulated ceremonial responsibility of the priest. Leiturgia, so conceived, made little space for lay participation, except for singing in the choir and processions, and during the celebration of the Eucharist the laity remained passive spectators. Individualistic devotion in the celebration of the sacraments, so at odds with our contemporary sense of Catholic identity, predominated during this period of Soviet occupation in Lithuania.

Conclusion

The Catholic Church carries out its mission to be a sign and instrument of communion with God in Christ and to be a source of unity among all human persons.[50] This is achieved in the most appropriate manner when martyria, koinonia, diakonia, and leiturgia are kept in balance. Historical, cultural, and geopolitical occurrences affect this balance. Whenever one of these areas is diminished or overemphasized, the other areas suffer. Martyria was emphasized more in the Lithuanian Roman Catholic Church under the conditions of Soviet communism than were koinonia, diakonia, and leiturgia. As a result, the Lithuanian Catholic Church survived, but deeply suffered.

In post-communist times, the Roman Catholic community has worked to coordinate these four areas of Church life. Such coordination will be necessary if the Church can hope to meet the challenges and opportunities of democracy in contemporary Lithuania.

NOTES

1. See Karl Rahner, *Zur Theologie des Todes* (Freiberg, Germany: Herder, 1958), 73.

2. See "Lumen Gentium," "Gaudium et spes," and "Apostolicam Actuositatem," in *Vatikano II Susirinkimo nutarimai* (Vilnius: Aidai, 2001).

3. See Lothar Lies, *Eucharistija* (Vilnius: Katalikų pasaulis, 2002), 24.

4. See Walter Kasper, *Zukunft aus der Kraft des Konzils* (Freiburg, Germany: Herder, 1986), 90.

5. See Medard Kehl, *Die Kirche* (Würzburg, Germany: Echter, 1994), 320–21.

6. See Lothar Lies, *Eucharistie in ökumenischen Verantwortung* (Graz, Austria: Styria, 1996), 239.

7. See Wolfhart Pannenberg, *Systematische Theologie 3* (Göttingen, Germany: Vandenhoek u. Ruprecht, 1993), 207.

8. See Miklos Tomka and Paul M. Zulehner, eds., *Religion im gesellschaftlichen Kontext Ost (Mittel) Europas* (Vienna: Schwabenverlag, 1999), 20.

9. See "Gaudium et spes," para. 1.

10. See Edward Schillebeeckx, *Church: The Human Story of God* (New York: Crossroad, 1994), 184.

11. See Clement von Rome, "1. Brief an die Korinther Kap 41; 44, 2–6," in *Fontes Christiani*, vol. 15 (New York: Herder, 1994), 171–75.

12. See Jonas Boruta, "Lietuvos Katalikų Bažnyčios kronika ir žmogaus teisių sąjūdis Vakaruose," in *Lietuvos Katalikų Mokslų Akademijos Metraštis 22* (Vilnius: Katalikų akademija, 2003), 634–35.

13. See *Lietuvos Katalikų Bažnyčios Kronika 3*, vol. 17 (Chicago: Lithuanian Catholic Religious Aid Auxiliary Society, 1976), 63–64, 72–73.

14. See Mindauga Bloznelis, *Adelė Dirsytė: gyvenimas ir darbai* (Vilnius: Katalikų akademija, 2003), 334–35.

15. See Hubertas Smilgys, *Prie Hanzos kelio* (Šiauliai, Lithuania: Saulės Delta, 2001), 60.

16. See Vytautas Sadauskas, "'LKB Kronikos' medžiaga dvasinio ugdymo teologijos šviesoje," in *Lietuvos Katalikų Mokslų Akademijos Metraštis*, vol. 12 (Vilnius: Katalikų akademija, 1998), 22.

17. See Danutė Gailienė, ed., *Sunkių traumų psichologija: Politinių represijų padariniai* (Vilnius: Lietuvos gyventojų genocido ir rezistencijos tyrimo centras, 2004), 108.

18. See Regina Laukaitytė, *Lietuvos Vienuolijos XXa. Istorijos bruožai* (Vilnius: Lietuvos istorijos institutas, 1997), 155.

19. See Jonas Boruta, and Algimantas Katilius, "Klierikų ir dėstytojų sąrašai, sudaryti pagal spausdinamuose tekstuose pateiktus duomenis," in *Pogrindžio kunigų seminarija*, ed. Jonas Boruta, and Algimantas Katilius (Vilnius: Katalikų akademija, 2002), 707–8. After the lay Christian Petras Plumpa raised the idea of founding an underground seminary for priests and in cooperation with the religious orders, the idea became a reality. See Egidijus Jaseliūnas, "Vatikano II Susirinkimo nutarimų įtaka katalikiškojo pasipriešinimo formavimuisi Lietuvoje," http//genocid.lt/Leidyba/12egidijus,htm.

20. See Thomas Remeikis, *Opposition to Soviet Rule in Lithuania 1945–1980* (Chicago: Lituanus Foundation, 1981), 127.

21. See Antanas Saulaitis, "Kunigas Antanas Šeškevičius SJ," in *Katalikų Žinynas 2003* (Vilnius: Katalikų pasaulis, 2003), 286–87.

22. See Jonas Boruta, "Die Katholische Kirche in Litauen im postkommunistischen Umwandlungsprozess der Geselschaft aus der Sicht eines Bischofs," in *Lietuvos Katalikų Mokslų Akademijos Metraštis 18* (Vilnius: Katalikų akademija, 2001), 329–30.

23. See Živilė Račkauskaitė, "Pasipriešinimas sovietiniam režimui Lietuvoje septintame-aštuntame dešimtmetyje," in *Genocidas ir rezistencija 2*, no. 6 (Vilnius: Lietuvos gyventojų genocido ir rezistencijos tyrimo centras, 1999), 91–106.

24. See Jonas Kauneckas, "Išsivaduokime iš baimės," in *Naujasis Židinys-Aidai no 4* (Vilnius: Aidai, 2001), 167–71.

25. See Jurgita Straigytė and Ona Voverienė, *Lietuvos mokslo gedulo ir vilties diena* (Vilnius: Džiugas, 1995), 3.

26. See Manfred Spieker, "Die Kirche im postkommunistischen Transformationsprozesse," in *Die Mission der Kirche* (Paderborn, Germany: AMATECA, 2002), 367.

27. See Paulius Subačius, "Daugumos ir mažumos paradoksai, Bažnyčia Lietuvoje 1990–1995 metais," in *Naujasis Židinys 1–2* (Vilnius: Aidai, 1996), 15–25.

28. See Algirdas Jurevičius, *Die Katholische Kirche Litauens* (Hamburg, Germany: Dr. Kovač, 2004), 47.

29. See *Lietuvos Katalikų Bažnyčios Kronika 7, no. 55* (Chicago: Society of the Chronicle of Lithuania, 1984), 348.

30. See *Lietuvos Katalikų Bažnyčios Kronika 6, no. 44* (Chicago: Society of the Chronicle of Lithuania, 1983), 258–59.

31. See Arūnas Streikus, *Sovietų valdžios antibažnytinė politika Lietuvoje (1944–1990)* (Vilnius: Lietuvos gyventojų ir rezistencijos tyrimo centras, 2002), 251.

32. See Sigitas Tamkevičius, "LKB Kronikai 25-eri metai," in *Lietuvos Katalikų Mokslo Akademijos Metraštis 12* (Vilnius: Katalikų akademija, 1998), 14. See also Vaclovas Aliulis, "Rinkau, mačiau," in *Naujasis Židinys-Aidai 3–4* (Vilnius: Aidai, 2005), 77–80.

33. See Martynas Purvinas and Marija Purvinienė, "Stalinizmo urbanistika Lietuvoje," in *Lietuvos Katalikų Mokslų Akademijos Suvažiavimo darbai 15* (Vilnius: Katalikų akademija, 1996), 494.

34. See Algirdas Jurevičius, *Die Katholische Kirche Litauens* (Hamburg, Germany: Dr. Kovač, 2004), 40.

35. See Ausra Malinauskaitė and Andrius Navickas, "Religion und Kirche in Litauen," in *Religion und Kirche in Ost (Mittel) Europa: Ungarn, Litauen, Slowenien*, ed. Paul M. Zulehner, Miklos Tomka, and Niko Tos (Vienna: Schwabenverlag, 1999), 170.

36. See *Lietuvos Katalikų Bažnyčios Kronika 1, no. 4.* (Chicago: Society for the Publication of the Chronicles of the Catholic Church in Lithuania, 1974), 173; *Lietuvos Katalikų Bažnyčios Kronika 4, no. 28* (Chicago: Society for the Publication of the Chronicles of the Catholic Church in Lithuania, 1978), 275.

37. See Juozas Stankevičius, *Mano gyvenimo kryžkelės* (Vilnius: Katalikų akademija, 2002), 453.

38. See Hans-Friedrich Fischer, "Bewährung in Freiheit," in *Herder Korrespondenz 57*, no. 3 (2003): 143–46.

39. See Algirdas Jurevičius, *Die Katholische Kirche Litauens* (Hamburg, Germany: Dr. Kovač, 2004), 41.

40. See Josef Pumberger, "Unsichere Aussicht," in *Herder Korrespondenz 54*, no. 12 (2000): 293.

41. See Jonas Boruta, "Ganytojas, pirmasis ėjęs į mirtį, kad kiti liktų drąsūs ir nepalaužiami," in *Vyskupas Vincentas Borisevičius straipsniuose ir dokumentuose*, ed. Jonas Boruta, Milda Klimkaite, Elena Neniskyte, and Algimantas Katilius. (Vilnius: Katalikų akademija, 2002), 3–4.

42. *See Arūnas Streikus,* Sovietų valdžios antibažnytinė politika Lietuvoje (1944–1990) (Vilnius: Lietuvos gyventojų ir rezistencijos tyrimo centras, 2002), 116.

43. See Nerijus Šepetys, "Katalikų kalendorius-žinynas sovietmečiu," in *Naujasis Židinys-Aidai 11–12* (1988): 455–67.

44. See Jonas Aničas and Jonas Rimaitis, *Tarybiniai įstatymai apie religinius kultus ir sąžinės laisvė* (Vilnius: Mintis, 1970), 23.

45. Tarybų Socialistinių Respublikų Sąjungos Konstitucija (Vilnius: Mintis, 1977), para. 23.

46. See Stanislovas Kiškis, *Aš padarysiu jus žmonių žvejais* (Kaišiadorys, Lithuania: Kaišiadorių vyskupijos kurijos leidykla, 1999), 99, 120.

47. See Juozas Fabijonavičius, "Maldos namų griovimo banga Lietuvoje okupacijų metais," in *Lietuvos Katalikų Mokslų Aakademijos Suvažiavimo darbai 15* (Vilnius: Katalikų akademija, 1995), 247.

48. See Kęsturis Girnius, "Nelygi kova tęsiasi," in *Krikščionybė Lietuvoje* (Chicago: Lietuvos krikščionybės jubiliejaus komitetas, 1997), 528.

49. See Juozas Jermalavičius, *Ateistinis auklėjimas tarybų Lietuvoje* (Vilnius: Mints, 1977), 133–34.

50. See "Lumen Gentium," in *Vatikano II Susirinkimo nutarimai* (Vilnius: Aidai, 2001), para. 1.

Traumatized Society, Democracy, and Religious Faith: The Lithuanian Experience

Danutė Gailienė

Severe traumatization has a deep and long-lasting impact on individuals and societies. In societies that have experienced mass political, economic, and cultural crises, the effects of trauma remain even after the crises have abated. Today, more than twenty years after regaining democratic independence, the people of Lithuania are still experiencing the traumatic effects of successive occupations of their country by the Soviet Union in 1940, Nazi Germany between 1941 and 1944, and the Soviet Union from 1944 to 1990. One might argue that Lithuania's efforts at building democracy have been hampered by the effects of social trauma.

Why does this trauma persist? How do Lithuanians cope with this experience? How might Lithuania emerge from this trauma and regain the social trust and optimism necessary for a healthy democracy? Does religious faith have a bearing on any of these issues?

Traumatizing History

In 1939, the Soviet Union and Nazi Germany signed the Molotov-Ribbentrop Pact that divided Europe into Soviet and German spheres of interest. Lithuania was placed within the Soviet sphere. Mass arrests and deportations of Lithuanian citizens by the Soviet Union began in the summer of 1940, even before Lithuania's formal incorporation into the USSR. These early victims were educated individuals and their families, people who were socially, politically, and economically active in Lithuanian society as public servants, teachers, university professors, high school and university students, leaders of farmer organizations, and members of civic institutions and political parties. During these arrests, men were usually separated from their families and sent to concentration camps.[1] Most of these men, along with nearly a third of all Roman Catholic priests in Lithuania, died during this first wave of Stalinist terror.[2]

Nazi Germany occupied Lithuania in June of 1941. Arūnas Streikus notes in this volume that many Lithuanian Catholics refused to participate in the Nazi policy against the Jews. Nevertheless, enough Lithuanians of every background participated in this policy so that two hundred thousand Lithuanian Jews were killed during the three-year Nazi occupation.[3]

As the Nazi regime collapsed at the end of the war, the Soviet army re-established its control of Lithuania and began a period of occupation that lasted almost fifty years. During the Stalin phase of that occupation, from 1940 to Stalin's death in 1953, more than a million Lithuanian people, or about 33 percent of the population, were imprisoned, sentenced to death, deported, or forced to emigrate.[4] The thousands imprisoned in Lithuania each year for political "crimes" were humiliated, tortured, and robbed by both their guards and the common criminals with whom they were held.

An even greater number of Lithuanian political prisoners were sent to Siberian gulag camps. They traveled there in cattle cars under conditions of severe physical and mental pain. Once in Siberia, the captives undertook grueling labor in forests, clay pits, coal mines, construction sites, and road projects. In the worst climatic conditions imaginable, the captives were forced to work continuous twelve- to fourteen-hour shifts with little rest. In many cases, the captives walked over six miles a day to reach their work-sites.[5] The annual mortality rate in the gulag between 1941 and 1944 was extremely high: well over 50 percent in most camps and as high as 93 percent in some camps. From 1945 to 1947, approximately 37,000 more Lithuanians perished in the camps.[6]

Long-Term Persecution after Imprisonment and Deportation

Most deportees never returned to Lithuania. They either died in Siberia or suffered circumstances that never allowed them to return. The Soviet system of deportation and repression required the vast majority of political prisoners to remain in Russia even after their sentences were served. Some former prisoners tried to move to areas as close to Lithuania as possible, such as Latvia or the Kaliningrad region. For the fortunate few who made it back to Lithuania after imprisonment, the average time for return after release was ten years.[7]

Those able to return to Soviet-occupied Lithuania could rarely find jobs or regain their permanent residency. This was because the local authorities were unwilling to register these returning "enemies of the people" and without a registration stamp on one's passport, access to regular employment was nearly impossible. Even for those who managed to obtain a *propiska* (registration at a permanent address), finding a job was very difficult. If a former prisoner was fortunate enough to find a job, he or she often faced continuous KGB observation, harassment, and persecution.

Former political prisoners and deportees lived in a state of perpetual fear that others would discover their past. If they had a job, they needed to hide their past from their coworkers. Such information would threaten their jobs and subject their families to discrimination and persecution. As one former prisoner remarked, "We who had returned from the Gulag camps continued to live as in some kind of pressurized environment, a pressurized chamber, and we lived this way for two or three generations. All the baggage of our traumas and problems of our future life and adaptation weighed heavily on those close to us."[8]

Former detainees were lucky if they had anyone they could trust, even within their own families. Finding trustworthy people was made more difficult by the fact that the unregistered former prisoners and deportees were banned from living in large urban areas and prohibited from returning to the districts where they lived prior to deportation. Often, their only confidants (and future marriage partners) were fellow political prisoners and exiles. Finding a safe haven where one could share one's experiences was extremely difficult.

Children were often protected from these conversations. A study of the trans-generational transmission of trauma surveyed adult children of repressed former exiles and found that most parents who experienced past repression kept that history away from their children. In cases where children were told, they were strictly warned not to tell anyone outside the family.[9] In this and countless other ways, the trauma induced by Soviet repression spread throughout Lithuanian society and across future generations.

The Problem of Recognition

Research on the *in situ* effect of political repression is difficult to conduct. Because such research is usually impossible to pursue until the repressive regime has collapsed, it is hard to arrive at an accurate assessment of the trauma as it is experienced.

Trauma research depends on people understanding what trauma is and recognizing it as a political and social reality. When a society acknowledges the reality of trauma among its citizenry it opens the way for serious scientific research and potential healing.

The history of trauma research shows an oscillation between periods of recognition and non-recognition.[10] After the Second World War, important social and political decisions were made in Western Europe that left a positive, long-lasting impact on studies of severe, prolonged trauma. Nazism was condemned as a criminal ideology and convicted Nazis were punished for their heinous crimes. The victims of Nazism were recognized and their suffering was acknowledged as traumatic. As such, efforts were made in the postwar years to redress harms done to victims of Nazi occupation. Intense research programs on the effects of traumatic experiences among this population were begun by mental health professionals and continue today.

Lithuania suffered the traumas of both Nazi fascism and Soviet communism. The later trauma lasted for fifty years after the end of the Second World War. To this day, however, Soviet communism has not been classified as a crime. The failure to identify the criminality of Soviet communism has created a major research imbalance in trauma studies. Unlike the enormous research done on survivors of the Holocaust and anti-Nazi resistance movements, little research has been conducted on the trauma experienced by post-communist societies and the former Soviet republics.

This presents a serious lack of understanding about social trauma. Millions of people fell victim to Soviet repression. Victims were exposed to horrifying degrees and duration of physical and psychological violence. Hundreds of thousands died of hunger, extreme cold, and exhaustion in the Siberian forced labor camps. Most of the survivors continued to be persecuted for the rest of their lives. However, as Vytautas Kubilius sharply remarked, "The commandant of the Auschwitz concentration camp was hanged, while the commandant of Ozerlag draws a colonel's pension."[11]

It is of vital importance to human understanding that studies of trauma in Lithuania be undertaken. It is tragic that they have not. The Lithuanian case is important to study and analyze because of its multiple stages and excruciating duration. Yet such study remains difficult because official recognition of the crime committed by Soviet communism has never been given. The world courts and the world's most powerful democratic governments have turned away from this reality.

The Traumatizing Effects of Soviet Repression in Lithuania

In 2005, a beginning was made on this research. This project analyzed the suffering of Lithuanians under Soviet repression by studying 1) deportees from the two waves of Siberian deportation in 1941 and 1948, 2) resistance fighters, and 3) political prisoners. The comparison group was of similar age and from the general Lithuanian population. Over fifteen hundred people participated in the project.[12]

Because the extreme severity of the first Soviet occupation in 1940 left very few survivors, the majority of the survey participants (77 percent) were victims of repression from the second Soviet occupation period that began in 1944. All the survey participants had been subjected to various forms of repression over long periods. This included political imprisonment and/or exile (the mean duration was 7.4 years) and political persecution lasting up to the collapse of the Soviet Union and the restoration of Lithuanian independence in 1991.

No one escaped trauma during the Soviet occupation. It was a matter of degree. Consequently, the comparison group in the study also experienced trauma. As one might expect, the level of exposure to trauma was much higher among people who were imprisoned, tortured, and exiled. Of those studied, 48 percent of the victims of repression were subjected to torture, compared with 5 percent in the comparison group. The percentages of people who experienced persecution were 55 percent and 8 percent, respectively.

As noted above, even after victims had served their prison sentences or completed their term of deportation, it was many years before they were allowed to return to Lithuania. When they did come back, they received little social support. Only 7 percent reported that their reintegration had been successful. Soviet repression had made reintegration virtually impossible. Victims had a lower educational level than the control group because the system prevented them from pursuing their professional and educational goals, as reported by 83 percent of the former prisoners and deportees. As expected, Soviet repression deteriorated the health of the victims (83 percent) and prevented them from being with family members who had died during their absence (55 percent).

The results of the 2005 research project confirmed that severe and prolonged exposure to trauma creates effects that last for decades. Almost half of the victims in the study continued to experience invasive memories long after the downfall of the Soviet occupation. Nearly one-third suffered from nightmares. Because of their severe traumatic experiences, some of the victims lost self-confidence and suffered deep feelings of inferiority. The victim-attempted suicide rate is higher than the national average. The victims of repression developed many post-traumatic stress symptoms, in addition to negative stress responses and impaired personality characteristics.

The trauma of political prisoners differed somewhat from that of the deportee and resistance fighter victims. Symptoms of loneliness, sadness, chronic tension, and uncontrollable crying were less prevalent among political prisoners. They tended to have intrusive symptoms of post-traumatic stress disorder, such as flashbacks and nightmares, while depressive symptoms were more pronounced among the other two victim groups.

Though the intensity of post-traumatic symptoms among the political prisoners was severe, it did not exceed that experienced by other groups. Former political prisoners were often participants in active resistance against the Soviet regime. Their motivations, risk-taking, and coping strategies may have served to mitigate some degree of the political prisoners' encounter with trauma and repression.

In studying the effects of Soviet repression, it is necessary to recognize that people who were not directly subjected to deportation or political repression were still living in country under oppressive communist rule. In a diary written from 1948 to 1949, Lionginas Baliukevičius-Dzūkas, the commander of the partisan district of Dainava,[13] offered a grim picture of the occupied country:

> Overwhelming poverty! Not a ray of hope for a more beautiful life.
> The only entertainment is drinking samogon often followed by a
> drunken brawl. The village is completely overtaken by samogon. It is
> brewed and drunk by everyone, even children. Drowned in a sea of
> blood, tears and black despair, the nation seems to have found its only
> solace and temporary comfort in samogon. How many idiots, criminals, degenerates, embezzlers, prostitutes and morons will these god-
> damned years bring to Lithuania? Some say that the years of the
> Bolshevik occupation and fighting will make the nation stronger.
> What remains will be steel, they say. Perhaps some will remain,
> strong as steel, melted and tempered in this struggle. But there will
> be few of them.[14]

The Soviet Union was a totalitarian state in which no one could feel safe. The individual was utterly helpless: her opinions did not matter, her choices did not matter, and she could do nothing to resist the system. Living under Soviet occupation required leading a double life: publicly declaring allegiance to official Soviet values but privately disowning them.

This double life put enormous stress on the Lithuanian family. Instead of being the social bedrock for education and upbringing, the family in Lithuania became a secret place for the preservation and exchange of forbidden values and stories. Children heard things from family members privately at home that would be publicly denied by social authorities such as teachers, political leaders, and even the family members themselves.

Living this kind of duplicitous lifestyle in an oppressive society creates moral trauma. It deeply affects individual self-consciousness and behavior. In Lithuania today, one can observe individuals behaving with the distrust, cynicism, negative attitudes toward the state, and incongruity between private and public morality that was formed during the Soviet occupation.

The Role of the Religious Faith

Trauma twists the very core of one's being. It causes one to question their most treasured views about both the world and themselves. Deep, existential questions invariably arise for victims of political persecution. The results of the aforementioned 2005 study revealed that for the victims of repression, religious faith, spiritual values, and the ability to find meaning in suffering were vital survival factors. This was true in three principal areas: coping, identity, and resistance.

RELIGION AND COPING

According to the 2005 study, the coping strategies adopted by people subjected to repression differed from those of the comparison group. The coping factor most frequently identified by the victims of repression was belief in God. In the comparison group, the most important coping factor was support from family and friends. Victims of repression often told stories about the importance of prayer as a coping strategy: "I knelt in front of Our Lady, said three Hail Marys, stood up and said: now we can go."[15]

The victims of repression also distinguished themselves in identifying multiple coping factors in their strategy for survival. For example, the repressed group identified coping factors such as support from friends and political involvement more than ten times as often as the comparison group (39.6 percent and 3.4 percent, 32.1 percent and 2.5 percent, respectively). Political prisoners identified still more coping factors when compared to the other groups of people subjected to repression. In addition to belief in God, they identified hope and spiritual strength, political participation, and political beliefs as coping mechanisms. Many of the former political prisoners and deportees pointed out that it was their faith in the liberation of Lithuania and in their sense of moral superiority over the occupying regime that helped them survive in prison and exile. Below is a selection of comments from members of this group:

> We prayed . . . . We begged God, we believed that only God could help. Only God could deliver us from the hell in which we were suffering. I found support in thoughts about my family. In hoping that we all still have to be happy. God cannot abandon His people. (D. P.)

> During interrogation, most of the support came from above . . . through prayer. (A. K.)

> Even though going to church was forbidden, I still went; and I also cleaned the church. I was mad that they would not let us go to Church. Faith in God was what helped us survive the deportation and overcome difficulties. (G. O.)[16]

The data on politically repressed people from the 2005 survey indicates that the connections between faith and the effects of trauma is complex.[17] Statistical analysis indicated a positive connection between faith in God and severity of the trauma. Statistics also showed a positive connection between religious faith and the strength of the post-traumatic symptoms.[18] This tells us that the more a traumatic experience intensified, the more people would increase their faith in God. Perhaps those who suffered more were also more likely to turn toward religious faith. Maybe once a person is no longer able to rely on herself or her surroundings, she looks for the kinds of support offered by religious faith. Such quests for meaning in the context of suffering and sacrifice are themes discussed by Holocaust survivor Viktor Frankl: "The crowning experience of all, for the homecoming man, is the wonderful feeling that, after all he has suffered, there is nothing he need fear any more—except his God."[19]

Throughout the long-term process of psychotherapy for people affected by Soviet traumatization, a patient's effort to overcome traumatic experiences often opens them up to the themes of religious faith. As Gražina Gudaitė remarks:

A prayer and seeking a connection with the Almighty. This is familiar to most of those who have been traumatized: In a case of unavoidable necessity, [prayer] remains the only available way of coping. Prayers help one concentrate and seek a connection with higher powers, thus helping to withdraw from the destructivity of the situation. On the one hand, it is a withdrawal; on the other hand, it is a switching toward relationship with someone higher.[20]

Clearly, religious faith was important for the exiled Lithuanian people as a means of coping with the horrors of their exile. As Vidmantas Šimkunas points out in this volume, clandestine acts of religious devotion and education were critical for the psychological balance of many Lithuanian Christians. For those who remained in occupied Lithuania, the choice about their faith was a sign of either resistance or submission to the aggressively atheistic government. Consequently, church attendance became an important part of personal identity.

RELIGIOUS IDENTITY

From the very beginning of the Soviet occupation, people were forced to prove their loyalty to the regime. The most obvious demonstration of one's loyalty was joining communist organizations, such as the Communist Party or the Union of the Communist Youth (*Komsomol*). In the popular imagination, these organizations were associated with atheism and demanded that a person relinquish their religious identity in order to join. In contrast, keeping one's faith and attending church became an expression of one's religious identity and commitment to the dream of an independent, democratic Lithuania.[21] Both personally and publicly, the choice was clear: either join the *Komsomol* or stay true to your faith. Nijolė Sadūnaitė remarks:

At school, the teachers forced me and my brother to join the pioneers [a school-level Communist organization for people too young to join the *Komsomol*], and later the komsomol. I was often kept until midnight in the teachers' lounge, and my brother and other students were forced to write application letters to Komsomol at gunpoint by partorg Ubagevičius. . . . Having disobeyed him, we were thrown out of the school. When our mother was called to the school, she said, "If only pioneers and Komsomol members can study, my children won't go to school. I'd rather let them stay uneducated, and grow up to be decent people, rather than be two-faced suck-ups." . . . Two weeks later our teachers themselves invited us back to school. We were protected by our mother's strength! But how many mothers dared not protect their children back then.[22]

Others who did not dare such open resistance considered church attendance and the celebration of Christian holidays a form of resistance in its own right. It was a measure of preservation for their autonomy, dignity, and distance from the Soviet system.

> I was pious, even though I used to be a member of the komsomol, I believed in God. . . . I had to join the Party. My wife was also a member, but in her heart not a Party person. She was a member, she taught political classes against religion, and now she has been persuaded by the school to teach religion, which even she herself found funny. Most of the instructors knew that my wife was religious and anticommunist, but we were friends, so they kept their mouths shut. . . . I was a Party member, but I took my son to First Communion. When my daddy died, I went to church and no one said a word about it. My cousin is a priest, and wouldn't advertise that, but as I entered the parsonage, I would still greet him with "Praise the Lord."[23]

RELIGION AS RESISTANCE

As noted in the chapters by Streikus and Šimkunas, the Lithuanian Catholic community was active in resistance against Nazi and Soviet occupation. The Catholic community was responsible for establishing the underground movement during Nazi occupation that later transformed into an armed resistance movement during the first decade of the second Soviet occupation. This underground movement and the popular periodical the *Chronicle of the Catholic Church in Lithuania* were the strongest and most articulate forms of anti-Soviet resistance.[24] Lead by priests, religious women, and laypeople, the *Chronicle* kept Catholics informed of religious activities as well as incidents of religious persecution in schools and workplaces. Such people who bravely resisted the Soviet regime became pillars of moral resistance.

Sister Ksavera Veriankaitė kept a diary from her youth until the time she spent in the Catholic underground. She secretly entered the religious order of the Handmaids of the Sacred Heart of Jesus (ACJ) in the summer of 1940, though her community's convent had been destroyed by the Soviets. She took her solemn vows during the German occupation in 1943. After the Soviet reoccupation in 1944, Sister Ksavera worked as an accountant in the government forestry department while secretly continuing her underground ministry as a religious sister. Her diary reflects her courageous efforts to resist the demoralization caused by Soviet repression.

> The foresters seem to drink a little less. I've had some serious talks about this with the deputy. I don't demand they all turn to abstinence, I tell them they can and sometimes even should "drink" (for instance, under great stress, especially nowadays), but not to the point of blacking out, as Lithuanians have recently learned. I don't scold them anymore when they're drunk, and if they start explaining themselves, I don't argue, but I am strictly abstinent myself, and I try to do that in an unemphatic way, so I don't lose their respect.[25]

Conclusion

Research on collective trauma is difficult and multifaceted. Some intellectuals have even begun to refer to a "fashion of victimization" and an "obsession with uniqueness" among those who claim to suffer from trauma and those who study them.[26] To complicate things even more, calls to never forget social oppression have given rise to a countermovement: the "apologia for forgetfulness." Some argue that "half a century on, grief as a genuine feeling is no longer possible" and that "any effort to stimulate it is a moral exploitation of the dead."[27]

None of these developments corresponds to the Lithuanian experience. In this case, the full extent of the trauma and the suffering of its victims still wait to be recognized. The challenging effects of long traumatization under extreme conditions are painfully evident in Lithuania's contemporary effort to rebuild a democratic nation. If practices of religious faith and religious community aided in trauma resistance during Lithuania's long night of oppression, possibly these traditions can be drawn on during its long dawn of democracy.

NOTES

1. See Dalia Kuodytė, "Traumatising History," in *The Psychology of Extreme Traumatisation: The Aftermath of Political Repression*, ed. Danutė Gailienė (Vilnius: Akreta, 2005), 13–25.

2. See Arūnas Streikus, "Democracy and Catholicism in Twentieth-Century Lithuania," in this volume.

3. See Kuodytė, "Traumatising History," 17.

4. See Arvydas Anušauskas, *Lietuvių tautos sovietinis naikinimas 1940–1958 metais* (Vilnius: Mintis, 1996).

5. See Nijolė Gaškaitė-Žemaitienė, *Lageris, Juodųjų dienų sakmės* (Vilnius: Genocide and Resistance Research Center of Lithuania, 2001), 520–31.

6. See Anušauskas, *Lietuvių tautos*, 151.

7. See Danutė Gailienė and Evaldas Kazlauskas, "Fifty Years On: The Long-Term Psychological Effects of Soviet Repression in Lithuania," in *The Psychology of Extreme Traumatisation: The Aftermath of Political Repression*, ed. Danutė Gailienė (Vilnius: Akreta, 2005), 67–107.

8. See Danutė Gailienė, "Politinių represijų psichologiniai padariniai," *Genocidas ir rezistencija* 2 (2002): 124.

9. See Ieva Vaskelienė, "Ilgalaikės politinių represijų pasekmės antrajai kartai" (PhD diss., Vilnius University, 2012).

10. See Lars Weisaeth, "Psychotraumatology: An Overview from a European Perspective," in Gailieneė, *The Psychology of Extreme Traumatisation*, 26–66.

11. Vytautas Kubilius, "Kelias į niekur per lūžtantį iliuzijų ledą," *Metai* 8–9 (2003): 125.

12. See Gailienė and Kazlauskas, "Fifty Years On," 67–107.

13. After the Second World War, the organized Lithuanian partisan resistance to Soviet occupation lasted for ten years.

14. Lionginas Baliukevičius, *Partizano Dzūko dienoraštis: 1948 m. birželio 23 d.–1949 m. birželio 6 d.* (Vilnius: Lietuvos gyventojų genocido ir rezistencijos tyrimo centras, 2002), 112. *Samogon* is homemade vodka.

15. See Irena Šutinienė, "Sovietinio laikotarpio atminties bruožai autobiografiniuose pasakojimuose," in *Socialinė atmintis: minėjimai ir užmarštys*, ed. Eugenija Krukauskienė , Irena Šutinienė, Inija Trinkūnienė, Anelė Vosyliūtė (Vilnius: Eugrimas, 2003), 13–66.

16. Quotations from semi-structured interviews of repressed persons.

17. See K. Allden, Ch. Poole, S. Chantavanich, K. Ohmar, N. Aung, and R. Mollica, "Burmese Political Dissidents in Thailand: Trauma and Survival among Young Adults in Exile," *American Journal of Public Health* 86 (1996): 1561–69; Lawrence G. Calhoun, Amie Cann, Richard G. Tedeschi, and Jamie McMillan, "A Correlational Testing the Relationship between Posttraumatic Growth, Religion, and Cognitive Processing," *Journal of Traumatic Stress* 13 (2000): 521–27; C. V. O. Witvliet, K. A. Phipps, M. E. Feldman, and J. C. Beckham, "Posttraumatic Mental and Physical Health Correlates of Forgiveness and Religious Coping in Military Veterans," *Journal of Traumatic Stress* 17 (2004): 269–74.

18. See Evaldas Kazlauskas, "Politinių represijų ilgalaikės psichologinės pasekmės" (PhD diss., Vilnius University, 2006).

19. Viktor Frankl, *Man's Search for Meaning: An Introduction to Logotherapy* (Boston: Beacon Press, 2002), 100.

20. See Gražina Gudaitė, "Psychological After Effects of the Soviet Trauma and the Analytical Process," in *The Psychology of Extreme Traumatisation*, Gailenė, 108–26.

21. See Šutinienė, "Sovietinio laikotarpio," 13–66.

22. Nijolė Sadūnaitė, *Skubėkime daryti gera* (Vilnius: Katalikų akademija, 1998), 45. A *partorg* was the head of the Communist party at school.

23. Šutinienė, "Sovietinio laikotarpio," 26, 52.

24. See Streikus's chapter in this volume.

25. Ksavera Variankaitė, *Viskas praėjo* (Kaunas, Lithuania: Naujasis Amžius, 2009), 134.

26. See Virgis Valentinavičius, "Holokaustas Amerikos gyvenime: atminties kultūros vingiai," *Naujasis židinys* 12 (2001): 667–74, and Ofer Zur, "The Psychology of Victimhood," in *Destructive Trends in Mental Health: The Well-Intentioned Path to Harm*, ed. by Rogers H. Wright and Nicolas A. Cummings (New York: Routledge, 2005), 45–64.

27. Rudolf Burger, "Atminties politikos klaidos: užmaršties apologija," *Naujasis židinys* 12 (2001): 666.

Christianity and Politics in Post-Soviet Lithuania: Between Totalitarian Experience and Democracy

Nerija Putinaitė

Stereotypes about Christianity and attitudes of Christians toward public action were engrained into the minds of Lithuanian people during the Soviet regime and are evident in contemporary Lithuania. As clearly outlined in the chapters by Streikus and Šimkunas, the Soviet ideological apparatus sought to annihilate the influence of Christianity from the lives of people. From the beginning of the Soviet occupation of Lithuania in 1940–1941, and especially from 1944 until Stalin's death in 1953, the Christian churches in Lithuania were brutally attacked as "the biggest obstacle to the smooth sovietisation of the occupied country."[1] Many priests were deported, parishioners were intimidated, and churches were transformed into "useful" buildings, such as cinemas, stores, sports halls, or museums.[2] Christian beliefs, rituals, symbols, and morality were expelled from the public sphere. Christianity was identified as a residue of the past that would gradually disappear from the lives of Soviet citizens.

Anti-Christian and anti-Catholic propaganda was part of the Soviet regime's widespread atheist campaign. As the humor journal *Šluota* (*The Broom*) said in 1979:

The Catholic Church fooled people by thrusting various kinds of "saints" on them, setting their statues and hanging their images everywhere. The simple folk worshiped them by falling on their knees, but the "servants of God" treated [the saints] like simple daily objects—bed, table or chair.[3]

As evidence for the mere material nature of saints' statues, the journal presented an archival account from 1642 that fixed the sums for renovation of statues damaged during war. The public sphere was filled with this manner of simplistic argumentation.

Such propaganda against religious faith and atheist indoctrination in schools bore fruit. By the 1980s, most people younger than thirty had retreated from participating in the Christian religion or were afraid openly to declare personal religiosity. According to Antanas Balsys, "More than 40% of boys and girls of that age had never been believers, about 20% of their contemporaries were believers, but during the maturation process, through learning and education, they developed a materialistic world-view."[4]

To replace Christianity, the Soviet regime imposed a way of life based on values that contradicted Christian morality. The regime's totalitarian ideology subjected people to a kind of normative-totalitarian morality that rejected the freedom of the citizen in public life and put strict limits on his or her personal responsibility. The morality that supported the totalitarian order rejected the possibility of human will to change the world. Change was based on deterministic social and political factors. According to this ideology, the actions of the individual could succeed only if they corresponded to the determined course of events. The Soviet state claimed to know these determinations and be the main agent leading to the accomplishment of these historical necessities.

These developments had deep consequences on personality. People learned to lead a double life, as Danutė Gailienė explained in her chapter in this volume. People learned that their personal attitudes and values could have no influence on the state's political and social judgments. To survive, one's public persona required a quiet, stoic compliance while one's true inner feelings had to be guarded carefully. A person could trust no one, not even one's family members. Steady erosion of natural social links between people characterized daily life in Soviet society.

Even though the Soviet atheistic campaign was total and unrelenting, the regime neither closed all the churches nor criminalized all church activity. Through this cynical tactic, the regime could maintain the ruse of religious freedom to the outside world. Meanwhile, what remained for Christians was private adult religious practice, outside the public eye. As such, the alternative Christian worldview and model of community based on trust and love was never utterly extinguished.

Where it could be practiced, religious faith helped preserve authentic human relationships and prevent the personal breakdowns caused by the Soviet experience.[5] It is true that the Catholic Church in Lithuania played a crucial role in resistance to the regime and in the rise of public movements leading to the declaration of independence in 1990. However, the larger reality is that after years of government attack on Christian faith and morality, people either left the faith or learned—as Vidmantas Šimkunas points out in his chapter in this volume—to restrict its practice to the private sphere. The majority of Lithuanians lost the habits and imagination necessary to build and maintain a society inspired by Christian principles and values. The Soviet heritage for a Christian in today's democratic Lithuania is the separation of private and public life, disillusionment regarding possibilities to have a personal impact on political life, and acceptance of the inevitable incongruity of private and public morality.

The Legal Faces of Christianity in Soviet Lithuania

The Soviet regime in Lithuania depicted Christianity in two general ways. The first way was expressed in the phrase "opium of the people." This phrase from Karl Marx was used repeatedly to further Lenin's revolution and present Christianity as an instrument of fraud. The second way was to identify Christianity as the destroyer of Lithuania's "genuine" national identity.[6] Both of these negative faces were attributed to Christianity in general, but more specifically to the Catholic Church as the dominant Christian church in Lithuania.

"Opium of the People"

Soviet ideology identified the Catholic Church and its representatives as an exploiting class of priests and hierarchs that kept the mass of people suppressed by superstitious lies. This ideology became a literary cliché in popular novels. Soviet novels presented priest characters as incarnations of evil, protected by the Catholic Church as they engaged in fraud, lying, adultery, greediness, and even murder.

One of the most popular Soviet crime novels was *Prelatas Olšauskas* by Jonas Kauneckis. This novel (referred to as a "documentary" by the Soviet press) follows the story of a crime in the 1930s.[7] A woman, identified as the mistress of a priest, is found murdered. The investigation gradually reveals the priest's destructive social activities, his huge influence upon people through Christian organizations, and his debauched personal life. There are suspicions that he had earlier murdered a son he had with the mistress. The final tribunal finds him guilty of murdering his mistress.[8]

In Soviet ideology, not all priests were depicted as wicked. The honest and consistent priests were those who came to their senses and broke away from the Catholic Church as the ill organization. The Soviet regime searched for men who would tell their story of having renounced their priesthood, left the Church, and replaced service to Christians with service to the Soviet people. In Lithuania, two such stories were well-known.

Jonas Ragauskas renounced his priesthood in 1948 and became a public propagandist for atheism. He wrote several books that were reissued many times with large print runs. The most famous was the 1960 *Ite, missa est!* For this and other works, Ragauskas was awarded the highest official state prize in Lithuania. From the regime's standpoint, Ragauskas liberated the minds of the people from the fairy-tale teachings of the Catholic Church, teachings that had made them afraid to construct their own lives by their own "natural" impulses. Ragauskas admonished people to "understand what religion is, how far it is from real life, how much it contradicts the basic demands of human nature."[9]

Ragauskas's story was appealing to a mass audience but less so to Lithuanian intellectuals.[10] To this latter group, the biography of the Lithuanian writer and poet Vincas Mykolaitis-Putinas was more compelling. Putinas was ordained a Catholic priest but did not practice his priesthood among people in a parish. Rather, he spent his time writing a semi-autobiographical novel *In the Shadow of the Altars* (*Altorių šešėlyje*), which was published in 1933. *In the Shadow of the Altars* tells the story of the inner doubts and searches of a young, talented, and sentimental seminarian Liudas Vasaris. He investigates his feelings and thoughts about life and his mission in the world and engages in long intellectual discussions with his friends and colleagues. Vasaris gradually decides to reject anything that blocks his calling to produce literary and creative work, including the priesthood and the Catholic Church. As a Soviet critic says, "the greatest worth of the book is the emphasis on humanity in the individual biography of an ex-priest."[11]

In 1935, Putinas himself renounced his priesthood and became a member of the Soviet Lithuanian Academy of Sciences during the first Soviet occupation (1940–1941). The Soviet regime used Putinas as an exemplar of an intellectual. His book was constantly republished and included in the obligatory reading list for secondary schools.[12] The idea that social and spiritual life should be exclusively focused on the human being, with no reference to God, was the basis for Soviet-style humanism.

Soviet humanism was a post-religious ideology that satisfied the creative and cultural needs of the Communist intelligentsia in Khrushchev era.[13] From this perspective, Christian spirituality was regressive and the activity of the Catholic Church was repressive. The regime made every effort to form the attitudes and feelings of people according to this perspective. As a totalitarian regime, it possessed every means to spread and impose its ideas: through schools, books, state prizes and awards for the most loyal citizens, and employment privileges for those who devoted their talents to this ideology.

"Genuine" National Identity

The idea of an independent Lithuanian national state was born in the nineteenth century. Part of that development required finding authentic grounds for Lithuanian national self-identification. Lithuanians have a very old language and a rich folklore that predates the arrival of Christian missionaries at the beginning of the eleventh century.[14] During some periods of history, Lithuania had a very close relation with Poland, a people for whom Catholicism was an essential part of national identity. As such, Catholicism could always be considered "a firm basis for alliance with the Poles."[15] However, in the nineteenth century this relationship with Poland was considered a threat to Lithuanian national revival. Fears existed that Lithuanian identity would be absorbed and lost in Poland's Catholic culture. This led many Lithuanian intellectuals to look for an "authentic" Lithuanian identity, an identity rooted in traditions that predated the arrival of Christianity. To the extent that Lithuanian strength came to be seen as rooted in its pre-Christian culture, Christianity and the Catholic Church came to be seen as a diminishment of that strength.[16]

This idea became stronger in the late Soviet period of the 1960s and 1970s, empowered by the work of historians and the writings of poets.[17] This latter group was part of a broad interest among young people in retrieving "authentic" Lithuanian folk culture.[18] This was further strengthened by university students doing archaeological research that involved going to villages, visiting the elderly, recording folk songs and proverbs, and gathering many forms of folklore.[19]

By the 1970s, the folklore movement was stretching dangerously beyond the confines of Soviet ideology. Yet, the movement was useful for local Soviet officials who wanted to strengthen their power in Lithuania against political domination of the central authorities in Moscow. Supporting Lithuanian nationalism was a way for local communists to show, albeit cynically, that they really cared for the Lithuanian people.[20]

Folklore groups were infiltrated by people who reported on their activity, but they were not overtly persecuted except for one massive arrest and interrogation by the KGB in 1973.[21] The number of groups grew, from folk dance groups to closed neo-pagan groups that practiced rituals of nature worship. As the movement grew, it came to be seen by the participants as a resistance movement against non-authentic official Soviet culture.

As this complex movement for authentic Lithuanian culture grew, so too did its anti-Christian and anti-Catholic emphasis. The more Christianity was seen as an alien imposition on "authentic" Lithuanian culture, the more it was regarded as irrelevant for dealing with Lithuania's moral, social, and political issues. A prevalent stereotype in contemporary Lithuania is that Catholicism and "authentic" Lithuanian culture represent two opposing worldviews.

Post-Soviet Reality: Christians in Politics

During the fifty years of Soviet totalitarianism in Lithuania, a generation of young people grew up under the ideology of atheism, constantly barraged by negative images of Christianity and vilification of Christian laypeople and clergy. Many young people were not baptized because their parents either lost their faith or did not want to have problems with Soviet authorities.

The experience of systemic atheist thought and practice has left today's post-Soviet Lithuanians with a four-fold view of the place of Christianity in public affairs. Some take an instrumental view of Christianity, seeing a social benefit to Christian-inspired charitable activities and moral attitudes. Others take a personalized view of Christianity and society. Here, Christianity is viewed as an exclusively private matter that should have no bearing on public affairs and should not be "tarnished" by involvement in politics. There are also those who retain the Soviet view of Christianity as a regressive ideology alien to Lithuanians' authentic identity and irrelevant to the demands of contemporary life. Despite the fact that this view is most obviously linked to the recent past, all three have been influenced by the Soviet mentality toward Christianity.

Finally, for the post-totalitarian mind that did not have a lived experience of religious faith, Christianity is easily marginalized into a kind of cultural heritage for tourists, cultural anthropologists, and historians. It is easy to look upon surviving Christian churches as pretty places to have weddings and funerals. One often hears stories of young couples who are planning their weddings but are not satisfied with a modest church interior or a priest who is not sufficiently famous for their ceremony. There are cases where people have expressed anger when priests refuse to perform a funeral mass because no one in the party is a practicing Christian. In an increasingly consumer society, more and more people look at the Christian church as a decorative service that should be available to anyone willing to pay.

Christianity is likewise not taken seriously as a basis for thought and action in public life. This is not only the attitude of post-Soviet atheists. Many Lithuanian Christians themselves are skeptical about the relationship between their faith and public life. This is exemplified in the activity of the the Christian Party.

In Lithuania, there are two political parties with the word "Christian" in their names: the Lithuanian Christian Democrats (LCD) and the Party of Christians (PC). The Lithuanian Christian Democrats[22] is actually a sub-party of the united party Union of Homeland–Lithuanian Christian Democrats.[23] The Party of Christians was established in 2010 after the merger of two smaller Christian parties.[24] Both the LCD sub-party and the main party have very low popularity among Lithuanian voters. About 80 percent of their members are declared Catholics. The LCD received only 1.4 percent of the vote in the 2004 parliamentary election. The PC received some mandates after the municipal election of 2011, but according to public opinion polls, the party had very low chances of getting into Parliament after the election of 2012. It eventually got about 1 percent of the vote, putting no members in Parliament.[25]

The Christian basis of the PC is highly problematic. An applicant to the party is not asked if he or she belongs to any Christian denomination.[26] Furthermore, the the PC program includes within it no discernible Christian goals and principles. It states:

> Our goal is to cherish spiritual and moral values and cultural traditions of the nation, and the democratic society and state governance that is subject to the modern citizen, to encourage development of the economy and private business initiative, to guarantee to every citizen minimal welfare correspondent to the economic conditions as means to social security of society and personal welfare, insistently defend rightful interests of all citizens of Lithuania at home and abroad.[27]

While the party program advocates moral politics, a socially oriented market economy, and support for the traditional family, the words "Christian" and "God" are never used.[28] These words do appear in the LCD program: "The values that we follow are based on the Christian concept of human being as a person and on the acceptance of his responsibility to God."[29] Nevertheless, the LCD party is not popular.

One might think that in Lithuania, with a majority of its population still identifying itself as Catholic, the word "Christian" would have a place in political discourse. This is not the case. "Christianity" and "Catholicism" are not words significant for framing any political discourse. Later chapters in this volume, by Russell Powell and David Ingram, present excellent studies of the complex issue of the place of religious language and commitment within democratic political discourse. The comparisons made in these chapters between Lithuania and Indonesia, Peru, the United States, and even Muslim Turkey, are highly informative.

In the case of Lithuania, many Christians want to keep Christianity separate from politics because the political sphere is an environment of "discredited morality."[30] In other words, Christian moral standards may be relevant to personal attitudes, but not to public debate. Many Christians do not see how they can be involved in politics without compromising their moralities. This may explain the decline in popularity of the LCD and the inadequate program statements of the PC.

At the same time, Lithuanian society as a whole is currently passive toward the public life and unwilling to take active responsibility for social and political matters. In the Soviet state, Lithuanians developed a feeling of resistance to the Soviet public values and the Soviet state structures. Lithuanian Christians shared an overall feeling of resistance and now, like most Lithuanians, transfer it to the Lithuanian democratic state.

The complex situation of Christianity and Lithuanian politics is revealed in the ongoing discussion of public policy regarding the family. The subject appeared on the stage in 2008, with the parliamentary discussion on the National Concept of Family Policy.[31] It emphasized the idea of traditional family as opposed to non-traditional family, the latter most associated with heterosexual couples living together outside of marriage. The National Concept was adopted in September 2008, stating, "Family is an essential good of society that derives from human nature and is based on free marital commitment of man and woman to dedicate their lives for creation of family relationship."[32] Although the word "Christian" was not used in the National Concept, most people understood the idea of traditional family as consistent with the teachings of the Catholic Church.

From the beginning, the National Concept met with strong political opposition. Some saw it as an effort by a minority of active Catholic believers to impose a restrictive definition of family on the majority.[33] A group of Parliament members, led by the Social Democrats, appealed to the Constitutional Court, claiming that the National Concept contradicted basic human rights and legalized discrimination against non-traditional families.

In September 2011, the Constitutional Court declared that the National Concept of Family Policy contradicted the constitution insofar as it identified family with marriage. The Constitutional Court declared that marriage is only one among other relationships upon which to build a family. Thus, the idea that marriage is the sole basis for defining a family was found unconstitutional.[34] This decision stimulated a wave of debate in Parliament. This discussion resulted in an initiative to introduce language into the Constitution that would prioritize the marriage-based family over other forms of partnership.[35] In June 2012, Parliament rejected this initiative by one vote short of the two-thirds necessary to make the correction. However, the defeat of the initiative did not close the debate.

Some claimed that the argument about marriage and family was more about form than content, that the language of "traditional family" was really a code phrase for remaking society according to a "particular political and religious ideology."[36] Some also identified this as the ideas of an older generation of Christians out of touch with the contemporary world. Public opinion polls revealed more support for "traditional family" among older people than younger people.[37] There were calls to move beyond the ideology of the traditional family and to look at the real, human problems in families, such as adequate care for children, protection against violence, and securing the careers of mothers.

The National Concept debate reveals the main tension Christianity faces in a post-totalitarian democratic state. The debate lacked open-minded, civil argumentation that would have permitted clarification of moral positions on all sides. The main agents of the discussion were politicians promoting positions for the purposes of power, not arguments for the purpose of clarity and civil communication.[38]

The indifferent attitude of the Lithuanian population toward the political debate indicates general skepticism about the significance of serious moral discourse in the public sphere. Indeed, when arguments came close to serious moral analysis, most participants raised the "danger of ideologization" and questioned the legitimacy of any moral discussion that would go deeper than meeting the immediate, utilitarian needs of the day.

As the discussion of the Concept of Family Policy reveals, society is suspicious of political participation that includes serious articulation of moral Christian positions. Politicians do not investigate or disclose the bases of their positions for fear that they would lose public attention and support. Such an approach ensures that political debate remains at a superficial level and that Christian principles are not given a hearing in civil society.

Does Post-Soviet Democracy Need Christianity?

The Soviet regime separated the church from the state and dissociated society from the state. Citizens could not play a critical role in the political order. The folk-group activity at the end of the Soviet order played a kind of critical role but not a productive one. It did not encourage positive participation in government and it delegitimated the credibility of Christian participation in Lithuanian culture and politics.[39]

The post-totalitarian inheritance in Lithuania is weak citizen involvement in the life of the state and society, weak social solidarity, and a diffident attitude toward social values and ideals. The situation is a national danger. Like any other society, Lithuania needs common normative grounds to survive. A positive attitude toward the state and democratic practices is required for the protection of human rights and human freedom.

It would be difficult to agree with the position of some scholars and politicians who believe that Christianity is implicit in practices of contemporary democracy. There is scant evidence for the idea that Christianity subtly underlies Lithuanian politics and public discourse. It may that the "old democracies" of Europe and North America retain democratic and social practices rooted in religious traditions. If such traditions existed in the pre-Soviet Baltic states, they were effectively eliminated by the habits, practices, and attitudes formed by fifty years of aggressively atheistic totalitarianism.

The desire to practice authentic democracy in a manner respectful of religious values has yet to break through Lithuania's non-democratic and anti-Christian Soviet legacy. Even though the Christian churches in Lithuania, especially the Catholic Church, were the only institutions to offer an alternative to the Soviet view of the human being and society, that alternative had yet to resurface. Twenty-three years of independence and freedom has not been long enough to form a new openness to religion as a basis for personal life and civic engagement.

In post-Soviet Lithuania, Christianity is either dismissed outright or used to further one's political ambitions. The repression of religion is characteristic not only of Soviet Lithuania but also post-Soviet Lithuania. As

C. S. Lewis has the devil say in *The Screwtape Letters*: "Certainly we do not want men to allow their Christianity to flow over their political life, for the establishment of anything like a really just society would be a major disaster."[40] On the other hand, there is a role for Christianity in politics acceptable even to the evil spirit. The nature of Christianity can be distorted, and it can be used for evil, when it is seen as a means to achieve "good" political ends, such as social justice.

The contemporary skepticism of Lithuanian citizens and government leaders toward political ideas and actions based on Christian ideas is a residue of the Soviet experience. Thus far, the twisted view that Christian ideas promote evil, inhumane goals has not fundamentally changed in Lithuanian society. There is no doubt that an untwisting of this complex relationship will take time. The work on social trauma by Danutė Gailienė in this volume makes this clear. Nevertheless, the future of democracy in Lithuania relies on hope that Lithuania can enter a new period of historical honesty, restorative civic practices, and inclusion of religious discourse in the public sphere.

NOTES

1. Arūnas Streikus, "Represijos prieš Bažnyčią Lietuvoje," in *Pilietinis pasipriešinimas Lietuvoje ir Lenkijoje: sąsajos ir ypatumai, 1939–1956*, ed. Arvydas Anušauskas (Vilnius: Lietuvos gyventojų genocide ir rezistencijos tyrimo centras, 2004), 367.

2. Because of the high ceilings, some of the churches suffered overlays that destroyed the interior, such as the Evangelical-Lutheran Church in Vilnius. Some churches were transformed into museums. The Church of St. John survived being a paper store and in 1979 became the Museum for Science.

3. *"Šluotos" kalendorius, 1978* (Vilnius: Leidykla Mintis, 1978), 30. Another example is the joke about a grandchild who does not understand the religious stories told by his grandmother and reacts by saying that God's occupation should be an electrician, because he makes the light appear. *"Šluotos" kalendorius, 1971* (Vilnius: Lietuvos TSR Žurnalistu sajungos leidinys, 1970), 194.

4. Antanas Balsys, "Ateizacijos ypatybės ir veiksniai," in *Ateizmas ir dabartis*, ed. Jonas Mačiulis, Jonas Aničas, and Antanas Balsys, 41–66 (Vilnius: Mintis, 1983). However, the same inquiry revealed that 13 percent of working citizens and students were convinced Christians.

5. Danutė Gailienė, *Ką jie mums padarė. Lietuvos gyvenimas traumų ir psichologijos žvilgsniu* (Vilnius: Tyto alba, 2008), 201.

6. In 1965, the Central Committee of the Lithuanian Communist Party discussed the necessity of establishing a Museum of Peoples' Life (Liaudies buities muziejus) to satisfy ideological needs. See "LKP CK biuro nutarimas dėl muziejų vaidmens padidinimo ideologiniame darbe. Vilnius, 1965 m. sausio 13 d.," in *Lietuvos kultūra sovietinės ideologijos nelaisvėje 1940–1990. Dokumentų rinkinys*, ed. J. R. Bagušauskas and A. Streikus (Vilnius: Lietuvos gyventojų genocide ir rezistencijos tyrimo centras, 2005), 345. By "Peoples' Life," the Central Committee meant the "natural" life of the peasant. In Lithuanian, the word *liaudis* is used as both "folk" in the ethnographical sense and "people" in the Marxist sense. Therefore, its use in the name of the museum is more of a reference to Marxism than to ethnography. The museum was supposed to be an open-air ethnographic village, including authentic wooden peasant houses and technical facilities brought from different Lithuanian regions. The museum was established in 1966. During this period, the "local heritage movement" (Kraštotyros judėjimas) arose, which focused on looking for remnants of pagan culture, usually stones or other objects used for pre-Christian rituals. An established Lithuanian society called Lietuvos kraštotyros draugija was formed for this purpose.

7. The first version of the novel was published in the official Writers' Union magazine *Pergalė* (*The Victory*) in 1957. Later, the rewritten story was published as a separate novel in 1961, with a second edition 1962. A third edition of twenty thousand copies was published in 1984. The film version of the story came out in 1984 as *Nine Circles of the Fall* (*Devyni nuopolio ratai*). Because new books and Lithuanian films were extremely rare, Kauneckis's story would have reached nearly every Soviet Lithuanian family in one way or another.

8. Jonas Kauneckis, *Prelatas Olšauskas, dokumentinė apybraiža, trečias leidimas* (Vilnius: Vaga, 1984), 219.

9. Jonas Ragauskas, *Nenoriu dangaus* (Vilnius: Vaga, 1970), 414.

10. In a propaganda collection of a hundred answers to actual questions on religion to Ragauskas, a separate question on reasons to reject the priesthood and religion is presented. See Feliksas Mačianskas, *Šimtas religijos mįslių* (Vilnius: Vyturys, 1985), 378–81.

11. Janina Žėkaitė, "Kunigo drama altorių šešėly," in *Žmonės ir religija* (Vilnius: Vaga, 1977), 70.

12. The first Soviet edition was published in 1946 as Vincas Mykolaitis-Putinas, *Altorių šešėly* (Vilnius: Valstybinė grožinės literatūros leidykla, 1946). This edition was followed by nine more Soviet editions.

13. The symbolic turning point for Soviet humanism is the poem "Human being" (*Žmogus*) by Eduardas Mieželaitis. It was first published 1959 and awarded the Lenin state prize in 1962. The poem develops secular

human-cosmic and human-centric images, like "My body—the body of my earth." See Eduardas Mieželaitis, *Žmogus* (Vilnius: Vaga, 1971), 18.

14. The name "Lithuania" was first mentioned in chronicles in relation to the martyrdom of Saint Bruno in 1009.

15. This was the view of the patriarch of Lithuanian independence, Jonas Basanavičius in *Gabija, Praktinė knyga, paaukota Lietuvos dainiaus vyskupo Antano Baranausko atminimui* (Krakow, Poland: Gebethnerio & Co. Knygynas, 1907), 3.

16. The impulse for further development of this nationalist anti-Catholic idea was given by the 1970 publication of a censored edition of selected works by Jonas Basanavičius, especially his article "Iš krikščionijos santykių su senovės lietuvių tikyba ir kultūra" ("On the Relationships of Christianity and the Ancient Lithuanian Faith and Culture"), in *Rinktiniai raštai*, ed. Jonas Basanavičius (Vilnius: Vaga, 1970).

17. One of the most prized Soviet Lithuanian poets was Justinas Marcinkevičius. In his poem *Mažvydas*, Marcinkevičius has Lutheran pastor Martynas Mažvydas participating in strange pre-Christian rituals. See Justinas Marcinkevičius, *Mindaugas, Mažvydas, Katedra, draminė trilogija* (Kaunas, Lithuania: Šviesa, 1988), 102–5.

18. Ethnologist Norbertas Vėlius and archaeologist Pranė Dundulienė were the most prominent academic researchers. See Norbertas Vėlius, *Senovės baltų pasaulėžiūra* (Vilnius: Mintis, 1983), and Pranė Dundulienė, "Senovės lietuvių religijos klausimu," in *Lietuvos TSR Aukštųjų mokyklų mokslo darbai, Istorija* 10 (1969): 181–207.

19. On the various forms of ethno-cultural movement, see Jūratė Kavaliauskaitė and Ainė Ramonaitė, eds., *Sajūdžio ištakų beieškant: Nepaklusniųjų tinklaveikos galia* (Vilnius: Baltos lankos, 2011), 41–58.

20. Arūnas Streikus, "Sovietų režimo pastangos pakeisti Lietuvos gyventojų tautinį identitetą," *Genocidas ir rezistencija* 20, no. 1 (2007): 20.

21. Arvydas Anušauskas, et al., *Lietuva, 1940–1990: okupuotos Lietuvos istorija* (Vilnius: Lietuvos gyventojų genocido ir rezistencijos tyrimo centras, 2005), 524.

22. The party derives from Party of Lithuanian Christian Democrats, which was founded in 1917, a year before Lithuania's first experience of independence. The party was re-established in January 1990 as the Lithuanian Party of Christian Democrats. This was before the restoration of the Lithuanian state, which occurred the following March. In 2001 the party took the name Lithuanian Christian Democrats.

23. The parties united before the parliamentary election of 2008 and from 2008 to 2012 was the largest member of a ruling coalition.

24. The Social Union of Conservative Christians and the Lithuanian Party of Christian Democracy had no noticeable role in Lithuanian political life at the time.

25. Party leader Linas Karalius publicly discussed his participation in "swinger parties." Eventually, he lost his mandate as a member of Parliament because of disregard for his duties.

26. See Krikščionių partija, "Narystes anketa," http://www.krikscion iupartija.lt/index.php?option=com_autoledi&view=addons&layout=become amember.

27. Translation by Nerija Putinaite. "Krikščionių partijos programa," http://www.krikscioniupartija.lt/programa/straipsnis?view=main.

28. References to the "traditional family" indicate a Christian political orientation in Lithuania, so it is safe to say that the program indirectly indicates Christian values.

29. See Tėvynės Sąjunga, Lietuvos krikščionys demokratai, "Jungtinės partijos," http://www.lkdp.lt/programa/36-jungtins-partijos-tvyns-sjunga -lietuvos-krikionys-demokratai-bendrijos-lietuvos-krikionys-demokratai -programa.html.

30. As indicated by a public opinion poll conducted in April 2012, only 4.8 percent of the Lithuanian population is positive (to 71.2 percent negative) about Parliament and only 4.0 percent are positive about political parties (to 74.9 percent negative). In public opinion, only the president of Lithuania was regarded as a "politician" with "moral authority": 56.9 percent positive to 15.2 percent negative. See Vilmorus, "Visuomenės nuomonės tyrimas, pasitikėjimas institucijomis, 2012–04–13/23," trans. Nerija Putinaitė, http://www.vilmorus.lt/index.php?mact=News,cntnto1,detail,0&cntnto1 articleid=2&cntnto1returnid=20.

31. "Dėl Valstybinės šeimos politikos koncepcijos patvirtinimo," Parliamentary resolution No. 10–1569, 2008–06–03.

32. "About the National Concept of Family Policy," "Dėl Valstybinės šeimos politikos koncepcijos patvirtinimo," Parliamentary resolution No. 10–1569, 2008–06–03, clause 1.4.

33. At the beginning of the debate, the question of same-sex couples was not discussed. Aušra Marija Pavilionienė, a Social Democrat and member of Parliament opposed the National Concept. She stressed the possible discrimination of children that were born outside the family and women that decide to bear a child without marrying. She was the first to open the discussion to the question of same-sex relationships. In September 2011, Pavilionienė proposed the Law of Cohabiting Partnership that proposed a broad concept of partnership as complementary to the concept of traditional family.

34. Case No. 21/2008: "Nutarimas dėl Lietuvos Respublikos Seimo 2008 birželio 3 d. nutarimu Nr. X-1569 'Dėl Valstybinės šeimos politikos koncpcijos patvirtinimo' patvirtintos Valstybinės šeimos politikos koncepcijos nuostatų atitikties Lietuvos Respublikos Konstitucijai," Vilnius, 2011–09–28.

35. The Project of Amendment to the Constitution was registered in Parliament on April 5, 2012 (XIP-3981–2), and proposed an additional statement that "the family also derives from maternity and paternity." See http://www3.lrs.lt/pls/inter3/dokpaieska.showdoc_l?p_id=421 621.

36. This is according to lawyer and professor of Vilnius University, Vytautas Mizaras in "The Concept of Family: Discrimination, or When Form is Above the Content." See http://www.delfi.lt/archive/article.php?id=44879063.

37. In October 2011, the Baltic News Service agency conducted a public opinion poll revealing that 41 percent of the population supported marriage-based family, 46 percent supported a broader understanding of family, and 13 percent were indifferent.

38. As a consequence of the resolution of the Constitutional Court, a parliamentary group "for the traditional family" was founded. It included 91 out of 141 members of Parliament. The Baltic News Service public opinion poll revealed that the percentage of supporters of the traditional family in Parliament is much bigger than the percentage of supporters in Lithuanian society.

39. Ainė Ramonaitė, "Pilietinė visuomenė sovietų Lietuvoje?," in *Demokratija Lietuvoje: Pilietiškumas ir totalitarizmas XX amžiaus istorijos lūžiuose*, ed. Mingailė Jurkutė and Nerijus Šepetys (Vilnius: Naujasis židinys-Aidai, 2011), 45.

40. C. S. Lewis, *The Screwtape Letters*, (London: Centenary Press, 1944), 23.

Montaigne, Julian, and "Others": The Quest for Peaceful Coexistence in Public Space

David M. Posner

In this note on the Lithuanian Voices, we reflect on a piece by David Posner. Posner suggests that many of the themes present in contemporary discussions on the intersection of democracy and Catholicism—the relationships between persons and persons, the relationships between persons and institutions, the phenomenon and experience—both internally and externally—of "otherness," etc.—can trace their roots back, at least in part, to the sixteenth-century French philosopher Michel de Montaigne.

According to Posner, Montaigne both internalized and externalized discussions of "otherness" throughout his life. He identifies four "others" who must be accounted for in both public and private space: the Protestant, the Jew, the Cannibal, and God. Looking to the Roman emperor Julian the Apostate, Posner, via Montaigne, notes that, when it came to encountering "others," Julian successfully navigated this terrain by tolerating difference and "otherness," rather than suppressing it. Montaigne sees this as model behavior for religious persons, and particularly religious rulers, in the public square. The moral and political structures necessary for democratization rely upon the concept of toleration, particularly in those contexts where irreducible ideologies encounter each other. When considered in the light of the "double-life" required for survival in Soviet-controlled Lithuania, Montaigne's differentiation between public and private makes for an interesting comparison and contrast.

Lithuania, as we have seen, has been—and continues to be—a land of irreducible ideologies and social trauma. In light of this, Posner's turn to Montaigne proves both interesting and timely. Even more so given the specific attention Montaigne pays to the interactions between cultural, political, and religious spheres.

In the present weak state of humane Nature, surrounded as we are on all sides with Ignorance and Error, it little becomes poor fallible Man to be positive and dogmatical in his Opinions.

—Benjamin Franklin, "Dialogue Between Two Presbyterians"

In his brief essay "De la liberté de conscience,"[1] Michel de Montaigne
(1533–1592) holds up as his hero the fourth-century Roman emperor Julian,
surnamed by later (hostile) generations the Apostate. Julian (331–361/363
CE) was so labeled for having abandoned, upon becoming emperor, the
Christian faith in which he was raised, and further for restoring paganism to
the empire, thereby disestablishing Christianity as the empire's official religion. This caused Saint Augustine to make of Julian one of the principal
villains in his *City of God*, a view that subsequent church fathers and other
Catholic thinkers were only too happy to share.[2]

Montaigne's praise of Julian appears a rather odd move for an allegedly
"good Catholic." At least a few of Montaigne's earliest readers did indeed
find it odd; the *Essais* were first published in 1580, and by 1581 the author
was already in trouble with Catholic Church authorities. In fact, Montaigne had to travel to Rome in person to persuade Vatican censors to allow
him to publish his work. One wonders what Montaigne could possibly
have said to get himself off the hook, as the essay lauds the pagan Julian as
an exemplum of moral and political virtue, praising the religious pluralism
he fostered as a civic ideal, while ridiculing his Christian opponents as
narrow-minded bigots.

To Montaigne, writing during the Wars of Religion, the questions of
freedom of conscience, of religious toleration, and of the kind of state or
society most likely to foster internal and external peace were not abstrac-
tions but real, concrete problems. At the heart of Montaigne's thought are
two fundamental questions: First, what are we to do when confronted with
the Other, a person who is unlike us and whose very being therefore constitutes a radical challenge to our values and existence? Second, what moral
and civic structures, what ethical and political frameworks, are most likely
to provide the conditions necessary for peaceful, even fruitful, coexistence
with that Other?

The following discussion addresses the first of these questions by suggesting that there are three categories of Others in Montaigne's thought,
categories arising directly from his experience and from his processing of
that experience in the *Essais*. The first of these is the Protestant (or, more
precisely and, as it were, ecumenically, the Protestant and the Catholic
viewed through each other's eyes). The second of these is, famously, the
Cannibal, the exemplum of what *not* to do when face-to-face with those
different from ourselves. The third is a little closer to home for Montaigne.
This Other, the paradigmatic Other for Christendom and for the Catholic
Church, is the Jew. As will be seen, the Jew is in some sense, for Montaigne,
the Internal Other for several reasons: because Christianity cannot do with-

out Judaism; because the Jew remains present (even when absent) in Christian society and the Christian psyche; and because of Montaigne's own ancestry (he descended, through both his parents, from Spanish Jews who fled religious persecution in their homeland). Finally, it is possible to say that there is a fourth category of Other in Montaigne, one that perhaps subsumes the other three, or to which we gain access through the figures of the Protestant, the Cannibal, and the Jew, but I will defer a definition of this Other until the end.

Montaigne is careful to make clear from the outset that the problem of the Other is not one that admits of facile solutions. He does not subscribe to the theological platitude that "we are all God's children," since that misleadingly effaces real differences without making either those differences or their potentially destructive effects disappear. Nor will he take refuge in philosophical abstraction; Montaigne understands that any ideal of purely disinterested action must remain an (abstract) ideal. For Montaigne, we as human persons are always already embodied, engaged with our own interests, and any possibility for right action in the world, whether between individuals or within a society, must take this prior engagement into account. Nor will it be sufficient merely to have good intentions; as he writes at the beginning of "De la liberté de conscience," "Il est ordinaire de voir les bonnes intentions, si elles sont conduites sans moderation, pousser les hommes à des effects tres-vitieux."[3] This is true, he says, even for allegedly Good Catholics.

So something else is needed, some more profound understanding of what makes us different, in order to contain, and if possible prevent, lethal conflict. And in the meantime, we need a practical solution, a provisional course of action that will keep us safe from one another. Montaigne tells us what form this might take in the second sentence of the same essay: "En ce debat par lequel la France est à présent agitée de guerres civiles, le meilleur et le plus sain party est sans doubte celuy qui maintient et la religion et la police ancienne du pays."[4] Montaigne clearly indicates here why he is pro-Catholic: not for any theological reasons—neither here nor elsewhere in the *Essais* does he enter deeply into the theological debates that agitate both sides—but because Catholicism, simply by virtue of its being the pre-existing state religion of France, best preserves civic order and stability. Indeed, Montaigne often hints that he finds certain key Protestant theological positions more appealing than their Catholic counterparts, and when he does criticize Protestantism as such it is more because of what he sees as its disruptive effects on society than because of its allegedly heretical doctrines. Hence, when he examines Protestant religious practice, as

for example in "Des prières," where he calls into question the Protestants'
singing of psalms and reading of the Bible in the vernacular, he attacks not
their doctrinal error but the potential for anarchy—both interpretive and
societal—that might result from the valorization of the individual conscience inherent in such practices.[5]

Montaigne sees at the root of such social disruption not a deviation
from the True Faith, but rather an unjustified presumption that anyone,
Protestant or Catholic, can fully know what the truth of that faith might
be. Yet, even as he criticizes this presumption, as in the "Apologie de Rai-
mond Sebond," he does not offer the traditional argument that we must
simply accept the limits of reason while trusting in faith to give us access
to what lies beyond. Neither does he merely assert that the time-tested
authority of the Church solves the problem. Instead, he concludes that,
since we dare not presume to know what we cannot know, we also cannot
presume that we know more than others know; that is, we cannot claim
that the religious position we stake out has any absolute claim to truth over
and against the similar claims of our (Protestant) neighbors. What he does
say is that—in the absence of any a priori guarantee of truth—the best set
of religious practices is necessarily that which guarantees a stable public
order. Therefore, for Montaigne, the Catholic religion—the *practice* of
Catholicism—is essentially a phenomenon of the public sphere, one whose
primary purpose is to ensure social stability. What one does in the private
sphere is (almost) irrelevant, and in any case, as the "Apologie" demonstrates at considerable length, no human is in a position to know precisely
what beliefs are or are not conducive to salvation.

This relationship between the public practice of religion and a stable,
peaceful society is precisely what is at stake in the essay "De la liberté de
conscience," and it is the Emperor Julian's handling of this problem that
makes him exemplary in Montaigne's eyes. Montaigne insists, at some
length, that Julian was a paragon of every moral and philosophical virtue:

> C'estoit, à la vérité, un tres-grand homme et rare, comme celuy qui
> avoit son ame vivement tainte des discours de la philosophie, ausquels
> il faisoit profession de regler toutes ses actions; et, de vray, il n'est
> aucune sorte de vertu dequoy il n'ait laissé de tres-notables exemples.[6]

After enumerating in detail the various ways in which Julian was superior to his contemporaries, and especially to his Christian opponents,
Montaigne shows us that even his alleged apostasy, his supposed betrayal
of the Christian religion, is in fact no such thing; instead, it is an illustration of precisely the kind of civic virtue, with regard to the practice of

religion, that Montaigne considers so essential. Yes, says Montaigne, he was a pagan:

> En matiere de religion, il estoit vicieux par tout; on l'a surnommé apostat pour avoir abandonné la nostre: toutesfois cette opinion me semble plus vraysemblable, qu'il ne l'avoit jamais euë à coeur, mais que, pour l'obeissance des loix, il s'estoit feint jusques à ce qu'il tint l'Empire en sa main.[7]

In other words, Julian—as long as he was a citizen and subject of the (Christian) empire, rather than its ruler—conducted himself with the most perfect virtue in the public sphere, conforming to the practices of the state religion for the sake of civic order ("pour l'obeissance des loix") even though his private beliefs were very different. Once he became emperor, however, he was free to change both his own religious practice and that of his empire as he saw fit. And even after becoming emperor, Julian's approach to religious legislation, to what Montaigne (and we today) might call the relationship between church and state, continued to be guided by the same virtuous dedication to order and stability in the public sphere. There is a paradox here: while Montaigne praises the state religion, Catholicism, as the guarantor of public order in his own society, he simultaneously praises Julian's policy of radical religious toleration for accomplishing exactly the same thing in the Roman Empire, even though it comes at the expense of Christianity:

> Pour parvenir à son effet, ayant rencontré en Constantinople le peuple descousu avec les prelats de l'Eglise Chrestienne divisez, les ayant faict venir à luy au palais, lesamonnesta instamment d'assoupir ces dissentions civiles, et que chacun sans empeschement et sans crainte servit à sa religion. Ce qu'il sollicitoit avec grand soing, pour l'esperance que cette licence augmenteroit les parts et les brigues de la division, et emperscheroit le peuple de se réunir et de fortifier par consqeuent contre luy par leur concorde et unanime intelligence; ayant essayé par la cruauté d'aucuns Chrestiens qu'il n'y a point de beste au monde tant à craindre à l'homme que l'homme.[8]

Montaigne shows us Julian's dealings with seditious subjects, but not just any seditious subjects; they are "les prelats de l'Eglise Chrestienne," who are resisting his civil and religious authority and cannot even get along with each other. Julian's response is to enforce, not a monolithic state religion, but instead a radical toleration of any and all forms of worship, and he does so in order to prevent sedition and to preserve the stability of the state.

Furthermore, in case we miss the point, Montaigne remarks that it is the Christians, not some barbarous pagans, who have taught Julian—as they have taught Montaigne—just how viciously people can behave. The end of this anecdote is surely meant to evoke the horrors of the Wars of Religion, and it shows Julian wisely and virtuously preventing exactly what Montaigne himself wants to forestall in his own society. That Christianity is particularly adept at making people behave very badly indeed is a point Montaigne makes many times, and not just in this essay. One example from the "Apologie" may stand for many:

> Il n'est point d'hostilité excellente comme la chrestienne. Nostre zele faict merveilles, quand il va secondant nostre pente vers la haine, la cruauté, l'ambition, l'avarice, la detraction, la rebellion. A contrepoil, vers la bonté, la benignité, la temperance, si, comme par miracle, quelque rare complexion ne l'y porte, il ne va ny de pied ne d'aile.
>
> Nostre religion est faicte pour extirper les vices; elle les couvre, les nourrit, les incite.[9]

In this list of the dire effects of misdirected Christian zeal, the term that occupies the final position, and that therefore carries the greatest rhetorical force, is "rebellion." This suggests that, as in "De la liberté de conscience," Montaigne is most concerned with the negative *public* effects of religious dogmatism. Given that any claims to absolute doctrinal rightness are necessarily unfounded, and given that pressing those claims, in spite of their dubiety, inevitably leads to civil strife, the only proper course of action, for Montaigne, is that which preserves peace in the public sphere. And Julian does precisely this, both before becoming emperor (by conforming) and after becoming emperor (through his policy of religious toleration). Thus, the pagan emperor teaches us, as good sixteenth-century French Catholics, how to deal with the Protestant Other (and vice versa), without any reference to what people might actually believe privately; what matters is how they behave in public.

A detailed discussion of the second category of Others (i.e., *les Cannibales*) is superfluous here, since Montaigne's famous exaltation of the virtues of the indigenous inhabitants of the New World is familiar territory to most readers. I will simply emphasize that while Montaigne implicates all Europeans, including himself, in the corruption and destruction of New World civilizations, he assigns primary responsibility to one particularly reprehensible category of Bad Guys: the Spanish. This is consistent with the historical record of fifteenth- and sixteenth-century European contact with the New World, but there is clearly something additional at stake for Montaigne; this leads us to his third category of Others, namely the Jews.

The Spanish were notorious, in Montaigne's time, for being the most ardent persecutors of the Jewish people, and Montaigne would have been well aware of this even if those persecuted people had not included his own family. That Montaigne descended from Spanish Jews is well known to modern scholars, and was presumably also well known to Montaigne's circle of friends and acquaintances, many of whom may have had similar family histories. One example is the printer to whom Montaigne confided the first edition of the *Essais*, Simon Millanges; and it has been pointed out that the delivery date of March 1, 1580, that Montaigne carefully notes in the prefatory "Au lecteur" at the beginning of the *Essais*, happens to have been the Jewish holiday of Purim. Purim was a holiday of particular significance among the Jewish diaspora community after 1492 because it commemorated the liberation of the Jews from a particularly nasty set of oppressors, as narrated in the Book of Esther. It takes on particular significance in this context because it also commemorates (in the figure of Esther) a kind of coming-out, a revealing of Jewish identity that had needed to remain hidden as long as the villainous Haman was in power.

With regard to this question about the revelation of identity, we must remember that Montaigne's project in the *Essais* is an explicitly autobiographical one, meant to reveal to the reader Michel de Montaigne unvarnished, exactly as he is. Montaigne claims repeatedly to be telling not just the truth about himself but the whole truth, and indeed in many respects he does. Nevertheless, there are certain things about himself that he never mentions, and one of them is the truth about his own ancestry. Montaigne omits certain important facts about his family—for example, that they descended from Spanish Jews—and he deliberately adjusts or obscures certain elements from his family history to make it seem as though his family had been in France, and had enjoyed their status as French nobility, much longer than was actually the case. More generally, and throughout the *Essais*, Montaigne consistently (and profoundly) calls into question the possibility of any truly self-revelatory discourse, even as he attempts (in a quite unprecedented way, as he also points out) to create one. Of particular interest to us is the way that Montaigne conceives of the difference between our outer and our inner selves. He describes the outer self, the public self, as a kind of performance, one which adapts and conforms to circumstance; the inner self is an entirely different matter, inhabiting the famous "arriereboutique" described in "De la solitude": "Il se faut reserver une arriereboutique toute nostre, toute franche, en laquelle nous establissons nostre

vraye liberté et principale retraicte et solitude."[10] In the context of our
discussion, it is hard not to see this as a space Montaigne reserves to himself, for his "true" self. He seems to be suggesting that to reveal that self,
whatever it might be, would be so difficult, so potentially dangerous, that it
must remain hidden. This, in the end, is precisely what he does in the
otherwise apparently so self-revelatory *Essais*. He offers to the reader an
amazing amount of information about himself, but there are critical lacu-
nae; while he does talk about his religious *practices*, which are always framed
as activities in the public sphere, he says very little about his private religious beliefs, and nothing at all about his family's religious history.

The essay that immediately precedes "De la liberté de conscience," "Du
dementir" ("Of Giving the Lie"), is the one essay where Montaigne spends
the most time explaining and justifying his autobiographical project. That
he does so in an essay with that title is already suggestive, and some of the
things he says in that essay should cause us to wonder further. For example,
when discussing, or more accurately *not* discussing, his ancestry, he laments:
"[1580] Quel contentement me seroit ce d'ouir ainsi quelqu'un qui me
recitast les meurs, [1595] le visage, la contenance, les parolles communes
[1580] et les fortunes de mes ancestres! Combien j'y serois attentif!"[11] He
claims here not to have certain information about his family history that he
would dearly love to have. While this may be true, in that much of his
family history may indeed have been lost to him in the course of exile, he
certainly has more information than he gives to his readers, and here he
offers, somewhat disingenuously, only the complete absence of any information whatsoever. Thus, even as Montaigne invites us to know him as he
knows himself, to encounter him as an Other that-unlike any other Other,
Protestant, Catholic, Cannibal, whomever—can be fully known, he deliberately withholds crucial information from his readers, information that
would seem to be essential to his self-portrait but that instead he keeps in
that *arrièreboutique* to which nobody else can ever have access.

One particularly interesting moment of (possible) partial self-revelation
and/or concealment comes not in the *Essais* themselves but in the *Journal de
voyage*. While in Rome for his visit with the Vatican censors, Montaigne
makes a point of going to synagogue and records a rather accurate description of what the Shabbat service was like. This is in itself somewhat unusual,
since one would not ordinarily find Catholics in a synagogue in Rome on
Shabbat; that Montaigne would have been invited suggests that he had at
least a casual connection to the Jewish community there. He goes on to
describe how he was also a guest, on January 30, 1581, at "la plus ancienne
ceremonie de religion qui soit parmy les hommes,"[12] namely a *bris milah*, a
circumcision. He notes that this ceremony is performed not in a synagogue

but in a private home, making it all the more remarkable that Montaigne, ostensibly a French Catholic and not a Roman Jew, would have been invited to such a ceremony in the first place. He offers a lengthy and detailed description of the entire ritual, astonishing in its precision and accuracy. It is hard not to wonder not only what Montaigne was doing at this ceremony in the first place, but also how he manages to describe it as though he has seen the ritual not once but many times. One also wonders why he dedicates so much space (two full pages) to describing this ritual in a text (the *Journal de voyage*) otherwise remarkable for its telegraphic concision, sometimes to the point of obscurity. These details suggest, at the very least, a familiarity with, or interest in, this ritual that goes beyond the interest of the average tourist. That he chooses a circumcision—why not a wedding, for example?—a circumcision, which is *the* ritual that marks and defines Jewish identity as such, is also suggestive. It is tempting to read Montaigne's account of a *bris milah* in the *Journal de voyage* as an account of the circumcision that Montaigne himself (presumably) did not have. Its textual presence might serve as a displaced marker of identity, a sign—for those who have eyes to see—of his connection to this community of Others that he knows perhaps only imperfectly and that likewise knows him only imperfectly or not at all.

To assert, however, that Montaigne is actually a crypto-Jew, retaining his Jewish identity for himself while hiding it from his interlocutors, would be to stray too far into a form of specious argument from the absence of evidence. What remains clear, though, is that Montaigne's contemplation of the Jew as Other, coupled with his complex sense, however obscured— even from himself—of his connection to the Jewish community, leads him to an understanding of Otherness as such that he would not otherwise have had. Throughout the *Essais*, there remains an uncomfortable tension between public self and private *arrièreboutique*, a tension that is as difficult to live with as it is unavoidable. In "Des prières," in the context of a discussion of Protestant and Catholic religious practices and the foolishness of dogmatism in this domain, Montaigne tells us of someone who, due to his position in public life, felt compelled to conform outwardly to a set of religious practices at odds with his private beliefs:

> Et celuy qui, se confessant à moy, me recitoit avoir tout un aage faict profession et les effects d'une religion damnable selon lui, et contradictoire à celle qu'il avoit en son coeur, pour ne perdre son credit et l'honneur de ses charges: comment patissoit-il ce discours en son courage?[13]

How, Montaigne asks, did this person—"confessing" his dilemma to Montaigne, revealing his true inner self—reconcile his outward acts with his inner convictions? Montaigne tells us nothing of who this person was and leaves the question floating in midair. It is easy enough to imagine him to have been one of Montaigne's colleagues in the *Parlement* of Bordeaux. It is also easy to imagine him to have been Montaigne himself, grappling with his own internal Other without ever being able to bridge the gap between that Other and himself. In any case, this unnamed person finds himself in exactly the same position as the Emperor Julian before becoming emperor: conforming to the religion of the state for the sake of civic order, while remaining internally Other. Ultimately, the question of whether Montaigne feels, or suspects, some connection to his Jewish family history is not especially relevant. The precise content of this internal otherness is less important than the fact of its existence. We all have an *arrièreboutique* that must ultimately remain Other, even, at times, to ourselves.

In the end, then, Montaigne remains Other, despite his claims to be effacing the boundaries between himself and his interlocutors: he always remains partly inaccessible, unknowable. In the course of his autobiographical undertaking, Montaigne offers himself as, among other things, an image of the Other as such. Whether Protestant, Cannibal, or Jew, there is always something else, something beyond our knowing, beyond our understanding, about the Other. If this fundamental unknowability is constitutive of the Other, if it is in ways its defining characteristic, it is also the defining characteristic, as Montaigne shows us especially in the "Apologie," of the fourth category of Other alluded to at the beginning of this essay. This fourth category of Other, which we may say subsumes the other three, or of which the other three are avatars or manifestations, is God. Therefore, if it ill befits us, as Montaigne claims, to be dogmatic about things of which we are and must remain ignorant, this must be as true of Cannibals or Jews as of the Divinity itself.

Montaigne explicitly draws the analogy between the Other and God: We can fully know neither the Other nor God, and yet we are called, indeed commanded, to extend our hand to both. This identification of God and the Other gives particular urgency to the second question we posed at the beginning of the chapter: What moral and civic structures, what ethical and political frameworks are most likely to provide the conditions necessary for peaceful, even fruitful coexistence with that Other? Montaigne has shown us the beginnings of an answer through his rejection of a monolithic authoritarianism and his support for a radical toleration that looks suspiciously proto-democratic. It will be fruitful to keep Montaigne's insights in mind as later chapters in this volume also explore the tensions between authoritarianism and toleration in twentieth-century

Indonesia (Baskara Wardaya and Albertus Budi Susanto) and Peru (Soledad Escalante and Gonzalo Gamio).

To return to Julian the Apostate, Montaigne's epic hero in questions of religion, politics, and otherness, we can now see that Julian was perhaps onto something. If, as Montaigne suggests, we live in a world populated only by Others, it is only by approaching these Others as we would approach God, with openness and humility, that we can hope to live in peace.

NOTES

1. All essays can be found in Michel de Montaigne, *Essais*, ed. Pierre Villey (Paris: Presses Universitaires de France, 1965).

2. See, for example, *The City of God*, 18.52 and elsewhere.

3. Montaigne, "De la liberté" [1580 edition]. "It is usual to see good intentions, if they are carried forward without moderation, push men to very vicious results." All translations are author's translations.

4. Ibid. "In this strife which is currently agitating France with civil war, the best and wisest choice is undoubtedly that which maintains the old religion and civil order of the country."

5. He also attacks these practices in the name of what he describes as the discontinuity between the exalted, even holy, language of worship and the (inevitably) sorry spiritual state of the worshipers; this (heretical) position is one of the things that got him into trouble with the Church censors, since Catholic doctrine held (and holds) that the efficacy of prayer is independent of the spiritual state of the person praying. Montaigne's position here is remarkably, one might say suspiciously, close to the Jewish notion of *kavanah*.

6. Montaigne, *Essais*, 669. "He was, in truth, a very great and rare man, someone who had his soul thoroughly imbued with the discourses of philosophy, according to which he professed to regulate all his actions; and indeed there is no sort of virtue of which he did not leave very remarkable examples."

7. Montaigne, *Essais* [1580], 670. "With regard to religion, he was entirely bad; he was called the Apostate for having abandoned ours. However, this opinion seems to me more probable: that he had never really been a believer, but in order to obey the laws, he pretended to be until he had the Empire in his hands."

8. Montaigne, *Essais* [1580], 671. "In order to achieve his end, having encountered the people of Constantinople in disorder and the prelates of the Christian Church divided, he summoned them to the palace, and admonished them to put an immediate stop to these civil dissensions, and ordered that everyone without hindrance or fear serve his own religion. He promoted this with great care, in the hope that this freedom would augment the factions

and divisions among the people, and would hinder them from uniting against him through concord and unanimous agreement; having discovered through the cruelty of some Christians that there is no animal in the world more to be feared by man than man."

9. Montaigne, *Essais* [1595], 444. "There is no hostility so excellent as the Christian version. Our zeal works marvels, when it supports our inclination to hatred, cruelty, ambition, avarice, slander, rebellion. On the other hand, toward goodness, benevolence, temperance, unless, as by a miracle, some rare character pushes us that way, we'll never move in that direction. Our religion is made to extirpate vices; it covers them, nourishes them, incites them."

10. Montaigne, *Essais* [1580], 241. "We must reserve for ourselves a backshop, entirely our own, entirely free, where we establish our true liberty and our principal retreat and solitude."

11. Montaigne, *Essais*, 664. "How happy I would be to listen to someone who would tell me about the habits, the faces, the comportment, the words and fortunes of my ancestors! How attentive I would be!"

12. Michel de Montaigne, *Journal de voyage*, ed. François Rigolot (Paris: Presses Universitaires de France, 1992), 101. "The oldest religious ceremony that exists among men."

13. Montaigne, *Essais* [1595], 320. "And this man who, confessing himself to me, told me how he had spent his life professing and practicing a religion which according to him was damnable, and contrary to the one he had in his heart, in order not to lose his reputation and the honor of his office: how did he justify this to himself?"

Indonesian Voices

What profoundly marks Catholicism's relationship to democracy and culture in Indonesia is the fact that Catholics are a minority in a majority Muslim country. Yet, given the profound commitment of Indonesians to the principles of democracy, Catholics have often found themselves at the table of political and civic discourse and involved in the processes of democratization. Nevertheless, the contributions Catholics have made to Indonesian society and government have always remained in the shadow of their minority status. Because of this status, Indonesian Catholics struggle to find their voice and to come to terms with the reality of precisely how effective this voice has been, and can continue to be, in a democratizing Indonesia.

Baskara Wardaya begins this section by articulating the process of democratization in Indonesia, most prominently in the mid- to late twentieth century, and the role of Catholicism, as a minority religion, therein. Catholics in Indonesia played an important role in the Indonesian democratization process but have since become less of a presence in Indonesian political circles. In a nation that has prided itself on being a bastion and exemplar of positive democratizing tendencies, Wardaya notes that Indonesia today is experiencing an increase in inter-religious conflicts. What the results of these conflicts within Indonesia's democracy will be, and what the future of Catholicism in Indonesia will be, remain ambiguous questions for Wardaya that call for attention and analysis.

Paulus Wiryono Priyotamtama approaches the relationships between democracy, culture, and Catholicism in Indonesia by analyzing the process from which the principles of the social and political order in Indonesia have emerged. *Musyawarah* is "a traditional system of mutual dialogue, consultation, deliberation, and decision-making based on consensus" that grounds *pancasila*, the official state philosophy of Indonesia. Wiryono's task is to evaluate the effectiveness, and continued relevance, of this deliberative process for developing future lay Catholic activists. In the end, Wiryono finds that the process of musyawarah retains its effectiveness in the process of developing such activists, especially when their religious, social, and political commitments are coupled with social entrepreneurship and responsibility.

Francisca Ninik Yudianti takes up the question of social responsibility and democratic practices in Indonesia and asks, with an eye to the Catholic community: Do the principles and frameworks provided by Catholic social teaching have any effect today on the processes of democratic practices and corporate social responsibility in Catholic-owned businesses? The results of Yudianti's research indicate that, in fact, yes, the democratic practices of Catholic social teaching do have a positive effect on the adoption of corporate social responsibility by businesses in Indonesia, specifically in the Yogyakarta Special Region, whose owners identify as Catholic. What this means for the impact of these practices in other regions of Indonesia, and around the world, remains to be researched, but Yudianti's contribution to the conversation indicates that such research should be undertaken, since her preliminary findings show positive results.

Albertus Budi Susanto, who takes a more culturally oriented approach via the people's performing arts (known as *kethoprak*), draws a connection between the democratizing tendencies of kethoprak and the process of Ignatian spirituality. Kethoprak is subversive and satirical. It looks to the social, political, and religious elites and holds up before them a funhouse mirror of distortion that, not without irony, often exposes their shortcomings and failures to the wider public. More than these results, however, kethoprak is about an interior orientation, about a way of subjectively perceiving and processing the external world. That is to say, kethoprak is about the methodological practice of attuning oneself, and one's audience, to seeing things differently. It is here that Susanto draws the comparison to Ignatian spirituality. He identifies in both kethoprak and Ignatian spirituality a process whereby one learns to see more clearly and to attend to one's surroundings more critically. As a result, the relationships between democracy, culture, and Catholicism are intimately tied to the internal movements, and the external experiences, of the performers and audiences and of all Indonesians whose lives take place outside the elite circles of power.

Catholics in Indonesia and the Struggle for Democracy

Baskara T. Wardaya, SJ

Colonized for over 150 years and gaining independence only after World War II, Indonesia is relatively new to the idea and practice of democracy. In the first two decades of Indonesian independence, democracy was difficult to put into practice because the country was undergoing a transitional period from being a colonial territory to an independent nation. Under the threat of domestic rebellion and the impact of the Cold War, Indonesia tried to democratize, but it never fully succeeded.

Beginning in the mid-1960s, Indonesia was ruled by an authoritarian government that paid only lip service to democracy. This facade was used to cover its political and economic interests. It is interesting to note how, as explained in Arūnas Streikus's earlier chapter in this volume, similar causes and effects were at work during Lithuania's 1926 slide into authoritarian government. Only after the fall of authoritarianism in 1998 did Indonesia gain the freedom necessary to begin making democracy a reality. As in earlier periods, this attempt has faced many challenges.

As in the case of Lithuanian Catholics, Indonesian Catholics have participated in Indonesia's struggle for democracy. A major difference between the two, however, is that Indonesian Catholics are a very small religious minority. Nevertheless, the history of this participation has had a powerful impact on both the self-understanding of Indonesian Catholics and the strength of the Indonesian Catholic Church. To grasp the main lines of the story of Catholicism and democracy in Indonesia, a sense of the country's broad historical context is needed.

Historical Background

Prior to the arrival of Western colonial powers, the area currently known as Indonesia was a vast archipelago made up of politically independent or loosely connected feudalistic sovereignties.[1] Each of these sovereignties kept its own traditions regarding politics, culture, language, and beliefs. In the sixteenth century, the Portuguese arrived as the first European colonists. They came after capturing Malacca in 1511 and continued their quest for spices in the eastern part of Indonesia. The islands in the cluster were called the Spice Islands or the Moluccas.

Following the Portuguese, Dutch explorers arrived in the Indonesian ports in 1595. In 1602, Dutch merchants established the Dutch East India Company (Vereenigde Oostindische Compagnie [VOC]). Three years later the company defeated the Portuguese in the Moluccas and took control of the area's spice trade. In a short time, the VOC exerted economic control over Indonesia's commercial centers. When the VOC went bankrupt in 1799, control of the islands was assumed by the Dutch colonial government. For the next 150 years, the Indonesian islands were a Dutch colony.

In March 1942, at the height of their power during the Second World War, the Japanese army took over the Dutch East Indies. The Japanese forces easily defeated the Dutch and absorbed all Dutch colonial possessions. The Dutch colonial government fled to Australia and formed a government-in-exile. Following the Japanese surrender on August 15, 1945, Indonesia proclaimed independence. Instead of returning to the precolonial feudal system of government, the Indonesian leaders declared that the new nation would be a democratic republic formed of the entire former Dutch East Indies. Sukarno became the first president.[2] The Indonesian leaders declared that the new republic would be based on a commitment to five fundamental values: belief in one God, a just and civilized humanity, the unity of Indonesia, democracy guided by the inner wisdom of unanimity, and social justice. They called this unifying philosophy "Pancasila."[3]

Despite this declaration of independence by the Indonesian people, the Dutch government-in-exile sought to reclaim and recolonize Indonesia after the Japanese surrender. This attempt met the fierce resistance of

Indonesian freedom fighters. Over the next four years, a bloody conflict waged between the Indonesians and the Dutch colonialists. On December 27, 1949, the Dutch conceded defeat and officially acknowledged Indonesian independence.

As president of the new republic, Sukarno was overwhelmingly popular and revered by Indonesians. In foreign policy, the president was very critical of the developed capitalist nations of the West. In the midst of Cold War tensions, he urged the newly independent nations of Asia and Africa to take neutral positions toward the United States and the Soviet Union. Soon, Sukarno's anti-capitalist rhetoric and Cold War neutrality were viewed as a threat by anti-Communist circles in Indonesia and around the world. The United States feared that a left-leaning Indonesia would become an ally of the communist bloc and spread communism over Indonesia and other parts of Southeast Asia.

This latter circumstance incited anti-Communist military and civilian groups to launch a brutal anti-Communist purge in 1965 with covert support from Western nations. More than half a million Indonesians were killed during the purge. Many more were imprisoned and exiled. This bloodbath became known as the 1965 Tragedy. In its aftermath, Sukarno's political power diminished until he was pushed from power and replaced in 1966 by military general Suharto.[4]

Suharto's regime was authoritarian and militaristic. As an indication of his intention to reverse Sukarno's policies, Suharto called his government the "New Order." The name was meant to suggest that the new government under Suharto would be better than the "old" style of President Sukarno's rule that was considered inefficient and Communist leaning. As it began to carry out its task of governing the country, however, the New Order government under Suharto demonstrated undemocratic ways of ruling the nation and was gradually subservient to the economic and political interests of many Western governments, especially the United States.[5] Pancasila remained the state ideology, but it was used mainly as a political tool to suppress critical voices against the government. This is point is well illustrated by Budi Susanto in his chapter on the role of *kethoprak* performances in the process of democratization. As Pancasila became co-opted by the powers that be, kethoprak sought to subvert this dominating tendency by offering alternative means for performing social and political democratization in the face of political totalitarianism and widespread human rights violations.

President Suharto himself used a variety of ruthless means to stay in power. For him democracy was merely a formality and was never a true principle on which his government was based. With regard to the presidential elections, for instance, there was indeed a presidential election every five years, but in each of these elections Suharto made himself as the only presidential candidate. If there were any other potential candidates he either would discourage or pressure that person so they would not run for president. As a result, for thirty-two years in every presidential election Suharto was always "elected" president.

In the face of such a political situation religious groups—including the Catholic ones—could not do much to change the situation for fear of political consequences. On the eve of the 1997 presidential election, however, there were some acts of resistance against the government's policies among some Indonesians, including Catholics. In a pre-Easter pastoral letter signed by the Indonesian Bishop Conference, the bishops bravely stated that if Catholics felt that the existing political parties were not representing their choices and they decided not to cast a vote, they would not commit sin.[6] Despite such forms of resistance, Suharto won the 1997 presidential election.

Suharto's autocratic and ruthless government came undone during the deepening Asian economic crisis of the mid-1990s and the rising student riots against the Suharto regime. As the economic crisis reached Indonesia in 1997, a growing number anti–New Order movements spread, spearheaded by university students in major cities across Indonesia. In the capital Jakarta, demonstrations against the government often turned violent and a number of demonstrators were killed. By the spring of 1998 Suharto and his New Order government were in a politically difficult position, and in May of 1998 he was forced to step down.

The period of political upheavals preceding the fall of Suharto was known as the *Reformasi* (Reformation). At that time, most Indonesians (especially university students) sought to reform the country into a functioning democracy with citizen participation, social and economic justice, and elimination of government corruption. This was a period of high expectations. Indonesians expected that with the departure of President Suharto's undemocratic and militaristic New Order government the Indonesians would have more freedom and would live under true democratic principles, including greater participation of the people in the political affairs of the nation. They also expected that the new government would guarantee the people's freedom of speech and the freedom of forming public associations.

In general, the fall of Suharto was indeed followed by significant growth of democracy in Indonesia. People had more freedom of speech and had greater participation in the nation's politics. Presidential elections, which during the Suharto years were done through a representative system under tight control of the government, were now carried out through a direct and open election system. In each of the elections the candidates were no longer merely one but several. The media, which used to be under a strong control of the government, was now guaranteed freedom to publish. People were also provided freedom to form political parties and other public associations.

At the same time, powerful anti-democratic forces continued to disrupt the democratization process. Within a few years after the fall of President Suharto, for example, politicians and groups that used to be the supporters of the former leader's undemocratic system of government began to re-emerge in the country's political scene. Golkar or Golongan Karya—the powerful political party that was used by Suharto to stay in power—gradually reassembled and grew in membership.

Meanwhile, the freedom of speech and freedom of association were often used by radical religious groups to attack religious minorities. In 1999, barely one year after Suharto's downfall, one such religious group attacked another in the province of the Moluccas. The communal violence that followed resulted in the deaths of thousands of people from both sides of the conflict. Similar communal violence took place between Muslim and Christian groups on the island of Celebes, also causing many deaths, especially among the Christians.

In recent years, in certain areas of Indonesia, there have been attempts to implement *Sharia* (Muslim) bylaws, which are a challenge to the nation's democratic principles. At the same time, any efforts to address Indonesia's past human rights abuses have always been blocked by former perpetrators of the abuses and their supporters, many of whom were also supporters of Suharto's undemocratic New Order government.[7]

Indonesian Religion and Catholicism

Indonesia's seventeen thousand islands contain hundreds of ethnic and sub-ethnic communities with diverse cultural and religious traditions. For centuries, each of these communities maintained their traditions in almost complete isolation. The coming of religious missionaries and traders from the West and the Middle East challenged these traditions. In the face of this challenge, many Indonesians abandoned their traditional beliefs and embraced the new religions. Some of this change was due to force; some was due to the appeal of new religious ideas. At the same time, some people retained their native religions and did their best to adapt to changing circumstances.

The first of the major "new" religions that came to Indonesia was Hinduism. This was brought by traders from India around the fourth and fifth centuries. Shortly thereafter, these same Indian traders and immigrants brought Buddhism, making it the second oldest organized religion in Indonesia. At nearly the same time, a new group of traders and immigrants from China began introducing Confucianism to Indonesia.

Another major religion that came to the Indonesian archipelago during the precolonial period was Islam. Like Hinduism, Islam was brought by traders from India, China, and the Middle East. The religion began to spread rapidly in the thirteenth and fourteenth centuries.[8] Today, Islam is the most widely practiced religion in Indonesia. With 87 percent of the Indonesian population declaring themselves Muslim, Indonesia is the largest Muslim-majority country in the world.

Along with the arrival of Portuguese colonists in the sixteenth century came Catholic missionaries. One of these missionaries was Saint Francis Xavier, a Spaniard and one of the first members of the Jesuit Order. Xavier arrived in the Moluccas in 1546.[9] When Xavier left in 1547, Dominican missionaries continued where he left off, working on nearby islands such as Flores. In 1574, Muslim rulers expelled the Portuguese and forcibly converted or killed all Catholics in the northern parts of the Moluccas.[10]

Those Catholics who survived Muslim aggression in 1547, and subsequent years of Muslim rule, further suffered when the Dutch East Indies Company (VOC) took over the islands in 1605. Under VOC rule, Catholic priests were either expelled or executed and the Catholic laity was forced to convert to Protestantism.[11] With the collapse of the VOC in 1799 and the subsequent legalization of Catholicism in the Netherlands, Dutch Catholic missionaries re-entered the colony.[12] On the large island of Java, however, Catholic missionary activity did not resume until 1898. At that time, a mission site was established in the small town of Muntilan, located about thirty kilometers north of Yogyakarta.[13]

The Muntilan mission site was led by Dutch Jesuit priest Frans van Lith. At first, the mission did not go well. There were few converts to Catholicism.[14] However, in 1904 four Javanese village leaders came to van Lith and asked for instruction in the Catholic faith. Van Lith agreed and by the end of the year the four leaders were baptized along with over 170 of their fellow villagers. This baptism triggered a wide interest in Catholicism in Java and other islands. By 1940, the growing number of Indonesian Catholics had their first native bishop, Albertus Soegijapranata, SJ.

With the Japanese defeat in World War II and Indonesia's declaration of independence in 1945, Catholics gradually resumed their faith-based activities. These early years of independence were not easy. Dutch colonists were combating the Indonesian freedom fighters, while many Indonesians associated Catholicism with the Dutch, as it was clear from Indonesia's history that many missionaries who brought Catholic faith to Indonesia were Europeans. The hatred toward the Dutch (and Europeans in general) was often expressed by attacking both native Catholics and foreign missionaries. Father Richardus Kardis Sandjaja, a Javanese Diocesan priest, and a Dutch Jesuit by the name of Herman Bouwen SJ, for example, were attacked and murdered in Muntilan by a group of Muslim youth who considered these Catholic figures as a symbol of continuing Dutch presence in postcolonial Indonesia. Muntilan, the town where these two Catholic figures were killed, was significant: it was the twentieth-century "birthplace" of Roman Catholicism in Java.

After the Dutch recognized Indonesian independence on December 27, 1949, and Sukarno acquired power, Catholics enjoyed relative freedom. This was partly because President Sukarno kept an open mind to all religions (his parents were Muslim and Hindu). Though the regime's philosophy of Pancasila encouraged belief in one God, this was always understood within the context of Indonesia's rich religious pluralism. In fact, Sukarno's government officially acknowledged six religions: Hinduism, Buddhism, Confucianism, Islam, Protestantism, and Roman Catholicism.

Good relations between Sukarno and the Catholics continued throughout most of his presidency and the period saw rapid growth in the Catholic population outside their usual areas of eastern Indonesia. The population was also enhanced after the massacres of 1965 when many Indonesians joined Christianity, including the Catholic Church, to avoid being labeled communist.[15]

The situation for the Catholics in Indonesia changed when General Suharto came to power at the end of 1965. Under Suharto, the freedom of Roman Catholics became more limited, as the Indonesian government began to control the number of European missionaries who could come to Indonesia and, by government's control of religious foreign aid, intended to support Indonesian Christian communities, including the Catholics.

Since the time of Suharto, the Catholic population has fluctuated. According to the census on religions in Indonesia taken between 1971 and 2010, the percentage of Catholics in Indonesia between 1980 and 1990 increased from 2.98 percent to 3.58 percent of the total population.[16] After 1990, the percentage went down. In the 2010 census, the total number of

Catholics was increasing, but their percentage within the whole population dropped to 2.91 percent. During the same period, the percentage of other Christian groups rose from 6.04 percent to 6.96 percent of the total population.

The decline in Catholic population may be due to the Catholic trend toward smaller families and a decrease in converts to Catholicism. Public attacks against Chinese Indonesians during the political upheavals of 1998 may be another reason. Many Chinese Indonesians are Catholic and their departure from Indonesia during the upheavals no doubt reduced the Catholic population in Indonesia. The fact that Catholics in recent decades are less nationally noticeable in Indonesia's political, economic, and social affairs could be yet another factor. The self-perception among certain Catholics that they are just a minority religious group—and therefore should not rock the boat—helps make Indonesian Catholics less prominent in the eyes of their fellow citizens.

Catholic Participation in the Struggle for Democracy

In the period prior to the proclamation of independence, the Catholic role in the struggle for democracy was very limited. This is understandable because the number of native Indonesian Catholics was very small and most lived far from the center of the colonial administration in Java. The island of Flores, where most Catholics of the period lived, for instance, is located in the eastern part of the Indonesian archipelago, far away from the colonial center.

After the proclamation of independence, Catholic participation in the democratic movement increased dramatically. Catholics like Agustinus Adisucipto and Ignatius Slamet Riyadi actively fought and died in the struggle to establish the Indonesian Republic.[17] It was here too that strong leadership came from Bishop Soegijapranata. When the town of Semarang became part of the Dutch-controlled territory, Bishop Soegijapranata moved his office from Semarang to Yogyakarta, the temporary capital of Indonesia. In so doing, he demonstrated his stand against the Dutch and his loyalty to Indonesia. When the war of independence was over, Bishop Soegijapranata maintained close personal relations with President Sukarno. In 1963, Sukarno recognized Bishop Soegijapranata's important role in the struggle for independence by declaring him a national hero.

The early years of President Suharto's New Order government were marked by active Catholic participation in politics. In the second half of Suharto's rule, however, Catholic political activity waned. There are several reasons that account for this decline: Suharto's growing authoritarianism, growing pressures from the Muslim community on religious minorities, and a declining interest among Catholics in the political process.

In the final days before Suharto was forced to resign, a brief period of Catholic political action occurred when large numbers of Catholic university students joined in the protests against the government. However, this did not stop the overall downward trend of Catholic participation in politics. In recent years, more and more Catholics have been retreating from political activity just as the Muslim community has become more politically outspoken. An interesting comparison exists here in relation to Lithuania's contemporary decline in Christian political participation, as noted in this volume's earlier chapter by Nerija Putinaitė. Both declines are oddly occurring in post-authoritarian periods, yet the former context is one of heightened non-Christian religious activity while the latter context is one of heightened non-Christian secular activity. As in Lithuania, fewer Indonesian Catholic intellectuals are following political careers. The majority of Catholics have elected to work as non-political writers, artists, businesspersons, educators, journalists, and publishers.

Sadly, this is a time when Catholic participation in Indonesian democracy is sorely needed. While Indonesia is considered one of the world's largest democratic nations, anti-democratic forces remain strong. Many of these forces originate from religious movements that commit violence against religious minorities. On February 6, 2011, for example, a group of about fifteen hundred people (mostly young men) attacked the small village of Cikeusik, Banten, in West Java in the name of their religion. Cikeusik is home to Muslims belonging to the Ahmadiyya community. Government officials were absent during the event.[18] Two days later, three churches (one Catholic, two Protestant) were attacked by over one thousand people claiming to be Muslims. Meanwhile, in the city of Bogor, West Java, a Protestant congregation of the Taman Yasmin Church was denied the right to worship.[19] A report produced by the Setara Institute— a non-government organization promoting social justice and religious tolerance   stated that since 2009 religious based communal violence has been on the rise. In 2010 alone there were 216 known cases of human rights violations against religious minorities.[20]

A few Indonesian Catholics have joined their fellow Indonesians in fighting against religious intolerance, but most have preferred to avoid any direct participation in democratic politics. This is an interesting development, particularly in light of the professed Indonesian national philosophy of Pancasila—already noted at the beginning of this chapter and more directly discussed in the following chapter by Paulus Wiryono on *musy-awarah*. Wiryono identifies Pancasila as bringing, and holding, Indonesians together through participatory governance, yet the contemporary situation in Indonesia seems to problematize this vision as participation in democratic politics becomes less and less pronounced. External pressures against such participation, it must be noted, are strong. The dominance of Islam in every aspect of the Indonesian society dissuades small religious minorities from speaking out. Many Indonesian Catholics prefer to direct their time and energy inward, focusing on local parish life, prayer, and sacraments.

As is well known, the Roman Catholic Church is not formally organized as a democratic institution. It is an institution with leadership granted from higher authorities and not from local people. Church decisions are validated by a clerical minority, not by the lay majority. With this long-standing structure, Catholic laypeople in Indonesia tend to look to the clergy for direction and endorsement in taking action for democracy in society. In the delicate social context of contemporary Indonesia, Catholic laypeople look for encouragement and support from Church authorities for active participation in democratic politics.

Although the Catholic population of Indonesia is less than 3 percent and a growing number of this minority are reluctant to assume active political roles in democratization efforts, there may be other ways for Indonesian Catholics to help their nation build democracy. For example, the Catholic community could be served if a research facility could be developed to record the history of Indonesian Catholicism and strategically discuss the best practices for community participation in Indonesian democracy. Such a facility could include programs to inspire Indonesia's Catholic youth and student organizations, rekindling their past enthusiasm for democratic nation building. In addition, a research facility could assist Indonesian Catholics in networking with Catholic communities facing similar challenges in other parts of the world, including the Middle East, Africa, and Latin America.

In recent years, a growing number of young Catholic Indonesians have been participating in the World Youth Day, an international gathering that is organized by the Catholic Church and is held every two or three years in different parts of the world. An international opportunity like this should be used by Indonesian Catholics to build networking with Catholics from around the world and to learn from them about how to be active participants in the democratic struggles in each of their countries. At the same time, the Indonesians could share their own experiences in the struggle to Catholics from other countries.

Conclusion

There is a marked difference in Catholic political participation in Indonesia from the period between 1945 to the early 1980s and the period between the mid-1980s to the present. In the earlier period, Catholics were very active in Indonesia's struggle for democracy. Despite their minority status, Catholics found that their Church leaders and their faith were sources of inspiration and energy for political engagement. In the later period, the public engagement of Indonesian Catholics has diminished. Due to external and internal pressures, Catholics have turned inward, focusing on spiritual life and matters internal to the Catholic community. At the same time, membership in the Catholic Church has waned.

Indonesian history suggests that the more active Catholics are in the struggle for democracy, the greater is the growth of Catholicism in Indonesia. In addition, the greater the Catholic Church grows in faithful leadership and faithful members in Indonesia, the more is provided for the growth of a religiously plural and culturally rich democracy in Indonesia. Learning from this lesson of history it is necessary that Indonesian Catholics begin to encourage each other to get involved as much as they can in the democratic struggle of their nation.

NOTES

1. The term "Nusantara" is commonly used to refer to the Indonesian archipelago prior to the Proclamation of Independence in 1945.

2. Like many native Indonesians, Sukarno has only one name.

3. *Pancasila* is a set of five principles agreed upon as the ideological foundation of the Indonesian Republic. See http://www.indonesianembassy.org.uk/aboutIndonesia/indonesia_facts.html.

4. Also often spelled "Soeharto."

5. Bradley R. Simpson, *Economists with Guns: Authoritarian Development and U.S.-Indonesian Relations, 1960–1968* (Stanford, CA: Stanford University Press, 2008), 207–48.

6. Kees van Dijk, *A Country in Despair: Indonesia Between 1997 and 2000* (Jakarta: KITLV, 2001), 21–23.

7. See, for instance, Katharine McGregor, "Mass Grave and Memories of the 1965 Indonesian Killings," in *The Contours of Mass Violence in Indonesia, 1965–68*, ed. Douglass Kammen and Katharine McGregor (Singapore: NUS Press, 2012), 245–62.

8. See M. C. Ricklefs, *A History of Modern Indonesia since c. 1300* (Stanford, CA: Stanford University Press, 1993), 3–14.

9. See Karel Steenbrink, *Catholics in Indonesia: A Documentary History, 1808–1900* (Leiden, Netherlands: KITLV, 2003), 6–7, and Ricklefs, *Modern Indonesia*, 25.

10. See Adolf Heuken, SJ, "Catholic Converts in the Moluccas, Minahasa and Sanghie-Talaud, 1512–1680," in *A History of Christianity in Indonesia*, ed. Jan Sihar Aritonang and Karel Steenbrink (Leiden, Netherlands: Brill, 2008), 68, and Azyumardi Azra, "1530–1670: A Race between Islam and Christianity?," in Aritonang and Steenbrink, *History of Christianity*, 19.

11. Steenbrink, *Catholics in Indonesia*, 7.

12. Robert Cribb, *Historical Dictionary of Indonesia* (Metuchen, NJ: Scarecrow Press, 1992), 72–73.

13. Aritonang and Steenbrink, *History of Christianity*, 695–703, and Frans Seda, "Simfoni Yang Tidak Pernah 'Rampung,'" in A. Budi Susanto, SJ, *Harta dan Surga* (Yogyakarta, Indonesia: Penerbit Kanisius, 1990), 62–77.

14. It was a common view among the Javanese that Catholicism was a religion of the colonists.

15. For conversion of many Javanese-Indonesians to Christianity during this period, see Robert Heffner, *Conversion to Christianity: Historical and Anthropological Perspectives on a Great Transformation* (Berkeley: University of California Press, 1993), 113–15.

16. See United Nations Department of International Economic and Social Affairs—Statistics Division, *Demographic Yearbook 1979 (Population Census Statistics)* (New York: United Nations, 1980), 641, and Badan Pusat Statistik, "Penduduk Menurut Wilayah dan Agama yang Dianut [Population by Region and Religion]," in *Sensus Penduduk 2010*, by Badan Pusat Statistik (Jakarta: Badan Pusat Statistik, 2010).

17. Adisucipto (1916–1947) was an Indonesian air force pilot shot down by Dutch colonists during Indonesia's war of independence (1945–1949). Slamet Riyadi (1927–1950) was an Indonesian army officer killed during a military campaign to suppress a rebellion against the Indonesian government in the Moluccas islands.

18. See Philip Shishkin, "The Persecution of Indonesia's Ahmadi Muslims," *Newsweek*, February 13, 2011.

19. See Ismail Hasani and Bonar Tigor Naipospos, eds., *Negara Menyangkal: Kondisi Kebebasan Beragama/Berkeyakinan di Indonesia, 2010* [Government Denies: Freedom of Religion/Religious Belief Situation in Indonesia, 2010] (Jakarta: Pustaka Masyarakat Setara, 2011), x.

20. See Hasani and Naipospos, *Negara*, vi–x.

Musyawarah and Democratic Lay Catholic Leadership in Indonesia: The Ongoing Legacy of John Dijkstra, SJ, and Ikatan Petani Pancasila

Paulus Wiryono Priyotamtama, SJ

The postcolonial Indonesian farmers organization Ikatan Petani Pancasila was founded in 1954 by the Jesuit priest John Baptista Dijkstra, SJ.[1] From this organization was born Bina Swadaya, a rural community development institution which became the largest NGO in Indonesia. The key figure in the development of Bina Swadaya was Bambang Ismawan.[2] Since their respective beginnings, Ikatan Petani Pancasila and Bina Swadaya have trained lay Catholics to build democratic processes and structures into social movements under the inspiration of the philosophy of *musyawarah* (mutual dialogue). In order to develop a long-term strategy of Catholic lay formation in democratic leadership, it is important to understand what musyawarah meant for the founders of Ikatan Petani Pancasila and Bina Swadaya and how it might be communicated today.

Musyawarah and Local Democracy in Indonesia

Musyawarah (also called *tradisi berembug* or *rembug*) is a traditional Indonesian system of mutual dialogue, consultation, deliberation, and decision-making based on consensus.[3] The word originates from the Arabic word *syawara*, which means having deliberations or consultations between persons. Though the word is Arabic, Indonesian people practiced musyawarah many years before Islam came to the archipelago. Analogues to musyawarah can be found in in the languages of many native Indonesian ethnic groups:

Javanese: *arisan, tengelan, selapanan, sambatan, lebotan*
Balinese: *pela*
Ambonese: *masori*
Batak: *marsi adapara*
Florinese: *arong, engko, gemoking*
Minahasan: *mapa/us*
Sundanese: *resaya, tabur*
Kalimantanese: *pulodow, pengerih*
Lampung: *sakai sambahyangan*
Sumbanese: *basiru matag siru*
Timorese: *partei, mepu tabua, kawok*

To explore the meaning of musyawarah in the lives of people, several local group leaders were interviewed for this chapter. These groups ranged from the Kelompok Tani (Local Farmer Group), Gapoktan (Association of Local Farmer Groups), PKK (Empowerment and Family Welfare Movement), the STN-HPS (World Food Farmer's and Fishermen's Movement Indonesia), and the Farmer Cooperative Movement. The method of these in-depth interviews will be discussed later in this chapter.

The spirit and practice of musyawarah is part of Indonesia's cultural identity.[4] For generations, the power of musyawarah has expressed the spirit of democracy through the sensibilities and customs of local people. Musyawarah has aided in a wide array of deliberations within villages and communities. It has played a role in discussions ranging from childbirth, weddings, and funerals, to crop failure, pest control, earthquake damage, increased food prices, and the effects of global warming. In every case where the principles of musyawarah were followed, groups explored and presented more than one solution to a given problem and permitted everyone to contribute his or her viewpoint. Experts could be invited to provide information on a given topic or facilitate the decision-making process, but the community would make the final decisions. In the wake of these deliberations, follow-up discussions were often held to discuss the impacts of the community's decisions. The key to the musyawarah process was maintenance of respect for each participant by giving them the freedom to express their own opinions.

A more formal way people understood musyawarah was through the concept of *permusyawaratan*. This is expressed in the fourth principle of the Indonesian national ideology, Pancasila. As stated in the 1945 Constitutional Preamble, and as alluded to by Baskara Wardaya in his chapter on the history of Indonesian democratization, found in this volume, Pancasila contains five principles or values:

1. Belief in one God
2. Just and civilized humanity
3. The unity of Indonesia
4. Democracy guided by the inner wisdom in unanimity arising out of deliberation among representatives
5. Social justice for the whole people of Indonesia

As related to the fourth principle above, musyawarah is deliberation aimed at discovering a community's inner wisdom and deep unanimity. Deliberation in the manner of musyawarah involves applying longstanding cultural values to new problems. These values include collaboration (*gotong royong*), egalitarianism, tolerance, mutual respect, hospitality, piety, sincerity, humility, harmony, and loyalty.[5] The application of these values in community deliberation is the best way to describe the practice of democracy in the Indonesian context.[6] However, community deliberation is not the only sphere within which these values apply. As Francisca Ninik Yudianti's analysis in the next chapter suggests, many of the values noted above also apply to social and economic entrepreneurship through the lens of corporate social responsibility. As Yudianti argues, this can be especially seen when said corporations identify, or can be identified as, Catholic and, therefore, as potential adoptees of the tradition of Catholic social teaching. While this analysis will focus on the sphere of community deliberation, the parallel to economics and corporate social responsibility must be noted.

Overall, it can be said that musyawarah was a necessary way for democracy to be practiced in Indonesia. Democracy is more than just casting a vote. It is a process by which attitudes and ideas are gradually formed and shared through respectful listening and deliberation. It is an inclusive process that places special value on the wisdom of the elders in the community. It is a process open to advice from outside experts but never to the exclusion of local knowledge and experience. This does not, however, prevent the possibility of musyawarah succumbing to domination and manipulation. In his chapter in this volume, Albertus Budi Susanto shows how Indonesia's *kethoprak* performances have served as a cultural outlet for exposing these manipulations. Before discussing current ways musyawarah is being introduced into the formation of lay Catholic leaders, however, more needs to be said about the historic role of John Dijkstra, SJ, and the farmer's organization, Ikatan Petani Pancasila, that he inspired. For future success, Catholic practitioners of musyawarah will need to continue drawing on the spiritual inspiration and practical experience of John Dijkstra.

John Dijkstra's Understanding and Practice of Musyawarah

From the point of view of the Jesuit missionary John Dijkstra, SJ, musyawarah deeply resonated with his understanding of the revelation of God's spirit in the person of Jesus Christ. In a 1989 interview conducted by F. Wahono Nitiprawira, SJ, John Dijkstra explained how he began using musyawarah in 1949 to revitalize parish groups (*kring*) while he was an assistant priest at Bintaran Parish in Yogyakarta.[7] At that time, many of his parishioners were jobless and living in absolute poverty. Young people wanted to go to school, but their families could not afford to send them. People wanted to work, but no work was available.

To address this issue in the spirit of musyawarah, John Dijkstra invited the parishioners to discuss joblessness and poverty in the community. Among the parishioners in the discussion were people skilled at managing households, running businesses, and promoting social change. Everyone shared the experiences and problems they faced. In the end, the process led parishioners to devise new ways of creating jobs in the community. John Dijkstra recalled a village tailor named Yuharman who was very active in the discussions. Inspired by the musyawarah dialogue, Yuharman ended up providing training to many unemployed young people in the village who, in turn, also became tailors.

Dijkstra repeated these practices when he moved to Gedangan Parish, Semarang in 1952. The musyawarah process again created positive results. Building on parish discussions, Dijkstra established an employment bureau named Biro Pengantar Kerja (Bureau for Offering Jobs). This bureau collected information about industrial factories owned by Catholics. With this information, Catholic business leaders were contacted and asked to help run the bureau. This put the factory owners and operators into direct contact with members of the parish community who needed jobs. This was another example of the spirit of musyawarah in action.

Through musyawarah, Dijkstra was able to identify, develop, and mobilize the community's potential for addressing social and economic problems. In Dijkstra's view, successful musyawarah required the following conditions:

Each participant's authentic faith can be freely expressed

All participants have the opportunity to share their experiences

Each idea for solving a problem is fully explored so each participant can understand what is being proposed

Direction and control of the discussion flows equitably and naturally from the subjectivity of the participants

Deliberation is conducted with mutual respect, support, and inspiration

Dijkstra believed musyawarah contained "nilai manusiawi tertinggi rakyat dan bangsa Indonesia," or "the highest human value owned by Indonesia as people and nation." From a social-psychological perspective, musyawarah could be interpreted as "an emergent property of life representing the epitome of psychosocial maturity" or "the pinnacle of insight into the human condition and about the means and ends of a good life."[8] From a cultural perspective, musyawarah, like its related principle of Pancasila, came from the heart of the Indonesian people. As Indonesian President Sukarno said about Pancasila:

> If someone should say that Pancasila is made by man, I would only reply: "I do not feel that I made Pancasila; I do not feel that I created Pancasila." . . . I am not the creator of Pancasila. I merely put into words some feelings existing amongst the people, to which I gave the name Pancasila. I dug in the ground of the Indonesian nation and I saw in the hearts of the Indonesian people that there were five living feelings there. . . . I formulated what we know today as Pancasila because these five feelings had already lived for scores of years, even for hundreds of years, in our innermost hearts.[9]

Though Dijkstra felt this value came from the bottom up and not from the top down, it was closely linked to his understanding of God's grace. Dijkstra once remarked:

> Within musyawarah, God is present as a spring of clean and fresh water. God's grace will accompany the hearts of all participants in musyawarah. God's grace is always available for all those who are searching for it.[10]

Dijkstra believed God's presence in the musyawarah was powerful enough to bring transformation in the hearts of the people:

> God's grace will facilitate the process of transformation within the heart of people without outside forces. As a result, the desire for justice

based on faith will come from the people themselves. God will accompany people in carrying out musyawarah because where there is openness, there God's love is dwelling and appearing more significantly through those involved in it.[11]

How can such a process really happen in the heart of people? According to Dijkstra, three factors must be present:

1. An awareness among people of a common basic faith and common moral values
2. The presence within people of a holy desire
3. An openness in the human heart to God's love

Ikatan Petani Pancasila and Musyawarah

Essential to the story of John Dijkstra and musyawarah is the postcolonial Indonesian farmer's organization Ikatan Petani Pancasila. This organization was founded in 1954, nine years after Indonesia proclaimed its national independence and seven years before the establishment of the Indonesian Catholic Church as an independent hierarchy in 1961. John B. Dijkstra, SJ, was known as its founder, though he never considered himself as such. He would say that he was only assigned as the spiritual adviser of this organization. However, because of his full involvement in the preparation and the running of the Second Indonesian Catholic Congress (1954) from which this organization was born, the claim that he was the real founder can be justified.

Shortly after Indonesian independence, Catholics began thinking about starting an organization to support farmers and fishermen. Some thought the organization should be named Ikatan Petani Katolik to emphasize its Catholic identity. Instead, the name Ikatan Petani Pancasila emerged, largely through the influence of Monsignor Albertus Soegijapranata, SJ, Vicariate Apostolic of Semarang and person in charge of the steering committee for the Second Catholic Congress in Semarang in 1954. It was during this Congress that Ikatan Petani Pancasila was chosen as the name of the new organization.

Monsignor Soegijapranata was the first native-born bishop in Indonesia. He had a special friendship with Sukarno, the first president of Indonesia. By naming the organization Ikatan Petani Pancasila, a bond was acknowledged between the democratic spirit of musyawarah and the fourth principle of Sukarno's national Pancasila philosophy. Here, Soegijapranata was able to position the Indonesian Catholic minority as an integral component in the formation of the new nation. The Indonesian Catholic Church would no longer be seen as a mere extension of the Dutch or Western Catholic Church. It would now be recognized as an *Indonesian* Catholic Church. Such a position allowed Catholic activists to grow, build identity according to their religious beliefs, and perform actively as national citizens in a situation of political equality with the other groups. This enhanced the democratic contribution of Catholics to the newly formed Indonesian state.

In 1955, Dijkstra was chosen by Soegijapranata to be his secretary. Dijkstra agreed that Pancasila and musyawarah were deep, collaborative values in which all Indonesians, whether Catholic or non-Catholic, could share *iman dasar bersama* (or, "common basic faith"). Dijkstra expected all members of Ikatan Petani Pancasila to be committed to the common faith expressed in Pancasila and the practice of musyawarah.

In 1964, President Sukarno published a new law named Keppres No. 72/1964 that required all organizations to spread their activities so that the whole country would be covered. Communists, anti-Catholics, and other opponents of Ikatan Petani Pancasila were hoping the organization would be banned by the president because this Catholic organization would not be able to meet the requirement. Surprisingly, Dijkstra and his colleagues were able to meet the requirement. Within a short time, Ikatan Petani Pancasila was able to spread its activities over the whole country. By 1967, Ikatan Petani Pancasila had one million members in all twenty-six Indonesian provinces. Approximately 90 percent of the members were non-Catholic.

How did Ikatan Petani Pancasila so successfully serve the needs of not only local farmers and workers but also Indonesia as a whole? Dijkstra taught that a musyawarah discussion begins by asking someone in the group to be an initiator. That person presents the issue under discussion. All members are asked to give their viewpoints on the issues. Through respectful speaking and listening, participants agree on concrete actions. Agreement is then made on the right person or persons to carry out the group's decision.

The word "right" here indicates a person who has compassion for the issue and the community's solution. Such compassion is vital to the spirit of musyawarah. It gives the community confidence that the person in charge will seek out further assistance from people who are likewise respectful of the community's desires. Technical skills in strategic planning, networking, and managerial operations are certainly needed for project success, but nothing replaces compassion as the central value of musyawarah. Indeed, an increase in compassion in the community is the hoped-for, long-term result of practicing musyawarah month after month, year after year, generation after generation.

These are the values and practices still identified by the social activists and focus group members interviewed for this study. This legacy of John Dijkstra has been carried forward by the organization Bina Swadaya, a rural community development institution born out of Ikatan Petani Pancasila.

The picture of musyawarah as presented above is taken from case studies. These studies were pursued with a qualitative approach involving literature review, in-depth interviews, and focus group discussions.[12] The in-depth interviews were conducted with four social activists who have practiced musyawarah. They were asked several questions regarding the practice of musyawarah and their personal experience of musyawarah's values and results.

The first interviewee was Haryanto, a forty-year-old farmer. Haryanto is a member of the Tani Muda Pagerharjo (Pagerharjo Young Farmer Group), vice chair of the Usaha Makmur Farmer Group, and an activist from the Karisma Kaliasih Credit Union. The second activist interviewed was Handoko Saptoto Adi, a thirty-three-year-old farmer and secretary of three local organizations (the Karisma Kaliasih Credit Union, Usaha Makmur Farmer Group, and Tani Muda Pagerharjo). The third activist was Tri Riyani, a fifty-five-year-old farmer, member of the Ngudi Mulyo Farmer Group, treasurer of the FMA Farmer Training Group, and an activist from Gapoktan (Farmers' Group Alliance). The final activist interviewed was Hemy Saraswati. He is a forty-nine-year-old farmer and member of the Wana Lestari Menoreh Cooperative Movement. At the time of the interviews, all four men were members of the World Food Farmers' and Fishermen's Movement and were living in the Kulon Progo and Sleman regencies of Yogyakarta Special Province.

The focus group discussion was conducted with four members from Bina Swadaya. The group was asked what impact they felt musyawarah has had on the formation of democratic lay Catholic leaders in Indonesia. The members of this group included Bambang Ismawan, Janu Ismanik, Emmanuel Haryadi, and Koeswandi. Janu Ismanik has been a close friend of Bambang Ismawan and was a participant in Bina Swadaya from 1975 to 1983. Emmanuel Haryadi was second only to Bambang Ismawan in the leadership of Bina Swadaya. Koeswandi was responsible for developing the organization's social entrepreneurship program.

New Expressions of Musyawarah

Since the contemporary era of Indonesian democratization began in 1999, the musyawarah-inspired rural community development institution Bina Swadaya has adopted more business-oriented training programs. The organization remains committed to its long-term goal training in compassion and empowerment. The organization's motto includes these four principles:

Bermartabat: respect for the dignity of every human being in open dialogue and collaboration

Mandiri: assistance in knowledge, management skills, and personal development

Sejahtera: focus on social and economic welfare

Maju Bersama: building progress through community solidarity

During the interviews conducted for this study, Bambang Ismawan noted that the key issue for the organization was not a choice between business or empowerment training, but an integrated training program in business *and* empowerment known, popularly, as social entrepreneurship.[13] This integrated educational program in social entrepreneurship has five characteristics:

1. Focus on the poor and marginalized as target groups
2. Development of products that have empowerment value
3. Creation of values-based business collaborations
4. Emphasis on the social reinvestment of profit
5. Formation of leaders in knowledge, networking, and compassion

Guided by these characteristics, Bina Swadaya empowers community members through programs such as micro-financing, civil society empowerment, and agribusiness. Each of these programs has business units that need professional management. As of 2013, Bina Swadaya had seventeen community-based businesses in operation. Because of this success, Bambang Ismawan was chosen as an Indonesian representative to the 1996 Social Development Summit in Copenhagen, the 1997 Micro-Credit Summit in Washington, and the 1997 International Leaders Forum on Development Finance. In 2006, Ismawan was presented with the Social Entrepreneur of the Year Award by Indonesia's Ernst & Young and Switzerland's Schwab Foundation.

Conclusion

The impact of musyawarah as an adaptive democratic value in the formation of Catholic lay activists in Indonesia can be related to three factors:

1. The faith-related inspiration found within musyawarah
2. The empowerment skills learned by practicing musyawarah
3. The nature of musyawarah as a carrier of local wisdom

When combined with the modern skills of social entrepreneurship pro-vided by Bina Swadaya, musyawarah remains a powerful democratizing practice in Indonesia today. The lives and testimonies of John Dijkstra, the pioneers and key leaders of Bina Swadaya, and the four Catholic lay activists of the Secretariat of the World Food Farmers' and Fishermen's Movement of Indonesia gave evidence to this ongoing value of musyawarah.

NOTES

1. Ikatan Petani Pancasila (IPP) is a national social movement and union. On John Dijkstra, SJ, see Wahono Nitiprawira, "Kerasulan Sosial, Kerasulan BerMusyawarah Wawancara Dengan John Dijkstra," in *Harta dan Surga*, ed. A. Budi Susanto, SJ (Yogyakarta, Indonesia: Penerbit Kanisius, 1990), 268–69. Also see Bambang Ismawan and John Dijkstra, *Dijkstra, People's Dialogue Facilitator* (Jakarta: Bina Swadaya, 1992).

2. Eka Budianta, ed., *Bambang Ismawan Bersama Wong Cilik* (Jakarta: Yayasan Bina Swadaya, 2008), 48–99.

3. Pius S. Prasetyo, "Village Democracy: The Interaction between Local Culture and Modern Political Patterns," in, *Pancasila's Contemporary Appeal: Re-Legitimizing Indonesia's Founding Ethos*, International Conference Book Series No. 2, Indonesian History Studies Centre, Sanata Dharma University, ed. Thomas J. Conners, Mason C. Hoadley, Frank Dhont, and Kevin Ko (Yogyakarta, Indonesia: Yale Indonesia Forum, 2010), 325–52. Prasetyo argues that musyawarah as a village democracy is really the Indonesian democracy or Pancasila democracy that can be categorized as deliberative democracy.

4. Emil Salim, "Mungkinkah Ada Demokrasi Di Indonesia?," in *Demokrasi Politik, Budaya dan Ekonomi: Pengalaman Indonesia Masa Orde Baru*, ed. Elza Peldi Taher (Jakarta: Yayasan Paramadina, 1994), 155–64. In 1982, UNESCO defined cultural identity as "a treasure that vitalizes mankind's possibilities of self fulfillment by moving every people and every group to seek nurture in its past, to welcome contributions from outside that are compatible with its own characteristics, and so to continue the process of its own creation." See "Mexico City Declaration on Cultural Policies," *World Conference on Cultural Policies*, Mexico City, July 26–August 6, 1982, http://www.portal.unesco.org.

5. See Frank Dhont, "Introduction: Indonesia's Pancasila," in Conners, Hoadley, Dhont, and Ko, *Pancasila's Contemporary Appeal*, 2. Frank Dhont states: "Pancasila, which even under fire remains uniquely Indonesian and forms the backbone of the Indonesian nation. To be Indonesian means to know the Pancasila. Even those who reject it have internalized it in so far to define their opposition."

6. See also, Hastangka, "Pancasila Education in Post Reform Era Senior High Schools (SMA): A Study in Yogyakarta," in Conners, Hoadley, Dhont, and Ko, *Pancasila's Contemporary Appeal*, 163–65.

7. The entire interview can be found in Wahono Nitiprawira, SJ, "Kerasulan Sosial, Kerasulan BerMusyawarah Wawancara Dengan John Dijkstra," in A. Budi Susanto, SJ, *Harta dan Surga*, 261–86.

8. Carol Hoare, "Work as the Catalyst of Reciprocal Adult Development and Learning: Identity and Personality," in *Handbook of Adult Development and Learning*, ed. Carol Hoare (New York: Oxford University Press, 2006), 358–561.

9. Michael O'Shannassy, "(Re)Imagining Community: Pancasila and National Identity in Contemporary Indonesia," in Conners, Hoadley, Dhont, and Ko, *Pancasila's Contemporary Appeal*, 47–72.

10. Alfons Taryadi, *Johannes Dijkstra SJ: Menjadi Garam Dunia* (Jakarta: Penerbit Yayasan Bhumiksara, 2006), 117.

11. Ibid.

12. Fred N. Kerlinger, *Foundations of Behavioral Research* (New York: Holt, Rinehart, and Winston, 1973), 479–80, and Carolyn Boyce and Palena Neale, "Conducting In-Depth Interviews: A Guide for Designing and Conducting In-Depth Interviews for Evaluation Input," at Pathfinder International, May 2006, http://www2.pathfinder.org/site/DocServer/m_e_tool_series_indepth _interviews.pdf.

13. In 1993, Bambang Ismawan was asked to join Tim Penanggulangan Kemiskinan Bappenas (Poverty Alleviation Team of National Development Planning Board) to design the Inpres Desa Tertinggal (IDT, or Presidential Instruction for the Underdeveloped Villages) program. This involved training four thousand facilitators and the monitoring of IDT execution. By 1996, 120,000 KSMs (*Kelompok Swadaya Masyarakat*, or community self-help groups) were established with 3.6 million members. All were involved in executing the program.

The Influence of Catholic Social Teaching on the Democratic Practice of Corporate Social Responsibility: A Study from Indonesia

Francisca Ninik Yudianti

Corporate Social Responsibility (CSR) is driven by the idea that businesses are part of society and therefore ought to contribute positively to social conditions and goals. Some of these conditions and goals include the democratic principles of respect for human rights, the rule of law, and transparent decision-making. CSR proponents argue that businesses should be held accountable not only for their economic impact on society but also for the other non-economic consequences of their activities on society and the natural environment.[1] There is growing pressure on businesses to respect human rights and the rule of law wherever they operate, to undertake expenditures to compensate for their social and environmental impact, and publicly account for this impact through transparent annual reporting.[2] Well-known corporate scandals and the increasingly international context within which businesses operate have intensified pressure on corporations to behave ethically in both social and environmental spheres.

In response to this intensifying pressure, some companies have begun to accept these new social responsibilities. Research conducted by David Hackston and Markus Milne found that some of the determinants for change in business social behavior and disclosure in New Zealand are a company's size, profitability, and the nature of its industry.[3] Other research has revealed that investors significantly influence corporate behavior. A sampling of seventy-nine manufacturing companies listed on the Indonesia Stock Exchange revealed that investors react positively when firms accept corporate social responsibility.[4]

An interesting question with regard to corporations and their acceptance or rejection of corporate social responsibility is the degree to which a corporation's leadership and overall culture is influenced by religion. Geoffrey Williams and John Zinkin used a sample of nearly twenty thousand observations across twenty-one countries and found that "Muslim countries" (Indonesia included) are less drawn to the idea of corporate social responsibility than "non-Muslim countries" and that these differences do not appear to be explained by demographics, socio-political factors, or cultural differences.[5]

Other research has shown an increase in the number of religious groups seeking to influence business conduct. One example of this is the 1994 Interfaith Declaration of International Business Ethics. This declaration was developed by Christian, Muslim, and Jewish scholars to identify "shared moral, ethical and spiritual values" and "draw up a number of principles that might serve as guidelines for international business behavior." An example characterized by more direct action is the Interfaith Center on Corporate Responsibility. This organization is committed to using the "power of persuasion backed by economic pressure from consumers and investors to hold corporations accountable."[6]

More research needs to be done on the noneconomic factors that go into a business's decision to accept corporate social responsibility. Such research will need to carefully analyze corporate culture. Corporate culture can be defined as the moral, social, and behavioral norms of an organization based on the beliefs, attitudes, and priorities of its members. Though not all businesses consciously set out to create a specific culture, every business has one. A corporation's operative culture is typically an unconscious creation that reflects the values of the organization's founder(s), top management, and day-to-day leadership. Whether conscious or unconscious, corporate culture is a power that can either assist or derail an organization's ability to reach its goals. A healthy corporate culture can result not only in a profitable business but also in positive results for society and the environment.

When looking at the relationship between corporate social responsibility, corporate culture, and religion, one might hypothesize that the probability of a business's acceptance of corporate social responsibility would increase in proportion to the degree to which religion influences its culture. However, this hypothesis does not appear to be borne out in research exploring the impact of Islam on business leaders' decisions to accept corporate social responsibility. It would seem that the degree to which a religion has explicit teachings similar to the norms of corporate social responsibility, along with the degree to which those teachings are embedded in a business's culture, proportionally increases the probability a religion might have increased influence on a business's decision to adopt corporate social responsibility.

Roman Catholicism is a religion with explicit teachings similar to the norms of corporate social responsibility. In its social teaching, Roman Catholicism offers moral perspectives on business practices that are applicable to all people, regardless of whether one is Catholic. Catholic social teaching honors the contribution of business to society but also stresses the democratic principles of human rights, rule of law, and transparent decision-making. These principles are vital for protecting employees, customers, and the environment.[7]

With this in mind, the following discussion reports on research conducted on the relationship between corporate social responsibility, corporate culture, and Catholic social thought in small and medium-sized enterprises (SMEs) located in the Yogyakarta Special Region of Indonesia. The designation "special region" indicates that Yogyakarta remains the only region in Indonesia still governed by a precolonial monarchy. The Sultan of Yogyakarta serves as the hereditary governor of the Yogyakarta Special Region.

The discussion begins with contextual information concerning corporate culture, Catholic social teaching, and corporate social responsibility. It then moves to the specific research hypothesis pursued in this study, the research design, and the results.

Corporate Culture

Shinichi Hirota, Katsuyuki Kubo, and Hideaki Miyajima used mission statement data from large Japanese firms to show that corporate culture has a significant impact on corporate policies that determine employment, board membership and process, and financial decisions.[8] Their research revealed that more than firms with weak cultures, firms with strong cultures are likely to retain employees, promote managers, hold less debt, and possess a higher percentage of interlocking shareholdings. This suggests that firms financially benefit from strong cultures. It also shows that some firms have intentionally adopted policies to preserve and further promote strong cultures. This shows that culture must be taken into account to understand corporate performance.

Most Indonesian businesses are led by family groups. A family business is an enterprise in which ownership, management, expenses, and profits are controlled by people in a kinship relationship. Benny Simon Tabalujan explored the impact of culture on corporate governance by looking at family relationships in companies listed on the Jakarta Stock Exchange (JSX).[9] In the Indonesian business context, the family is important because a great deal of economic activity revolves around companies controlled by a small group of powerful families. The values of these families affect how their companies operate and, by extension, how the Indonesian economy runs. Listed Indonesian corporations, even if family controlled, are regulated and subject to more disclosure requirements than unlisted, small and medium-sized enterprises. This means that families in unlisted companies have more latitude in terms of business decisions about corporate social responsibility.[10]

Catholic Social Teaching

Catholic social teaching is the Church's presentation of moral norms regarding human relations in society. It takes into consideration human relations within various arenas of life, including the political, economic, social, and cultural institutions of society. It identifies the social realities confronting persons and highlights the benefits and dangers those realities present to full human flourishing. It critiques harmful realities and encourages positive change based on the moral values of Catholic faith.

The principles of Catholic social teaching address the relationships between employer and employee, workplace conditions, and policies for morally improving business practices.[11] The body of these principles is rich and complex. The research in this analysis focuses on four specific principles: the dignity of workers, the democratic rights of workers, just wage, and worker equity.

In Catholic social thought, the measure of business success is not limited to profit margins and market shares but includes the quality of a business's relationship with workers, customers, investors, and the environment.[12] Catholic social teaching places particular emphasis on the moral necessity to see that workers have a safe environment for their work and a living wage that allows workers and their families to live decent lives. Calculating workplace conditions and wages solely on a market cost-benefit mechanism does not ensure that a worker's rightful needs will be met.

Compared to a large corporation, a small or medium-sized business can make the work experience more humane in terms of providing closer personal relationships in the workplace and more opportunities for personal and professional initiative. On the other hand, leadership and culture within a small or medium-sized business can often be unjust and oppressive.[13] The research in this study looks at which of these alternatives predominates in the Yogyakarta Special Region.

Corporate Social Responsibility

In an era of increasingly globalized markets and attention to environmental sustainability, corporate conduct has come under increased scrutiny from investors and governments. More and more institutions and citizens are expressing the view that companies must realize their profits in a manner that respects society and the environment. Companies that do so are following the guidelines of corporate social responsibility. Some companies disclose their compliance with corporate social responsibility in annual CSR reports.

CSR is a multilayered concept differentiated into economic, legal, ethical, and philanthropic responsibilities. Social responsibility requires that businesses address all four levels consecutively.[14] In descending order of application, these responsibilities are:

Economic Responsibility: Companies have shareholders who demand
    a reasonable return on their investments, employees who want safe
    and paid jobs, and customers who demand good quality products at
    a fair price.
Legal Responsibility: The legal responsibility of corporations requires
    that businesses abide by the law and play by the rules of the game.
    Laws are understood, in part, as a codification of society's moral
    views. Abiding by these standards is a necessary prerequisite for
    taking on greater social responsibilities.
Ethical Responsibility: These responsibilities oblige corporations to do
    what is right, just, and fair even when a corporation is not legally
    compelled to do so. Meeting these ethical responsibilities is a social
    expectation, over and above economic and legal expectations.
Philanthropic Responsibility: These responsibilities include the corpo-
    ration's efforts to improve the quality of life for employees, local
    communities, society, and the environment. This aspect of CSR
    includes such things as charitable donations, building recreation

facilities for employees and their families, supporting local schools, or organizing pollution clean-up events.

The advantage of the four-part CSR model is that it prioritizes social responsibilities while still acknowledging that in a market system of economy a firm must be profitable. One limitation of the CSR model is that it does not offer a guideline for action when two or more responsibilities come into conflict.

CSR Research

Krishna Udayasankar has shown that SMEs constitute 90 percent of businesses worldwide.[15] She found that firms of this size are less likely to engage in CSR initiatives. Udayasankar did not explain this finding. This leaves open the question: Why is there a relatively low rate of SME participation in CSR?

Family-owned and -operated SMEs play a significant role in Indonesian society. For Indonesian SMEs that do support CSR, why are they doing so? The research here offers three hypotheses:

Catholic social teaching influences corporate culture
Religion influences corporate culture
Catholic social teaching, religion, and corporate culture each influence SME participation in CSR

To explore these hypotheses, research was conducted on SMEs in the Yogyakarta Special Region. The method used to gather data from the respondents was convenience sampling. This is a nonprobability sampling technique where respondents are selected because of their convenient accessibility and proximity to the researcher. This method was also chosen because the respondents are owners and/or managers of SMEs who are typically reluctant to be involved in academic research. I approached potential respondents personally, through my membership in several social organizations. Seventy standardized questionnaires were distributed and forty of them were returned for a 57 percent response rate. The questionnaire consisted of the following parts:

Company profile
Manager/owner profile
Statements to determine the degree of Catholic social teaching applied in companies

Statements to determine the values, beliefs, and norms applied in
  companies
Statements to reveal the practices of CSR in companies

The data collected from the respondents was analyzed by using descriptive statistics, linear regression, and nonparametric statistics. The following is the legend for variable measurement:

Corporate Culture: The importance of a set of values, beliefs, and
  norms that apply in the company
Religion: The owner's religious affiliation. Islam = 0; Catholic = 1;
  Protestant = 2; Other = 3
Catholic Social Teaching: The degree of company recognition of the
  democratic rights of workers, safe working conditions, just wage,
  and environment protection
Corporate Social Responsibility:
  Index CSR = ratio of the number of CSR activities applied in the
  company and the total number of CSR activities proposed
  CSR score = aggregate score of weighted CSR activities applied in
  the company with criteria:
  0: If the firm had no plans to participate in a CSR activity
  1: If the firm already had a plan to apply a CSR activity
  2: If the firm already applied a CSR activity but not on
  a regular basis
  3: If the firm already applied a CSR activity regularly

The research sample consisted of forty companies established between
1952 and 2009, with the average age of the companies at 24.2 years. Of the
company owners, 43 percent were Catholic, 28 percent were Muslim, 18
percent were Protestant, and the rest were Confucian or Buddhist. The
oldest owner was eighty-seven years old and the youngest owner was
thirty-one years old. This made for an average age of company ownership
at 50.6 years.

Most of the respondents were well educated, with 68 percent possessing
bachelors or masters degrees. Most respondents indicated that they participated directly in the daily operation of their firm, accompanied by
family and nonfamily workers. The types of business represented in the
survey were from the areas of food and beverage, furniture, pharmaceu-
ticals education, handicrafts, plastics, leather, bookstores, medical products, agricultural machinery, contracting, gold, minimarkets, distribution
centers, motorcycle service, stationery, luggage, chemical and laboratory
products, and transportation. The average of annual sales of the respon-

dents' businesses was Rp6,745,000,000 ($674,500), with a maximum annual sales at Rp85,000,000,000 ($8,500,000) and a minimum annual sales at Rp120,000,000 ($12,000).

Table 1 responds to the first hypothesis, that Catholic social teaching influences corporate culture. The table shows that there is a relationship between Catholic social teaching and corporate culture at a 05.1 percent significance level. This means that when Catholic social teaching is present it does positively influence the moral, social, and behavioral norms of an Indonesian SME in the Yogyakarta Special Region.

TABLE 1. The influence of Catholic social teaching to corporate culture

Model	Unstandardized Coefficient		Standardized Coefficient		
	β	*Std. Error*	*β*	*t*	*Sig*
1 (Constant)	22.634	4.409		5.134	.000
CST Score	.104	.052	.301	2.011	.051

Dependent variable: CC Score

Further results (as seen in Table 2) are shown by looking at the split between the different religions (0: Islam; 1: Catholic; 2: Protestant; 3: Other). Here, the research suggests that the presence of the Roman Catholic religion among participants in the firm has a positive influence (at a 5 percent level) on whether Catholic social teaching will have an impact on the culture of the firm. The other three categories of religion did not show this relationship with a high percentage of significance.

TABLE 2. The influence of corporate culture and Catholic social teaching (split by religion)

Model	Unstandardized Coefficient		Standardized Coefficient		
	β	*Std. Error*	*β*	*t*	*Sig*
0 (constant)	25.893	11.821		2.190	.056
CST Score	.074	.135	.180	.550	.596
1 (constant)	14.422	6.627		2.176	.046
CST Score	.195	.078	.539	2.479	.026
2 (constant)	37.692	17.108		2.203	.079
CST Score	-.057	.196	-.130	-.292	.782
3 (constant)	32.322	9.481		3.409	.042
CST Score	-.031	.122	-.144	-.252	.817

Dependent Variable: CC Score

Tables 3 and 4 respond to the second hypothesis, that religion influences corporate culture. The results show that religion in and of itself does not significantly influence corporate culture. Most of the respondents (85 to 100 percent) choose very important and important for all items related with values, beliefs, and norms applied in their companies, regardless of their religious affiliations. This result suggests that Indonesian culture writ large, and not qualified by religious affiliation, recommends noneconomic values, beliefs, and norms to business owners in the Yogyakarta Special Region.

TABLE 3. Mean rank of corporate culture score based on religion

	Religion	*N*	*Mean Rank*
CC Score	0	11	23.59
	1	17	17.79
	2	7	24.21
	3	5	17.70
Total		40	

TABLE 4. Test statistics[a,b]

	CC Score
Chi-Square	2.696
Df	3
Asymp.Sig	.441

[a] Kruskal-Wallis Test
[b] Grouping Variable: DReligion

Hypothesis three proposes that Catholic social teaching, religion, and corporate culture encourage small and medium-sized enterprises to participate in corporate social responsibility. The research results shown in Tables 5, 6, and 7 reveal that there is enough positive influence from Catholic social teaching on SMEs to encourage their participation in CSR at a 01.1 percent level when measured by the CSR index. The results show that there is not a similar influence coming from corporate culture or religion that is comparable to the influence coming from Catholic social teaching. This suggests that Catholic social teaching has a comparatively higher influence on company practices that recognize the democratic principles of respect for the human rights of workers and consumers, the rule of law, decision-making transparency, protecting the environment, and providing philanthropic aid to the surrounding community.

TABLE 5. Model summary[a]

Model	R	Rsquare	Adj Rsquare	Std Err of the Estimate
1	.493[a]	.243	.180	.23183

[a] Predictors: (Constant), CC Score, DReligion, CST Score

TABLE 6. Anova[a]

Model	Sum of Squares	df	Mean Square	F	Sig
1 Regression	.623	3	.208	3.861	.017[b]
Residual	1.935	36	.054		
Total	2.557	39			

[a] Predictors: (Constant), CC Score, DReligion, CST Score
[b] Dependent variable: CSR Index

TABLE 7. Coefficient[a]

Model	Unstandardized Coefficient		Standardized Coefficient		
	β	Std. Error	β	t	Sig
1 Constant	-.076	.332		-.229	.820
DReligion	-.039	.039	-.149	-1.007	.321
CST Score	.008	.003	.417	2.685	.011
CC Score	.004	.009	.064	.422	.676

[a] Dependent Variable: CSR Index

It should be noted, however, that based on the descriptive statistics provided by this research, Islamic firms were revealed to have higher mean scores than Catholic firms in the three variable areas. Within the Catholic social teaching variable, Islamic firms received an average score of 87 out of 114, compared with Catholic firms that only had 83 out of 114. The corporate culture score for Islamic firms was 32 out of 33, compared with Catholic firms that scored 30 out of 33. For their CSR score, Islamic firms again received 87 out of 114, compared with the Catholic firms, which, again, received an average score of 83 out of 114. This suggests that although there does not appear to be strong evidence that CSR is directly influenced by corporate culture or religion in either Catholic or Islamic firms, nevertheless, the Islamic firms encountered in this research demonstrated a high level of interest in the implementation of CSR in their firms and businesses.

Conclusion

Three conclusions can be drawn from this research. First, Catholic social teaching does influence corporate culture in the Yogyakarta Special Region. Catholic social teaching has had a positive influence on corporate culture at a level of 5 percent. Second, there is no significant influence from religion in general on corporate culture in the Yogyakarta Special Region. Third, Catholic social teaching motivates small to medium-sized enterprises in the Yogyakarta Special Region to practice corporate social responsibility. This influence is greater than any influences detected from either religion in general or corporate culture per se. In other words, Catholic social teaching contributes positively to the democratic principles of respect for human rights, the rule of law, transparent decision-making, care for the environment, and public philanthropy in the economic sphere of society in the Yogyakarta Special Region.

It is interesting to note that in the Lithuanian and Peruvian contexts further explored in this volume, Catholic social teaching is also shown to have had a positive moral impact on social institutions. As Arūnas Streikus stated in his earlier essay, "Catholic social teaching constituted a large obstacle for the Sovietization of society at large." When discussing the Peruvian Catholic bishops' advocacy for the rights of indigenous people in the Amazon, Oscar Espinosa's essay later in this volume notes the importance of Church social documents such as *Gaudium et spes* for validating and empowering the bishops' moral stand. Though sometimes criticized as a collection of noble but abstract and ineffectual principles, Catholic social teaching has been shown to have a positive moral impact not only in the limited circumstances analyzed in this study, but also in larger institutional contexts elsewhere in the world.

These research results are drawn from a limited region and a relatively small number of samples, but they do introduce a set of conclusions that merit further research. As it is, research into corporate social responsibility usually links participation to financial or political incentives. There is very little research exploring the influence of corporate culture, religion, or Catholic social teaching on CSR participation. The findings here invite further research as to whether Catholic social teaching has a positive influence on the corporate reception of the democratic principles of human rights, rule of law, and transparency in decision-making over a wider geographical region and among a larger pool of respondents.

NOTES

1. Isabelle Maignan, O. C. Ferrell, and Linda Ferrell, "A Stakeholder Model for Implementing Social Responsibility in Marketing," *European Journal of Marketing* 39, no. 9/10 (2005): 956–77.

2. Fred Robin, "The Future of Corporate Social Responsibility," *Asian Business and Management* 4 (2005): 95–115.

3. David Hackston and Markus J. Milne, "Some Determinants of Social Environmental Disclosures in New Zealand Companies," *Accounting, Auditing and Accountability Journal* 9, no. 1 (1996): 77–108.

4. Yohana Premavari and Francisca Ninik Yudianti, "The Influence of Corporate Social Responsibility's Disclosure Published in Annual Report to the Investor's Reaction: Empirical Study on Manufacturing Companies Listed in Indonesia Stock Exchange 2005–2007" (paper presented at the Fourth International Conference on Business and Management Research: The New World Order after the Crisis, Indonesia University and University of Adelaide Australia, Sanur, Bali, 2009).

5. Geoffrey Williams and John Zinkin, "Doing Business with Islam: Can Corporate Social Responsibility Be a Bridge between Civilizations?" (working paper, Nottingham University Business School, Malaysia, 2005).

6. Stephen Brammer, Geoffrey Williams, and John Zinkin, "Religion and Attitudes to Corporate Social Responsibility in a Large Cross-Country Sample" (working paper, The University of Nottingham Malaysia Campus, 2006).

7. See Susan J. Stabile, "Workers in the Vineyard: Catholic Social Thought and the Workplace," *University of St. Thomas Legal Studies Research Paper* 31, no. 7 (2007): 1–41, and Leo L. Clarke, Bruce P. Frohnen, and Edward C. Lyons, "The Practical Soul of Business Ethics: The Corporate Manager's Dilemma and the Social Teaching of the Catholic Church," *Seattle University Law Review* 29, no. 1 (2005): 139–204.

8. Shinichi Hirota, Katsuyuki Kubo, and Hideaki Miyajima, "Does Corporate Culture Matter? Evidence from Japan" (working paper, Waseda University, Japan, 2008).

9. See Benny Simon Tabalujan, "Family Capitalism and Corporate Governance of Family-Controlled Listed Companies in Indonesia,"*University of New South Wales Law Journal* 25, no. 2 (2002): 486–514.

10. See Syahrial Syarif, "Characteristics of Small-Scale Enterprises in West Sumatra," *Asian Academy of Management Journal* 9, no. 2 (July 2004): 87–95.

11. Stabile, "Workers in the Vineyard," 2.

12. Clark, Frohnen, and Lyons, "The Practical Soul," 154.

13. See Pontifical Council for Justice and Peace, *Compendium of the Social Doctrine of the Church* (Rome: Libreria Editrice Vaticana, 2004).

14. See Archie B. Carroll and Ann K. Buchholtz, *Business and Society: Ethics and Stakeholder Management* (Cincinnati, OH: Thomson Learning, 2000).

15. See Krishna Udayasankar, "Corporate Social Responsibility and Firm Size," *Journal of Business Ethics* (2007), doi:10.1007/s10551-007-9609.

The Performing Art of Kethoprak and the Democratic "Power to Will" in Indonesia

Albertus Budi Susanto, SJ

Since the fall of the thirty-year military regime of President Suharto in May 1998, Indonesia had been widely considered the largest democracy in the world. Twelve years later, the 2010 Economist Intelligence Unit's Democracy Index, however, only ranked Indonesia sixtieth out of 167 countries with a "flawed democracy."[1] The ranking was based on five categories: electoral processes and pluralism, the functioning of government, political participation, political culture, and civil liberties.

The ranking invites the question: How can Indonesia reverse this decline in democratization? Are there indigenous Indonesian traditions that can assist democratization? Paulus Wiryono Priyotamtama has pointed out the importance of *musyawarah* in a previous chapter in this volume. The present chapter explores another cultural resource for building democracy. This is *kethoprak*, the traditional Javanese theatrical performing arts. The following discussion suggests how kethoprak performances contribute to democracy. A particular focus is placed on the ways kethoprak encourages popular participation in public affairs, heightens a sense of political equality in a community, and facilitates the local handling of social conflict.[2]

The discussion begins by showing how democratic practices are expressed through kethoprak performances. Next, the discussion moves to kethoprak as a form of social criticism and its relation to other forms of Javanese artistic social expression. Finally, the importance of kethoprak for Indonesia's minority Catholic population is explored. In this last section, a suggestion is given as to how kethoprak supports a form of Catholic identity linked to the spirituality of Saint Ignatius of Loyola.

Kethoprak and the Practice of Democracy

Kethoprak has been a Javanese form of popular dramatic entertainment since the early 1900s. A typical kethoprak performance intermingles traditional storytelling, contemporary social drama, and Indonesian gamelan music. An analogous Western artistic genre might be an operetta, though there tends to be more dialogue in a kethoprak performance. In the beginning, kethoprak performances could last up to seven hours on makeshift, village stages. By the early 1990s, kethoprak plays were produced on more permanent city stages, with performances lasting up to four hours.

The themes of kethoprak plays have always developed around local events or stories and histories from the Javanese kingdoms of the past.[3] Narratives from the kingdoms of the ninth through the sixteenth centuries are particularly popular because these dynasties rose and fell through scandal, romance, and intrigue. Various kethoprak communities—of directors, actors, and spectators-create links between these ancient events and contemporary life.

The periods of Dutch colonization and military dictatorship in the nineteenth and twentieth centuries, discussed in the opening chapter of this section by Baskara Wardaya, presented another set of experiences for kethoprak commentary. Here, Indonesians used kethoprak to interpret their experience of colonial and authoritarian oppression. Postcolonial theorists Jacqueline Lo and Helen Gilbert describe how oppressed people can use art:

> to expose gaps, absences and ambivalence in historical representations,
> to identify moments of rupture where the exercise of imperial power
> is incomplete and/or compromised by colonial resistance, to elicit sup-
> pressed or forgotten (subaltern) histories, and to problematize the very
> mode through which "history" has accrued its authority as "truth."[4]

Barbara Hatley, an Australian expert on Indonesian performing arts, also notes how the entertainment of the wong cilik (common people) articulates their oppressive links to people of all social classes. Kethoprak performances can include people from all strata of society: workers, business people, university presidents, civil servants, military officers, and even convicts. This social mixture gives performers and their audiences a wider perspective on local, regional, and national issues, a perspective less shaped by the narrower, elite-dominated mass media.[5]

One way such widening of perspective occurs in kethoprak performance is through the theme of deconstruction. Here, what the audience thinks is reality turns out to be virtuality. An example is the popular story of Suminten Edan (or, *The Crazy Suminten*). This story relays the love between Suminten, the daughter of a powerful Javanese regent, and a poor traveler. Suminten Edan goes crazy because she loves the traveler, but her father will not allow her to see him. In fact, the traveler is the son of another regent, who has disguised himself as a poor man so that he can learn about the conditions of his father's kingdom.

During and after the oppressive Suharto military regime, many Suminten kethoprak stories were performed, such as *Not Crazy Suminten* (*Suminten Ora Edan*), *Crazy Suminten, Canceled* (*Suminten Ora Sida Edan*), *Not Crazy, Yet Suminten* (*Suminten Durung Edan*), and *Really Crazy Suminten* (*Suminten Edan Tenan*).[6] This is no doubt an artistic, democratic expression of the fact that when the reality of Indonesia was one of suffering and oppression, Suharto's government promoted the illusion of peace and tranquility. Through the Suminten kethoprak, lower- and middle-class Indonesians could speak indirectly about the reversals they experienced in their world.

Another way kethoprak approaches the falsehoods and pretensions of social authorities and power holders is by head-on exposé. Kethoprak dialogue can be filled with complex mockeries and sarcasm that directly address social oppression. For example, President Susilo Bambang Yudhoyono was elected to a second term of office in 2009 in the wake of bank fraud and tax-grafting scandals. In response, kethoprak groups in Yogyakarta staged satirical performances criticizing the Yudhoyono regime. One such performance was *Gonjang Ganjing Kabar Miring* (*Rattling Bad News*).

Kethoprak gives democratic voice to the social and political frustrations of the Indonesian people. In bringing people together through shared entertainment, kethoprak expands the imagination, invites self-transformation, and creates solidarity across class, religious, and ethnic lines. It is a creative way of breaking down pockets of power and oppression that remain as a legacy of Indonesia's colonial and autocratic past. By giving voice to the less powerful, kethoprak helps develop a democratically oriented imagination and a democratic hope within Indonesian citizens.[7] A proper democracy certainly needs a strong sense of citizenship staged at a kethoprak performance. As discussed in the next section, this form of democratization stands in uneasy relationship to the Indonesian national philosophy of Pancasila. While Paulus Wiryono Priyotamtama has noted in his earlier chapter that Pancasila grew out of musyawarah, it is also the case that this philosophy became complicit in the totalizing and authoritarian rule of Suharto. When used by Suharto, the word "Pancasila" became disconnected from democratic actions and, as such, suffered from compromised credibility in the eyes of many Indonesians. Kethoprak, as a subversive form of social, political, and cultural engagement, remained outside of Suharto's authoritarian grip and, therefore, remains for many a viable alternative space for democracy and democratization in Indonesia today.

Kethoprak Social Criticism and Growth

At the end of Ramadan on September 13, 2011, the Conthong kethoprak group in Yogyakarta performed *Putri Cina* (*The Chinese Lady*). Three years earlier, the performance was staged in the Chinese section of Semarang during the city's celebration of National Awakening Day.[8]

Putri Cina is based on a novel of the same name by Sindhunata, SJ, an Indonesian Catholic priest of Chinese descent. The novel is a series of compelling stories about a female Chinese Indonesian kethoprak artist who is married to a Javanese nobleman. Through these stories, the author takes the audience through the experience of discrimination suffered by Indonesians of Chinese descent. From 1965 to 1998, the Suharto regime deliberately treated the Chinese Indonesians as a national *kambing hitam* ("black sheep," scapegoat) and passed discriminatory legislation against them. To make matters worse, several Chinese Indonesian women were harassed and raped in Jakarta during the anti-Suharto riots of May 14–15, 1998.

Kethoprak *Putri Cina* criticized the horrific treatment of Chinese Indonesians through sharp and ironic comedy, including vulgar and lewd lines mastered by the Conthong kethoprak actors. In this way, the kethoprak performances offered social critique and defused barbaric and vengeful mob action. Marshall Clark, a reviewer of the *Putri Cina* novel, called Father Sindhunata's work a form of "shadow-boxing," a way of "indirectly provoking or confronting the powers-that-be, and undermining their symbolic authority."[9]

There are other forms of artistic expression in Indonesia in subtle competition with kethoprak. These are engineered by ruling elites to forestall democratization and keep lower classes in their "traditional" positions. Some portrayals of Suharto's state ideology of Pancasila promoted the idea of a classless society guided by a respected, faultless *bapak* (father).[10] The bapak ideology portrayed Indonesian people as vulnerable children who needed the government's fatherly supervision. This supervision was communicated through Hollywood-style forms of mass entertainment that lulled Indonesians into consumerist delusions that led them away from the practice of democratic citizenship. When a conventional elite-backed theater production says, "Look, my play resembles real life," a kethoprak production says, "Only my kethoprak will show you what everyday appearances conceal."[11]

From the beginning, kethoprak performers and audiences have recognized the distance between their world and the world of the ruling elites. Remembering the imposed ideologies of European colonists, capitalists, traders, and missionaries, the kethoprak community prefers to explore reality on its own terms. This exploration focuses more on the ways ordinary people construct meaning in their lives and less on arriving at an approved or final interpretation of reality.[12]

Members of the kethoprak community know by experience how to deal with the dangers and sufferings of daily life. This is how their experiences of desire and hope are expressed and supported. With its satirical interpretations of elite dress, music, and discourse, kethoprak helps ordinary people cope with and respond to oppressive practices of the more powerful members of Indonesian society. According to Albert Alejo, kethoprak expresses a "power to will" in the community rather than an elitist "will to power."

> The will to power is often associated with either domination (power over) or resistance (power against). The power to will is more of the moral and spiritual and creative resource to be or to remain or sometimes to become a people with self-confidence and self-affirmation.[13]

The images of the common people found in kethoprak are not imposed from the outside but are located in the minds and imaginations of the community members. These images represent the shared meanings that are constantly being created and recreated in everyday life. Even in *gandrung* scenes (sensual, romantic scenes between male and female actors from different social classes, ethnicities, and religions), the most favorite one awaited by the female audience, spectators listen in on ordinary conversations of intimate life, where over and over again differences are negotiated, contested, and re-evaluated within a dynamic, fluid process. These performances subtly communicate the people's "power to will" a more democratic way of life.

The concept of *adiluhung* (the past Golden Age) in kethoprak indicates that the traditional prestige of the governing elites is declining among the Javanese people. Ironically, this development is attracting more members to kethoprak performances from all social classes. For example, people in Yogyakarta have witnessed in recent years a growing popularity of EXSEL Kethoprak, a kethoprak group of actors from the upper class. As this group has increasingly focused on corruption in Indonesian national politics, it has brought together like-minded people from all social classes.

At one level, the success of EXSEL Kethoprak indicates how Indonesians of all classes increasingly perceive themselves as outsiders relative to those holding social power and authority. For example, three days after the 2009 celebration of *Lebaran* (the celebration ending Ramadan, the holy month of fasting for Muslims) a kethoprak play entitled *Kalagemet* was performed in Yogyakarta. Kalagemet is a nickname for Jayanegara, a fourteenth-century Majapahit Javanese king who faced intrigue related to the selection of his prime minister. The play was a commentary on the scandal surrounding Indonesian President Susilo Bambang Yudhoyono's selection of a new Indonesian cabinet minister. In this, as in many other examples, kethoprak is increasingly becoming a creative outlet for members of all social classes to express democratic opposition against corrupt rulers.

Kethoprak and Catholicism in Indonesia

Sanata Dharma University in Yogyakarta celebrated its fifty-sixth anniversary in 2011 by staging a kethoprak. The performance was entitled *Ontran-Ontran Sekar Kedaton* (*Turbulence of the Palace Daughter*) and was an interpretation of the *Suminten Edan* story. In this version, a noble family is worried about their eldest daughter's interest in finding a suitable partner. This simple story became the medium to explore complex questions about sexuality and marriage in contemporary Indonesia. In this way, the story's traditional message of *esuk dele sore tempe* ("a soybean in the morning can easily become fermented by evening") warned of the necessity for honesty in contemporary matters of sexuality and marriage.

The Sanata Dharma kethoprak was distinct in that it explored sexuality and marriage within the context of a Catholic institution, with actors who were both laypeople and clergy in the Roman Catholic Church. The performance was also distinct in other ways. The performers were all university faculty, staff, and administrators. Indeed, one of the actors was the university's president. The popularity of the performance earned it a new title: *Kethoprak Paling Konyol* (*The Most Absurd Kethoprak*), or KPK for short. This title added another level of irony because KPK stands for *Komisi Pemberantasan Korupsi* (Commission of Corruption Eradication) in Indonesia. This play on acronyms was an exemplary display of the subversive nature of kethoprak.

After the performance, the university sponsored a discussion among the actors. The participants acknowledged that their experience of acting together had a democratic spirit in that it broke down both the usual sense of being in the administrative hierarchy of the university and of being a part of the social hierarchy of traditional Javanese culture. At the same time, the performance opened up discussions on sexuality and marriage not common within a Catholic setting.

In effect, *Kethoprak Paling Konyol* created what Victor Turner calls a "liminal experience." Turner notes that in the liminal state between two phases, individuals are "betwixt and between." During the kethoprak performance, a kind of social ritual, the actors and audience were lifted out of their typical social context and relocated in an imagined society—a "liminal space" between the old realities and new possibilities.[14] As is typical of kethoprak, traditional and modern assumptions about hierarchy, status, and cultural norms were dissected and deconstructed in this "betwixt and between."[15]

This calls for a deeper look into the relationship between kethoprak and Catholicism in Indonesia. One way to do this is to explore the subtle similarities between kethoprak performances and the spiritual practices articulated in Saint Ignatius of Loyola's *Spiritual Exercises*.[16] Both of these actually endorse that kind of a liminal community. Roland Barthes, an expert in both semiotic studies and the *Spiritual Exercises*, has written:

> [Ignatius's] methodically seeking of spiritual self identity in the Exercises is in fact a semiophany. What he is striving to obtain is more the symbol, the sign, of God than knowledge of Him/Her or His/Her presence; language is his definitive horizon and articulation an operation he can never abandon in favor of indistinct—ineffable—states.[17]

In a similar way, kethoprak is more concerned with the process and practice of articulating knowledge than it is with the actual production of knowledge. The importance of kethoprak lies not in its communication of facts but in its creative interpretation of them through imagination and symbolism. In contrast to personal and cultural tendencies to assume that language exists to communicate a truth about the world, language is better understood as a process of instantiating or hinting at the ineffable.

Just as in Saint Ignatius's *Spiritual Exercises*, a performance of kethoprak has no fixed script; it is a triumph of the signifier (a floating and duplicating sign) over the signified (a fixed, meaningful sign). Barthes further notes that sight comes first for Ignatius, then hearing and touch. In following Ignatius's *Spiritual Exercises*, one creates an image (in the sense in which this word is used in graphic art) depicted by the five senses. By comparison, kethoprak artists consider worldly events and experiences as more than just scenes in a play. They see them as scenarios for articulating the audience's ways of thinking and acting.[18]

This kind of kethoprak enactment has been adapted by some Javanese Catholics, especially when they observe the Christmas and Holy Week celebrations. In recent decades, several urban parishes in the Archdiocese of Semarang have organized a kethoprak performance of Jesus's Passion on Holy Friday. During the 2011 Christmas celebrations in the Rembang Parish of the Central Java Province, a kethoprak performance was undertaken by twenty-five Catholic actors, including two parish priests. The organizer of this kethoprak said that the Christmas celebration in Rembang was a genuine and harmonious enactment of interfaith dialogue. The gamelan music played during that Christmas Kethoprak performance was played by non-Catholic musicians. What these lay Catholics, non-Catholics, and priests, in performing kethopraks at certain Christian celebrations in contemporary Indonesia, have done is in a similar in spirit to what Saint Ignatius does in the *Exercises*. More important than an official theological information and communication of the facts of Christ's birth, was a creative kethoprak interpretation of the possible *meaning* of Christ's birth—for *all* people—through imagination, symbolism, and performed religious pluralism. Kethoprak helps people "read" their lives as well as "write" them. In this process, democratic equality and negotiation is performed and actualized between actor and audience.

Conclusion

The performing arts are a way for performers and audiences to freely challenge and shape their identities and beliefs. In a democratic spirit, they allow people to express new ideas, visions, and demands. The Indonesian ruling elite have known this for a long time and, with this knowledge, recklessly have manipulated memory, interpretations, and ceremonial representation in Indonesia to support their interests. Here, a rich comparison can be made with the point made in Nerija Putinaitė's earlier chapter in this volume concerning the political interpretation and use of Lithuania's pre-Christian culture by the secular opponents of both the USSR and Lithuanian Christianity.

Kethoprak has been, and continues to be, a democratizing cultural resource in Indonesia for challenging the cultural hegemony of the ruling elite. In contrast to other forms of Javanese art, kethoprak creates a relationship between actor and audience that both mimics and engages public affairs, political equality, and social conflict to establish a sense of citizenship needed by liminal or imagined communities.[19] An imagined community that is needed, for instance, to actualize a (democratic) nationalism in a country—such as Indonesia—with vulnerable (engineered) social class, religious, and ethnic discriminations.

Based on his notion of semiophany, Barthes argues that the Jesuit founder, Ignatius Loyola, invites people to reinterpret the entire world by way of deconstructing language that leads them into a new state of being where images are created and all words are traced back to a scenario of divine interaction (with God) discovered in liminal contexts. At the same time, kethoprak has reinforced Ignatian spirituality that also acknowledges liminality based on the semiophany search of the (democratic) ultimate virtue[20] and thereby contributed to the enrichment of Indonesia's minority Catholic population. Through both its social and spiritual contributions, one hopes that kethoprak will continue to encourage democratic practices in Indonesia and move the country from a "flawed" to a "healthy" democracy.

NOTES

1. Veeramalla Anjaiah, "Economic Boom, 'Democratic Recession' in ASEAN," *Jakarta Post*, March 28, 2011. It was reported that on a one to ten scale, Indonesia received a score of 6.92 in electoral process and pluralism, 7.50 in functioning of government, 5.56 in political participation, 5.63 in political culture, and 7.06 in civil liberties.

2. See Nicolas Warouw, "Approaching Conflict and Democracy in South and Southeast Asia," *Journal of Power, Conflict and Democracy in South and Southeast Asia* 1, nos. 1 and 2 (2009), 36.

3. See James R. Brandon, *Theatre in Southeast Asia* (Cambridge, MA: Harvard University Press, 1967).

4. Jacqueline Lo and Helen Gilbert, "Postcolonial Theory: Possibilities and Limitations" (paper presented at the International Research Workshop on Post-Colonialism and the Question of Modern Indonesian Literature, University of Sydney, May 29–31, 1998).

5. Barbara Hatley, "Staging Identities, Constructing Communities in Contemporary Indonesian Theatre" (paper presented at the Cultural

Performance in Post-New Order Indonesia: New Structures, Scenes, Meanings International Conference, Yogyakarta, Indonesia, June 28–July 1, 2010). See also, Barbara Hatley, *Kethoprak: Performance and Social Meaning in a Javanese Popular Theater* (PhD diss., University of Sydney, 1985), 44.

6. See Budi Susanto, SJ, *Kethoprak: The Politics of the Past in the Present-day Java* (Yogyakarta, Indonesia: Kanisius-Lembaga Studi Realino, 1997).

7. See Matthew Isaac Cohen, *The Komedie Stamboel: Popular Theater in Colonial Indonesia, 1891–1903*, Ohio University Research in International Studies, Southeast Asia Series, no. 112 (Athens: Ohio University Press, 2006), 341.

8. Celebrated nationally and annually on May 20, the Indonesian National Awakening Day (Kebangkitan Nasional Indonesia) commemorates the first few decades of the twentieth century, during which people from many parts of the archipelago first began to develop a sense of national consciousness as "Indonesians."

9. Marshall Clark, "Shadow Boxing: Indonesian Writers and Ramayana in the New Order," *Indonesia* 72 (October 2001), 187.

10. The Pancasila consists of (1) belief in the one and only God, (2) just and civilized humanity, (3) the unity of Indonesia, (4) democracy guided by the inner wisdom in the unanimity arising out of deliberations among representatives, and (5) social justice for all of the people of Indonesia.

11. Benedict Anderson, *Language and Power: Exploring Political Cultures in Indonesia* (Ithaca, NY: Cornell University Press, 1990), 165–66.

12. Dick Hebdige, *Subculture: The Meaning of Style* (London: Methuen, 1983), 118.

13. Albert E. Alejo, *Generating Energies in Mount Apo* (Quezon City, Philippines: Ateneo de Manila University Press, 2000), 7.

14. Victor Turner, *The Forest of Symbols: Aspects of Ndembu Ritual* (Ithaca, NY: Cornell University Press, 1970), 99.

15. Rudolf Mrazek, *Engineers of Happy Land: Technology and Nationalism in a Colony* (Princeton, NJ: Princeton University Press, 2002), 190.

16. Ignatius of Loyola (1419–1556), the founder of the Society of Jesus, composed a thirty-day retreat handbook (published in 1548) titled *Spiritual Exercises*, designed to help people to experience a deepening experience of God in their daily lives.

17. Roland Barthes, *Sade, Fourier, Loyola* (Baltimore, MD: Johns Hopkins University Press, 1997), 53.

18. Ibid., 61.

19. Benedict Anderson argues that, "it is imagined because the members of even the smallest nation will never know most of their fellow-members, meet them, or even hear of them, yet in the minds of each lives the image of

their communion." Benedict Anderson, *Imagined Communities: Reflections on the Origin and Spread of Nationalism*, rev. ed. (New York: Verso, 2006), 6.

20. Considering that human being is created to praise, reverence, and serve God our Lord, and by this means to save his/her soul, Ignatius of Loyola wrote, in the introduction to his *Spiritual Exercises*, "in everyday life, then, we should keep ourselves indifferent or undecided in the face of all created gifts when we have an option and we do not have the clarity of what would be a better choice. We ought not to be led on by our natural likes and dislikes even in matters such as health or sickness, wealth or poverty, between living in the east or in the west, becoming an accountant or a lawyer. Rather, our only desire and our one choice should be that option which better leads us to the goal for which God created us." David L. Fleming, *Modern Spiritual Exercises: A Contemporary Reading of the Spiritual Exercises of St. Ignatius* (New York: Image Books, 1983), 25–26.

Alter/native Democracies:
Muslim and Catholic Negotiations
of Culture, Religion, and Citizenship
in the Twenty-First Century

Marcia Hermansen

Can the lessons learned from the encounters between democracy, culture, and Catholicism have a ripple effect upon, or serve as models for, the encounters between democracy, culture, and other religious identities? In this note, and in the light of the analysis of democracy, culture, and Catholicism in Indonesia, we hear from two scholars who attempt to answer this question from the Muslim perspective. This is a perspective that, not unlike Catholicism, is often perceived to be incompatible with democracy and democratization. At a time when the contemporary Muslim world is dealing, every day, with struggles between movements to democratize and the faith claims of Islam, this conversation could not be more timely, and the lessons that might be learned from the Catholic experience could not be more important.

Marcia Hermansen looks to the Catholic Church and its encounters with democracy, particularly in the recent history of the Catholic Church, for examples from which the Muslim world can learn about navigating these inevitable encounters. Noting that Catholics have held both minority and majority positions in different democratic countries, Hermansen argues that the history of Catholic engagements with democracy can be a model for the Muslim world as it continues to deliberate over whether or not democracy is the most appropriate political system for it to embrace. Through an analysis of the practice of reserving seats for religious minorities in government bodies, and an analysis of how this practice affects the identities of said minorities, Hermansen suggests that, in the wake of the Catholic experience, Muslim countries can responsibly and faithfully envision the possibility of creating alter/native democracies.

Russell Powell focuses on the experience of democracy in the nation of Turkey, a Muslim nation with a strictly secular constitution. In looking to Turkey and the recent legal and political shifts that have taken place there, particularly regarding the type of secularism they practice and the rise of religiously inspired political parties, Powell suggests that the possibility of a shift in Turkey from an assertive secularism (e.g., the French model) to a more passive form of secularism (e.g., the United States model) might actually have a positive effect on Turkish politics and the Turkish people. The dangers, however, that religiously motived political parties present to democracy cannot be underestimated. In the end, religion can have a transformative, prophetic voice in secular society if it continues, as it has in some strands of Catholic and Muslim thought, to emphasize authenticity and justice within the structures of democratic governments.

In June 2009, Pope Benedict XVI issued an encyclical letter entitled *Caritas in veritate*. This letter was directed to Christians and all those interested in seriously engaging questions regarding democracy, justice, and development in the modern world. The pontiff concluded by stating that in our times democracy offers the best political system for providing justice and freedom.[1]

In many modern democratic nations where Catholics live together with Muslims in majority/minority relationships, challenges to justice and equality persist and are addressed constitutionally in a variety of ways. However, both older and newer issues that challenge the ability of democratic processes to ensure full equality of citizenship continue to be debated in the public sphere.

The purpose of this chapter is to interrogate the relationship between democracy, culture, and Catholicism by considering certain practices and perceptions in modern democracies that place Catholics and Muslims in dialogue and, at times, contestation with one another. Two specific areas are researched here and the results of each inquiry are subsequently integrated into a broader reflection.

The first inquiry considers the practice of reserving electoral seats for religious minorities in a number of contemporary democratic states with Muslim majority populations. The more theoretical second piece of the project reviews, and puts into context, discussions of cultural or multicultural citizenship that have emerged with the rise of Muslim immigration into the traditionally Christian nations of Western Europe and North America.

Some historical remarks are, therefore, necessary before discussing these two topics, particularly as we attempt to understand the comparative responses of the Catholic and Islamic communities to the so-called third wave of democratization since 1974 and the Arab Spring since 2010.[2]

The nineteenth century marked the emergence of state nationalism that continues to be a major factor in geopolitical organization up to the present. During this time, nationalism constituted and sustained imagined communities of citizens in a variety of ways.[3] Particular religious allegiances and identifications have sometimes acted as solidifying elements in constituting national identities. In other instances, religious identification has torn the

fabric of national identities that were originally premised on other compo-
nents of popular consciousness.

In the case of emergent Muslim nation-states, the religion of Islam has
played a variety of roles in the twentieth century. Majority Muslim nation-
states in the Arab world largely emerged in the wake of the dismember-
ment of the Ottoman Empire at the close of the First World War. During
the same period, new Muslim nations in Asia and Africa gained independence in the wave of postwar decolonization. Scholars of Islam speak of
various articulations of nationalism during this period. For example, there
are the well-known cases of Turkey under Kemal Atatürk (d. 1938) and
Iran under Reza Khan Pahlavi (d. 1944) where each leader implemented
modernization by promoting linguistic and historical factors of national
solidarity over religious ones.

In other Muslim states, Islam provided the primary basis for national
identity, such as the 1947 creation of Pakistan to be a homeland for the
Muslims of the Indian subcontinent. In these and other cases, the emphasis on shared Muslim identity has struggled to overcome local ethnic and
linguistic divisions and, at the same time, has put significant pressure on
non-Muslims in being seen and treated as full citizens in these nation-
states.

In most of these new Muslim nation-states, democratization was never
total. Dictatorial powers, military rule, or absolute monarchies remained
the norm. Pakistan, for example, struggled for decades to find a constitutional framework that could be both Islamic and democratic.[4] More recently,
the Arab Spring saw uprisings across North Africa and the Middle East
aimed at ending decades of autocratic rule.

The balance between allegiance to an Islamic system and the principles
of citizen equality in a democratic state has been negotiated in various ways
as nations have been created, built, and rebuilt. Against this background,
one can better understand the diverse responses of Muslim nations to
democratizing trends, like the 1948 United Nations Declaration of Human
Rights.[5]

Reserved Seats and Minority Rights in Democratic Nation-States

An interesting practice in which to observe the evolving relationship
between Islam, Muslim nation building, and democracy is the allocation of
reserved seats or quotas to members of religious minorities in some Muslim nation-states. Three specific examples will be discussed here: Jordan,
Lebanon, and Pakistan.

This practice raises two questions for students of religion and democratization. First, are electoral quotas for religious minorities a form of unequal citizenship and an obstacle to full democratization, or are they steps toward achieving it? Second, do such quotas in majority Muslim states reflect a specifically "Islamic" theological ethos or legal practice? Criticism of reserved seats or quotas arises from a range of positions. Liberal critics argue that granting rights to identity groups fails to acknowledge the dynamism and fluidity of the groups, as well as the internal injustices suffered by some members. Since the oppression is ultimately suffered by individuals, liberal institutions can respond more effectively by legal means than by the practice of electoral quotas.[6] Conservatives claim that group-differentiated rights undermine common citizenship and deteriorate the public good toward which society should be oriented.[7] Libertarians allege that collective rights benefit the already privileged, increase in-group inequality, and aggravate social divisions.[8]

The three cases of minority Christian religious representation in predominantly Muslim state legislatures considered here are quite distinct. The distinctions show in each legislature's actual and symbolic response to minority religious identity. Jordan, Lebanon, and Pakistan differ in how they interpret the meaning of minority religious identity. Only in Lebanon are Christians a strong minority in the population. In Jordan, Christians constitute a smaller minority, yet they are recognized as a community established before the Islamic conquest. In South Asia, the minority Christian presence is pre-Islamic yet also associated with conversions that took place during the colonial period in British India.

LEBANON

The Lebanese parliament is unicameral with 128 elected deputies from eleven confessional identities that are distributed across these seats. There are sixty-four seats for Muslims of various sects and sixty-four for Christians, including thirty-four for Maronites, fourteen for Greek Orthodox, eight for Greek Catholic, and one each for Armenian Catholic, Evangelical, and "Minority" groups of Christians.[9] Though the seats are allocated by confession, voters from any background elect the candidates. This arrangement reflects one rationale for reserved seating, which argues that "in such 'cosociational' or 'consensus' polities, each group is guaranteed a share of power to preclude secession and civil war."[10]

While anthropologist Clifford Geertz wrote admiringly of the Lebanese way of negotiating electoral pluralism in his 1970s classic, *Interpretation of*

Cultures.[11] By the middle of that decade Lebanon was racked by prolonged civil wars fought largely along communal lines. While a range of external factors, such as the influx of Palestinian refugees and Israeli and Syrian interference, have contributed to persistent instability in Lebanese government, shifts in population, in particular the rising numbers of Shi'a Muslims in Lebanon, have proved a daunting challenge to the persistence of the electoral quota system.

JORDAN

The case of Jordan bears one similarity to Lebanon in that all seats of the national legislature are reserved. Otherwise, the Jordanian Catholic population is much smaller than the Lebanese Catholic population. A 2009 article counted Catholics in Jordan at about 109,000, this number including members of the Melkite, Roman, Armenian, and Syrian Catholic rites.[12]

When Jordan achieved independence from the British mandate in 1946, Catholic Church authorities considered the Jordanian constitution the most liberal among Arab countries regarding the status of Christians.[13] Given this context, Geraldine Chatelard observes that the Catholic Church vacillates between autonomy and dependency in relation to the Jordanian government.

On the one hand, the worldwide Church seeks global spiritual authority over its faithful and total independence from civil authorities in that regard.[14] On the other hand, the Vatican is a state and thereby plays a leading international role with regard to the question of Jerusalem.[15] Jordanian authorities must then take into account two factors in their treatment of local Catholic churches. First, the Jordanian government must recognize that it has no oversight with respect to the internal organization of the Catholic Church. Second, the Jordanian government has not been able to bring Catholic communal social activities under as great a degree of compliance with legislation as they would like.[16]

PAKISTAN

Pakistan has a colonial legacy of seats being assigned (in British India) based on religious communal identity.[17] Today, 10 of the 342 seats of the Pakistani national assembly are reserved for non-Muslim minorities and another 60 for women. The reserved seats for non-Muslim minorities are elected in one national district based on the total number of seats won by each party in the national assembly, using a list proportional representation system, in which the percentage of votes received determines the seats allocated to parties. Currently, four seats each go to Christians and Hindus, one to Sikhs/Buddhists and Parsis, and one to Qadianis (Ahmadis).

In 1985, the Separate Electorate System Act was established wherein Christians had their votes restricted to only electing seats in federal and provincial assemblies reserved for their religious minority. Christians saw this as a disenfranchisement, as being cut off from fully participating in elections and from being able to support major political parties.

The Catholic Bishops' Conference of Pakistan (CBCP) actively lobbied to get the 1985 restriction modified so that Christians could fully participate in Pakistani politics. In 2002, the representatives of nearly twenty-three leading political parties joined their voices with the CBCP to abolish the separate electorate system. These restrictions were subsequently lifted in 2002 when General Pervez Musharraf took over control of the country. In an address to the ambassador of Pakistan on May 15, 2003, Pope John Paul II applauded the abolition of the separate electorate system.[18]

Other forms of restrictive legislation from 1985, however, were not eliminated. Christians have been victimized by a blasphemy law, for example, that includes the death penalty for offenders. Later governments tried to amend the law but dropped their efforts because of opposition from Islamist groups. To a certain extent, support for this law arose in response to Salman Rushdie's writings, which were deemed insulting to the Prophet Muhammad and symbolic of the conflict of values between the West and the Muslim world.

The blasphemy law continues to be a point of contention. In 2009, Pope Benedict XVI urged Pakistani President Asif Ali Zardari to guarantee protection of minority Christians who had been targets of blasphemy-related violence. In 2011, the governor of Punjab Province in Pakistan, Salman Taseer, was assassinated. He had spoken out against the law and visited a Christian woman held in jail on blasphemy charges. In March 2011, the only Pakistani Christian cabinet minister, Shahbaz Bhatti (a Catholic), was killed for expressing his opposition to the blasphemy laws.[19] These assassinations have fueled religious tension and have cast doubt over the wisdom of the government's abolishing the separate electorate system.

Reflections on Reserved Seats, Democracy, and Christian-Muslim Relations

Arguments can be made that having separate electoral seats in some Muslim countries is a fair way of incorporating minorities into the democratic process, even though such practices seem to conflict with secular liberal notions of equal citizenship. In many Muslim states, expectations have been shaped by the majority religious tradition, meaning that just political representation is not based on the idea of equality but on shari'a constructions of Muslim/non-Muslim relations that mandate asymmetrical reciprocity. This entails a conceptualization of rights and duties anchored in a specifically Islamic ethic. We know, too, from the debates surrounding the 1948 ratification of the Universal Declaration of Human Rights that certain Muslim states, democratic and otherwise, have been reluctant to embrace the universality or equal allocation of certain legal rights.[20]

The remaining questions, in this regard, include whether reserving seats for non-Muslim minorities represents a stage along the way to full democratic participation and equal citizenship in Muslim states. Will some degree of unequal citizenship become embedded in Muslim countries even as they democratize?

With these questions in mind, the history of the contentious encounter between the Roman Catholic Church and democracy in the nineteenth and twentieth centuries may offer some interesting points of comparison with the experience of Muslim nation-states. Sociologist José Casanova notes that:

> As in the case of Catholicism before, the internal and external debates over the compatibility between Islam and democracy and modern individual freedoms is taking place at three separate yet interrelated levels: (a) debates over the proper articulation of a Muslim *ummah* in diasporic contexts outside of Dar al-Islam; (b) in debates over the democratic legitimacy of Muslim political parties in Turkey and elsewhere, which like their at first equally suspect Catholic counterparts may establish new forms of Muslim Democracy, akin to Christian Democracy; and (c) in debates over the alleged clash of civilizations between Islam and the West at the geopolitical level, with clear parallels with earlier debates on the clash between "republicanism" and "Romanism."[21]

Casanova's analysis anticipates that democratic processes will succeed in the Muslim world, as they have elsewhere, including predominantly Catholic countries. Just as Church opinion was updated in new socio-historical contexts, so will Muslim practices ultimately adapt to new social and political realities and human aspirations.

Another scholar of Muslim democratization, Vali Nasr, concurs that Catholic precedents augur well for the possibility of religious values to inspire forms of "Islamic democracy." Similar forces are now at work in some Muslim-majority countries, with ripple effects that will likely be felt throughout the Muslim world. Like the Catholic Church in the last century, Islamic-oriented parties are grasping the need to relate religious values to secular politics. As was also the case in Europe, secular parties and politicians are sensing the benefits of including appeals to religious values in their platforms. Thus Muslim democracy, like Christian democracy before it, is emerging as a political tendency that is strongly tied to both the democratic process and the use of direct appeals to the concerns of religious voters.[22] Indeed, Arūnas Streikus showed in his earlier chapter in this volume how Christian democracy functioned in this exact capacity in Lithuanian history.

These analyses suggest that reserved seats for non-Muslim minorities may indeed represent a stage along the way to full democratic participation and equal citizenship in Muslim states. So too, even with a degree of unequal citizenship embedded in Muslim countries, a unique and valuable Muslim-style democracy may be emergent.

Democratic Citizenship and Religious Identity

In the second section of this chapter I address developments and challenges posed by religious identities to evolving notions of democratic citizenship in a globalizing world.[23] For example, post 9/11, a number of scholars in Western societies have suggested that despite receiving the right to vote and other benefits when achieving naturalization, Muslim immigrants are held to notions of cultural citizenship that exclude them from being full participants in society in other important ways.[24] The process of immigration and the possibility of becoming a naturalized citizen of a particular nation-state are more open in North America, less so in Europe, and almost impossible in many Muslim majority nation-states that have constitutional systems that structure electorates along religious lines. How does this disparity in accepting others as citizens affect perceptions of democracy?

How are we to bring religious factors, whether Catholic or Muslim, into conversation with theoretical debates about these issues of incorporation and religious identity in democracies? The archipelago of Indonesia presents an interesting case with respect to these several patterns of relationships between religious minorities in Muslim majority democracies and Muslim minorities in Western democracies.

As noted in Baskara Wardaya's chapter in this volume, the Indonesian government has been officially democratic and secular since its independence in 1949. Though Indonesian society prides itself on a tradition of religious tolerance and diversity, increased tensions have erupted between Muslims and Christians in recent years. For example, the East Timor independence movement was widely perceived in religious terms by Muslims in Indonesia, and elsewhere, since East Timorians are overwhelmingly Christian. Tensions around inter-religious conflicts in the Maluku Islands increased from 1999 to 2002, and in continuing incidents elsewhere in Indonesia, churches have been burned and Christians persecuted. The rise of Islamist movements in Indonesia, with certain groups agitating for an Islamic state, has also put pressure on religious minorities. John T. Sidel has observed that violent incidents up until 2005 had taken an increasingly strident tone against religious minorities, though these attacks were largely perpetrated by small extremist sects, rather than by broad-based communal sentiment.[25]

However, in the case of Indonesia, the issue is less that of a Muslim majority state struggling to enact a legitimate democracy than it is the nature of a secular democratic state being called into question by the rising religious sentiments of local Muslims. Such cases embody the tension between the Western "secular" model of democracy, enacted after Indonesian independence in the 1940s, and the growth of Islam-specific ideas of citizenship among Muslims since the 1970s. In these cases, the question of religious minorities emerges quickly.

In Indonesia, religious freedom is a matter of special concern to Catholics. About 7 percent of Indonesia's population is Christian and about one-third of that population is Catholic. As a thicker Muslim interpretation of democracy grows, will people remain free to convert from Islam to Christianity without social or political reprisal?

At the same time, a related, but reverse debate has been going on in Europe where the immigrant Muslim population has been considered by some as inassimilable, ostensibly due to religious commitments and cultural practices that are thought alien to a perceived European consensus on values and habits. Many such instances have emerged, ranging from former Pope Benedict XVI's 2006 Regensburg address, to the Swiss vote banning the construction of new minarets, to French laws seeking to penalize the wearing of certain forms of female Muslim attire such as headscarves and burqas.[26]

In most European countries, Muslims now constitute the largest religious minority. After World War II, Muslims were welcomed to Europe to fill the labor shortage. In the 1970s, many countries tightened their laws, limiting immigration to those seeking family reunification. There remains, however, a perception that increasing numbers of large Muslim families put pressure on schools, hospitals, and prisons to accommodate religious differences.

Given each nation's unique history of state-church relations, patterns of accommodation that Muslims encountered across Europe varied widely. In Britain, for example, a major concern was whether the state would finance separate religious schools as it had for other faith groups.[27] In Germany, the question was whether Muslim religious institutions should be granted public corporation status.[28] As noted above, the prominent issue in France was Muslim dress codes, especially female forms of conservative dress.[29]

Exacerbating the fear of Muslims as outsiders and their treatment as unequal citizens in Europe are the special provisions given to guest workers, the rise in right-wing xenophobia, and the "war on terror" mentality subsequent to the 9/11 attacks in the United States and the 7/7 bombings in London. In both Europe and the United States, high profile debates have been held to ask whether Muslims can be fully loyal to the state and "assimilate" to Western values.

Numerous scholars have pointed out similar anxieties regarding earlier waves of Catholic immigrants to the United States and the integration of Catholics in largely Protestant European states during the nineteenth century.[30] Catholics have at times been perceived as allied with Muslims in Europe in advocating for the human rights of immigrants both on purely social justice grounds and with a sense of expediency in terms of the reciprocal treatment that Christians in Muslim majority countries might in turn receive.[31]

As we have seen, the debate about the compatibility of Catholicism and democracy touches on the debates about Islam and democracy in a number of ways. Catholics, like Muslims, were considered religious outsiders in the Protestant-dominated United States. As will be noted in Bren Ortega Murphy's later chapter in this volume, on Catholic immigrants to the United States, the group was generally perceived as people of lower socio-economic background poor education who were liable to religious allegiances that would preclude full loyalty to the new nation. However, do the racialization of Muslim identity and the fact that many Muslims are more visibly different from Catholics mean that their equal incorporation in Europe and America will be more difficult than their Catholic counterparts?

In comparing the possible trajectory of the Muslim relationship with democracy to the Catholic experience, José Casanova notes the following crucial difference between their respective *"aggiornamentos"*:[32] The eventual acceptance of democracy by Catholics had the character of an official, relatively uniform, and swift reform from above that found little contestation from below. It was encouraged across the Catholic world, generating a remarkable homogenization of Catholic culture. Islam, by contrast, lacks centralized institutions and administrative structures to define and enforce official doctrines. As such, ongoing Muslim openings to democracy are likely to be plural, with diverse and often contradictory outcomes.[33]

On the other hand, is it possible that a global form of Muslim solidarity around democracy could develop, parallel to that of the Catholic Church's international support for political democracy? Casanova imagines three possible models. The first would be some sort of international system of Muslim states in a geopolitical alliance. To some extent this has been the mission of the Organization of Islamic Cooperation (OIC), established in 1972.[34]

The second model would be a reconstitution of the traditional central authority of the caliph, a Muslim leader who combined religious and Ottoman claimant to the title and was deposed in the 1920s. However, Muslim groups advocating this model today tend to be fringe, extremist, and disinterested in democracy or operating within the nation-state system.

Casanova's third possibility seems most realistic now: a series of transnational networks and movements of Muslim renewal, separate from either state-sponsored Islam or transnational jihadism. Such groups include grassroots pietistic movements such as Tablighi Jamaat,[35] Sufi and neo-Sufi mobilizations, and transnational Muslim feminist networks.[36]

Comparing Catholic and Muslim experiences with democracy does not answer the vexing problems of incorporating religious minorities in democratic states or honoring their rights to citizenship. It does warn us, however, against adopting a too sanguine view of the protection of religious minority rights and general citizenship rights for religious minorities in either "secular" Western democracies or Muslim majority nation-states. Respecting such rights will remain a challenge as these democracies develop over time.

Conclusions

This discussion of current tensions in religious minority identity and democratic citizenship, as disclosed in debates over electoral processes and religious accommodation, has attempted to shed light on the multiple ways in which religion has interacted with democratic movements in diverse cultural contexts. In particular, we have selected and examined specific situations in which both Catholics and Muslims have a direct stake. They both share experiences as minorities and have come into conflict with each other as majorities.

Just as theorists of modernity and secularism, such as Dilip Gaonkar and Charles Taylor, conclude that "alter/native modernities" will emerge as part of a globalized future,[37] the varied national approaches to addressing ethnic and religious diversity in instituting democratic and electoral processes suggest that in diverse cultural and religious contexts, some version of alternative democracies will emerge. Certainly, in the Muslim world, attempts to theorize and even implement Islamic democracy have competed with attempts to formulate systems of Islamic socialism, Islamic theocratic statehood, and so on.[38] The future trajectories of developing democracies in Muslim majority contexts will clearly remain an important topic for the foreseeable future.

NOTES

1. Benedict XVI, *Caritas in veritate*, Encyclical letter, Vatican website, June 29, 2009, http://www.vatican.va/holy_father/benedict_xvi/encyclicals/documents/hf_ben-xvi_enc_20090629_caritas-in-veritate_en.html.

2. The formulation of three waves of democratization was made by Samuel Huntington in his influential book *The Third Wave*. According to Huntington, the first wave of states moving from autocratic to democratic rule lasted from 1826 to 1926. The second wave followed World War II and was followed in the 1960s and early 1970s by a swing away from democracy. The third wave began in 1974. Samuel Huntington, *The Third Wave: Democratization in the Late Twentieth Century* (Norman: University of Oklahoma Press, 1991).

3. See Benedict Anderson, *Imagined Communities: Reflections on the Origin and Spread of Nationalism* (London: Verso, 1991).

4. See Leonard Binder, *Religion and Politics in Pakistan* (Berkeley: University of California Press, 1963).

5. See Ann Mayer, *Islam and Human Rights: Tradition and Politics* (Boulder, CO: Westview Press, 1998).

6. Adam James Trebble, "What Is the Politics of Difference?," *Political Theory* 30, no. 2 (2002): 259–81, and David Miller, "Group Rights, Human Rights, and Citizenship," *European Journal of Philosophy* 10, no. 2 (2002): 178–95, cited in Mala Htun, "Is Gender like Ethnicity? The Political Representation of Identity Groups," *Perspectives on Politics* 2, no. 4 (September 2004): 440.

7. See Jean Elshtain, *Democracy on Trial* (New York: Basic Books, 1995).

8. Thomas Sowell, *Preferential Policies: An International Perspective* (New York: William Morrow, 1990), qtd. in Htun, "Is Gender like Ethnicity?," 440.

9. International Foundation for Electoral Systems, "The Lebanese Electoral System" (IFES Lebanon Briefing Paper, March 2009).

10. Htun, "Is Gender like Ethnicity?," 440.

11. Clifford Geertz, "The Integrative Revolution: Primordial Sentiments and Civic Politics in New States," in *The Interpretation of Cultures* (New York: Basic Books, 1973), 255–310.

12. Catholic News Agency, "Church Office Publishes Latest Data on Holy Land," May 5, 2009, http://www.catholicnewsagency.com/news/church_office_of_statistics_publishes_latest_data_on_the_holy_land/.

13. Geraldine Chatelard, "The Constitution of Christian Boundaries and Spheres in Jordan," *Journal of Church and State* 51, no. 2 (2010): 476–502, 481.

14. Chatelard, "The Constitution," 492, citing Emile Poulat, *L'Eglise, c'est un monde* (Paris: Le Cerf, 1986), 260.

15. See J. Bryan Hehir, "The Catholic Church and the Middle East, Policy and Diplomacy," in *The Vatican, Islam, and the Middle East*, ed. Kail C. Ellis (Syracuse, NY: Syracuse University Press, 1987), 109–24; Fred J. Khouri, "The Jerusalem Question and the Vatican," in Ellis, *The Vatican, Islam, and the Middle East*, 143–62; and Andrej Kreutz, *Vatican Policy on the Palestinian–Israeli Conflict* (New York: Greenwood, 1990).

16. Chatelard, "The Constitution," 492.

17. In pre-independence India, legislative reservations for communal groups were introduced by the British. Muslims received allocations of seats in 1909, and Christians and Sikhs in 1919. Untouchables (Dalits) and women also received reservations. The 1950 Indian constitution rejected communal quotas except in the case of scheduled castes and tribes. Later, in the early 1990s, women did begin to receive a quota of one-third of the seats on local and rural councils. Htun, "Is Gender like Ethnicity?," 448–49.

18. John Paul II, "Address of the Holy Father John Paul II to the New Ambassador of the Islamic Republic of Pakistan to the Holy See," Vatican website, May 15, 2003, http://www.vatican.va/holy_father/john_paul_ii/speeches/2003/may/documents/hf_jp-ii_spe_20030515_ambassador-pakistan_en.html.

19. "Pakistan Minorities Minister Shahbaz Bhatti Shot Dead," March 2, 2011, http://www.bbc.co.uk/news/world-south-asia–12617562, and Sara Angle, "Vatican Condemns Murder of Pakistani Minister for Minorities," March 2, 2011, http://www.catholicnews.com/data/stories/cns/1100847.htm.

20. Ann Mayer, *Islam and Human Rights: Tradition and Politics* (Boulder, CO: Westview Press, 1998).

21. José Casanova, "Catholic and Muslim Politics in Comparative Perspective," *Taiwan Journal of Democracy* 1, no. 2 (2005): 96–97.

22. Vali Nasr, "The Rise of 'Muslim Democracy,'" *Journal of Democracy* 16, no. 2 (2005): 13–27.

23. Michael W. McConnell, "Believers as Equal Citizens," in *Obligations of Citizenship and Demands of Faith: Religious Accommodations in Pluralist Democracies*, ed. Nancy L. Rosenblum, 90–110 (Princeton, NJ: Princeton University Press, 2000). Whether secular or religiously plural, some individuals living in modern democratic states will face tensions between the demands of allegiance to the state and to religion.

24. See Katherine Ewing, *Being and Belonging: Muslims in the United States since 9/11* (New York: Russell Sage Foundation, 2008), and Sunaina Maira, *Missing: Youth Citizenship and Empire After 9/11* (Durham, NC: Duke University Press, 2009).

25. John T. Sidel, *Riots, Pogroms, Jihad: Religious Violence in Indonesia* (Ithaca, NY: Cornell University Press, 2006), 222.

26. Ralph M. Coury, "A Syllabus of Errors: Benedict XVI on Islam," *Race and Class* 50, no. 3 (2009): 30–61.

27. As of 2005 Britain funded seven thousand Church of England and Catholic schools but only five Muslim schools for a population of 1.6 million Muslims. Nancy Foner, afterword to *Citizenship, Political Engagement and Belonging*, ed. Deborah Reed-Danahay and Caroline Brettell (New Brunswick, NJ: Rutgers University Press, 2008), 250.

28. Christian denominations and Judaism have this status that entitles federally collected taxes to be used for religious institutions and the right to run state-subsidized social services and hospitals.

29. Joel S. Fetzer and J. Christopher Soper, *Muslims and the State in Britain, France, and Germany* (Cambridge: Cambridge University Press, 2004), 2–3.

30. Robert Kahn, "Are Muslims the New Catholics? Europe's Headscarf Laws in Comparative Historical Perspective," at http://works.bepress.com/cgi/viewcontent.cgi?article=1001&context=robert_kahn, and Casanova, "Catholic and Muslim Politics," 95–96.

31. Mitchell Landsberg, "In Italy, Protecting Immigrants Crosses the Faith Line," *Los Angeles Times*, July 19, 2010, http://articles.latimes.com/2010/jul/19/world/la-fg-catholic-muslim-20100719.

32. *Aggiornamento* ("bringing up to date") was one of the key words used during the Second Vatican Council. It was used to mean a spirit of change and open-mindedness.

33. Casanova, "Catholic and Muslim Politics," 101.

34. In 2011 the name was changed from "Organization of the Islamic Congress" to "Organization of Islamic Cooperation."

35. Tablighi Jamaat is a global Islamic pietistic movement with millions of followers that originated in India in the 1920s. See Khalid Masud, *Travellers*

in Faith: Studies of the Tablīghī Jamā'at as a Transnational Islamic Movement for Faith Renewal (Leiden, Netherlands: E. J. Brill, 2000).

36. Casanova, "Catholic and Muslim Politics," 95.

37. Dilip Gaonkar. *Alternative Modernities* (Durham, NC: Duke University Press, 2001).

38. Nasr, "The Rise of 'Muslim Democracy,'" 13–27.

Comparative Insights Regarding Religion and Democracy in a Muslim Context

Russell Powell

> We think that secularism has to do with the relation of the state
> and religion, whereas in fact it has to do with the response
> of the democratic state to diversity.
>
> —CHARLES TAYLOR

Considering the role of democracy in the United States, Peru, Lithuania, and Indonesia presents opportunities for comparing the influence of culture and dominant religion on the development of political and legal systems. In particular, it invites inquiry into similarities and distinctions between predominantly Muslim societies and predominantly Christian or Catholic societies in their approaches to democracy. Examining the role of Islam in Turkish law and politics as a comparative example, this chapter explores approaches to reconciling religious identity with legal secularism (the mechanism states use to insulate themselves from religious influence) in liberal democracies.

Some liberal political philosophers presume that religious ideology is incapable of tolerating dissent or pluralism. By way of contrast, in this chapter I examine Turkish constitutional secularism as well as the "Islamist" Justice and Development Party (Adalet ve Kalk nma Partisi or AKP) and its electoral victories in 2002 and 2007 in order to explain the AKP's ability to shift away from dogmatic ideology to conservative, yet democratic, positions. I compare this with similar developments in predominantly Catholic and Protestant countries. Contemporary, US-based scholarship in the social sciences on Turkish secularism may be viewed as identifying trends toward versions of secularism more open to religious sentiment and expression.

This chapter examines frameworks for considering democratic secularism in Muslim contexts, the legal and constitutional status of secularism in Turkey, the political shifts affecting views of Turkish secularism over the past twenty years, the role of religious identity in Turkish politics, modes of secularism, and the construction of Turkish national identity, with comparisons to Catholic examples. A thoroughgoing comparison between the Turkish situation and the influence of the dominant religion on politics in the United States, Peru, Lithuania, and Indonesia would require a second study. However, I will make some comparative remarks in this regard, especially in view of the relationship between religion and politics in Indonesia.

For the purposes of this chapter, democracy is presumed to be constituted by representative government, multiparty elections, government protection of individual rights (those of minorities in particular), constitutionalism, and secularism. Although each of these elements has implications for religious communities and identities, secularism, at least in principle, addresses the need for governmental neutrality in the treatment of religious groups and persons.

The development of Turkish secularism is in many ways analogous to the development of secularism in predominantly Catholic countries, such as eighteenth-century France. In both cases, religion had been, arguably, the principal basis for political unity and authority. When these systems of empire were replaced by revolutions, political leaders attempted to replace religious and imperial discourses with nationalist ones. In both France and Turkey, revolutionary governments played active roles in dismantling the political power of religious institutions in order to prevent the return of religiously principled systems of imperial governance.[1]

Although this form of separation between religion and the state appeared to be an innovation, it had roots in both Christian and Islamic traditions. The dynamic tension between the papacy and the Holy Roman Empire led to distinctions between religious and state jurisdiction.[2] Similarly, the jurisprudential theory of *siyasa-shari'a* within the Islamic context created a basis for the legitimate exercise of state power outside those areas clearly regulated by religious rules.[3]

Theories of secularization popularized during the development of industrialization in the eighteenth and nineteenth centuries created bases for the reassessment of these traditional approaches to the relationship between religion and the state.[4] Rights discourses, republicanism, technology, civil society, education, and legal reform all created challenges to the balance between religious and state power. This was as true of the Ottoman Empire in the period of Tanzimat as it was for England, Switzerland, and the German principalities during the Enlightenment. Ultimately, the American, French, and Turkish Revolutions institutionalized formal principles of secularism into their constitutions.

In furtherance of explicit modernization projects, some countries, such as Turkey, have created structural barriers between religion and government so that discourses rooted in faith are generally removed from legislative and legal discourse, even though they undoubtedly influence lawmakers, judges, and voters. Some scholars identify such strict separation between faith and public discourse as problematic, particularly within the broader context of democratic commitments.

Abdullahi Ahmed An-Na'im argues that democracy and state secularism (as opposed to societal secularism) are liberating and authentically Islamic approaches to government.[5] He describes an essentialized and totalizing understanding of Islam as a colonial creation developed to create uniformity and assure control. Such an understanding is not consistent with the diverse and contextualized understandings of Islam that arose historically within Muslim cultures.[6] An-Na'im argues instead that Muslims would be better served by systems of state secularism that do not seek either to control religion or to remove it from public life.[7]

He proposes that this position is the one most likely to contribute to broader protections of human rights. Although An-Na'im does not identify Turkey as a model for Muslim state secularism, the transformation of religiously identified political movements in Turkey, along with recent constitutional amendments, may represent a more authentically Islamic approach to government according to his view.

Secularism in the Turkish Constitution

From the outset, any discussion of Turkey's Constitution faces problems that can be traced back to the context within which the current 1982 Constitution of the Republic of Turkey as Amended was drafted and ratified.[8] While the Kemalist elite suppressed many expressions of Islam in the early years of the republic in the 1920s, religious sentiments re-emerged in the public sphere with the advent of multiparty politics in the 1950s.[9] Religion, artfully linked to neoliberal economics, was used to counter leftist strategies after the 1980 coup.[10] Because it was arguably not adopted as the result of primarily democratic processes, the Constitution has always lacked some degree of legitimacy—at least in the eyes of those who were subject to military and governmental oppression during and after the coup. This includes many marginalized political groups, particularly leftists and religiously inspired groups.[11]

Since the Turkish Republic was founded in 1923, understandings of secularism in Turkey have varied. The Constitution was amended in 2001 in order to bolster the strict approach to secularism taken by Turkish courts and the military as a follow-up to the "Soft" or "Postmodern" Coup of 1997, which resulted in the end of the Refah Party-led coalition government.[12] The AKP-proposed constitutional amendments, which were approved in 2010, are likely to transform understandings of strict secularism in the courts over time, but these shifts remain politically contentious.[13] Although secularism in Turkey is also a product of its legislators, judges, and bureaucrats, it is most basically and importantly rooted in the language of the Turkish Constitution.

Secularism has been a core principle of Kemalist ideology from the founding of the Turkish Republic in 1923[14] and appears as a central theme throughout the Turkish Constitution. Significantly, the preamble establishes a theoretical wall of separation to prevent religion from influencing the state, but it does not necessarily restrict state involvement in religion:

> The recognition that no protection shall be accorded to an activity contrary to Turkish national interests, the principle of the indivisibility of the existence of Turkey with its state and territory, Turkish historical and moral values or the nationalism, principles, reforms and modernism of Atatürk and that, as required by the principle of secularism, there shall be no interference whatsoever by sacred religious feelings in state affairs and politics.[15]

The language used throughout the Constitution highlights the importance of secularism to its drafters. Article 2 further establishes that "the Republic of Turkey is a democratic, secular and social state governed by the rule of law."[16] Articles 13 and 14 describe the boundaries between state protection of and limitations on individual rights:

> These restrictions shall not be in conflict with the letter and spirit of the Constitution and the requirements of the democratic order of the society and the secular Republic and the principle of proportionality.[17]

> None of the rights and freedoms embodied in the Constitution shall be exercised with the aim of violating the indivisible integrity of the state with its territory and nation, and endangering the existence of

the democratic and secular order of the Turkish Republic based upon human rights.[18]

The Constitution also protects secularism in two oaths of office[19] and in a provision for legitimizing certain reform laws.[20] Chapter 4, which addresses the role of political parties, provides a basis for prohibiting activities opposing secularism:

> The statutes and programs, as well as the activities of political parties shall not be in conflict with the independence of the state, its indivisible integrity with its territory and nation, human rights, the principles of equality and rule of law, sovereignty of the nation, the principles of the democratic and secular republic.[21]

In order to guarantee conformity with the constitutional vision of the secular republic, Article 136 provides for direct governmental oversight of religion. "The Department of Religious Affairs, which is within the general administration, shall exercise its duties prescribed in its particular law, in accordance with the principles of secularism, removed from all political views and ideas, and aiming at national solidarity and integrity."[22] This approach to secularism is found in other constitutional democracies. France, for example, has the Ministry of Worship that is analogous to the Turkish Department of Religious Affairs. This approach reflects a completely different understanding of the relationship between religion and the state, and many American readers find this sort of state control over religion problematic. This distinction between approaches will be discussed in greater detail below.

The ban on certain religious forms of dress (such as the ban on head coverings on women in universities and public institutions) is emblematic of the Turkish approach to religious expression in the context of its deep commitment to secularism. Once the Ottoman Empire and the caliphate were dismantled, the leaders of the republic had deep and legitimate concerns that public religiosity would weaken the fledgling secular state. While the Ottoman Empire maintained cohesion in Islamic tradition in part due to shared faith and governmental institutions, the new Turkish state sought cohesion in the philosophy of Atatürk (the arrows of Kemalism, including secularism, republicanism, nationalism, etc.).[23]

More than any other principle in the Constitution, secularism has come to represent the final defense against a return to the theocratic imperial model of governance of the Ottoman Empire. Historically, this battle has been fought most publicly over the issue of whether women have the right to wear a head covering in accordance with Islamic tradition. The Constitutional Court has read beyond the plain language of the Constitution and added an absolute prohibition against threats to secularism, which trumps statutes and even competing sections of the Constitution itself.[24] In stark contrast with First Amendment jurisprudence in the United States, Turkish constitutional secularism attempts to restrict any religious speech that may be considered to have a socially coercive impact. The current ban on head coverings, for example, was formalized by the Council of Higher Education after the adoption of the new Constitution in 1982. Since then, the ban's presence in institutions of higher learning has been vigorously upheld by the Constitutional Court (although in recent years, the government has not required universities to enforce it).[25]

The high judiciary is strongly committed to the principle of secularism. This commitment abides despite repeated attempts by both the Turkish Parliament and the lower courts to loosen the ban, whether by statute, amendment, or legal opinion.[26] In recent years, after nearly a decade of AKP governance, there has been an increase in popular and political pressure to protect religious speech in this context. At the same time, this issue has had a polarizing effect on Turkish politics, with nationalist parties, the military, and the courts standing in opposition to political parties with Islamist roots and the majority of Parliament.

In 2010, the dynamic of Turkish secularism shifted significantly. Perhaps surprisingly, the Turkish Constitutional Court allowed recent proposed amendments to the Constitution to be decided by referendum.[27] These amendments, which were approved as a package, will have a profound long-term impact on Turkish law and may indicate a move toward more passive or softer secularism (as in the United States, India, or the Netherlands). Among other things, they remove some structural barriers to democratic input and accountability within the judiciary and the military, which were established in the 1982 Constitution.

Secularism in the Indonesian Constitution

Although Indonesia's legal system is often identified as "secular," religion plays a significant role in legal theory and practice. As noted in Baskara Wardaya's earlier chapter, the preamble of Indonesia's Constitution of 1945 expresses the five core values of the state's ideology (*Pancasila*): "the belief in one God Almighty,[28] humanity that is just and civilized, the unity of Indonesia, democracy guided by the wisdom of representative deliberation, and social justice for all Indonesians."[29] While Islam played an influential role in the historical development of Indonesia, the world's most populous Muslim country,[30] Indonesia is a non-Islamic, secular state.[31]

As such, sharia is not enforced, and in fact, "an effort to include a provision imposing on the state an 'obligation to carry out the *sharia* for the adherents of Islam' in the Indonesian constitution was rejected . . . on the ground that it would threaten national unity in a multi-religious polity."[32] The government has maintained its positivist legal system by "limit[ing] formal recognition of Islamic law to specified areas of family law and finance, codifying the relevant principles and enforcing them through Islamic courts,"[33] essentially absorbing those elements into positive law.[34] In 1989, "the Legislature passed and the President signed a Religious Courts Act which significantly strengthened both the legal and institutional standing of the Islamic judiciary."[35] Prior to the act, decisions of Islamic courts had to be ratified by a civil court in order to be enforceable: "The 1989 Act redressed the subordinate status of the Islamic courts by making their decisions enforceable in their own right."[36] The state, "by taking control over the recruitment, training and employment of those bureaucrats and judges responsible for enforcing Islamic law, has been able to ensure that these actors give predominance to state law in their policy and decision-making, rather than giving effect to their own understandings of Islamic doctrine."[37]

Although both Turkey and Indonesia legally self-identify as secular, Indonesia acknowledges a role for Islamic jurisprudence that is not accorded to the tradition in Turkey. It is possible that as a diverse multiethnic nation without a history of hegemonic religiously affiliated rule as in France or Turkey, Indonesian legislators and jurists have not considered religious sentiment as problematic. This has probably been truer since the democratic reforms of the 1990s than the earlier periods of more-authoritarian rule.

Notable Shifts in Turkish Perceptions of Secularism

There is a growing consensus among social scientists that the political victories of the AKP over the past ten years have paralleled a shift away from dogmatic ideology to conservative, yet democratic positions.[38] Hakan Yavuz calls this a " 'conservative revolution' based on civil society, in which political change has followed social and political change—a bottom-up and gradual revolution in society to control the political language and society; and eventually the state."[39]

Yavuz asserts that the AKP has embraced elements of secularism by reimagining "the meaning and function of authoritarian secularism" as well as encouraging "a thickening of civil society."[40] Berna Turam claims that the AKP has transformed by embracing elements of democracy, secularism, and rule of law.[41] Brian Silverstein attributes these sorts of shifts to a synthesis between traditional Islamic worldviews and Western modernity, transforming the understanding of both Islam and democratic institutions.[42] He observes a shift toward integration of Turkish expressions of Islam with a softer form of secularism that has a greater emphasis on free exercise.[43]

Scholars studying the role of Islam in Turkish politics, like Ahmet Kuru and Soner Çağaptay, would likely agree that the AKP has been able to draw broader support by abandoning polarizing critiques of Kemalism proffered by the Refah party and other predecessor parties. Even so, some scholars remain skeptical that current party leaders, with ties to those predecessor parties, have fully recanted the rhetoric of earlier Islam-inspired political movements.[44]

Yavuz presents an optimistic view of religious parties' ability to reconcile ideology with democracy, a view that may have parallels to the experience of early Catholic political mobilization in Europe. Although the Catholic Church was highly critical of much of the Enlightenment and the political events that followed, by the nineteenth century Catholic-inspired civil society organizations formed the early basis for Christian democratic parties that were able to integrate elements of Catholic ethics and social teaching with a commitment to elements of democracy.[45]

Emergent Political Islam in Turkey

One of the most helpful studies of religion and secularism in contemporary Turkey is Jenny B. White's *Islamist Mobilization in Turkey: A Study in Vernacular Politics*. Based on extensive interviews in poorer Istanbul neighborhoods from the mid-eighties through the nineties,[46] White makes sense of the growing appeal of religiously identified parties, such as Refah, particularly among the working poor.[47] She calls this "vernacular politics," which is "a value-centered political process rooted in local culture, interpersonal relations, and community networks, yet connected through civic organizations to national party politics."[48] Secular political organizers were not as successful in these communities arguably because they did not identify with or appeal to local community values, including religious values.[49] A significant number of wealthier residents came to identify with Refah, perhaps because of its identification with community values.[50] Within poorer urban communities, secularism (in the Kemalist sense) tended to be identified with government elites.[51] Refah opposed established government elites in the early and mid-nineties by challenging corruption, particularly within local government.[52] Thus, religiously oriented political movements identified Islam as a liberating force.[53]

Focusing on developments of the 1990s, Alev Çinar argues that Islamist ideology generated an alternative modernization project that applied the same strategies and techniques as the modernizing state to produce and institutionalize its own nationalist program. In this context, the process of veiling is symbolic of both "liberation" from the West and the struggle to reclaim a national culture.[54] Çinar incorporates elements of critical and postmodern geography, for example, noting the importance of Islamist parties focusing their efforts in Istanbul as the economic and cultural center of Turkey rather than Ankara, the political capital. She attributes the success of the AKP to its incorporation, perhaps even cooptation, of key Kemalist values in order to transform itself into a broad-based conservative party.

Yael Navaro-Yashin also considers the development of Turkish political Islam in the 1990s.[55] She considers the role of secularism in Istanbul to reveal the tension between state power and the struggle to maintain religious identity. She examines Refah victories in the nineties and the roles ostensibly played by secularists and Islamists therein. She concludes that hard Turkish secularism created social tension, while Islam provided opportunities for liberation, creating a dialectic between the secular and the religious.

The characterizations of White, Çinar, and Navaro-Yashin bear similarities to the experiences and movements of Catholic liberation theology in Latin America, which embraced democratic principles as a means to empower the poor. In both the Turkish Muslim context and the Latin American Catholic context, the social justice and liberationist aspects of religion provided opportunities for education, consciousness raising, civil society organizations, and political mobilization for marginalized people of faith. However, in both contexts, successful liberationist political movements tended to be replaced or coopted by religious movements more sympathetic to neo-liberal economics. This dynamic will be further explored in this volume in the chapters by Gonzalo Gamio and Oscar Espinosa.

As in Turkey, the state has largely remained the principal source of legal and social meanings in Indonesia.[56] Islamic political parties "have always played a role in Indonesia, but have never achieved dominance."[57] Post-independence, "Islamic politics flourished . . . but [were] brought under increasingly tight controls after the mid-1950's."[58] And "although Islamic parties hold seats in Indonesia's national parliament, the majority parties are not associated with Islam and most of the so-called Islamic parties are associated with moderate Islamic organizations."[59] In fact, many of Indonesia's influential Muslim leaders actually "oppose the formation of religiously based parties on the ground that they would promote social division."[60] That said, the existence and success of overtly religious parties in Indonesia distinguishes it from Turkey.

Turkish Identity and Secularism

Both Turkish identity and its constructions of citizenship provide critical insights into the relationship between religion and the state within the republic. One such approach understands "Turkishness" as three concentric circles.[61] The outer circle includes those who live legally within the territorial borders of Turkey but who are not Muslim (and presumptively of non-Turkish ethnicity).[62] The middle circle is populated by non-ethnic Turkish Muslims (including Kurds, Laz, Circassians and others).[63] Turkish governments, even the AKP, have attempted to enforce linguistic and cultural conformity in order to perpetuate a narrative of unity in this circle.[64] The inner circle consists of ethnic Turks (who are presumptively Muslim according to the dominant narrative).[65] Ethnicity and language are thus central, and although religion is a signifier of "Turkish" identity, it is arguably of less importance.[66] Secularism provided a mechanism for creating national identity and unity that transcended religious difference, and was thus a powerful tool for defining both citizenship and intranational power relations.[67]

The shaping of national identity in terms of language, religion, and territory is not unique to Turkey. It has been employed in the Americas in order to legitimize and solidify colonial power (particularly over indigenous peoples). It is being used in Europe to challenge immigration and the status of Muslims in predominantly Catholic countries, such as France and Austria. In this sense, secularism can be used in both Catholic and Muslim contexts to marginalize religious out-groups by identifying membership with politically dominant religious groups.

In Indonesia today, sharia remains a significant aspect of life for many Muslims—a gauge for what actions are obligatory, recommended, neutral, disapproved of, and prohibited by Islam.[68] However, it is only formally applicable or enforced in the "fields over which the religious courts have jurisdiction, which include marriage, divorce, inheritance, trusts, gifts, and Islamic finance."[69] The traditional texts of Islamic law are not the direct sources of the rules governing society, and instead, the Indonesian Constitution is the highest law.[70] While "modern Indonesian Islamic thought and practice is radically diverse,"[71] most Indonesian Muslims accept interpretations of Islamic law that are "read in light of rapidly evolving social, economic and political contexts."[72] The state's treatment of Islam, rather than being considered anti-Islamic, might accurately be described as resembling some of these more progressive understandings of the tradition, which likely support a balance between free exercise and nonestablishment (as in so-called passive secularism).[73]

Modes of Turkish Secularism

One of the most insightful taxonomies of secularism is Ahmet Kuru's analysis of the United States, France, and Turkey.[74] He identifies two basic approaches to legal secularism. The first is a softer or "passive" secularism exemplified by the balance of free exercise and government nonestablishment of religion found in the United States.[75] France and Turkey are models of harder or "assertive" secularism, where government actively regulates religious institutions in an attempt to minimize the risk of religious coercion in the public square.[76] Kuru explains that both revolutionary Turkey and France adopted assertive secularism in order to contain renewed control by hegemonic religion, which had previously provided legitimacy for the monarchies.[77] In contrast, no single religion or religious institution had comparable influence in the American colonies, perhaps explaining why the United States took a different approach. Kuru's analysis concludes that secularism in Turkey tends to assert more control over religion than French *laïcité*, as a result of single-party rule in the first thirty years of the Turkish Republic.[78] However, he makes principled arguments in favor of the applicability of American-style secularism in the Turkish context and identifies a movement in that direction.[79]

It might be possible to infer from this study that harder forms of secularism tend to be more stable in societies that are no longer predominantly religious (such as France). When hard secularism is imposed on societies that continue to hold religion as a core part of communal identity, it tends to result in political friction (such as in Turkey or Mexico). If that is true, softer forms of secularism might ultimately be more compatible with strong religious identification, as in both Turkey and Indonesia. A fascinating parallel to explore here is the relationship Jeffrey Klaiber points out later in this volume between the Catholic Church and the "hard secularist" regimes of South America's "New Populist" states.

Conclusion

It is clear that religion is playing an increasingly important and public role in Turkish politics. Islam plays a role both as a potential source of liberation and as an alternative to imposed national identities. These developments may result in a shift to a softer form of secularism than was envisaged at the founding of the republic in the 1920s or in the 1982 Constitution.

It can be argued that the religious inspirations and discourses of parties like the AKP actually contribute to more vibrant political exchanges and to a richer sense of public reason. The shift toward softer secularism may validate local values, including religious values, and reveal the approach of strict secularism as being less representative of Turkish communities. This could explain the success of parties like the AKP and suggest a more inclusive vision of secularism. The move toward a more passive secularism in Turkey and an increasing role for religion in public discourse may be descriptively accurate and predictively helpful. As another predominantly Muslim "secular" legal system, Indonesia demonstrates the viability of softer secularism in an Islamic context. To the extent, however, that religiously inspired politicians intend to enforce their vision of the good upon those who disagree, those who defend traditional Turkish secularism are likely to have important normative arguments to critique this trend (in the same way that US secularists criticize some of the religious rhetoric and policies of US administrations).

These developments reflect tensions similar to those found in Protestant and Catholic contexts. Protestants in England and the United States were largely responsible for shaping passive secularism in the context of the Reformation, the Enlightenment, and an emerging pluralism. Predominantly Catholic countries such as France and Mexico took a much more assertive position in challenging institutional religious participation in political life and public discourse. However, Vatican II provided Catholic legitimacy for democracy, religious freedom, tolerance, human rights, and perhaps even passive secularism. Today, some of the most prominent Turkish Islamic scholars, including Fethullah Gülen[80] and Yaşar Nuri Öztürk,[81] also argue for passive secularism. Although the preference for passive secularism over assertive secularism might be pragmatic, secular principles have become as embedded in much of contemporary Turkish Islamic thought as they are in Catholic social thought. This similarity may provide important insights into just and sustainable approaches to tensions between states and religions in democratic societies.

Although both Islam and Catholicism have adapted to the growth of democratic institutions and various forms of secularism, there is a sense in which institutionalized religion continues to play conservative and sometimes oppositional roles in democratic states. In his final interview, Cardinal Martini, the former Archbishop of Milan, asserted that the Catholic Church was "200 years out of date" and needed to live out its mission of justice and hope more thoroughly.[82] Martini, like Gülen, expressed the desire for religious voices to be prophetic, transforming, and liberating. Both make a case for the opportunity for greater effectiveness and authenticity within the freedom and boundaries created by democratic legal and political structures than exist under authoritarian regimes.

NOTES

1. See Ahmet T. Kuru, *Secularism and State Policies toward Religion: The United States, France, and Turkey* (Cambridge: Cambridge University Press, 2009), 14.

2. See William Chester Jordan, *Europe in the High Middle Ages* (New York: Viking Press, 2001), especially chapter 6 describing the Investiture Controversy, which resulted in a separation of religious and secular authority.

3. See Baber Johansen, "A Perfect Law in an Imperfect Society: Ibn Taymiyya's Concept of 'Governance in the Name of the Sacred Law,'" in *The Law Applied: Contextualizing the Islamic Shari'a,* ed. Peri Bearman, Wolfhart Heinrichs, and Bernard G. Weiss (New York: I. B. Tauris, 2008), 261.

4. Andrew Davison, *Secularism and Revivalism in Turkey: A Hermeneutic Reconsideration* (New Haven, CT: Yale University Press, 1998), 35–38.

5. See Abdullahi Ahmed An-Na'im, *Islam and the Secular State: Negotiating the Future of Shari'a* (Cambridge, MA: Harvard University Press, 2008).

6. See An-Na'im, *Islam and the Secular State,* 141–58, for a discussion of this dynamic in India.

7. Ibid.

8. *The Constitution of the Republic of Turkey,* November 7, 1982 (amended 2010).

9. Erik J. Zürcher, *Turkey. A Modern History* (London: I. B. Tauris, 2010), 221–40.

10. Cihan Tuğal, *Passive Revolution: Absorbing the Islamic Challenge to Capitalism* (Stanford, CA: Stanford University Press, 2009) 38–42.

11. Zürcher, *Turkey,* 281–90.

12. See Carter Vaughn Findley, *Turkey, Islam, Nationalism, and Modernity: A History, 1789–2007* (New Haven, CT: Yale University Press, 2010), 357–58.

13. Fazil Sağlam, "Orhan Pamuk ve Referandum," *Hakimiyet-I Milliye*, September 1, 2010, http://www.hakimiyetimilliye.org/index.php/hm-yazarlari/1075821-orhan-pamuk-ve-referandum-fazil-saglam.html.

14. See Bernard Lewis, *The Emergence of Modern Turkey* (Oxford: Oxford University Press, 1961). Kemalist principles such as secularism refer to the views of Mustafa Kemal Atatürk, the "Father" of the Turkish Republic established in 1923. The so-called Arrows of Kemalism include republicanism, populism, secularism, revolutionism, nationalism, and statism.

15. *The Constitution of the Republic of Turkey*, preamble.

16. Ibid., art. 2.

17. Ibid., art. 13.

18. Ibid., art. 14.

19. Ibid., arts. 81 and 103.

20. Ibid., art. 174.

21. Ibid., art. 68.

22. Ibid., art. 136.

23. See Findley, *Turkey, Islam, Nationalism, and Modernity*, 252–59.

24. Mehmet Uzun, "The Protection of Laicism in Turkey and the Turkish Constitutional Court," *Penn State International Law Review* 28 (Winter 2010): 383–426, at 408–10.

25. Ibid.

26. Ibid., 406–12.

27. "Turkey Backs Constitutional Changes," BBC News, September 12, 2010.

28. "The belief in one God Almighty" requires all citizens to declare one of five officially recognized religions: Islam, Catholicism, Protestantism, Buddhism, and Hinduism. Mark Cammack, "Islam, Nationalism, and the State in Suharto's Indonesia," *Wisconsin International Law Journal* 17 (1999): 27–63, at 48.

29. Cammack, "Islam, Nationalism, and the State," 63n115.

30. Ibid., 47, 28.

31. See Alfitri, "Expanding a Formal Role for Islamic Law in the Indonesian Legal System: The Case of Mu'Amalat," *Journal of Law & Religion* 23 (2008): 249–66, at 250.

32. Cammack, "Islam, Nationalism, and the State," 48.

33. Simon Butt, "Islam, the State and the Constitutional Court in Indonesia," *Pacific Rim Law & Policy Journal* 19 (2010): 279–300.

34. See Alfitri, "Expanding a Formal Role for Islamic Law," 252.

35. Cammack, "Islam, Nationalism, and the State," 50.

36. Ibid.

37. Butt, "Islam, the State and the Constitutional Court," 285.

38. See M. Hakan Yavuz, *Secularism and Muslim Democracy in Turkey* (Cambridge: Cambridge University Press, 2009); Berna Turam, *Between Islam and the State: The Politics of Engagement* (Palo Alto, CA: Stanford University Press, 2007); and Brian Silverstein, *Islam and Modernity in Turkey* (New York: Palgrave Macmillan, 2011).

39. Yavuz, *Secularism and Muslim Democracy*, xiii.

40. Ibid., 267.

41. Turam, *Between Islam and the State*, 139.

42. See Silverstein, *Islam and Modernity in Turkey*.

43. Ibid.

44. See Umut Uzer, "Secularism and Muslim Democracy in Turkey," *Middle East Policy* 16, no. 3 (Fall 2009): 172. "It is true that center-right parties and the Nationalist Action Party accord a crucial role to Islam without assigning it the central role in politics. The Islamists, on the other hand, want to redesign the Turkish society and polity according to the dictates of Islam. Yavuz's very definition of a religious party entails such a project. It follows that for [secularism as making Islam the major component of Turkish identity] to make conceptual sense, it should be confined to the center-right parties . . . and it should exclude the Islamists, who have no desire for secularism."

45. Stathis N. Kalyvas, "Commitment Problems in Emerging Democracies: The Case of Religious Parties," *Comparative Politics* 32, no. 4 (July 2000): 382–98, at 391: "The Belgian experience suggests that the politicization of religion is compatible with liberal democratic development, thus undermining arguments that posit 'the desacralization of politics and the depoliticization of the sacred' as preconditions for democracy in Muslim countries."

46. See Jenny B. White, *Islamist Mobilization in Turkey: A Study in Vernacular Politics* (Seattle: University of Washington Press, 2002).

47. See Yavuz, *Secularism and Muslim Democracy*, 59–64. The Refah Partisi (Turkish for Welfare Party) was an overtly Islamist party founded in 1983 by a group including, most notably, Necmettin Erbakan, who was a controversial figure. The party was initially successful in municipal elections and became the largest party in 1996, when Erbakan became prime minister. The coalition advanced a number of Islamist initiatives and was forced out of power by the military in 1997. The party was banned in 1998.

48. White, *Islamist Mobilization*, 27.

49. Ibid., 242.

50. Ibid., 137–48.

51. Ibid., 76.

52. Ibid., 137–48.

53. Ibid., 30.

54. See Alev Çinar, *Modernity, Islam, and Secularism in Turkey: Bodies, Places, and Time* (Minneapolis: University of Minnesota Press, 2005).

55. See Yael Navaro-Yashin, *Faces of the State: Secularism and Public Life in Turkey* (Princeton, NJ: Princeton University Press, 2002).

56. Ibid., 279.

57. Cammack, "Islam, Nationalism, and the State," 48.

58. Ibid.

59. Butt, "Islam, the State and the Constitutional Court," 300.

60. Cammack, "Islam, Nationalism, and the State," 48.

61. See Soner Çağaptay, *Islam, Secularism, and Nationalism in Modern Turkey: Who Is a Turk?* (New York: Routledge, 2006).

62. Ibid., 160.

63. Ibid.

64. Ibid., 159–60.

65. Ibid., 160.

66. Ibid., 156–62.

67. Ibid., 102–23.

68. See Alfitri, "Expanding a Formal Role for Islamic Law."

69. Butt, "Islam, the State and the Constitutional Court," 299.

70. Ibid.

71. Ibid., 281.

72. Ibid.

73. Ibid., 281–82.

74. See Kuru, *Secularism and State Policies toward Religion*.

75. Ibid., 10–14.

76. Ibid., 11–14.

77. Ibid., 32–34.

78. Ibid., 32–33.

79. Ibid.

80. Fethullah Gülen is a prominent religious scholar who has organized an influential Islamic movement that emphasizes education, inter-religious dialogue, nationalism, and free-market capitalism. Movements associated with Gülen now run hundreds of schools, several universities, and numerous foundations around the world.

81. Yaşar Nuri Öztürk is a Turkish theologian, lawyer, and columnist and a former member of Turkish parliament.

82. "In Final Interview, Liberal Cardinal Says 'Church 200 Years out of Date,'" September 2, 2012, http://www.msnbc.msn.com/id/48876172/ns/world_news-europe/.

Peruvian Voices

Of the four countries represented in this book, Peru is the most predominantly Catholic. What this means is that Peru represents some of the most established, yet complex, sets of relationships between democracy, culture, and Catholicism surveyed in this book. The Church's presence is seen and felt on all social and political levels. This means that the Catholic Church has, at one time or another, stood alongside opposing forces in Peru's continuing process of social and political democratization. The themes that run throughout the chapters in this section are the themes of power and authority: Who has it? Who should have it? How should Peru balance power and authority between the state and the Catholic Church?

Soledad Escalante analyzes the relationship between the Catholic Church and the Peruvian state in terms of patronage and legitimacy. With an eye to the great reforms of the twentieth century in the Catholic Church and the Peruvian state, Escalante looks at the nature and history of the relationship between these two institutions through the lens of the 1980 Concordat between the Holy See and the Peruvian state. While the relationship in questions remains tinged with struggles for power and influence, the struggle in contemporary Peru between the Church and the state is,

Escalante claims, moving in a more positive direction—away from the tutelage and patronage of the past, and toward a more mutual and responsible future.

Gonzalo Gamio looks to the important category of memory for insight into the history of both the Peruvian state and the Catholic Church during the authoritarian governments that defined Peru in the later part of the twentieth century. How do we remember? What do we remember? These are all debated questions in Peru today, with some arguing that we must remember the violent abuses of power in the past, and the complicity of church and state authorities in said abuses. Others, often the elites of the Catholic Church and the Peruvian government at the time of said abuses, would prefer to forget what happened because the memories are too painful and too politically volatile to be recalled. Gamio, in line with the Comisión de la Verdad y Reconciliación (or CVR, Peru's Truth and Reconciliation Commission), suggests that we must remember the past and unbury the truth not only for the sake of justice for the victims of this violent history but to ensure that we do not repeat the same mistakes in the future through a complex, yet willed, ignorance.

Oscar Espinosa looks to the local indigenous communities in Peru to surface some of the complexities constitutive of the relationship between the Catholic Church and the Peruvian state at the grassroots level. In looking to the indigenous communities in the Amazon region, Espinosa highlights one of the great internal and external challenges of the Catholic Church in Peru today—the tension between high-church authority and grassroots democracy. Within the Catholic Church, argues Espinosa, the commitment of the Amazonian bishops to their base communities has connected these shepherds to their flocks in intimate ways. Yet, this same act has alienated the Amazonian bishops from their brother bishops in the other regions of Peru, who see the commitment of the Amazonian bishops to the indigenous people as theologically problematic, not to mention politically dangerous. Espinosa highlights this political danger for the Catholic Church at the grassroots level in his recounting of the stories of individuals and groups being punished by the Peruvian state for their democratic activism. For Espinosa, the question becomes how a person ought to live their calling in Christ.

Jorge Aragón argues that, despite claims to the contrary, religion is, and remains, an important, positive political factor in Peru, and one that deserves more attention from both the academic community and the wider community at large. Aragón suggests that actively religious persons in Peru are well suited to contribute to the social and political order—

particularly a democratic social and political order—because of their religious identification. According to this argument, actively religious persons come together in, for example, a common system of beliefs, a distinctive way of life, and regular social interaction. These factors—among others—predispose actively religious persons to the civic responsibilities constitutive of the social and political organization of a democratic society. For Aragón, the future of democracy in Latin America depends, importantly though not exclusively, on religious factors.

The Relationship of Patronage and Legitimacy between the Catholic Church and the Peruvian State

María Soledad Escalante Beltrán

The goal of this chapter is to offer a brief overview of the relationship between the Roman Catholic Church and the Peruvian state in the modern era. This will include a discussion of church-state relations prior to the Second Vatican Council of the Roman Catholic Church (1962–1965) and an analysis of two key periods during and after the Council: 1958–1977 and 1978–1980. This complex history is discussed using the interpretive lenses of "legitimacy" and "patronage."

Church-State Relations Prior to the Second Vatican Council

Before the Second Vatican Council, it was a common theological and philosophical approach in Roman Catholicism to refer to the Church as a *societas perfecta*, or "perfect society." This phrase meant that the Church was a self-sufficient, independent institution possessing all the resources necessary to achieve its goal of the universal salvation of humanity. The Church was considered an institution prior to and of higher status than the state because it received its original legitimacy through its divine foundation in Jesus Christ. As canon law expert Juan Roger Rodríguez Ruiz puts it: "In her long itinerary, the Church has pointed out that she has her jurisdictional order, which is originary, primary, autonomous and independent, previous and different to any positive jurisdictional ordainment."[1] On this basis, whatever legitimacy the state might acquire would require the acknowledgement of the Church.

Along with its claim to original legitimacy, another important concept for understanding church-state relations prior to the Second Vatican Council is patronage. This is particularly true of the former colonial empires of Spain and Portugal. Patronage was an accord whereby both the Church and the state would agree to support one another in the occupation and colonization of the New World. For example, while the Spanish Crown was in charge of converting the New World to Catholicism, the tithes it received from the New World were to be used for financing works of evangelization. As such, the patronage agreement was considered mutually beneficial.

The effects of patronage continued long after the Spanish colonial power left South America. This is no less true in Peru than in any other South American state. During the struggle for Peruvian independence from Spain (1810–1824), patronage remained the effective relational model between the Church and the state, but the particular characteristics of this relationship had shifted. For example, some anti-clerical liberals opposed certain elements of patronage and certain decrees issued by the pope. Yet, many of these same anti-clerical liberals continued to honor other elements of patronage in order to maintain their own power and influence.

Peruvian independence resolved the political situation in the country but not the cultural situation. Even after political independence, an allegiance remained between Peruvian culture and the Catholic Church that the state had to recognize. The remnants of patronage continued to translate into favoritism. Rubén Vargas Ugarte states that:

> While studying the relations between State and Church during the
> Republic, the first thing that jumps out is its instability. There has
> been no unique direction, nor has there been one defined orientation,
> though the desire of adopting only one position was present. This
> position was the Concordat [i.e., patronage between the Catholic
> Church and the Peruvian state]. In the first years of independent life,
> many of our politicians, poorly or non-versed in canonic matters,
> judged that the Patronage exercised by the Kings of Spain was a trib
> ute to their sovereignty and considered themselves legitimate heirs to
> all their privileges and rights.[2]

Although patronage was maintained during the Republican period from 1822 to 1842, the situation was not easy. The Church in Peru had its privileges, but it lacked true autonomy. The state managed to keep the people united through religion, but it too lacked the kind of autonomy characteristic of the European and North American states where the relationship between church and state was one of separation. The government, for example, believed it had the legal right to choose bishops, even those from the canonical institution. Vargas Ugarte points out:

> In Peru, our first governors judged misguidedly that they had inherited this right, granted by the Supreme Pontiffs to the Kings of Spain, though neither the clergy nor religious people believed this right to be inherited, and even those who claimed it were unsure of possessing it legitimately.[3]

By 1920, the Peruvian Constitution legally recognized a citizen's freedom of conscience regarding religion and stipulated a specific prohibition against clergy holding parliamentary office. This did not end patronage altogether, but it became increasingly difficult for the state and the Church to maintain this relationship.

The Impact of the Second Vatican Council and Its Aftermath to 1977

Church-state relations in the period from 1958 to 1977 were first marked by the influence of the Second Vatican Council and the Episcopal Assembly of Medellín (1968). During this time, the Church addressed many fundamental questions concerning its nature and its relationship to the world. These questions included its relationship to the state and society as a whole.

The Catholic Church finally moved toward the modern principle of separation of church and state at the Second Vatican Council in its 1965 Declaration on Religious Freedom, *Dignitatis humanae*. This was consistent with the council's general move away from the language of the Church as a *societas perfecta* toward a recovery of the biblical notion of the Church as the *populus Dei*, the "pilgrim people of God."

This development was in line with the overall goals of the Second Vatican Council to redefine the relationships of the Church to the modern world, to other Christian churches, and to the poor. Isabel Larriera points out:

> The Council was more sensitive to the first two subjects [mentioned above], for the most active participants [had] better theological

instruments to deal with them. It could be said that the terrain was not yet mature enough to deal with the third theme, though conciliar perspectives created the space for experiences and reflections in the line of a Church to the Poor.[4]

Three years after the Second Vatican Council, the Latin American bishops met at the Episcopal Assembly of Medellín in 1968. It is here that the Church in Latin America directly addressed the relationship between the Church and the poor. At Medellin, the bishops took up Pope John XXIII's call in his encyclical letter *Pacem in terris* to work for peace and care of the poor.

In line with conciliar developments such as these, the Peruvian Episcopal Conference announced that state protection of a particular religious creed, along with the maintenance of patronage in Peru, were against the principles of religious freedom. However, it simultaneously argued that the separation of church and state meant neither that the state should no longer acknowledge the unique contributions the Catholic Church made to Peruvian society nor that the government of Peru should avoid collaborative relations with the Catholic Church.

Consistent with this development, the Peruvian Church took a more determined effort at supporting social changes addressing the conditions of poverty in Peru. This call for change included, for the first time, criticism of Peru's military government. In January 1969, the 36th National Episcopal Conference of the Peruvian Church was held. The prelates at this conference took up the work and inspiration of the 1968 Medellín Assembly and publically stated their concerns about the effects of Peru's military government on the people. Jeffrey Klaiber reflects on the importance of this move by the prelates:

> The Assembly affirmed the great lines of Medellín in the Peruvian context. In unusual language for an assembly of bishops, the Assembly denounced the existence of colonial feudalism, still existent in some regions of the country, and accused the nation's aristocrats, who in association with colonial imperialists had been the fundamental reason for poverty in Peru. This type of language, strong and almost aggressive, reveals the influence of Medellín and, at the same time, of the liberation theology. Following the example of John XXIII and the Second Vatican Council, it also submitted itself to self-criticism. Concretely, it proposed to examine all the properties of the Peruvian Church.[5]

Two other examples of this trend were the work of Juan Cardinal Landázuri Ricketts and Gustavo Gutiérrez. Juan Cardinal Landázuri Ricketts was the archbishop of Lima and made important statements regarding the dire situation of the poor in Peru during the 1965 Seventh National Eucharistic Congress. Gustavo Gutiérrez's groundbreaking book *A Theology of Liberation* was published in 1871. This book introduced the term "liberation theology" to the world, referring to the movement and ideas that had begun among priests and laity within the Catholic Church in the 1950s–1960s. Liberation theology interpreted the Christian faith through the experience of the poor and advocated for social justice.

The period from 1958 to 1968 was critical because it secured the separation of church and state as official teaching and enabled the Church to find its place in society as an advocate for justice. This meant that at any time the Church might support the state or criticize it, depending on how well the state was protecting and promoting the common good of society.

The Constitution of 1979 and the Concordat of 1980

The Constitution of 1979 put a formal end to patronage in Peru. The Constitution recognized the full independence of all religious groups in Peru and the autonomy of both the church and the state. This constitutional position was formally recognized by the Vatican in its 1980 Concordat with the state.

The 1979 Constitution was a watershed moment in the republican history of Peru because it constituted a movement toward democracy after years of military dictatorship. It recognized the freedom and autonomy of both the Peruvian state and the Catholic Church. According to article 86 of the 1979 Constitution:

> Within a regime of independence and autonomy, the State recognizes the Catholic Church as an important element in the historic, cultural, and moral development of Peru. The State affirms its willingness to aid the Church. It also may establish ways of collaborating with other confessions.[6]

In this way, the 1979 Constitution brought the legal relationship between Church and state in Peru to that of other modern states in Europe and North America.

The Constitution also established rights and liberties of citizens. For example, article 2, section 3 of the new 1979 Constitution states that every individual in Peru has:

> the freedom to choose their own religion, in an associated or individual way. There may be no legal persecution based upon . . . personal beliefs or ideals. The public exercise of all confessions is granted,

assuming that this public action does not offend moral principles or alter public order.[7]

Through its treatment of both the Church and the citizen, the constitution sought to place Peru on the pathway to greater democracy.

In other ways, however, the Constitution reflected the legacy of Peru's history of church-state relations. For example, state financial assistance to Church-sponsored community organizations and social service groups would continue, with these organizations understood as non-taxable. In addition, a military vicariate would continue to offer religious assistance to Catholic members of the armed forces, police forces, and civil servants. Finally, the Church would be allowed to establish and operate educational institutions at all levels, in accordance with national regulations. Therefore, while the Constitution establishes respect for and protection of other religious confessions, there remains a special cultural relationship between the Catholic Church and the Peruvian people.

While the seeming intent of the Constitution was to develop a language of separation in the church-state relationship, the actual language used was that of collaboration. Klaiber points out: "Instead [of the word 'separation'], the more positive word 'collaboration' was chosen, because it points to the environment of harmony and good will which should reign between the two."[8]

In the year following the establishment of the 1979 Constitution, the Church issued its own declaration on the state of the relationship between Peru and the Holy See. This was the 1980 Concordat. According to Juan Roger Rodríguez Ruiz:

> This international agreement between the Peruvian State and the Holy See is the most significant achievement in Peru in its attempt to establish relations with the Holy See. . . . This international, jurisdictional instrument . . . recognizes the Catholic Church as an entity with its proper jurisdictional ordainment, which is primary, autonomous and independent of the international community. Thus, the Peruvian State recognizes the Church as an important element in the historical, cultural, and moral formation of Peru, and provides the Church the necessary aid to allow it to reach its goal. With the promulgation of the Concordat, the institution of the "National Patronate" is overcome by the absolution of the Dictatorial Decree of 27 January 1870, because it did not adapt itself to the social and jurisdictional reality of the moment, nor translate the true independence and autonomy of the Church.[9]

The Church becomes, then, an independent jurisdictional personality and finally overcomes the patronage relationship between the state and the Church.[10]

Conclusion

The relationship between the Catholic Church and the Peruvian state in the nineteenth and twentieth centuries was a complex interplay of legitimacy and patronage. Due to the depth of this legacy, there remains today a belief that the rights of all individuals to follow their religious convictions is not fully recognized in Peru and that the Catholic Church still receives disproportionate government preference. In the next chapter, by Gonzalo Gamio, the effects of this will be seen in the conflict over the 2003 Final Report of the Truth and Reconciliation Commission. Oscar Espinosa's chapter also explores this topic in terms of the Peruvian government's response to the rights of Amazonian indigenous people and the role of the Catholic Church.

Nonetheless, the relationship between the Catholic Church and the Peruvian state today is an improvement over the past. The Second Vatican Council, the Medellín Assembly, the 1979 Constitution, and the 1980 Concordat remain institutional instruments and mechanisms through which the relations between the Peruvian state and the Catholic Church have been improved. Although church-state tensions remain in Peru, the legitimacy of the Catholic Church and the Peruvian state has foundations that have been built over time and are recognized by the majority of the Peruvian population.

NOTES

1. Juan Roger Rodríguez Ruiz, *La Relevancia Jurídica del Acuerdo entre la Santa Sede y el Perú* (Lima: ROEL S. A. C., 2006), 8.

2. Rubén Vargas Ugarte, *De la Conquista a la República* (Lima: PACIFICO, 1970), 189.

3. Ibid., 191.

4. Isabel Larriera, *II Conferencia Episcopal de Medellín* (Río: MAGIS, 2012), 2.

5. Jeffrey Klaiber, *La Iglesia en el Perú* (Lima: PUCP, 1987), 384–85.

6. *Constitución Política del Perú*, 1979. Translation by María Soledad Escalante Beltrán.

7. *Constitución*.

8. Klaiber, *La Iglesia*, 475.

9. Rodríguez Ruiz, *La Relevancia*, 27–28.

10. In 2010, the Law of Religious Freedom was passed in an effort to provide equal treatment to all religious confessions in Peru. The law guarantees confessional freedom and equality to all religious communities. It also guarantees a person's right to change their religious affiliation or to have no religious affiliation at all. Concern for respecting the indigenous religions of the Andean and Amazon peoples is highlighted in this law. This was done to amplify the freedom of conscience noted in article 2 of the 1979 Constitution and in the 1993 Constitution: "To the freedom of conscience and religion, individually and collectively. There is no persecution sustained upon belief or ideal. There is no crime in opinion. The public exercise of all confessions is free, while it does not offend the moral or affect public order."

Catholicism and the Struggle
for Memory: Reflections on Peru

Gonzalo Gamio Gehri

The work of memory is an ethical act. Among its foci can be the recollection of violence. In 2001, a truth and reconciliation commission, or Comisión de la Verdad y Reconciliación (CVR), was established by the transitional government of Valentín Paniagua to examine atrocities committed during the 1980s and 1990s, when Peru was plagued by the worst violence in its history. The CVR was given a two-year term to produce a rigorous research on the violence. The final report was completed and published in 2003.

The CVR is a rich but shocking place to investigate the condition, roles, and relationships between the state, the Catholic Church, and the people in contemporary Peru. This chapter offers a reflection on these complex realities. It begins by a general discussion of the ethics of memory and then moves to an analysis of the struggles over memory that marked the CVR's work and the public debate on the project of transitional justice in Peru. In the process, this chapter focuses particular attention on the relationship between these matters and the moral and intellectual tradition of Roman Catholicism.

The Ethics of Memory and "Pasts That Do Not Pass"

For the Roman Catholic Church, commitment to, and dependence upon, memory is beyond question. Celebration of the Mass is an act of remembering the teachings, passion, and death of Jesus Christ.[1] The reading of the Gospels refurbishes Jesus Christ's message and invites believers to live this message in their daily lives. The Eucharist of bread and wine recalls the mystery of faith, recreating the Last Supper at Christ's request. The Catholic Church remembers the suffering and sacrifice of Christ, and remembers it in a variety of ways.

From this theological standpoint, the Catholic Church has often acknowledged the relationship between memory, perspective, and ethics. Two examples are John Paul II's exhortation *Reconciliatio et paenitentia* and the International Theological Commission's document *Memory and Reconciliation*. Theologians such as Johann Baptist Metz and Gustavo Gutiérrez have focused on memory and the perspective of the suffering poor. Metz, for example, argues that Christian political theology "forces us to contemplate the *theatrum mundi* not only from the perspective of those who have achieved their goals, but also from the defeated and the victims' perspectives."[2]

Reflections such as these highlight the importance of taking up the point of view of victims when reflecting on the relationship between violence and memory. By putting oneself in the shoes of victims, one can begin to understand the damage they have suffered and attempt to address it with the tools of justice. Some societies have undergone extended periods of neglect within the "democratic" system. Some have faced terrible armed conflicts. Consequently, some have decided to undertake retrospective evaluations of this violence in hope of understanding its causes and effects on citizens and institutions.

Such acts of remembering are instruments of justice. They can be called works of "transitional justice," since they undertake remembering within the process of democratization. The principle idea underlying these acts of justice is that a democratic ethos requires not only the honest acknowledgment of past violence but also the proper distribution of liabilities for violence done. Required too is the assurance of institutional and educational reform, so the violence does not happen again.

This is not the only view of memory in situations of social violence and repression. People who support a policy of silence take a very different view. They argue that the past should be left alone and that old social wounds should not be reopened. One example of this is the transition to democracy in Spain after the fall of General Francisco Franco. Here, the return to democracy and rule of law occurred on condition of silence about crimes committed during the Civil War. While this proclamation had effects in the political realm, over time it was less successful in extra-political contexts. The flood of books and films exposing the crimes committed under Franco's dictatorship, like *La Lengua de las Mariposas* (1999) and *El Laberinto del Fauno* (2006), show that the Spanish public has had a deep need to surface the memories of their society's past. A rich comparison could be made here to the role of *kethoprak* theater and public memory in Indonesia, as discussed in Albertus Budi Susanto's chapter in this volume.

Recovering the past is a complex activity. Tzvetan Todorov teaches that memory is a selective process. It is a form of discernment that enables human beings to distinguish between images of the past that deserve to be retained and images that might as well be discarded. A perfect and complete memory of that past is not feasible; in fact, it might be viewed as a curse if it were so (as we see in Jorge Luis Borges's short story *Funes el memorioso*).

The real enemy to the genuine exercise of memory is the construction of an official history by the ruling elite and those in positions of power. Such an official history fails to grasp the victims' experiences and refuses to address any form of injustice or oppression, particularly insofar as the ruling elites might be implicated.[3] This kind of memory is not the result of civil deliberation about what needs to be remembered, nor does it acknowledge the voices of those directly affected by violence. To this point, Paul Ricoeur's dual understanding of memory and forgetting is helpful.

On the one hand, there is the forgetting of those who come to terms with their past, take measures to prevent the past from returning, and move forward without the burdens of grief and pain. On the other hand, there is the forgetting of those who choose "voluntary blindness," something akin to the tradition in Greek tragedies where one "does not want to see, does not want to become aware of something."[4] This type of forgetting is deliberate omission: an agent has seen something, but they choose to look the other way.[5]

The CVR and Peru's Struggle for Memory

In contemporary Peru, all the positions on memory discussed above have surfaced in the public debate about the CVR. The task of the CVR was to research, analyze, and allocate responsibility for the violence experienced in Peru in the 1980s and 1990s. In addition, the CVR was to propose recommendations for reform of institutions to prevent violence from recurring in the future. Special attention was to be given to violence linked to intranational terrorist groups, such as Sendero Luminoso (Shining Path) and Tupac Amaru, and government forces, such as the military and the police.

The CVR's final report pointed to the Sendero Luminoso as the main perpetrator of violence. While the report acknowledged many of the heroic acts performed by the government's own forces at this time, it also uncovered substantial evidence that some members of the government forces undertook the "systematic practice of Human Rights violations."[6] The commission determined that the administration of Fernando Belaúnde (1980–1985) and the first administration of Alan García (1985–1990) bore much political responsibility for the violence in Peru throughout the 1980s. In the case of Alberto Fujimori and his administration (1990–2000), the CVR found sufficient evidence of crimes against humanity to recommend a judicial investigation into the criminal liability of Fujimori himself. Under his administration, the power of the state was concentrated in the hands of an elite few who destroyed democratic institutions and turned Peru into a military dictatorship. Baskara Wardaya's earlier chapter in this volume pointed out a similar development in Indonesia with the rise of the Suharto regime.

The final report of the CVR acknowledged the important roles played by Catholic and Protestant churches in the fight against terror and the defense of human rights during the armed conflict in Peru. The churches reported acts of organized violence by terrorist groups and the nation's own armed forces.[7] One example of this occurred in the Southern Andean region, where the churches successfully resisted the attempts of Sendero Luminoso to convert people into their terrorist organization.

The report pointed out that the churches in the Ayacucho area, which was an epicenter of violence, did not successfully oppose either the terrorists or the government forces. A similar judgment was passed on the churches of the Apurimac and Huancavelica areas. Juan Luis Cardinal Cipriani Thorne, then bishop of Ayacucho and now cardinal archbishop of Lima, was a controversial figure in this regard. As cardinal, he had a relationship with the Comisión Episcopal de Acción Social (CEAS, or Commission of Peruvian Bishops for Social Action), but kept the commission's members from reporting on the violent areas. Cardinal Cipriani supported Fujimori's authoritarian regime and made public statements against human rights organizations that reported the violent actions of the government forces.[8]

The CVR exposed complicity among clerical and military authorities in the violence that occurred in the Ayacucho, Apurimac, and Huancavelica areas. Among those who saw the Catholic Church and the Peruvian military as the protector institutions of the country, there was a tendency to look at the CVR with suspicion. As pointed out in Soledad Escalante's chapter in this volume, Peru has a long history of church and state relations shaped by the Spanish tradition of patronage and the Church's theology of legitimation. All of these factors combine to politicize memory and favor selective recollection.

FERNÁN ALTUVE-FEBRES AND THE TRADITIONALIST CRITIQUE OF THE CVR

Fernán Altuve-Febres, a former congressman from Fujimori's political party, is a lawyer and historian who has worked with some of the most important conservative newspapers in Peru: *Expreso*, *La Razón*, and *Correo*. As an expert in the history of the Peruvian nation and its institutions, he promotes what he calls the "classic right-wing" perspective. This is the so-called traditionalist perspective that identifies its legacy in the critiques of Western modernity begun by nineteenth-century thinkers, such as Joseph de Maestre and José Donoso Cortés.[9] Traditionalists support a strong link between the state and both the Catholic Church and the military. It defends the Church and the military against "the menaces incarnated by modernism, progressivism and socialism."[10] In his book *La Democracia Fuerte* (*Strong Democracy*), Altuve-Febres expresses this conservative point of view as he defends the authoritarianism of the Fujimori regime: "Once in power, President Fujimori found that the state was weakened to the point that he could not combat the serious problems of terrorism, bureaucratic collapse, fiscal bankruptcy, and the persistent problem of extreme poverty."[11]

Altuve-Febres made his stand against the CVR in an article "El ministerio de la Verdad" ("The Ministry of Truth"), which was originally published in *La Razón* one day before the official presentation of the CVR final report. The article raised jurisprudential and political objections to the CVR. Altuve-Febres claimed the CVR could do nothing about human rights violations since "they have no legal standing in our criminal justice system."[12] He also said that in cases where the CVR might suggest individual responsibilities in criminal offenses, it would be usurping judicial power and the Public Ministry's functions. Cynically calling it the "Lerner Commission" and not the "Truth Commission," Altuve-Febres called on the CVR to proceed with "veracity," meaning: "we, the Peruvian people, suffered an unjustified aggression by *Sendero Luminoso* . . . . there really was not a national armed conflict."[13]

The CVR acknowledged that it was not its charge to legally judge or punish the perpetrators of crimes against humanity. Rather, its task was to conduct research to clarify the prevalence of the violence experienced in Peru, allocate responsibility, and recommend institutional measures to prevent future violence. The case studies undertaken by the CVR have amassed useful information for judicial investigations into the homicides, torture, and disappearances that took place during the years of armed conflict. In cases such as these, Altuve-Febres disagrees with the CVR. In his view, the report's focus must be on the liability of the terrorist aggressors and "*the exemption of the use of force undertaken by the attacked party* [i.e., the military] in order to restore the Peruvian State and the community's rights."[14]

Federico Prieto Celi: Truth as Silence

One of the most controversial figures in Peru's contemporary political scene is Federico Prieto Celi. He is a journalist, a political theoretician, a former lecturer at the University of Piura, and a member of the conservative Catholic organization Opus Dei. Prieto Celi's response to the CVR and his defense of Cardinal Cipriani are in his book *El Trigo y la Cizaña* (*The Wheat and the Tares*). The book develops a conspiracy theory approach to the CVR; that is, he has the view that events in Peru have been secretly directed through political intrigue and clandestine activity.

Against the supposed conspiracy undermining Peru, *El Trigo y la Cizaña* vindicates the authoritarian policies of repressive state administrations like that of former president Fujimori.[15] The actions of military personnel who "allegedly went beyond the call of duty" should be seen as justified responses to terrorism. In Prieto Celi's view, the final report of the CVR lacks this perspective: "[The CVR] should have further studied the ways in which the violence of the revolutionaries caused the violence of the military and paramilitary force."[16] Politicians who agreed with Prieto Celi supported the Amnesty Law passed during President Fujimori's regime.

Concerning the memories of past injustices noted in the final report of the CVR, Prieto Celi argues:

> It would have been best for Peru that it did not have to suffer the drama of terrorism for so many years, and once it did, *it would have been best that no one confronted the actors*, beyond the inalienable functions of the police forces and the law. Every important event in our national history demands to be researched and noted down. The protagonists, the facts, and the historical analysis are valuable. All these things must take place

in the life of society and the life of the Church *under the guidance of historians*. A silence that hides or obscures the truth is not an option. However, in the face of the anguish and pain that the people suffer, when what must be said at the time is said as complementary to the truth, it is also viable to keep a respectful silence for the suffering people, a silence that accompanies them with clarity and affection, not with exhibitionist manipulation. As [Pablo] Neruda once wrote, "I like you when you are silent because you look as if you were absent. / Distant and painful as if you had just died. / A word and a smile are then enough." It is a silence that has a peculiar meaning for the Christian, because it is the natural realm of divine contemplation, which would have purified the hearts of men in time.[17]

Putting Prieto Celi's hyperbolic style aside, one notices his emphasis on the need for silence regarding past violence during a period of transitional justice. Attention must be paid to his peculiar dialectic between truth and silence. His frequent allusions to Neruda's "Poem 15" are instructive: "Me gustas cuando callas *porque estás como ausente*. / Distante y dolorosa *como si hubieras muerto*" ("I like you when you are silent *because you look as if you were absent*. / Distant and painful *as if you had just died*."). Silence in response to tragedy conveys the sensation of its absence.

Ultimately, Prieto Celi thinks that the Peruvian Church and society should not explore their potential liability during the period of violence. For him, the CVR's public recuperation of memory is a "scandal." He says Catholic clergy should not have subscribed to the final report of the CVR. Such an approach is, in his view, "a frontal outrage against the Church."[18] This view is actually contrary to the position taken on memory and injustice by John Paul II in *Memoria y reconciliación*. Prieto Celi's book presents itself as offering the "balm of truth, justice and clarity, so that public opinion can get its normal spiritual health back."[19] However, *El Trigo y la Cizaña* does nothing of the sort. It is, rather, a deliberately confrontational text designed to undermine the CVR. Later in this volume, Barry Sullivan offers a chapter on secrecy and access to information that touches on the Church's handling of the clerical sexual abuse crisis in the United States. Comparative notes can be made between the divisions within the United States Church on that crisis and the Church divisions over the CVR.

Gustavo Gutiérrez and the Need to Unbury the Truth

Many Catholics have publicly rejected the positions of oblivion and silence about past social and political injustices. Among them is theologian

Gustavo Gutiérrez, a strong defender of memory for the sake of transitional justice.

As noted in Soledad Escalante's chapter, Gutiérrez is most widely known as one of the principle architects of liberation theology. This theology focuses a commitment to justice for the poor as the way to build the Kingdom of God. The poor are those who have been put aside by the powerful. The poor experience socio-economic, cultural, and sexual discrimination and are deemed socially insignificant and made subject to violence.

Less than two months after the delivery of the CVR's final report to the state's representatives, Gutiérrez published *Desenterrar la verdad*.[20] Here, Gutiérrez emphasizes the moral imperative "to seek the truth under the ground, covered by bushes of guilty amnesia, lies turned into currency and disenchanted indifference."[21] The metaphor of subterranean light is revealing. It is an allusion to the necessity of bringing the real facts about violence to light, such as the facts about the mass graves in Peru, some identified and opened while others remain closed.

Gutiérrez focuses not only on the violence but also on the deep social inequity behind the armed conflict. "Much of what happened," Gutiérrez points out, "would not have taken place if a large part of Peruvian society had not found itself, for a long time, trapped in the nation's basement."[22] Gutiérrez emphasizes that violence is not inevitable. Unlike natural catastrophes, violence is an action performed by a human being that has the potential to be prevented.[23] Political philosopher Judith N. Shklar has pointed out a similar distinction between misfortunes and injustices.[24]

According to Gutiérrez, it is pointless to call for reconciliation without taking care of memory and without doing the work of justice. While the CVR's final report was being prepared, many public figures called for the amnesty of police and army members implicated in crimes against humanity. From Gutiérrez's perspective, reconciliation via amnesty is empty. Amnesty keeps the wounds open and the secret mass graves closed. Silence and the suspension of justice are alien to the Christian attitude, since *ágape* implies both empathic projection and just action. The Christian attitude also assumes the mantle of the prophet, a mantle that calls for criticism of violence and abuse of power. Gutiérrez writes:

> In the style of James and for a better grasp of the prophetic text [Isaiah], we can say: "Beware those who introduce themselves to the God of justice and mercy with dried eyes!," because they didn't care to share their time, their concern and their feelings with those who saw their own

dignity as humans and as children of God trampled upon, with those
who have suffered in silence and oblivion.[25]

This prophetic legacy requires the biblical virtue of *parrhesía*—the disposition to tell the truth, even in extremely adverse circumstances. Biblical
examples include John the Baptist before King Herod and Jesus before
Pontius Pilate.

The CVR's reconciliation process is a long and demanding attempt to
repair the social tissue damaged by violence. Such repair involves working
on memory, making efforts toward reparations for victims, and building
justice for the future. In the words of the CVR:

> The CVR conceives of reconciliation as the reestablishment and refur-
> bishment of the fundamental links among all Peruvian people, links
> that had been voluntarily broken or deteriorated in recent decades due
> to the emergence of a violent conflict initiated by the Peruvian Com-
> munist Party, *Sendero Luminoso, in the heart of a society severely affected
> by a crisis.* The reconciliation process *is possible and is necessary* because
> of the unveiling of the true events that took place in those years—
> concerning both the records of violent acts and the explanations of
> their underlying motivations—and because of the repairing and sanc-
> tioning actions of justice.[26]

Gutiérrez believes that both the process and findings of the CVR have
contributed to the reconciliation process in Peru. In his view, "unburying
the country's truth from the truth of these two horrific decades, the CVR
reveals the evils to which we consistently used to have our eyes closed and
poses the idea of looking beyond to gain better insight into the road ahead
we need to walk."[27] After decades of neglect and suffering, the poor were
given a space by the CVR to bring out their testimonies and pleas for
justice.

Final Considerations: Prophecy against Voluntary Blindness

The Peruvian Church stands at a crossroads in view of the armed conflicts
of the 1980s and 1990s. Either the Church can respond to the prophetic
imperative, an imperative for truth, or it can take the stance of silence,
submitting to those in power who would want to block the road to justice
and reconciliation. There is no third alternative.

> From there [i.e., the prophetic imperative] stems the courage of a
> Church that resembles Mother Mary, faithful, poor, yet standing by
> the crucified of history. In spite of the fact that our two bishops don't

seem to conceive of this kind of Church, many of us try to do just that, to support and to be side by side with the innocent and the victims of violence. To do that, I believe, is our strength and our weakness without any pretensions.[28]

This quote comes from Carlos Flores Lizana, a young ex-Jesuit who undertook pastoral work in Ayacucho, the epicenter of the armed conflict in Peru. He wrote these lines on the anniversary of his priestly ordination and at a time when he discovered there was a price on his head because he had become an inconvenient figure in the eyes of the armed forces. Flores's 2004 book *Diario de vida y muerte: Memorias para recuperar humanidad* (*A Diary of Life and Death: Memories for Recuperating Humanity*) is a personal recounting of the nightmare that the people of Ayacucho endured. His words are harsh, something to be read from the perspective of *parresía*. He does not hesitate to confront clerical authorities who "want an oppressed, silent Church in favor of impunity."[29] He writes:

Their silence makes them complicit because it enables both sides to kill human beings every day, many of them Christians, sons of the Church. Their human poverty keeps them from seeing where they should be and how they should act as the Church of Jesus Christ.[30]

The heads of the Church hierarchy, according to the Flores, "become pawns in a larger game when they lose their positions as prophets and brothers . . . once they become 'authorities' and part of the power system, therefore [becoming] defenders of that system."[31]

Mrs. Angélica told me that she looked all over the place for her missing son, who remains among the "disappeared" up to this day. In the beginning, she could not stand the sight of such human carnage, but little by little she ended up getting used to seeing and smelling all that horror. . . . She told me that she addressed the bishop many times [in the first half of the 1980s], but she was not paid attention to; on the contrary, he accused her, and other people who approached him, of treachery, saying, "You could also be a Senderista, a terrorist—your sons might as well have been one of them . . . . how can I know if you are not one of them, too?"[32]

Flores's claims are powerful. It has been said that God's people were caught in the crossfire between the guns of terrorist fanatics and the guns of corrupt military officers during the years of armed conflict.

I am terribly hurt and mortified by the weight of these crimes being committed. What to do, God, in the middle of this complicit silence?

For myself, I believe that silence has many manifestations, and I think I will write something about it so that people can understand that there are many kinds of silence, that of God, that of the innocents who demand justice. There is the complicit silence of the cowards who should speak out but don't; while I write this, I am thinking of our Church, and most specifically, the bishops, who will someday be judged for their silence.[33]

Silence constitutes an expression of passive injustice, a giving up on what a citizen and a Christian should do. Giving in to violence and the suppression of memory are transgressions against civic courage and the practice of *ágape*. The attitudes of many lay and religious conservatives in Peru may remind us of the voluntary blindness portrayed in ancient Greek tragedies: the characters do not wish to watch what they *should* watch. Keeping silent in the face of innocent suffering is equivalent to granting death a definitive victory over life. This is a position to which a Christian, as one who believes in the resurrection, should not consent. Recovering the memory of injustice constitutes a necessary condition for the defense of life in times of darkness and sorrow.

NOTES

1. The author thanks César Mendoza L. for assistance with the English translation of this chapter.

2. Johann Baptist Metz, "El futuro a la luz de la Pasión," *Concilium* 76 (1972): 321.

3. Tzvetan Todorov, *Los abusos de la memoria* (Barcelona: Paidós, 2000), 15–16.

4. Paul Ricoeur, "El olvido en el horizonte de la prescripción," in *Academia Universal de las Culturas ¿Por Qué recordar?*, ed. Françoise Barret-Ducrocq (Buenos Aires: Gránica, 2002), 74.

5. In line with Ricoeur's reflections, Xabier Etxeberria develops a lucid, detailed analysis of various modes of ethical oblivion and forgetfulness in his book *El reto de los derechos humanos* (Santander, Spain: Sal Terrae, 1994).

6. Comisión de la Verdad y Reconciliación, *Informe Final (I)* (Lima: UNMSM–PUCP, 2004), 30.

7. In the specific case of the Catholic Church, the labor undertaken by the Episcopal Commission of Social Action (Comisión Episcopal de Acción Social—CEAS) and other organizations committed to the promotion of peace cannot be stressed enough.

8. Another example is the case of Father Carlos Schmidt. He was the head of the Office of Social Action in the archdiocese of Ayacucho, which fulfilled an important role in the areas of medical attention for the victims of

violence and human rights defense. His offices were closed down under "higher orders." See Comisión de la Verdad y Reconciliación, *Informe Final de la Comisión de la Verdad y Reconciliación (III)*, 292.

9. De Maestre and Cortés were early nineteenth–century conservative Catholic political thinkers opposed to post-French Revolution emergence of claims to universal rights and civil liberties. See Bela Menczer, *Catholic Political Thought 1789–1848* (Notre Dame, IN: University of Notre Dame Press, 1962).

10. Fernán Altuve-Febres Lores, *Democracia fuerte* (Lima: Quinto Reino, 2006), 74.

11. Ibid.

12. Ibid., 163.

13. Ibid., 165.

14. Ibid., 165. Emphasis added.

15. See Federico Prieto Celi, *El trigo y la cizaña. Radiografía de una conjura contra el Cardenal Cipriani* (Lima: [s.n.], 2007).

16. Ibid., 106.

17. Ibid., 81. Emphasis added.

18. Ibid.

19. Ibid.

20. English title: *Unburying the Truth*.

21. See Gustavo Gutiérrez, "Desenterrar la verdad," *Páginas* 183 (2003): 6.

22. Ibid.

23. See Gustavo Gutiérrez, "Pobreza y teología," *Páginas* 191 (2005): 14.

24. See Judith N. Shklar, *The Faces of Injustice* (New Haven, CT: Yale University Press, 1988).

25. Gutiérrez, "Desenterrar la verdad," 13.

26. Comisión de la Verdad y Reconciliación, *Informe Final (I)* (Lima: UNMSM–PUCP, 2004), 63. Emphasis added.

27. Gutiérrez, "Desenterrar la verdad," 13.

28. Carlos Flores Lizana, *Diario de vida y muerte. Memorias para recuperar humanidad* (Cusco, Peru: CADEP / CBC, 2004), 272.

29. Ibid., 270.

30. Ibid.

31. Ibid., 306.

32. Ibid., 219.

33. Ibid., 196.

The Catholic Church, Indigenous Rights, and the Environment in the Peruvian Amazon Region

Oscar A. Espinosa

In recent years, there have been signs of a renewed and more intimate relationship between the Catholic Church and the indigenous movement in the Amazon region of Peru. After almost two decades of little public activity, the Amazonian bishops have explicitly expressed their concern for, and solidarity with, the claims of indigenous persons to both their land and rights.

This chapter examines the public declarations of the Amazonian bishops in defense of indigenous rights and the environment. These declarations evolved in a new historical context in Peru marked by two opposing forces: the aggressive expansion of large enterprises in the Peruvian Amazon region under the government of President Alan García (2006–2011) and a growing concern in both the Catholic Church and the global community regarding the rights of indigenous persons and the environment.

The Amazonian Bishops' Renewed Meetings

The Catholic Church in the Amazon region of Peru changed after 1981. Between 1971 and 1980, the nine bishops of the Peruvian Amazon region had organized five regional assemblies and made several public statements regarding indigenous rights and adequate state policies regarding indigenous peoples. After 1981, the only regular meetings among the Amazonian bishops were meetings of *Centro Amazónico de Antropología y Aplicación Práctica* (CAAAP), a nongovernmental organization created and supervised by the bishops of the Peruvian Amazon region. While this became the new normal, some Amazonian bishops felt a need to meet among themselves, outside CAAAP, to freely discuss the pastoral issues unique to their region. In June 2006, the Amazonian bishops began meeting twice a year, in addition to their annual CAAAP meeting.

At this time, the bishops also renewed their support of the Pastoral Nativa, an umbrella organization for missionaries of all religious orders who work with indigenous peoples.[1] The support of Monsignor Gerardo Zerdin has been particularly important for this group. Before ordination as bishop, Gerardo Zerdin was a Franciscan missionary from Croatia working with indigenous communities in the Amazon region. His testimony and experience have given new hope to the older generation of missionaries and has encouraged younger missionaries to engage more fully in the lives of the indigenous peoples. Other bishops, especially Monsignor Juan Luis Martin and Monsignor José Luis Astigarraga, have also been active in the defense of human and indigenous rights for many years and have played an important role for their younger colleagues.

Most of these meetings of the Amazonian bishops since 2006 have ended with official public statements intended to inform journalists, academics, and politicians who are engaged in the political events affecting the Amazonian environment and indigenous rights. Of particular importance have been the public statements of February 2008, August 2008, May 2009, and February 2011.

Official Support from Aparecida

The situation of indigenous peoples was a controversial issue during the 2007 Latin American Bishop's Conference in Aparecida, Brazil. Pope Benedict XVI's inaugural speech at this conference offended the indigenous peoples because he neglected to mention the past actions of the Church in dominating and harming the indigenous peoples and cultures of the Americas. One Brazilian indigenous leader from the Amazon region, Jecinaldo Satere Mawé, described the pope's speech as "arrogant and disrespectful."[2] Some Catholics feared that Benedict's attitude would reverse Pope John Paul II's efforts at forgiveness for the Church's historical mistakes in the Americas. Soon after delivering this speech, Pope Benedict

XVI tried to rectify his statements by noting the ambiguity of evangelization of Latin America. However, he never directly acknowledged the Catholic Church's responsibility for harm to indigenous peoples of this continent. As he stated:

> Certainly, the memory of a glorious past cannot ignore the shadows that accompany the work of evangelization of the Latin American Continent: it is not possible, in fact, to forget the suffering and the injustice inflicted by colonizers on the indigenous populations, whose fundamental human rights were often trampled. But the obligation to recall such unjustifiable crimes—crimes, however, already condemned at the time by missionaries like Bartolomé de Las Casas and by theologians like Francisco de Vitoria of the University of Salamanca—must not prevent noting with gratitude the wonderful works accomplished by divine grace among those populations in the course of these centuries.[3]

The final document of the Aparecida conference also created controversy due to censorship changes in the section on indigenous peoples made by the committee responsible for the final redaction of the text. According to Margaret Hebblethwaite:

> A section on the indigenous suffered radical cuts, including the removal of the terms "indigenous protagonism," "their cultural symbols," "indigenous theological reflection" and "Indian Theology." The sentence, "It is urgently necessary to push forward with more dynamism the inculturation of the Church, of her ministers, of the liturgy and of indigenous theological reflection," was changed to, "We view with hope the process of inculturation discerned in the light of the Magisterium." Cardinal William Levada, the Prefect of the Congregation for the Doctrine of the Faith, is reported to have objected to an attempt by seven bishops' conferences to restore the term "Indian Theology" because the status of this theology was not yet clear.[4]

In spite of these controversies, the conference's final document reaffirmed the Church's commitment to the defense of indigenous rights and the environment in the Amazon region. As a result, positive references to Aparecida have occurred in nearly every Amazonian bishops' public statement since 2008.

The Indigenous Mobilizations of 2007 and 2008

In February 2008, the Amazonian bishops published in major Peruvian newspapers the first of a new series of public statements regarding the situation of indigenous peoples. This occurred just after the annual meeting of the Pastoral Nativa. At this meeting bishops, priests, religious women, and lay indigenous Catholics discussed the impact of the government's new regressive decrees regarding indigenous people and the environment in the Peruvian Amazon region.[5] This was the first meeting of the Pastoral Nativa after the Aparecida conference and the first meeting after the United Nations General Assembly approved the Declaration on the Rights of Indigenous Peoples in September 2007. As a result, the bishops were in a strong position to support the causes of indigenous rights and the environment in the Amazon.

At the February 2008 meeting, the bishops expressed their concern over the economic investment of large timber, mining, and oil companies in the Amazon and the legal decrees proposed of the García administration in support of these companies. The people of Amazonia sarcastically called one of these legal decrees (number 840) the "Law of the Jungle" because it affected the Amazon jungle and supported the exploitation of the forests by large corporations while expelling the indigenous and poor peasant communities from their lands. The bishops' document that emerged from the February 2008 meeting supported criticism of this decree and demanded that indigenous people be consulted in all decisions concerning the development of the Amazon region.

By the time the bishops published their Aparecida document, the indigenous communities had already begun a protest against the proposed governmental decrees. Indigenous mobilization spread rapidly throughout the Peruvian Amazon region. In August 2008, indigenous organizations stepped up their protests in the provinces of Condorcanqui and Datém del Marañón. The social movements disrupted commerce by cutting off the main roads and rivers in the region. This affected the circulation of agricultural products and manufactured goods, as well as people traveling to and from other regions. Thousands of people of all ages left their communities and traveled several hours by river to protest the government, making this the largest mobilization effort of indigenous people in the history of Peru.[6]

After more than two weeks of indigenous protest, the government agreed to abrogate two decrees (numbers 1015 and 1073) and promised to review other controversial decrees. The Peruvian National Congress established a special committee to study all recent decrees related to indigenous rights and the environment in order to evaluate their constitutionality and to consider if they violated indigenous rights.

On August 27, 2008, the Amazonian bishops published a new declaration expressing their concerns regarding the indiscriminate abuse of natural resources from the Amazon region and the occupation of indigenous territories by different types of enterprises.[7] Motivated by the principles of inclusive democracy and the framework of international law regarding indigenous rights, the bishops urged the government to dialogue with the indigenous peoples.

In President García's view, the indigenous peoples were "opposed to progress." Of course, this was "progress" as defined by the García government, without input from the indigenous people.[8] In their August 2008 declaration, the bishops opposed this viewpoint and insisted that indigenous peoples were open to responsible development. It was the Peruvian state and its allied multinational corporations that did not offer a responsible vision of progress. The bishops explained what indigenous peoples mean by authentic progress: the improvement of the quality of life, access to bilingual and intercultural education, access to intercultural health services, support for cultural identity, and respect for individual and collective rights.

In reference to the questionable legislative decrees passed by the García administration, the bishops made several suggestions that were consistent with those made by CAAAP's lawyers and other experts.[9] The bishops concluded their declaration by insisting that the government take a more comprehensive view toward national development, one not limited to macroeconomic statistics. The bishops urged the government to:

> Pursue an alternative development model, one that is comprehensive and communal, based on an ethics that includes responsibility for an authentic natural and human ecology, which is based on the gospel of justice, solidarity, and the universal destination of goods . . . and therefore, support our peasants and native peoples to organize themselves in order to achieve their just demands.[10]

The Indigenous Mobilizations of 2009

In December 2008, Peru's Special Commission of Congress presented its final report on the constitutionality of the Garcia government's decrees regarding the Amazon region. The final report stated that the decrees were unconstitutional and recommended their abrogation. Despite these recommendations, the president of Congress postponed all discussions until February 2009. When February 2009 arrived, the president of Congress did not put the matter on the congressional agenda.

Indigenous organizations wrote formal letters to the president of Congress and the prime minister, reminding them of the promises made to discuss the abrogation of the decrees. On April 9, 2009, the indigenous communities began a new period of mobilization after having received no acknowledgment of their letters. Once again, the region where the mobilization was most prominent was the Condorcanqui province. On May 5, 2009, the Amazonian bishops published another declaration.[11]

The May 2009 declaration began by proclaiming the cultural richness and biodiversity of the Amazon region and the responsibility all people have for protecting it. The bishops once more quoted the Aparecida document: "As prophets of life we want to insist that the interests of economic groups that irrationally demolish sources of life are not to prevail in dealing with natural resources, at the cost of whole nations and of humankind itself."[12] Two paragraphs followed this statement in which the bishops criticized the Peruvian state for permitting the environmental destruction of the Amazon region through deforestation and contamination of rivers. The Amazonian bishops also denounced the government's attempts to appropriate indigenous lands and resources through unjust decrees.

At the end of the declaration, the Amazonian bishops called on the García administration and the National Congress to engage in a true dialogue with the indigenous people. The bishops also urged the media to report accurate information about what was happening in the Peruvian Amazon. Finally, they repeated their call for the government to abrogate decrees that infringe upon the rights of the indigenous people and the environment.

Prime Minister Yehude Simon, Congressional President Javier Velásquez, and President García ignored the bishops' requests and remained unwilling to discuss the disputed decrees. They also ignored the protests of the indigenous peoples, hoping that by this action the mainstream national media would give little coverage to the protests. Despite this, indigenous protests and further mobilization efforts continued in different parts of the Peruvian Amazon region.

Early in the morning of June 5, 2009, police forces in Bagua released tear gas from helicopters and began shooting at protestors, despite the efforts of protestors to broker a negotiation with the government the night before. By the end of the day, more than thirty people were killed, including several police officers. A larger number of people were either wounded or missing. After these events, the indigenous Awajún and Wampís people who participated in the protests fled to the forests to hide. Eventually they went back to their own communities.

In other parts of the Amazon region, however, indigenous communities continued their protests. Finally, Prime Minister Simon met with a large group of indigenous representatives in Peru's central Amazon region and officially announced the overturning of two more legislative decrees (numbers 1064 and 1090). President García, however, maintained a bellicose demeanor toward the indigenous people. In a press conference held on the same day as the Bagua incidents, García declared that indigenous people did not deserve being treated as "first-class citizens."[13]

The García administration began actively persecuting indigenous leaders, independent journalists, media outlets, and Catholic missionaries. Alberto Pizango, a Shawi indigenous leader and president of the *Asociación Interétnica de Desarrollo de la Selva Peruana* (Interethnic Development Association of the Peruvian Rainforest, AIDESEP), the largest and most important Amazonian indigenous organization in Peru, was forced to flee the country. The brothers Saúl and Cervando Puerta, both Awajún leaders, were also forced to flee. The independent radio station in Bagua, La Voz de Bagua (Bagua's Voice), was forced to close down. The radio and TV stations of the Yurimaguas Vicariate (Radio and TV "Oriente") were accused of promoting violent acts. The bishop of Yurimaguas, Monsignor Astigarraga, was accused of inciting the indigenous peoples to violence. Two foreign-born missionaries were threatened with expulsion from Peru: Father Mario Bartolini, an Italian Passionist who was defending poor peasants in Yurimaguas, and Brother Paul McAuley, a British Christian Brother who was engaged in the Red Ambiental Loretana (the Environment Network of Loreto) in Iquitos.[14]

The Peruvian Bishops' Conference Steps In

After the tragic events in Bagua, the Peruvian Bishops' Conference took a special interest in the situation of the Amazon region. Unlike the divided Church response to the truth and reconciliation report on violence in Peru, as discussed in Gonzalo Gamio's chapter in this volume, the bishops were united in their support of the Amazonian peoples. Prior to these events, the general opinion of the conference was that what happened in the Amazon region was the concern of the Amazonian bishops alone. However, the national attention given to indigenous mobilization efforts in 2008 and 2009 brought to the fore of Peruvian society, and therefore the Peruvian Catholic Church, the issues and challenges facing the Amazon region. As the struggles of the indigenous Amazon people captured national attention, the president of the Peruvian Bishops' Conference, Monsignor Cabrejos, became increasingly involved in their struggle.[15]

After a special assembly in August 2009, the Peruvian Bishops' Conference published a statement on the tragedy in Bagua. The bishops decried the government's violent response to the indigenous protests and urged the government to take responsibility for the terrible events that unfolded there. To illustrate the horror of this event, the bishops cited a Wampís woman who exclaimed "¡Nos hemos matado entre hermanos!" ("We are brothers murdering brothers"). The bishops invited the whole country to reconciliation and mutual understanding and urged political authorities to recognize the just claims of the indigenous people. They concluded their statement with a quote from Pope Benedict XVI's encyclical letter *Caritas in veritate*, which invited everyone to work together toward the common good.[16]

Despite these supportive statements, the Bishops' Conference statement seemed more conciliatory in tone toward the Peruvian government and more critical of the indigenous people than the earlier declarations made by the Amazonian bishops. The fact that violence occurred on both sides during the confrontation in Bagua appeared to temper the bishops' criticism of the government and support for the indigenous people. The insinuation that the indigenous people instigated violence, however, does not correlate with the facts of what actually happened. The only violence used by the indigenous peoples came in response to attacks by the police. It is true that the protestors' violence was sometimes severe. The protestors were responsible for the deaths of several police officers. While these acts are rightfully condemned, it is important to understand them in the context of Awajún culture. When the police began their attack, the Awajún people assumed they were in a state of war. In war, the cultural norm of the Awajún is to defend the people by any means necessary. Even now, years after the Bagua incidents, many Awajún people do not understand why they were attacked by their own government, their own people. According to their culture, one can only attack an enemy, never one of your own.[17]

In July 2010, the Peruvian Bishops' Conference published a second declaration regarding the continuing conflict in the Amazon region. In this instance, the declaration does not begin by quoting Pope Benedict XVI or Aparecida, but rather it turns to the Second Vatican Council and the writings of Pope Paul VI. This fact may seem unimportant to one who is not familiar with internal politics and tensions within the Catholic Church. At least in Peru, the more conservative bishops of the past few decades have usually avoided appealing to Vatican II documents, preferring to quote in their declarations only the documents and/or speeches put forth since the beginning of the pontificate of Pope John Paul II. These quotes, however, mark a different tone and a change in attitude from previous declarations—for example, the declaration made one year before, in 2009. What happened in the Peruvian Church to explain such changes? One fact that likely accounts for this difference in tone is that the July 2010 declaration by the Bishops' Conference was prepared by Monsignor Cabrejos, who has expressed openly his commitment to the defense of human rights and of the environment.

Quoting first from *Gaudium et spes*, the declaration refers to the rights of citizens to defend themselves against abuse from political authorities.[18] The declaration also quotes from *Evangelii nuntiandi*, stating the Catholic Church's principles of justice, liberation, and peace.[19] Only after these initial paragraphs do the bishops quote from the Aparecida document and Pope Benedict XVI. The quote from Aparecida is a small phrase in which the bishops express their preferential option for the poor and support for human liberation. The quote the document takes from Pope Benedict XVI is itself a quote from Pope John Paul II, in which he relates world peace and the promotion of an ecological consciousness:

> John Paul II's appeal is even more pressing today, in the face of signs of a growing crisis that it would be irresponsible not to take seriously. Can we remain indifferent before the problems associated with such realities as . . . the pollution of rivers and aquifers, the loss of biodiversity? . . . Can we remain impassive in the face of actual and potential conflicts involving access to natural resources? All these are issues with a profound impact on the exercise of human rights, such as the right to life, food, health and development.[20]

Subsequent paragraphs in the July 2010 declaration explain the evangelical reasons for the arrival of missionaries to the Amazon region over five hundred years ago. It further explained the continued value of the Amazonian apostolic vicariates[21] for the indigenous people: "to promote their culture, improve their health and education, and take care of nature, which is the work of God, the Creator."[22] And once again, the declaration quotes the Aparecida document:

> Hence, as prophets of life we want to insist that the interests of economic groups that irrationally demolish sources of life are not to prevail in dealing with natural resources, at the cost of whole nations and of humankind itself. The generations that succeed us are entitled to receive an inhabitable world, not a planet with polluted air.[23]

The remaining paragraphs of the declaration recognize the important role played by the Amazonian bishops, the Peruvian Bishops' Conference, the Comisión Episcopal de Acción Social (Episcopal Commission for Social Action), and CAAAP in the negotiations between indigenous communities and the Peruvian state. The declaration even makes explicit reference to the letter written by the Amazonian bishops to President García on March 5, 2010, in which they demanded the president reopen avenues for honest and constructive dialogue with indigenous people.

In January 2011, the Peruvian government passed two decrees of urgency to eliminate the requirement of making social and environmental impact assessments before starting major building projects, including the construction of hydroelectric dams in the Amazon region. These decrees met strong opposition from indigenous organizations and several civil organizations. In a declaration made on February 4, 2011, the Amazonian bishops and the president of the Peruvian Bishops' Conference called for an end to these destructive decrees.

This declaration begins by expressing the bishops' concern over the new decrees. Quoting Aparecida, it states that the Catholic Church cannot accept policies that will destroy natural resources and thus lead to misery and desolation.[24] Such callous policies had spawned over two hundred social protests in Peru between the end of 2010 and the beginning of 2011. The declaration stressed that such conflicts further harm the poorest people. The bishops further claim, "water, air, earth, are essential elements of nature that God has generously given to us."[25] Quoting from Pope Paul VI, the bishops insist that all "development requires respect for the earth and its peoples."[26] The bishops end the declaration by quoting Pope Benedict XVI: "If you want to cultivate peace, protect creation."[27]

This declaration was widely referenced in the media and was supported by indigenous organizations and national and international NGOs. As a result of this pressure, the García administration was forced to modify the decrees. Here, again, evidence is shown for the role Catholic social teaching can play in improving social institutions when communicated through the official channels of the Church. Several authors in this volume make this point for Lithuania (Streikus), Indonesia (Yudianti), and the United States (O'Neill).

Conclusion

Despite their years of silence, the Amazonian bishops have become active supporters of the indigenous people. They have taken the indigenous peoples' struggles as their own and have insisted that indigenous rights be respected and that the environment within which they live be protected. This decision has brought government hostility and persecution to many bishops, priests, religious women, and laypeople in the Church. Father

Mario Bartolini and Brother Paul McAuley were accused of conspiracy and faced expulsion from Peru. Two bishops have also faced government persecution and are still facing charges of conspiracy at courts of law: Monsignor Astigarraga for supporting the indigenous mobilizations of 2008 and 2009 and Monsignor Paco Gonzales for supporting indigenous mobilizations in the Madre de Dios region. In September 2011, the Amazonian bishops expressed solidarity with Monsignor Gonzales in a formal declaration.

At the same time, the Amazonian bishops have been criticized by other Peruvian bishops. They have been accused of being too politically active, of replacing the teachings of the Gospel with environmental and or legal preoccupations. They have been asked by some of their brother bishops to leave these matters of indigenous rights and environmental protection to specialists and dedicate themselves to religious duties.[28] The Amazonian bishops see their commitment to indigenous rights and environmental protection as part of their religious duty. From a Christian point of view, these criticisms and others from governments and corporations may be interpreted in a positive manner: followers of Christ are usually misunderstood and persecuted by the powerful. It can be a sign that one is going down the right path with Christ.

NOTES

1. The Pastoral Nativa typically meets every year in January or February.

2. Margaret Hebblethwaite, "Opinions Divided over Pope's Gaffes in Brazil," *National Catholic Reporter*, June 8, 2007.

3. Ian Fisher, "Pope Softens Remarks on Conversion of Natives," *New York Times*, May 23, 2007.

4. See Aparecida, *Concluding Document of the Fifth General Conference of the Latin American and Caribbean Bishops' Conferences* (2007) at http://www .celam.org/aparecida/Ingles.pdf, and Margaret Hebblethwaite, "Speaking for the Church in a New Language," *The Tablet*, June 9, 2007.

5. In 2007 and 2008, the Garcia administration passed a series of legislative decrees that seriously affected indigenous rights in Peru and were later found unconstitutional. These legislative decrees concerned such matters as private investments for timber exploitation and agro-forestry in the Amazon region and promoting private enterprises in irrigation projects, land use, and water policy. For more detailed analyses of these decrees, see CAAAP, *Informe Legal sobre los decretos legislativos 1090, 1064, 1080, 1081 y 1089. Elaborado por algunos integrantes de la Comisión Consultiva de la Comisión de Pueblos Andinos, Amazónicos, Afroperuanos, Ambiente y Ecología del Congreso de la República*, at

http://www.caaap.org.pe/archivos/Comision_Consultiva_Informe-1
_DecretosLegislativos_Nov2008.pdf.

6. There were protests in Yurimaguas and Iquitos (January 2008), Pucallpa (March and June 2008), Lima (April 2008), Puerto Maldonado (July 2008), and Condorcanqui, Datém del Marañón, and the Urubamba Valley (August 2008). For a more detailed description of the 2008 and 2009 indigenous mobilizations in the Peruvian Amazon region and their social and political impact in Peruvian society, see Oscar Espinosa, "¿Salvajes opuestos al progreso?: proximaciones históricas y antropológicas a las movilizaciones indígenas en la Amazonía peruana," *Revista Anthropológica* 27 (2009): 123–68.

7. Obispos de la Amazonía Peruana, "Comunicado de los Obispos de la Selva Peruana," August 27, 2008.

8. Alan García Pérez, "El síndrome del perro del hortelano," *El Comercio*, October 28, 2007. In recent years the discussion about the indigenous concept of *vivir bien* (the good life) brings into question modern ideas of progress and development. For a more detailed discussion of what the indigenous peoples of the Amazon region view and desire as proper development, see Evaristo Nugkuag, "Futuro de la Amazonía. (Ponencia presentada por el Presidente de la COICA, Evaristo Nugkuag, ante las Naciones Unidas)," *IWGIA Bulletin* 9 (3–4): 3–16.

9. CAAAP, *Informe Legal.*

10. Aparecida, *Concluding Document*, no. 474.

11. Obispos de la Amazonía Peruana, "Pronunciamiento ante el paro de los pueblos amazónicos," May 5, 2009.

12. Aparecida, *Concluding Document*, no. 471.

13. In this press conference on June 5, 2009, President García said: "Ya está bueno. Estas personas no tienen corona, no son ciudadanos de primera clase. 400 mil nativos no pueden decirnos a 28 millones de peruanos: tú no tienes derecho de venir por aquí." The president's words at the press conference quickly circulated through different media outlets and most newspapers and radio and television news programs repeated them in the following days. See http://www.youtube.com/watch?v=3ekPeb6nMnw. "Alan García y los ciudadanos de primera clase-Bagua Perú," June 5, 2009, posted by Ricardo Marapí S. on June 9, 2009.

14. On these events, see Jorge Acevedo, "Libertad para unos, amenazas y restricciones para otros," Diario Pro & Contra, June 16, 2009 [unsigned article], "Cancelan residencia a Paul McAuley," July 2, 2010. During this period, over one hundred organizations and one thousand activists sent a letter to President García in order to stop persecution of indigenous leaders. See Lawrence Gist, "Peruvian Government Called Upon to Stop Persecution of Indigenous Leaders," examiner.com, August 11, 2009 at http://www

.examiner.com/article/peruvian-government-called-upon-to-stop-persecution
-of-indigenous-leaders.

15. Since the 2008 indigenous mobilization efforts, Monsignor Cabrejos expressed his concern and solidarity with the indigenous peoples. He played a crucial role for the two declarations of the Peruvian Bishops' Conference of 2009 and 2010 and included his signature on the declaration made by the Bishops of the Peruvian Amazonia in 2011. After the presentation of the Peruvian minister of justice at the United Nations forum explaining the tragic events of Bagua, Monsignor Cabrejos published a declaration questioning this official government presentation (August 6, 2009). A year later, he came back to insist on respect for indigenous rights and protection of the environment in his declaration *Nuestra patria, el Perú, es un don* (July 28, 2009).

16. The full quote from Pope Benedict XVI reads: "Awareness of God's undying love sustains us in our laborious and stimulating work for justice and the development of peoples, amid successes and failures, in the ceaseless pursuit of a just ordering of human affairs. God's love calls us to move beyond the limited and the ephemeral, it gives us the courage to continue seeking and working for the benefit of all, even if this cannot be achieved immediately and if what we are able to achieve, alongside political authorities and those working in the field of economics, is always less than we might wish. God gives us the strength to fight and to suffer for love of the common good, because he is our All, our greatest hope." Pope Benedict XVI, *Caritas in veritate*, no. 78.

17. The Awajún (also known as Aguaruna) share with the other Jivaroan peoples the same cultural traits related to war and the role of the warrior. See Michael F. Brown, *Una Paz Incierta: Historia y cultura de las comunidades Aguarunas frente al impacto de la Carretera Marginal* (Lima: Centro Amazónico de Antropología y Aplicación Práctica, 1984).

18. *Gaudium et spes*, no. 74, in Vatican Council II, *The Conciliar and Post Conciliar Documents*, ed. Austin Flannery, OP (Collegeville, MN: Liturgical Press, 1975).

19. *Evangelii nuntiandi*, no. 31, in Vatican Council II, *The Conciliar and Post Conciliar Documents*.

20. Benedict XVI, Message for the Celebration of the World Day of Peace, 1 January 2010.

21. An apostolic vicariate is one of the territorial jurisdictions through which the Catholic Church functions. It is usually established in regions considered "missionary territories." Once the Catholic Church is developed in these territories, the jurisdiction may be upgraded to a prelature, and then to a diocese, which is the most regular form of territorial jurisdiction within the Catholic Church. The head of an apostolic vicariate is also a bishop. In the Peruvian Amazon region there are eight apostolic vicariates and one apostolic

prelature. Therefore, there are nine Catholic bishops in the Peruvian Amazon region.

22. Conferencia Episcopal Peruana, *Rol de la Iglesia Católica en la Amazonia Peruana*, July 16, 2010.

23. Aparecida, *Concluding Document*, no. 471.

24. Presidente de la Conferencia Episcopal y Obispos de los Vicariatos Apostólicos de la Amazonía peruana, *Cuidar la casa de todos*, February 4, 2011.

25. Ibid.

26. Pope Paul VI, Encyclical Letter *Populorum Progressio* (1967), no. 20.

27. Benedict XVI, *World Day of Peace*.

28. Personal communication made by attendee at the Peruvian Bishops' Conference who wishes to remain anonymous.

Religion as a Political Factor
in Latin America: The Peruvian Case

Jorge Aragón Trelles

Research conducted in some Latin American countries has shown the existence of connections between self-reported levels of religious devoutness, church attendance, and specific political attitudes and orientations (e.g., trust in the government or satisfaction with the democracy). In light of this, the goal sought in this chapter is twofold. First, to contribute to a better understanding of the way religion can be considered as a political factor in Latin America. Second, through analyzing public opinion data, to provide an initial answer to the question as to whether Peru is a country where some religious beliefs and practices are associated with political perceptions and preferences.

Mainstream modernization and secularization theories suggesting a gradual decline of religion as an important individual and social experience have been challenged by the persistence of religious beliefs and practices in contemporary societies.[1] Furthermore, in recent years, religion has actually appeared as a powerful and sometimes decisive political force in several countries. The contemporary role of religion as an important political factor runs the spectrum from the rise of conservative, religiously oriented political groups to the impact of individual religious attitudes on political and electoral behaviors.[2] The earlier chapter in this volume by Russell Powell on Islam and politics shares this perspective on the inadequacy of the secularization thesis and the variety of ways in which religion affects political life.

In addition to historical instances where religion has played an important role in contemporary politics, there is also a theoretical argument for the importance of religion in studying politics. Christian Smith argues that religion is a system of beliefs and practices about the sacred thorough which meaning and direction are given to people's life experiences.[3] Similarly, Kenneth Wald and Allison Calhoun-Brown contend that humans can think in a sophisticated way about their place in the universe and consequently wonder about the meaning of life and the basis of ethical behavior.[4] If we accept that religion is an important source of meaning and direction for individuals, we should attend to the latent potential in religious beliefs and practices for shaping political attitudes and behaviors.

Religions also tend to develop in an institutional form. This means that a religious organization can have political interests, and they may also mobilize their members for social and political purposes. Several scholars have shown that religious organizations play an important role in civil society and that participation in religious organizations develops an individual's social capital (i.e., networks, norms, and social trust that facilitate coordination and cooperation for mutual benefit) and political capital (i.e., civic norms that support democratic governance and conventional political participation).[5] This mobilizing and educating role of religion for social and political action was clearly shown in the Indonesian case by Paulus Wiryono Priyotamtama in his earlier chapter and will be discussed by Bren Ortega Murphy in the case of the United States later in this volume.

Hence, there are many ways religion can be important in politics. As Daniel Levine points out, the challenge in making sense of religion in political life is to understand the precise mode of interaction between religion and politics in a given circumstance.[6] Harder still is making predictions about future relationships between religion and politics in a given community. It might seem unlikely, for example, that religion would be an important element for the development of democracy. John Anderson notes, however, that many scholars feel religion has played a marginal role in the process of nation-state democratization.[7]

To arrive at realistic expectations about the political role of religion, it is important to clarify the particular ways religion can become relevant in and to political life. There is significant scholarly consensus around three aspects of religion that are crucial for the study of politics: religious creeds, religious organizations, and social groups.[8] These three aspects may not capture all that occurs within a religion, but they do identify the central means through which religious people become involved in politics. It is also important to keep in mind that the political impact of religion can be relevant in some specific domains of society (e.g., core beliefs about politics, views about church-state relations, etc.) but not in others.

Religious creeds are the expressed beliefs, ideas, and ethical codes that are fundamental to a religious tradition. The emphasis here is on the content of religious teachings and the values the tradition encourages. Of course, it is not uncommon to find different interpretations of these fundamental teachings and values within a religious community. This is why Paul Freston warns that religious traditions should not be essentialized; the fluidity of interpretation makes it impossible to predict whether or not a religious community will be favorable to democratization.[9]

Regarding the role of religious organizations, it is important to note that religious communities are often organized, or institutionalized, in specific ways and, therefore, can be more or less hierarchical and more or less globalized. In all cases, religious leaders play a critical role in defining the official social and political orientations of their communities and deciding how to use their institutional resources. Again, religious communities as organizations and religious leaders will place demands on members, but there is no guarantee that the views and practices of individual members will always coincide with the official doctrine of the religious leadership.

Finally, religious experience implies the existence of believers who share a common status, a distinctive way of life, and regular social interaction. Members of a religious community share a collective experience and may come to develop a similar way of looking at the world. This dimension of religious experience is particularly important because it highlights how unintended effects can occur, such as the development of social capital among members or changes in gender relationships.[10] An undemocratic religious community may, for example, end up strengthening civil society and democracy.

Another way to approach the political impact of religion is to consider the direct or indirect influences religious organizations and practices can exert on civil society. Direct impact shows itself when religious organizations promote coordinated social and political actions. Two examples of such activity are, first, the involvement of Evangelical leaders and churches in backing congressional candidates from different mainstream political parties in Brazil since the 1980s and, second, the connection between grassroots organizations and the Catholic Church in several Latin American countries between the 1970s and 1980s. The indirect impact of religion can be seen in the social capital and individual political skills that religious participation can build.[11]

Religion and Politics in Latin America

To understand the role of religion as a political factor in contemporary Latin America, it is necessary to start by noting important changes in the religious landscape that have occurred in recent decades. First, there has been an important shift within the Catholic Church that has been experienced throughout Latin America. As Jeffrey Klaiber points out in the next chapter, the progressive nature of the Catholic Church during the 1960s and 1970s has been replaced today by a more conservative outlook. This shift is due to several factors. Many government decisions that have accompanied democratic transitions since the 1960s resulted in policies that challenged some of the traditional moral teachings of the Catholic Church. Many church leaders responded to this by adopting a more apolitical position, letting the new systems evolve without explicit direction. At the same time, Pope John Paul II carried out a conservative restoration of the Latin American episcopacy, assigning vacant positions to bishops and cardinals who were not sympathetic to either the political aspirations or the methods of popular Catholicism that had been earlier influenced by liberation theology.[12]

Alongside the decline of progressive Catholicism has been an unprecedented rise in Protestant Christianity in Latin America, specifically Evangelical Protestantism. There is no consensus on the exact numbers of Protestants in Latin America today. Some scholars claim the number has grown from a handful to 20 or 30 percent of the population. Other scholars think the number is closer to 10 percent. It is also worth noting that Evangelical Protestantism in Latin America is largely nationally run, institutionally fragmented and divided, and over-represented by poor, less-educated, and indigenous people. While the exact number is uncertain, it can be noted that the majority of these Evangelical Protestants in Latin America identify as Pentecostals. This unquestionable expansion has led several scholars to wonder about the political implications of this change in the religious landscape of Latin American countries.[13]

Despite the fact that Evangelical Protestants in Latin America do not show the political orientation of the Christian Right in the United States and have remained a diverse religious group, controversy still surrounds the political implications of their increasing numbers. To address this controversy with greater understanding of its political implications, more empirical research is needed.

Anthony Gill has begun research in this area.[14] He has found that Latin American Protestants and Catholics do not differ substantially in their political and economic preferences. According to Gill, age, gender, and socioeconomic status are more important variables in explaining people's political and economic preferences than religion. However, this does not mean that religious affiliation is unimportant. Similarly, findings in Brazil and Chile show that church attendance is highly correlated with participation in civic organizations. Church attendance is also linked favorably with trust in government in Mexico and Brazil. Also in Mexico and Chile, the more respondents consider God important in their lives, the more they will identify as political conservatives. Overall, Gill concludes that the religious effect on politics is based not on affiliation but rather upon one's degree of immersion in religious beliefs and practices. Gill also feels that studies of religious values should carefully consider the institutional and structural contexts at the local level.

In analyzing data from the Latinobarómetro (an annual public opinion survey that involves interviews in most Latin American countries) from the year 2000, focusing on the cases of Argentina and Chile, Eric Patterson classified respondents as devout Protestants, devout Catholics, not devout Protestants, and not devout Catholics. He addressed two questions: are members of one faith more likely to support democracy than members of another faith, and does the intensity of one's religious participation make a difference in their support for democracy? In the case of Chile, Patterson found that the most devout individuals, whether they were Catholic or Protestant, were more likely to trust others, be satisfied with democracy, and look positively on the civic culture of their fellow citizens. However, like Gill, he found that demographic variables (i.e., level of education and self-reported socioeconomic status) and political engagement variables (i.e., interest in politics and a sense of political efficacy) were stronger predictors of democratic attitudes. In the case of Argentina, he found that religious variables were not powerful predictors of democratic attitudes. Patterson warns, however, that these findings should not lead us to consider religion irrelevant to politics.[15]

Several points emerge from the works of Gill and Patterson on the relationship between religion and politics in Latin America. First, the intensity of one's religious experience is a more important indicator of political orientation than one's religious affiliation alone. Second, it is possible that the main effect of religion on politics is the role it plays in providing individuals with the experience of participating in an organization. It is widely known that mainline Protestant church organizations in the United States, for example, provide places for people to meet, foster informal social networks, develop leadership skills, inform people about public affairs, draw diverse people together, and encourage members to be actively involved in groups concerned with education, youth development, and human services.[16]

Research Design for Exploring Religion and Politics in Peru

The analysis of empirical data about the relationship between religion and politics in Latin America, especially at the micro or individual level, has been conducted in very few countries. This scarcity of empirical research poses serious limitations in our ability to make credible generalizations about the role of religion in Latin American politics. As a way to work against this limitation, I analyze empirical evidence from Peru, a case that has not been previously considered.

Specifically, I test hypotheses regarding the role of religion as a political factor using the results of a 2007 public opinion survey conducted monthly in Lima, Peru.[17] The sample size for this public opinion survey was 503 cases and all the interviews were conducted face to face in the month of February of that year. The sampling method was a random multiple-stage approach with a random selection of zones, blocks, and households. A final selection of interviewees was based on age and gender quotas.

The limitations of the data must be noted. The overall design of the survey was not tailored to address specific questions about the political role of religion. The purpose of the survey was to measure, on a monthly basis, public opinion trends about broad matters of political authority, political institutions, and current political events. The February survey did, however, include some basic questions about religious beliefs, attitudes, and practices. Some of the standard questions about the connection between religion and politics were included in this survey, but others were left out.[18] Specifically, there are questions about core religious beliefs, the frequency of attendance at religious services, the self-perception of one's level of religious commitment, and religious affiliation, but there are no questions about religious practices such as prayer outside of religious services or reading the Bible. There are also no questions about the role of religious institutions in providing answers to social, familial, or individual needs.

The survey questions regarding individual political perceptions and attitudes can be used to measure support for democracy, interest in politics, assessment of political representation, attitudes toward mandatory voting requirements, and attitudes toward the relationship between the president and Congress. This set of outcome variables covers not only some of the most standard individual political orientations (e.g., support for democratic institutions, interest in politics, the quality of political representation, etc.) but also some individual orientations that have been not been previously considered in research about the relationship between religion and politics (e.g., the preferred type of relationship between the president and Congress).

Building on previous research findings and information available in the 2007 Peruvian data, I developed the following hypotheses:

Hypothesis One (H1):Religious affiliation (i.e., Catholics versus Protestants) is not a significant determinant of individual political attitudes and orientations.

Hypothesis Two (H2): One's level of religious belief is a significant determinant of individual political attitudes and orientations.

Hypothesis Three (H3): One's level of individual religious devoutness is a significant determinant for individual political attitudes and orientations.

Accordingly, I have constructed different statistical models to account for each one of the main outcomes or dependent variables considered here:

Model One: The outcome or dependent variable is an index of support for democratic institutions that are based on three variables. Democracy is or is not possible without (a) political parties, (b) Congress, and (c) judiciary.[19]

Model Two: The outcome or dependent variable is the level of individual interest in politics.

Model Three: The outcome or dependent variable is an assessment of the quality of political representation provided by members of Congress.

Model Four: The outcome or dependent variable is the opinion about mandatory voting requirements.

Model Five: The outcome or dependent variable is the individual's preference on the relationship between the president and Congress (i.e., unconditional congressional support, critical congressional support, or congressional opposition to presidential initiatives).

Given the nature of the outcomes or dependent variables (categorical variables with either a nominal or ordinal scale), I use either logistic regressions or ordinal logistic regressions. A logistic regression provides an estimation of the effect of different explanatory variables on an outcome or dependent variable with a measurement scale composed by two unordered categories (e.g., thinking that voting should be mandatory or thinking that voting should not be mandatory). An ordinal logistic regression provides an estimation of the effect of different explanatory variables on outcomes or dependent variables with a measurement scale composed by a set of ordered categories (e.g., different levels of interest in politics: not interested at all, not very interested, somewhat interested, or very interested). The set of explanatory variables directly related to religion and individual religious experience includes:

1. An index of religious beliefs.
2. An index of religious commitment that includes the self-perception an individual has about the level of their religious devoutness or religious commitment, and frequency of attendance at religious services.[20]
3. Religious affiliation.

As control variables, I use the respondent's gender, age, and socio-economic level.

Findings and Discussion

In most logistic models, religious variables play a significant role in explaining different individual political perceptions, attitudes, and orientations. As such, it would be a mistake to neglect religion as a political factor in Latin American countries and, specifically, in Peru. However, the main challenge remains identifying and understanding patterns in the way religion shapes political outlooks and behaviors in this region of the world.

Regarding support for democratic institutions, Table 1 shows that a respondent's individual socioeconomic level is the only variable that has a significant effect (p-value 0.001). Therefore, there is significant evidence that individuals from the highest socioeconomic levels have a higher probability of supporting key democratic institutions. No other explanatory variable, religious or non-religious, is as significant a predictor of an institutionalized version of democracy (i.e., a democracy with political parties, Congress, and judiciary). Additionally, religion is not as significant a factor for supporting the idea of democracy without the conviction that having

TABLE 1. Support for Institutional Democracy

		Estimate	Std. Error	Wald	df	Sig.	95% Confidence Interval Lower Bound	Upper Bound
Threshold	[Support = 0]	-.183	.720	.064	1	.800	-1.593	1.228
	[Support = 1]	.640	.721	.789	1	.375	-.772	2.052
	[Support = 2]	1.792	.730	6.024	1	.014	.361	3.224
Location	Religious Beliefs	-.010	.060	.030	1	.863	-.128	.107
	Age	-.010	.007	2.048	1	.152	-.023	.004
	Gender	.275	.198	1.938	1	.164	-.112	.662
	Socioeconomic level	-.288	.087	11.049	1	.001	-.458	-.118
	Religious commitment	-.016	.147	.012	1	.914	-.305	.273
	[Catholics = 1]	.352	.531	.440	1	.507	-.688	1.393
	[Christians/ non-Catholics = 2]	.465	.599	.603	1	.437	-.708	1.638
	[No religion = 3]	0[a]			0			

Link function: Logit.

[a] This parameter is set to zero because it is redundant.

democratic institutions such as political parties and Congress are key for the development of a representative political regime. At least in this case, differences in religious beliefs and different levels of religious devoutness do not explain any significant variations in individual support for a liberal democracy.[21]

The findings are much more interesting when analyzing the determinants at the individual level of interest in politics. Table 2 shows that a respondent's socioeconomic level had a significant effect on the dependent variable (p-value equal to 0.000). Better-off individuals have a higher probability of being interested in politics. In addition, there is no significant difference between Catholics and non-Catholic Christians regarding their levels of interest in politics (p-value of 0.028 and 0.031 respectively). 22 However, significant differences exist between individuals with a religious affiliation (Catholic and Christian) and respondents who defined themselves as non-religious individuals. Thus, the important crevasse in this case is the one between religious and non-religious individuals, not between Catholic and non-Catholic Christians.

Two additional comments should be made about these findings. First, the fact that non-religious people appear to have a higher level of interest in politics could be seen as evidence in support of a secularization theory. However, it is important to note that they constitute a minority in this

TABLE 2. Interest in Politics

		Estimate	Std. Error	Wald	df	Sig.	95% Confidence Interval	
							Lower Bound	Upper Bound
Threshold	[Interest = 1]	-.299	.619	.234	1	.629	-1.512	.914
	[Interest = 2]	1.554	.623	6.221	1	.013	.333	2.774
	[Interest = 3]	3.247	.638	25.862	1	.000	1.995	4.498
Location	Religious Beliefs	.033	.053	.384	1	.535	-.071	.136
	Age	.003	.006	.357	1	.550	-.008	.015
	Gender	-.224	.177	1.602	1	.206	-.571	.123
	Socioeconomic level	.447	.079	32.062	1	.000	.292	.601
	Religious commitment	.415	.133	9.696	1	.002	.154	.677
	[Catholics = 1]	-.976	.444	4.843	1	.028	-1.846	-.107
	[Christians/ non-Catholics = 2]	-1.091	.506	4.650	1	.031	-2.083	-.099
	[No religion = 3]	0[a]	.	.	0	.	.	.

Link function: Logit.

[a] This parameter is set to zero because it is redundant.

Peruvian sample (6 percent). Second, religious affiliation does not exert a significant influence on the level of political interest. In other words, Evangelical Protestants are not less politically interested than their Catholic counterparts. Hence, no evidence has been found supporting the idea that a difference in political interest exists between Catholic and non-Catholic Christians.

Finally, regarding the variable of religious commitment, people who perceived themselves as devout and frequently attend religious services had a higher level of interest in politics (p-value of 0.002). This is a puzzling outcome if we note the conservative shift in the Peruvian Catholic Church in recent years and the belief that a strong level of commitment to religious practices might compete with political curiosity and interest.

Table 3 reveals that both a respondent's socioeconomic level and age had a significant impact on their assessment on the extent members of Congress in Peru are delivering political representation for the citizens. More specifically, the higher the socioeconomic level of the respondent, the higher the probability of a positive assessment regarding the capacity of members of Congress in Peru to provide political representation to their constituency (p-value 0.022). In the case of age, older respondents are much more critical about the political representation delivered by members of Congress in Peru (p-value 0.005). Interestingly, individual religious commitment indicated a higher probability of giving a member of Congress a positive evalu-

TABLE 3. Political Representation by Congress Members

		Estimate	Std. Error	Wald	df	Sig.	95% Confidence Interval Lower Bound	Upper Bound
Threshold	[Representation = 1]	-.013	.632	.000	1	.984	-1.252	1.226
	[Representation = 2]	1.797	.639	7.911	1	.005	.545	3.050
	[Representation = 3]	4.459	.724	37.923	1	.000	3.040	5.878
Location	Religious Beliefs	-.007	.054	.015	1	.902	-.113	.100
	Age	-.017	.006	7.858	1	.005	-.029	-.005
	Gender	-.054	.183	.087	1	.768	-.412	.304
	Socioeconomic level	.182	.079	5.250	1	.022	.026	.337
	Religious commitment	.447	.139	10.297	1	.001	.174	.720
	[Catholics = 1]	-.359	.450	.637	1	.425	-1.242	.523
	[Christians/ non-Catholics = 2]	-.667	.517	1.666	1	.197	-1.681	.346
	[No religion = 3]	0[a]	.	.	0	.	.	.

Link function: Logit.
[a] This parameter is set to zero because it is redundant.

ation (p-value much less than 0.01). Therefore, after controlling by gender, age, and socioeconomic level, there is strong evidence that individuals with a higher level of religious commitment are clearly less dissatisfied with one of the key dimensions of political representation.

Something very similar surfaces when the dependent variable is about whether voting in Peru should be mandatory or voluntary, as indicated in Table 4. Again, socioeconomic level and age are significant determinants for preferring voting to be mandatory. Better-off and older respondents have a clear preference for making voting optional in Peru. Taking into consideration the religious explanatory variables, individual religious commitment has a significant positive effect on the probability of preferring voting as mandatory (p-value of 0.02). It is possible to make the case that respondents preferring voting to be mandatory are expressing a higher level of civic responsibility (i.e., the participation of citizens in electoral processes). With this in mind, the results show that there is a relationship between individual levels of religious commitment and a higher sense of civic duty.

The last dependent variable was the perception about the relationship between Congress and the president. This binary variable separates the respondents who think that the main responsibility of Congress is to support all presidential initiatives from the respondents who believe that

TABLE 4. Voting as Mandatory

		Estimate	Std. Error	Wald	df	Sig.	95% Confidence Interval	
							Lower Bound	Upper Bound
Threshold	[Voting = 0]	-.175	.729	.058	1	.810	-1.604	1.254
Location	Religious Beliefs	-.038	.061	.398	1	.528	-.157	.081
	Age	-.019	.007	7.812	1	.005	-.033	-.006
	Gender	-.108	.203	.285	1	.593	-.505	.289
	Socioeconomic level	-.157	.089	3.134	1	.077	-.331	.017
	Religious commitment	.352	.153	5.314	1	.021	.053	.651
	[Catholics = 1]	.076	.533	.020	1	.887	-.968	1.120
	[Christians/ non-Catholics = 2]	-.011	.602	.000	1	.986	-1.190	1.168
	[No religion = 3]	0[a]	.	.	0	.	.	.

Link function: Logit.
[a]This parameter is set to zero because it is redundant.

Congress is supposed to provide critical support for or even, when necessary, oppose some presidential initiatives. As shown in Table 5, individuals from higher socioeconomic levels have a higher probability of considering the responsibility of Congress to be the providing of checks and balances to presidential initiatives (p value of 0.000). Regarding religious explana-

TABLE 5. Relationship between Congress and President

		Estimate	Std. Error	Wald	df	Sig.	95% Confidence Interval	
							Lower Bound	Upper Bound
Threshold	[Relationship = 0]	-1.120	.832	1.813	1	.178	-2.751	.510
Location	Religious Beliefs	.102	.072	2.045	1	.153	-.038	.243
	Age	.007	.008	.856	1	.355	-.008	.022
	Gender	-.033	.228	.021	1	.884	-.480	.414
	Socioeconomic level	-.639	.107	35.380	1	.000	-.849	-.428
	Religious commitment	-.427	.176	5.856	1	.016	-.773	-.081
	[Catholics = 1]	.148	.601	.061	1	.805	-1.029	1.326
	[Christians/ non-Catholics = 2]	.324	.678	.229	1	.632	-1.004	1.653
	[No religion = 3]	0[a]	.	.	0	.	.	.

Link function: Logit.
[a]This parameter is set to zero because it is redundant.

tory variables, a higher level of individual religious commitment has a significant impact on this dependent variable (p-value of 0.016). People who defined themselves as religiously devoted and frequently attend religious services are more likely to prefer a Congress that provides critical support or is able to oppose presidential initiatives.

As with the previous models, religious commitment appears to be associated with political orientations that are less problematic for the functioning of the current democratic regime in Peru. These individuals are less dissatisfied with the political representation provided by members of Congress, more interested in politics, and more inclined to believe that voting should remain mandatory; but they are also less inclined to support a democratic regime with low or nonexistent horizontal accountability.[23]

Conclusion

Taking into consideration these findings, and similar findings in other Latin American countries, it is very difficult to deny the relevance of religion as a political factor in Peru. Equally important to note, the empirical data makes it very difficult to advance an argument about the negative impact of religion on the development of individual political perceptions and attitudes. Within several Latin American countries, more actively religious people (Catholic and non-Catholic Christians) hold political orientations that could support the maintenance and stability of current democratic regimes. Finally, because the measure of religious commitment used here includes information about attendance at religious services, support seems to be in favor of the idea that religious participation develops civic skills and political orientations that are favorable to the maintenance and development of democracy.

There is no doubt that the fate of the current democratic regimes in Latin America will depend on more than religion alone. However, there is evidence for the indirect impact that religion plays in shaping individual political orientations. This indirect impact will be mostly related to the way religious organizations provide their members a collective or institutional experience. This seems to be important in terms of the development of civic skills and particular political outlooks. In this regard, people who perceive themselves as committed to their religion and attend religious services more frequently are quite different in terms of political attitudes and perceptions from the rest of the population. There is reasonable justification to hold the position that it is less the difference of religious creed or the position of the official hierarchy that affects one's political orientation and more the level of one's participation and/or commitment to one's religious organizations.

NOTES

1. For a revised version of modernization and secularization theories, see Pippa Norris and Ronald Inglehart, *Sacred and Secular: Religion and Politics Worldwide* (Cambridge: Cambridge University Press, 2004).

2. See Anthony Gill, "Religion and Comparative Politics," *Annual Review of Political Science* 4 (2001): 117–38; Anthony Gill, "Weber in Latin America: Is Protestant Growth Enabling the Consolidation of Democratic Capitalism?," *Democratization* 11, no. 4 (2004): 1–25; Christian Smith, *Disruptive Religion: The Force of Faith in Social Movement Activism* (New York: Routledge, 1996); Kenneth Wald and Allison Calhoun-Brown, *Religion and Politics in the United States* (New York: Rowman & Littlefield, 2007).

3. Smith, *Disruptive Religion*, 5.

4. Wald and Calhoun-Brown, *Religion and Politics in the United States*, 17.

5. See John Booth and John and Patricia Bayer, "Civil Society, Political Capital and Democratization in Central America," *Journal of Politics* 60 (1998): 780–800; Paul Freston, "Evangelical Protestantism and Democratization in Latin America and Asia," *Democratization* 11, no. 4 (2004): 21–41; Robert D. Putnam, Robert Leonardi, and Raffaella Nanetti, *Making Democracy Work: Civic Traditions in Modern Italy* (Princeton, NJ: Princeton University Press, 1993); Amber L. Seligson, "Civic Association and Democratic Participation in Central America: A Test of the Putnam Thesis," *Comparative Political Studies* 32, no. 3 (1999): 342–62.

6. See Daniel Levine, "Conclusion: Evangelicals and Democracy—the Experience of Latin America in Context," in *Evangelical Christianity and Democracy in Latin America*, ed. Paul Freston, 207–23 (Oxford: Oxford University Press, 2008).

7. See John Anderson, "Does God Matter, and If So, Whose God? Religion and Democratization," *Democratization* 11, no. 4 (2004): 192–217. Fred Halliday provides a very similar argument about the main obstacles to democracy in Islamic societies. According to him, within Islamic countries, the main obstacles to democracy are not related to their religious traditions but to the more social and political features of society. See Fred Halliday, *Islam and the Myth of Confrontation* (London: Tauris, 1996).

8. Kenneth Wald contends that these three religious aspects or dimensions constitute the human face of religion. See Wald and Calhoun-Brown, *Religion and Politics in the United States*.

9. Freston, "Evangelical Protestantism," 25–26. It is important to note that even in the case of the political implications of Protestantism in recently

democratized countries, there are different interpretations. Some scholars have emphasized, for example, the non-democratic nature of Pentecostal churches (i.e., a repressive and corporatist nature) and see them as perpetuating traditional and authoritarian political cultures. Other scholars have stressed Protestantism's democratizing potential: the churches offer a free social space, an experience of solidarity, and a new personal identity, as well as responsible participation in community and, for some, the development of leadership skills. See David Martin, *Tongues of Fire: The Explosion of Protestantism in Latin America* (Cambridge, MA: Blackwell, 1990).

10. See Charles H. Wood, Philip Williams, and Kuniko Chijiwa, "Protestantism and Child Mortality in Northeast Brazil, 2000," *Journal for the Scientific Study of Religion* 46, no. 3 (2007): 405–16.

11. It is important to mention here that in the context of Latin America, especially in recent years, the argument that both churches and religious experiences can be relevant to the development of civil society and civic life has been basically related exclusively to Protestant Evangelical churches. See Levine, "Conclusion."

12. See Manuel Vasquez and Philip Williams, "Introduction: The Power of Religious Identities in the Americas," *Latin American Perspectives* 32, no. 1 (2005): 5–26.

13. See Freston, "Evangelical Protestantism"; Paul Freston, "Introduction: The Many Faces of Evangelical Politics in Latin America," in *Evangelical Christianity and Democracy in Latin America*, 3–36 (Oxford: Oxford University Press, 2008); Martin, *Tongues of Fire*; Eric Patterson, "Different Religions, Different Politics? Religion and Political Attitudes in Argentina and Chile," *Journal for the Scientific Study of Religion* 43, no. 3 (2004): 345–62; David Stoll, *Is Latin American Turning Protestant? The Politics of Evangelical Growth* (Berkeley: University of California Press, 1990). It is worth noting that the political implications of the considerable rise of Evangelical Protestantism in Latin America have been appraised in starkly different ways. Sometimes they have been portrayed as a new religious right and as an undemocratic force. See Jean-Pierre Bastian, "The Metamorphosis of Latin American Protestant Groups: A Socio-Historical Perspective," *Latin American Research Review* 28, no. 2 (1993): 33–61; Rowan Ireland, *Kingdoms Come: Religion and Politics in Brazil* (Pittsburgh, PA: University of Pittsburgh Press, 1991); Stoll, *Is Latin American Turning Protestant?*. At other times, they have been portrayed as a force for democracy, economic development, and a strong civil society. See Freston, "Evangelical Protestantism"; Freston, "Introduction"; Martin, *Tongues of Fire*.

14. Gill, "Weber in Latin America."

15. See Patterson, "Different Religions."

16. Ibid.

17. Lima represents approximately one-third of Peru's population.

18. See the World Values Survey for a comprehensive list of the most standard and frequently used survey questions about religion and religiosity.

19. The alpha-Cronbach score for these three variables is 0.69.

20. The alpha-Cronbach score for these two variables is also 0.69.

21. See *Programa de las Naciones Unidas para el Desarrollo*, La Democracia en América Latina. Hacia una Democracia de Ciudadanos y Ciudadanas (Buenos Aires: Alfaguara, 2004).

22. The category of Christians, or non-Catholic Christians, includes Evangelical Protestants, Jehovah's Witnesses, Adventists, and members of the Church of Jesus Christ of Latter-Day Saints. It is worth noting that the large majority of these respondents—60 percent—classified themselves as Evangelicals.

23. See Guillermo O'Donnell, "Horizontal Accountability in New Democracies," *Journal of Democracy* 9, no. 3 (1998): 112–26. According to O'Donnell, this kind of accountability depends upon the existence of state agencies that are legally empowered to take actions in relation to potentially unlawful decisions or actions by other agents or agencies of the state.

The Catholic Church and the Leftist Populist Regimes of Latin America: Venezuela, Ecuador, and Bolivia

Jeffrey Klaiber, SJ

In this note on the Peruvian Voices, the questions of power and authority remain. In an attempt to understand what gave rise to these questions, Jeffrey Klaiber turns to the broader context of Latin America. Here, he surfaces the historical trends that, in his estimation, have cultivated the cultural, political, and religious environments found not only in Peru but also in other Latin American nations.

Specifically, Klaiber offers an analysis of the relationship between the Catholic Church and the leftist states of the South American continent over the past few decades. From this, he attempts to understand the process of democratization in Latin America and the role Catholicism has played therein. Prior to the rise of the leftist regimes, the Catholic Church was looked upon as a trusted mediator between the state and civil society. Today, the Catholic Church's position is more tenuous, and Klaiber queries into the possibility of the Catholic Church returning to its social, economic, and political role as mediator between the people and their government. Klaiber's analysis highlights the contentious history of the Catholic Church in Latin America and, as such, proves integral for understanding not only the Peruvian context but broader contexts and conversations on the relationships between democracy, culture, and Catholicism as well.

After Latin America returned to democracy in the 1980s, the Catholic Church faded as a subject of academic research interest. Many specialists turned to the new topic of evangelical growth. However, the Catholic Church did not disappear and it continued to wield much influence, especially on the grassroots level. In this regard, it is interesting to note that in public opinion polls the Catholic Church continues to receive the highest rating as the institution in which most people have confidence.[1]

A striking example of this is the Church's emergence in Cuba as the acceptable mediator between the regime and civil society. Though Cuba is not a leftist populist regime, it was the historical model that inspired the Hugo Chávez revolution in Venezuela and, to a lesser extent, the Evo Morales regime in Bolivia. As populist regimes experience greater internal fissures and economic woes, the question may be asked: Will the Catholic

Church reassume the role it once played during the last cycle of dictatorships as the acceptable mediator between government regimes and political opposition?[2]

The New Populists

"Populism" in Latin America refers to the mass-based parties and regimes
that arose throughout the continent in the decades following the Mexican
Revolution (1910–1920). These parties include the Partido Revolucionario
Institucional (PRI) in Mexico, the Alianza Popular Revolucionaria Ameri-
cana (APRA) in Peru, the Movimiento Nacionalista Revolucionario (MNR)
in Bolivia, the Perón movement in Argentina, and the Getúlio Vargas
movement in Brazil. These parties and movements were built on coalitions
of workers, peasants, and middle-class intellectuals who challenged the ruling oligarchies and sought to forge a nationalistic state favoring the lower
classes. Once in power they wrested control of natural resources from foreign oil or copper companies (principally American), put land reforms into
effect, and promoted universal health and education.

These movements were not communist. They opposed the Moscow-
dominated communist parties in the region. Culturally, they rejected the
Spanish or Portuguese past and promoted "national values." In the case of
Mexico and Peru, the movements romanticized the Indian past in their
countries. Leaders such as Perón in Argentina, Víctor Raúl Haya de la
Torre in Peru, and Getúlio Vargas in Brazil presented themselves as cham-
pions of the people's heroic struggle against the national oligarchies and
foreign interests. This serves as a fascinating parallel to the situation in
Lithuania described by Nerija Putinaitė in this volume. There, a romanticized version of a pre-Christian Lithuanian culture was developed to, in
part, oppose the Moscow-dominated communist control of the country.

Following a cycle of neoliberal governments in the 1980s and 1990s, a
new wave of populism spread over much of the region. The socialist presidents Luiz Inácio Lula da Silva (2003–2011) in Brazil and Chile's Ricardo
Lagos (2000–2006) and Michelle Bachelet (2006–2010) proved to be very
moderate and actually maintained many of their predecessors' liberal
economic policies. In Venezuela, Ecuador, and Bolivia the new populists
(Hugo Chávez, Rafael Correa, and Evo Morales) took a more radical
stance. Under the banner of "socialism of the twenty-first century" they
denounced foreign (principally American) interests and expressed their
admiration for Fidel Castro and the Cuban model. Although none went so
far as to impose Cuban type socialism in their countries, they did national-

ize major oil and gas companies and shunned free trade agreements with the United States. In every case, they experienced tense relations with the United States and expelled their American ambassadors.[3]

The new populist leaders also used a messianic type discourse in which God is on the side of the people. When Catholic bishops criticized the authoritarian tendencies in these governments, the leaders immediately cast the bishops in the role of the political opposition. Typically they pit the bishops against the people, claiming that the people are the real Christians. In reference to the pope being the representative of Christ on earth, Chávez once retorted, "Christ is in the people and in those who fight for justice and the liberation of the lowly."[4] While the use of religion to legitimize politics may have ceased to be of interest to most Europeans, Latin America's populist leaders know that religion still matters in politics.

At the same time, the new populists have taken up the banner of a radically "lay state" that goes beyond mere separation of church and state to the exclusion of the Church from the public sphere altogether. As Soledad Escalante observed in her earlier chapter, though church and state were legally separated in all of Latin America years ago, the Catholic Church continues to retain special status of tax exemptions and state support of Church-run health and educational facilities. On the level of ritual, Latin American presidents still attend a Te Deum mass on Independence Day and the army officially celebrates the feast of Our Lady of Mercy, the patroness of the armed forces, in several countries. Public officials are sworn in before a cross and a bible. In recent years, presidents have attended ecumenical services in recognition of the growing Protestant presence. The new populists have sought an end to these Church prerogatives.

Populists have gone beyond matters of formal church-state relations and have sought the elimination of Church influence in civil society as a whole. Relations between the populist leaders and the Catholic Church in Venezuela, Ecuador, and Bolivia have been characterized by acrimonious verbal exchanges. However, in moderate left-leaning regimes that have established secular states, such as Chile and Brazil, there have been no noticeable church-state tensions. One recalls here the earlier chapter by Russell Powell in which the useful distinction is made between "hard" and "soft" secularism.

The Church

The scenario the Catholic Church faces vis-à-vis the populist regimes has been full of ambiguities. To begin with, the populist regimes were all democratically elected and have enjoyed a high degree of popularity. In the days of the dictators, the Church could take the moral high ground and speak in the name of all the disenfranchised. The populists take this high ground from the Church but are careful to distinguish between the hierarchy and certain religiously affiliated organizations on the popular level. One example is Fe y Alegría, the chain of schools for the poor founded by the Jesuits throughout Latin America. The schools generally receive high praise as educational models from populist leaders.

To complicate matters, Pope John Paul II's naming of conservative bishops around the world left Latin America with a new generation of conservative bishops unsympathetic toward the populist regimes and lacking in the necessary diplomatic savoir faire to deal with them. In addition, issues that were once considered purely first world concerns, such as abortion and same-sex marriage, are now much discussed in Latin America. Abortion is legal in several Latin American countries, and same sex marriages or unions are recognized in Argentina, Brazil, and Uruguay. Finally, in all the secular states, Catholic religion courses in public schools have been under scrutiny. Religion courses in Venezuela were eliminated under the revised 2009 Constitution, and in Bolivia a new course on all the religious beliefs in that country has been proposed to replace the traditional course on Catholicism.

Given these and other situations, Church leaders find themselves in a dilemma: how to criticize the authoritarian tendencies of the populist regimes without alienating practicing Catholics at the popular level who support those governments. A further review of the situation in Venezuela, Ecuador, and Bolivia will shed light on the complexities of each case.

Venezuela

HUGO CHÁVEZ

Hugo Chávez burst upon the political scene in 1992 when he and fellow military officers attempted a coup d'état against the government of President Carlos Andrés Pérez. The coup failed and Chávez spent the next two years in prison. He received an indult from President Rafael Caldera and returned to politics as a candidate for the presidency in 1998, which he won with 56.5 percent of the vote. Venezuela's lower classes, reeling under ever-rising prices and deeply discontented over the country's traditional political parties, saw the maverick and outsider Chávez as their champion.

Once in power, Chávez called for a referendum to write a new Constitution that greatly expanded presidential powers. He won the referendum and the Constituent National Assembly produced the new Constitution. For two days in 2002, however, Chávez was forced to relinquish power by a group of businessmen who were backed by some military leaders and members of the hierarchy of the Catholic Church. The attempted coup failed for lack of sufficient support from the international community and the Venezuelan army.

Chávez returned to power amid popular acclaim. In another attempt to remove him, opposition forces organized a national referendum in 2004. Chávez won the referendum with 59.06 percent of the vote. He was re-elected in 2006 when his Castro-style war cry was ever more defiant: "Fatherland, Socialism, or Death!" He soon nationalized the country's principal telephone and light companies and refused to renew the license of Radio and Television Caracas. In 2009, he won another referendum that allowed him to be re-elected indefinitely.[5] In 2013 the ailing Chávez relinquished power, but the Chavistas remain in control of the government. This has likewise been true since his death in 2013. Although many Chavistas look upon the bishops as enemies of their revolution, the Catholic Church has been the only major organization that commands the respect of Venezuelans on both sides of the political divide.

The Church

The Venezuelan Bishops' Conference is made up of one cardinal, nine archbishops (including the cardinal), twenty-eight bishops, and four vicars apostolic. The conference in turn represents 1,365 diocesan priests. There are also 3,946 religious order priests and 3,724 religious women.[6] Five percent of all school children are in Fe y Alegría schools. The Catholic Church remains present among all social classes throughout the country and exercises considerable influence on public opinion. At the same time, the Church in Venezuela mirrors the divisions within Latin American society.

Ever since the changes set into motion by the Second Vatican Council and the bishops' assemblies in Latin America, especially at Medellín, Colombia (1968), when the bishops took a strong stand on social justice, the Catholic Church has experienced internal fissures. From the 1950s on, many priests and religious women began working in the poor districts surrounding the major cities, while others remained in the parishes and schools of the middle and upper classes. Pedro Trigo, SJ, a well-known Jesuit intellectual, expressed the view that the bishops still tend to be paternalistic in their ways of thinking and acting.[7] In addition, Chávez had his sympathizers among the clergy. One of the most well-known is Father Jesús Gazo, a Jesuit who teaches at the Catholic (and Jesuit) University of Táchira in San Cristóbal. Gazo was popularly known as Chávez's spiritual adviser and criticized the bishops and fellow Jesuits for blaming the president for Venezuela's ills. In his view, they should respect the will of the people and help the Chavistas carry out their plan to lift the people out of poverty.

Relations between the hierarchy and Chávez during his first year in office were relatively harmonious. The bishops called upon the public to participate in the elections for a new constitution and Chávez responded favorably to the bishops' request to retain mention of God in the preamble and not to include the right to abortion in the document. Yet the stage was set for future confrontations when the bishops questioned the transparency of the process to write a new Constitution in 2007 and retired Cardinal Rosalio Castillo Lara announced his intention not to vote for it. In typically coarse style, Chávez called the bishops "Judases" and "allies of the oligarchy."[8]

By far the principal source of tension between Chávez and the bishops was the Church's role in the 2002 coup. A few months before the coup, the Jesuit president of Andrés Bello Catholic University, Luis Ugalde, and Pedro Carmona, a businessman who assumed the presidency when Chávez was overthrown, called for a new national dialogue. Ugalde was unaware that the meeting was actually a first step toward a coup.[9] Once installed in the presidential palace, Carmona and the conspirators produced a document setting down the legal basis for the de facto government. Among the four hundred signatories of the document was Cardinal Ignacio Velasco, archbishop of Caracas. Velasco visited the deposed leader at the naval base of La Orchila and urged Chávez to resign.

After the failed coup, Chávez took a conciliatory approach toward the lay conspirators and offered them amnesty. He never, however, forgot the Church's role in the affair. As a likely snub, Chávez flirted with the *evangélicos* (Protestants represent around 5 percent of the population) and gave them public recognition. That support ended in 2005 when Pat Robertson suggested that the CIA assassinate Venezuela's president.

The other major bone of contention between Chávez and the Church has been education in state schools. In 2000, the government published a decree greatly broadening state control of education. The decree incited protest marches all over the country and the government backed down. Nevertheless, in August 2009 the National Assembly approved a new law of education that enshrined most of the government's earlier goals. The new law recognized the right of private education but greatly circumscribed that right. Article 5 declares that the "Teaching State" ("Estado docente") will be the maximum judge in all things referring to education. Furthermore, it declares that all education will be inspired by the doctrines of Simón Bolívar and his mentor, Simón Rodríguez, and "social humanism" (article 14). Article 7 declares that the state will maintain its "lay character" and be independent of all religious currents and organizations.[10] The religion course was eliminated from the state school curriculum. One of the law's transitory articles poses a veiled threat declaring that the state has the right to "close down" or "order the reorganization" of any private school that goes against the principles laid down in the Venezuelan Constitution and the new law.

In the opinion of the staff at the Jesuit-run Gumilla Center, the new law promised everything but solved none of the country's real educational problems. These problems include dysfunctional infrastructure, poorly paid teachers, and an overall lack of pedagogical vision. The bishops became increasingly fearful that Chávez was turning Venezuela into an authoritarian regime where freedom of expression would be given little or no respect. In December 2010, the National Assembly gave Chávez power to legislate by decree for the next eighteen months.

As Venezuela seemed to be slipping into an authoritarian chasm, the Catholic Church remained the only force capable of rallying Venezuelans around the banner of authentic democracy. In January 2011, the bishops leveled their strongest charge against the government, stating that the National Assembly had imposed an "ideological agenda" on Venezuelan society that aimed at establishing a "socialist and totalitarian system" in the country.[11]

Ecuador

Rafael Correa

Like Venezuela, Ecuador has suffered from chronic political instability. Between 2000 and 2007 the country was ruled by eleven different presidents, three of whom were overthrown by either military or popular uprising. In every case, the incumbents were accused of incompetent handling of the economy and political corruption. The 2007 election of Rafael Correa engendered hopes that Ecuador might take a new course. Correa seemed to be what the country needed: a relatively young political leader (forty-four when elected), an idealist, and a well-trained economist with degrees from the Universities of Louvain and Illinois at Urbana-Champaign. Unlike Evo Morales, he was neither the product of a movement from the lower classes nor a native Indian. His party was created by middle-class intellectuals and technocrats. Neither was he promoted by a movement created from above, as was Hugo Chávez.

Correa defined himself as a leftist Christian humanist and had knowledge of the social teachings of the Catholic Church, unlike Hugo Chávez and Evo Morales. In a speech at the University of Oxford in 2009, Correa praised Catholic social justice leaders Helder Câmara and Oscar Romero and cited the documents of the episcopal conference of Puebla.[12] Helder Câmara had been the archbishop of Recife, Brazil, and was a forerunner of the progressive Church in Latin America. Oscar Romero, the archbishop of San Salvador, was assassinated in 1980 for denouncing the Salvadoran death squads.

Correa won the presidency in a runoff election with 56.7 percent of the vote. Shortly after coming to power he spearheaded a move to elect a constitutional assembly to write a new Constitution. During the campaign he called for the "refounding" of the country, a theme he shared with Hugo Chávez and Evo Morales. Sixty-four percent of Ecuadorians approved the new Constitution in a plebiscite held in September 2008. Correa then ran for the presidency again in 2009 and won with 52 percent of the vote.

Correa gave Ecuador the stability and sense of direction that it needed. His detractors say he has had little patience for criticism. He has carried out an ongoing battle with the press, which he believes defames him. His other main critic is the hierarchy of the Catholic Church.

THE CHURCH

As in Venezuela, Catholicism is the predominant religion in Ecuador. Church members constitute close to 95 percent of the population. The forty-three archbishops, bishops, and vicars apostolic who make up the bishops' conference could be described as centrists who tend toward the conservative. The president of the conference is Antonio Arregui, the archbishop of Guayaquil. Arregui is Spanish-born and the only member of Opus Dei among the hierarchy.

Correa's proposal to write a new Constitution drew great attention within the Catholic Church. The document, largely the work of pro-Correa intellectuals (especially the economist Alberto Acosta), closely resembles the Bolivian Constitution from the same period. It emphasizes Ecuador's Indian cultures (25 percent of Ecuadorians are native Indian).

The preamble refers to the "Pacha Mama," the Mother Earth spirit to which many in the Andean countries pay tribute. The vast majority of Ecuador's native peoples practice popular Catholicism that frequently identifies the Pacha Mama with the Virgin Mary.[13] After its reference to the Pacha Mama, the constitution states: "We invoke the name of God in recognition of the many diverse forms of religiosity and spirituality."[14] The mention of both the Pacha Mama and God in the preamble attests to a new sensitivity toward the native Indian religions. The Constitution also drew attention by declaring that nature has "rights."

What drew the most criticisms from the bishops was the vagueness of the articles with regard to health, gender, and the family. Article 32 declares that the state will guarantee "permanent and opportune access without exclusion to programs, activities, and services which promote integral, sexual, and reproductive health." Article 66 upholds the "inviolability of life" but makes no mention of when life begins, thus leaving the door open to abortion. An ambiguous reference to "different types of families" seemed to open the door to same-sex unions. Overall, the bishops observed that the proposed Constitution accorded a too-dominant role to the state, seeming to identify the state as the very source of all human rights.

In response, Correa accused the bishops of turning their backs on him. After the successful referendum on the proposed Constitution, Archbishop Arregui announced that the bishops would accept the results and that the Church was always open to dialogue. The bishops' conciliatory message was not publicly reciprocated by Correa.

In a surprise move after the referendum, Correa invited nineteen Jesuit superiors and directors of different works (e.g., Fe y Alegría, the Center for the Working Boy, and Jesuit Refugee Service) for lunch at the presidential residence. No explicit reason was given for the meeting, but it was evident that Correa wished to send a signal that he was not opposed to the Church per se, only to certain conservative groups within the Church. In another move, Correa signed a decree in June 2009 empowering the state to enter into agreements with Catholic missions in the Amazon region and the Galápagos Islands to offer economic assistance to the Church's educational and pastoral projects among native peoples.

In yet another unusual move, Correa intervened in the naming of a bishop. In 2010, the Vatican named Rafael Ibarguren Schindler, a member of the ultraconservative group Heralds of the Gospel, to be the new bishop of Sucumbíos, a prelature in the Ecuadorian Amazon. Correa asked the pope to rescind the nomination and declared in public that Ecuador could do without "fundamentalist" sects. For all his defense of a "lay" state, Correa is not above taking sides in favor of progressive Catholics.

Bolivia

Evo Morales

The 2005 election of Evo Morales drew global attention because he was the first person of native Indian background to become president of Bolivia. For all of its history, Bolivia had been ruled by the minority white population of the middle and upper classes. Bolivia's Indian population includes two major linguistic groups: the Aymaras (23 percent), who are concentrated in the altiplano around La Paz, and the Quechua speakers (34 percent), located in the central plains. Although Morales's election was celebrated as a victory for Bolivia's native peoples, Morales was not the direct result of a pro-Indian movement. Rather, he rose to prominence as a leader of the coca growers' union.[15]

His first major move was to call for a constitutional assembly to write a new Constitution for the purpose of "refounding" the country. The constitutional debate divided the country into two warring regions: western Bolivia where the Indian population is greatest (La Paz and the central valley around Cochabamba), and eastern Bolivia that is dominated by wealthy white ranchers and businessmen of Santa Cruz. After a few violent clashes and a long, tortuous debate, the new constitution was approved in 2009 by a national referendum with 61.43 percent in favor.

Two novelties drew attention to the Constitution: its emphasis on Indian rights and culture and its insistence on the secular, "lay" nature of the Bolivian state. Several keywords appear as connecting links throughout the document: "plurinational," "decolonization," and "spirituality." The first refers to the multiple Indian communities in the country. The second refers to the country's colonial past, a reality that continues to weigh heavily on the present. Finally, the word "spirituality" was introduced to include non-Christian Indian beliefs and practices. As in the Ecuadorian Constitution, the idea was to include non-Christian beliefs along with Catholic Christian beliefs.

From the very beginning of his administration, Evo Morales celebrated his victory by participating in traditional Aymara rituals and ignoring Catholic celebrations such as the feast of Our Lady of Urkupiña in Cochabamba. This snub seemed unnecessary as the Bolivian Church emerged out of the 1960s very progressive. During the Hugo Banzer dictatorship (1972–1978) the Church defended human rights and legitimized a nationwide hunger strike that led to the dictator's downfall. All this would have seemed consistent with Morales's political views; indeed, in his inaugural address he included in his list of heroes Che Guevara, Túpac Katari (an eighteenth-century Indian leader), and Luis Espinal, a Catalan Jesuit who had been murdered by the military in 1980.

Though sympathetic to some groups in the Church, Morales resented the Church hierarchy that he perceived as part of the establishment. This simmering resentment came to the fore in numerous verbal attacks. He once accused the hierarchy of using prayer as an "anesthetic to put people to sleep."[16] He added, however, that he was not referring to priests working on the grassroots level.

THE CHURCH

The real test of wills between the president and the Church revolves around the question of education. In December 2010, the National Assembly promulgated a new education law promising to bring about a radical and sweeping change to the country's educational system. The Avelino Sinañi-Elizardo Pérez Law mirrors the Constitution itself. It declares that education in Bolivia will be "decolonizing, liberating, revolutionary, anti-imperialist, depatriarchalizing [meaning, anti-machista]."[17]

What most concerned Church leaders was the concept of decolonization. Given that the Catholic Church is the most important survivor of Bolivia's colonial past, many feared that the Marxist and anticlerical advisors surrounding Morales would seek to do away with Catholic instruction in the educational system.[18] When the current law was being discussed in June 2006, Minister of Education Félix Patzi, an Aymara sociologist, proposed precisely that. Arguing that the Church was the "primary colonial instrument" in the country, Patzi called for an end to Catholic religious education in state schools.[19] The Church and other private educational organizations reacted so strongly that his proposals were shelved and he resigned from office in January of the following year.

Church educators observed that the law did not take into account the point of view of other groups in society.[20] Also, they questioned the notion that the state has the exclusive right to educate. Finally, the critics pointed out that the law does not guarantee an integral education, which would include religious education. The law was to be put into effect over a six-year period. As of this writing, the battle for the hearts and minds of millions of schoolchildren, and eventually those of all Bolivians, is underway.

The Future

The tension between the Church and the new populist regimes is essentially a battle over influence. The regimes have all proposed sweeping ideological programs for their respective countries that can be compared to the attempts of the eighteenth-century French and Spanish Bourbons to accord the state supreme power over the political, economic, and religious life of society. In Venezuela, Ecuador, and Bolivia the new populists have written constitutions that aim to mold their citizens in the image and likeness of an all-encompassing secular state.

The Catholic Church, with its deep historical roots and still considerable influence in society, is the only institution that can compete with the state. The question for the future is: As the popularity of the these regimes wanes as a result of economic crises and the inevitable wear and tear of remaining in power too long, will the Church be able to position itself as the universally acceptable moral authority capable of creating dialogue between highly polarized factions? If so, it would be an agent of transition in each country toward more civil and less demagogic democracies.

NOTES

1. Edward Cleary, *How Latin America Saved the Soul of the Catholic Church* (Mahwah, NJ: Paulist Press, 2009), 3–4.

2. See Jeffrey Klaiber, *The Church, Dictatorships and Democracy in Latin America* (Maryknoll, NY: Orbis Books, 1998).

3. On the new populists, see Carlos de la Torre, *Populist Seduction in Latin America* (Athens: Ohio University Press, 2010), and Sebastian Edwards, *Left Behind: Latin America and the False Promise of Populism* (Chicago: University of Chicago Press, 2010).

4. See Alejandro Bermudez, "Catholic Church in Venezuela Braces for Uncertain Times after Chavez," *National Catholic Register*, March 3, 2013, http://www.ncregister.com/daily-news/catholic-church-in-venezuela-braces-for-uncertain-times-after-chavez.

5. A few recent works on Chávez include Barry Cannon, *Hugo Chávez and the Bolivarian Revolution* (Manchester, UK: Manchester University Press, 2007), Kirk A. Hawkins, *Venezuela's Chavismo and Populism in Comparative Perspective* (Cambridge: Cambridge University Press, 2010), and Allan Brewer Carías, *Dismantling Democracy in Venezuela: The Chávez Authoritarian Experiment* (Cambridge: Cambridge University Press, 2010).

6. Data on religious order priests is from 2003 and data on religious women is from 2008. See "The Hierarchy of the Catholic Church," http://www.catholic-hierarchy.org/.

7. Father Pedro Trigo, SJ, interview by author, Gumilla Center, Caracas, February 25, 2011.

8. See Nikolas Kozloff, "Hugo Chavez's Holy War," April 1, 2007, http://venezuelanalysis.com/analysis/2312?page=3.

9. Father Luis Ugalde, interview by author, Caracas, March 3, 2011.

10. *Ley Organica de Educacion Venezuela, 2009,* http://www.scribd.com/doc/19024603/Ley-Organica-de-Educacion-Venezuela-2009.

11. Conferencia Episcopal Venozolana, "Exhortación pastoral: anhelos de unión, justicia, libertad y paz para Venezuela," Caracas, January 11, 2011, 2.

12. Rafael Correa Delgado, Oxford Speech, El Universo, November 1, 2009, at http://www.eluniverso.com/2009/11/01/1/1363/oxford-speach.html.

13. Carol Damen, *The Virgin of the Andes* (Miami Beach, FL: Grassfield Press, 1995).

14. See Republic of Ecuador, 2008 Constitution, at http://pdba.georgetown.edu/Constitutions/Ecuador/english08.html.

15. Xavier Albó, *Movimientos y poder indígena en Bolivia, Ecuador y Perú* (La Paz, Bolivia: Centro de Investigación y Promoción del Campesinado, 2008), 82–89. Also see Martin Savak, *Evo Morales: The Extraordinary Rise of the First Indigenous President of Bolivia* (New York: Palgrave MacMillan, 2010).

16. Rodrigue Tremblay, "The Moral Dimension of Things," March 8, 2010, http://www.thenewamericanempire.com/tremblay=1122.htm.

17. Helen Strom, "The New Bolivian Education Law," *Revista: Harvard Review of Latin America,* Fall 2011, http://revista.drclas.harvard.edu/book/new-bolivian-education-law.

18. Bishop Eugenio Scarpellini (secretary to the Bolivian Bishops' Conference), interview by author, La Paz, Bolivia, March 4, 2010.

19. Albó, *Movimientos,* 85–86. Also, Xavier Albó, interview by author, La Paz, March 4, 2010.

20. Javier Reyes (Secretary of Education, Bolivian Bishops' Conference), interview by author, La Paz, Bolivia, July 24, 2010.

US Voices

What greatly marks the relationships between democracy, culture, and Catholicism in the United States are the particular political and theological contexts from which the identity of US citizens emerged. The republic was established on the principles of democracy, and its culture was greatly affected and influenced by the prominent place enjoyed by Protestant Christianity among the people. Catholicism was an "outsider" religion that was not to be trusted and, worse, appeared to be completely incompatible with the political and cultural milieu of the nation. What the authors in this section seek to illustrate is the positive role Catholicism has played—and continues to play—in the United States. Catholicism is not antithetical to democracy and, as the authors indicate, it can oftentimes serve and promote the goals and objectives of democratization.

Bren Ortega Murphy offers a look at the relationships between democracy, culture, and Catholicism in the United States by looking to those figures who have been (arguably) most responsible for protecting, promoting, and passing on the principles of democracy, the importance of culture, and the Catholic faith to both immigrants and citizens in the United States: women religious. Rather than looking to broad, generalized questions about the relationship between democracy, culture, and Catholicism, Ortega

Murphy looks to the specific examples and experiences of women religious. From this, she teases out the myriad ways Catholic nuns have been responsible for passing on the Catholic faith and imparting notions of democratic citizenship and civility to the immigrant populations they serve. Ortega Murphy suggests that good Catholics have become good democratic citizens because of the efforts of women religious. At the same time, however, Ortega Murphy notes that the relationships between women religious in the United States and the authorities of the Catholic Church have been—in spite of the tremendous impact women religious have had on the processes of civil discourse and democratization—both fairly uncivil and decidedly undemocratic.

William O'Neill takes a different approach to these topics and offers a provocative philosophical and theological reflection on the role of restorative justice, which he links tightly with the Catholic social tradition, in deliberative democracy. O'Neill argues that restorative justice, as opposed to the forms of retributive justice that predominate in the American penal system, more justly and more comprehensively attends, first and foremost, to the victims of violence, but, secondarily, it also attends to the perpetrators of violence (many of whom, often enough, are themselves victims of personal and/or systemic violence). O'Neill makes the theological turn to the narratives of Christian discourse, both ancient and contemporary, to stress the call made of all persons to act toward others not simply retributively but with compassion and empathy.

Barry Sullivan offers an insightful analysis of the relationship between government transparency, human dignity, and Catholic social teaching. Sullivan argues that, in democratic governments such as the United States, citizens have a right to the information necessary to make informed decisions about public policy and those they elect to enact such policy. The citizen's claim to such information is based on the belief that each citizen is respected and dignified as a human person when they are able to exercise this democratic form of governance and decision-making. This right, and the dignity it is based on, finds support in and through the insights offered in Catholic social teaching and in the work of the French Catholic philosopher Jacques Maritain. The problem, according to Sullivan, arises when this same call for transparency, based on dignity, is applied to the inner workings of the Catholic Church itself. The duplicity of the Catholic Church's position— a duplicity latent within the critique offered by Bren Ortega Murphy—when it supports human dignity and government transparency as applied to others but not to itself compromises its effectiveness in promoting the democratic right to information and the rights to respect and dignity.

Roman Catholic Sisters and the Cultivation of Citizenship in the United States: Rich and Contentious Legacies

Bren Ortega Murphy

In 2009, an extraordinary exhibit started touring the United States. What made this exhibit so remarkable was that it was telling a story to the US public about an important part of their history that few had heard before. *Women and Spirit: Catholic Sisters in America* presented the complex, compelling story of what Catholic sisters have contributed and continue to contribute to the lives of not just Catholic Americans but all Americans. Working in education, health care, social work, disaster relief, immigration aid, and numerous other fields, Catholic sisters built remarkable institutions and formed democratic citizens.

Roman Catholic women religious have had a positive impact on the culture of democracy in the United States. The cultivation of democratic ideals by Catholic sisters communicated a conscious pedagogy of citizenship and gradually incorporated democratic values within the processes and identities of their own communities. An essential element of the relationship between democracy and religious women in America is the difficulty they have had in reconciling their experience of effecting democracy with their experience of inequity with the structure of the Roman Catholic Church.

First Arrival

Catholic sisters began arriving in the United States in the early eighteenth century and immediately began addressing the needs of people, regardless of ethnicity, gender, religion, or social class. Although women religious in Europe had long cared for the sick, the orphaned, and the uneducated, the American experience was different. Sisters who first arrived in America did not come to established institutions but had to build them from the ground up. Unlike their European counterparts, most religious women in America were not "secluded in convents or monasteries" but were work-ing in tenements, on the streets, and across the frontier.[1] Even their tra-ditional vows of poverty, celibacy, and obedience functioned differently in the New World.

> Vowing to live a life of celibacy, agreeing to obey male superiors and living on a few dollars a month might seem hopelessly anachronistic to many modern women; to some, downright un-American. But the three vows created strong, disciplined, selfless organizations that adapted very well to the rigors of America.[2]

To be clear, the primary motivation of the Roman Catholic hierarchy in sending women religious was not to foster democracy. Rather, Church authorities were concerned that the immigrants from traditionally Catholic countries such as Ireland, France, and parts of Germany, and later from Italy and Central Europe, would be drawn away from their Catholic faith and assimilated into the predominantly Protestant American culture. Such concerns were not unfounded. The seventeenth-century Penal Laws imposed on Catholic Ireland by Protestant England seemed obvious in their goal: "simply to force all Catholics to become Protestant."[3] Moreover, every great wave of Catholic immigrants to America triggered a counter impulse of virulent anti-Catholicism manifested in riots and anti-Catholic organizations such as the Know Nothings.[4]

In this sociopolitical context, Church authorities petitioned European women religious to journey to the New World and minister to the immi-grants. They recruited specific religious orders or founded new ones focused on the needs of particular ethnic groups.[5] One of the perceived needs iden-tified by Church leaders was to "make Americans" out of immigrants.[6] To meet these needs, sisters established organizations and institutions focused on housing, medical care, and education, all the while teaching the immi-grants and their children how to grow strong in both Catholic faith and American citizenship.

This work was practically and ideologically difficult. Although state structures of governance in the United States were entirely fashioned by Protestants, the constitutional principle was clear: there was to be no state religion. Early English settlers had a deep antipathy toward Catholicism (often called "the whore of Babylon") but had experienced religious persecution themselves in England. Thus, the early Protestants rejected governmental exclusion based on creed. But this raised a serious question for them. Since Catholics had allegiance to a foreign monarch (the pope), how could a person be both a good Catholic and a good American?[7] "True Americans" were to revere the God-blessed United States and its Christian way of life.[8]

Catholic women religious educators had to take on a dual role. They had to educate immigrants and their American-born children in a faith that valued obedience to central authority and participation in a highly distinctive religious culture while at the same time equipping them to be sincere, functioning members of a growing democracy in a rapidly changing secular society. They accomplished this task with both overt and covert methods.

Laying the Groundwork

Teaching American citizenship to immigrants is a complex process that has intrigued scholars and activists for centuries.[9] Central questions on this subject include how American political identity can be forged without destroying other elements of a prospective citizen's identity. For example, how can a Polish immigrant retain his or her personal identity with Polish culture and still self-identify as an American?

Making immigrants "American" seemed comparatively simple at the beginning. America promoted itself as a country where one could economically start anew. The first step in becoming American seemed deceptively straightforward: find a place to live, shed one's peasant clothing, find a job, and learn English. The first goal of women religious was, then, to establish schools. These were to serve ethnic minorities, orphans, and others outside the cultural mainstream. Thus, the schools would need to be built in urban slums, along the delta bayous, and on the raucous frontier.[10]

Long accustomed to running exclusive schools for girls in Europe, religious sisters in America emphasized education for all children, regardless of sex. At the same time, there was "new pressure on schools from the Catholic press [which] argued for training young women to survive in a competitive world, or, in other words, to treat girls like boys."[11] When their regular teaching day was done, it was not uncommon for Catholic sisters to teach evening classes to adults. In all these venues, immigrant children and adults learned the language and history of their newly adopted country as well as the meaning and responsibility of living in a democracy. Gradually, these experiences affirmed students' sense of belonging in America.

The sisters' message of inclusion went beyond the classroom. Because Catholic women religious were often the first and only responders to epidemics such as yellow fever, cholera, and influenza, they interacted with Catholics and non-Catholics alike.[12] The sisters visited prisoners, helped secure employment for the jobless, and sheltered abandoned women. Nowhere was this undifferentiated civic engagement more evident than during the American Civil War when over six thousand sisters "from twenty-one different communities representing twelve separate orders nursed both Union and Confederate soldiers."[13]

It is important to note that unlike US Protestant women who admirably founded settlement houses and led campaigns against the ills of poverty and class discrimination, nineteenth-century Catholic women religious were more likely to themselves be products of the working class to whom they ministered. They knew the people they served because they were one of them. The first sisters from Ireland knew that Irish peasants fleeing the famine were neither educated nor particularly religious. They knew from firsthand family experience the destruction caused by alcoholism, domestic abuse, and ignorance.[14] At the same time, they also knew the potential for personal transformation through education and hard work because many of them had undergone the transformation themselves.

This realism contributed to the sisters' views on charity and justice. Suellen Hoy observes:

> Unlike middle-class reformers, sisters thought that class divisions were likely to endure and, therefore "did not imagine an end to the inequitable social and economic system that made charity necessary." Hence, they channeled their efforts towards alleviating the symptoms of poverty through personal works of mercy and charitable institutions.[15]

In other words, the first sisters who came to the United States focused more on caring for individuals than challenging social inequities. In doing so, they demonstrated to needy immigrants and other marginalized Americans the importance of personally performing the practices of citizenship and civic engagement. William O'Neill, in the following chapter, offers a contemporary manifestation of this commitment when he analyzes the problem of mass incarceration. Care of the individual, at the most basic and intimate level, which has been, and continues to be, at the heart of the mission of women religious, and performing the act of civic engagement are staples of contemporary Catholic social discourse, and the tradition, in large part, has women religious to thank for that.

This work, however, has not been met with universal enthusiasm. Those hostile to Roman Catholicism suspected sisters of using their schools, orphanages, hospitals, and charitable service to infect "good Protestants" with "diabolical Catholic doctrines."[16] At the same time as Catholic sisters were gaining respect for "civilizing the West," Protestant sects began training people to "save the West" from Catholics.[17] Underlying these efforts was the old fear that Catholics could not be "true Americans" because of their "allegiance to Rome."[18] Over time, the incredible service of women religious to humanity on America's battlefields, city streets, and vast prairies largely dispelled this suspicion.[19]

The determination of Catholic sisters to respond to all people as well as the full range of human needs reinforced the idea among immigrants and non-immigrants that the US Constitution applied to them, that they were indeed created equal and "endowed by their Creator with certain unalienable rights, that among these are life, liberty, and the pursuit of happiness." This determination also "laid a solid foundation for the diversified and specialized undertakings that Catholic sisters of various racial and ethnic origins would undertake in the nineteenth and twentieth centuries."[20]

Twentieth-Century Lessons

By mid-twentieth century, women religious in the United States had accomplished a great deal. Despite their growing reputation as caregivers and educators, Catholic religious women were becoming increasingly alarmed at what they perceived as their inadequate training. Very often, a young woman entered a religious community without a college education and was expected to teach immediately in a primary or secondary school classroom. Although they had guidance from seasoned teachers in their religious communities, such support did not sufficiently compensate for lack of formal training. Educational content and teaching methods had to keep pace with the vibrant and rapidly changing American society. Added to that, the numbers of vocations to religious life were growing.[21]

The Catholic school population was burgeoning too. In response to these pressures, a small group of religious women met in 1952. They decided to push for more systematic education of sisters. They did this by first creating a survey about teacher education for major superiors of religious communities across the country. The survey results revealed deep deficiencies in teacher training among women religious in Catholic schools.[22] This prompted a series of meetings and research that culminated in an "integrated sister formation process" that was formally titled the Sister Formation Conference (SFC).[23]

Among the many accomplishments of the SFC was a careful examination of what it meant to form effective educators and sustain a first-rate educational system. A key factor recognized for school success was the development of each individual sister's intellectual potential. This came to mean supporting college education in teaching, nursing, and other fields. Sometimes this extended to graduate level education. As a result of these initiatives, by mid-twentieth century American women religious were among the most highly educated women in the country.

For the SFC, the purpose of these developments was to increase the teaching competence of religious women and, through that, change the nature of Catholic education. An additional program in line with this movement was the Marquette Workshops. This was a series of summer workshops held at Marquette University from the mid-1950s through the early 1960s focusing on what was called the "Everett Curriculum." This curriculum was a comprehensive framework for the education of women religious that took great care in addressing contemporary issues. The effect of the Marquette Workshops and the Everett Curriculum was to energize sisters into being active, issue-conscious citizens of the United States and the world.[24]

These workshop and curriculum experiences changed how the sisters cultivated democratic values in Catholic schools. Improved pedagogy produced better citizens. A better citizen was not simply more law-abiding but a citizen with the critical thinking skills to promote justice in a democratic society. That Catholic religious women succeeded in forming such citizens can be seen in the increasingly prominent leadership roles Catholics have played in American public life since the 1960s.[25] By 2010, the vice president of the United States, the Speaker of the House, 156 congresspersons, and five out of nine Supreme Court justices were Catholic. Most had been educated in Catholic schools. One of these people, Senator Barbara Mikulski, gave this as one reason for her passion for public service: "I went to Catholic schools and was educated by the nuns. Their emphasis on leadership, service, and also the values of our faith contained in the Beatitudes, Matthew 5, the Sermon on the Mount. To hunger and thirst after justice."[26]

The people who designed these programs recognized that they would change women religious themselves. "At the heart of Sister Formation," writes Kenneth Briggs, "was an effort to refine a sister's identity from dependent child to thinking adult . . . . the life of the mind gained respect of its own. Nuns would begin to see themselves as individuals instead of cogs in an anonymous machine."[27] As Lora Ann Quiñonez and Mary Daniel Turner have noted, women religious:

> [grew] to understand that their identity as Americans and their identity as religious [were] not detachable but interactively related. Indeed, being American—living inside of the conditions that make up American reality, engaging the events and people that constitute American history, wrestling with the ties between American culture and whatever identity one claims—has been, if not a causal, then certainly a qualifying, factor of the changed identity of sisters as well as the changed dynamic of the life of religious communities.[28]

Another striking outcome of the SFC was a greatly expanded concept of where nuns belonged. "Rather than simply training sisters to be pious contributors to the everyday workings of Catholic schools and hospitals, the curriculum's objective was to train sisters for professional engagement in the world."[29] Women religious were encouraged to learn about and discuss a variety of issues that had direct bearing on democracy, such as racism, anti-Semitism, religious prejudice, the rights of migrant workers, structural poverty, and urban violence.

Advanced education for American sisters enhanced their capacity and credibility to engage in public discourse on social issues. Some of the most remarkable of these public contributions are two books by Mary Ellen O'Hanlon, OP: *Racial Myths* (1946) and *The Heresy of Race* (1950).[30] Sister O'Hanlon earned her PhD in biology and used her scientific expertise to make a strenuous case against the widely held belief that "negroes" were members of a genetically inferior race. Such research, combined with the sisters' experiences of working with the despised and the marginalized, prompted many religious women to "cross color lines" in ways that were rare at the time.

Schools became places to extend the promise of democracy, regardless of race. As Hoy notes:

> Believing that ignorance was the result of circumstance not race, missionary sisters built educational institutions in Chicago with the power to transform poor black youngsters into middle-class adults. . . . Since the sisters who staffed parish schools were mostly from immigrant Catholic families, they emphasized values learned in their working class homes and schools—hard work, thrift, honesty, reliability and

cleanliness. They also provided "adequate discipline and personal
attention for all students" treating everyone "with respect like human
beings."[31]

Given these developments, it is not surprising that many women religious became involved with the organized civil rights movement of the
1950s and 1960s. Sometimes this involvement was quite dramatic. In 1963,
seven Franciscan sisters in full religious habit joined a picket line denouncing racial discrimination at the Illinois Club for Catholic Women. Because
they were in full habit and because they were protesting a Catholic institution that itself was located on a Catholic university campus, the involvement of these women became national news and their images appeared in
newspapers across the United States.[32] Journalist John Fialka writes:

> By 1965 more than five hundred nuns, a rolling sea of black and white,
> joined a civil rights demonstration in New York. The momentum con-
> tinued to build. At Selma, Alabama when Sister Margaret Ellen
> Traxler, a School Sister of Notre Dame, led a line of ten sisters into
> the front ranks of the demonstrators, she was followed by Benedic-
> tines, Sisters of the Blessed Virgin Mary and Sisters of Loretto.[33]

There was less dramatic, more sustained involvement as well. What
some have termed a "racial apostolate" emerged out of the SFC discussions. Many sisters began to coordinate efforts with the newly formed
National Catholic Conference for Interracial Justice (NCCIJ).[34] Under
this organization's educational wing, Mary Peter (Margaret Ellen) Traxler,
SSND, developed the Traveling Workshops on Inter-Group Relations
program. These workshops emphasized practical ways to improve race
relations and were conducted primarily by women religious known as the
"sister-faculty." Sessions included lectures, discussions, and strategic planning tailored to the particular circumstances of each community.

Though initially focused on discrimination against African Americans,
the scope of the Traveling Workshops expanded to include other ethnic
groups and the growing concern over women's rights.[35] Through their
involvement in the civil rights movement, a number of women religious
became active participants in the early second-wave feminist movement in
the United States.[36]

> At a warm-up rally before one of Martin Luther King's Chicago
> marches, a nun, Sister Mary William, stepped up to the microphone
> to suggest that racial justice for African Americans—as messy and
> embarrassing as it was for the Church to deal with—was only part of

the agenda that was moving younger sisters. They had another issue. . . "Why are sisters like Negroes?" she asked. "Because they, too, are segregated, ghettoized and because leadership is not encouraged in their roles."[37]

US feminist historians often ignore the role of women religious in the feminist movement. Beginning in the 1960s, many sisters identified themselves as feminists or at least gave voice to the need for gender equity within both society and the Roman Catholic Church. Joel Read, SSSF, was one of the founding members of the National Organization for Women (NOW). She and her Alverno College colleague, Austin Doherty, SSSF (also an active member of NOW), worked tirelessly to educate people about women's rights and the rights of women religious.

John Fialka calls women religious "America's first feminists," arguing that they broke gender barriers in the professions and other leadership arenas far before most other American women even dreamed of doing so.[38] Despite their decidedly unfeminist vows of obedience and formalized subordination to male authority, sisters demonstrated that women could be smart, strong, and engaged in issues of public policy. They showed that women deserve respect as fully functioning citizens. No doubt, this sense of identity—rightfully claimed by women religious—was at least in part due to the strong, though not uncontested, claims made in Catholic thought about the inherent and inviolable dignity of every human person, a point highlighted by Robert John Araujo in his reflection on the legacy of Francisco de Vitoria at the end of this section of the current volume.

Complicated Messages

The irony is that while women religious had succeeded at keeping Catholic Americans faithful to the Church and adept at democratic citizenship, they found themselves working inside Catholic institutions that were growing more and more undemocratic. As the frontiers settled and the institutions they created stabilized, convents became more restrictive and the diocesan Church structure functioned more hierarchically.

To an extent, this growing tension is understandable. Well before the Roman Catholic Church opened the Second Vatican Council in 1962, sisters had been encouraged by Church authorities to become more relevant and accessible. Speakers at leadership assemblies often urged women religious to fuse their identities as American and Catholic. Quiñonez recounts this dynamic at one such assembly:

"Your special call," said Fr. Thomas E. Clarke, S.J., "is to be a channel by which the distinctly American experience of freedom and all that is noble and enduring in it is more fully assimilated into the life of the church all over the world." Indeed, Elise Krantz, SND, complained that whenever a member "tried to get the Conference back on the track" by speaking of the church and of loyalty to its teaching, six or seven other members would rise to the floor to counter: "that isn't important today. We're in America. This is the American church. We're women religious in the United States."[39]

It was a matter of challenging male hierarchies and challenging their own hierarchical structures. In 1972, what had been the Conference of Mother Superiors became the Leadership Conference of Women Religious (LCWR) in part to avoid using language that resonated with elitism.[40] The change was more than rhetorical.

> It expanded the vehicles for participation of the membership in the election of officers, the choice of goals, and the governance of the organization. It had, in the process, become more egalitarian and democratic, more intent on participating in the time honored American tradition of social reform.[41]

Individual organizations of women religious followed suit. No longer were women who ran colleges and hospitals required to ask permission to buy a tube of toothpaste. No longer did unquestioning obedience to authority trump critical thinking and individual moral agency. This process of becoming more democratic within their own community self-governance was complex, stressful, and not without internal resistance.[42]

Internal resistance was nothing compared to the resistance of authorities within the hierarchy of the Church. As Quiñonez and Turner report:

> In terms that anticipate recent fulminations of highly placed ecclesiastics on "radical feminism," Cardinal Antoniutti, the head of the Congregation for Religious, lamented the "erroneous ideas about the promotion of women" of some nuns, which "smothered their natural instinct towards humble and retiring self giving" (address to superiors general, November 24, 1969) . . . When the authors [Quiñonez and Turner] interviewed Archbishop Thomas C. Kelley, OP (March 11, 14–15, 1988), they asked him what he believed was the major objection of the Congregation for Religious to LCWR. Without a pause he answered, "Feminism."[43]

Perhaps no more striking example of the struggle between democratic self-governance and obedience to absolute authority can be found than in the 1968 confrontation between Los Angeles Cardinal John McIntyre and the Sisters of the Immaculate Heart of Mary. According to Anita Caspary, then Mother General of the Sisters, Servants of the Immaculate Heart of Mary (IHM) community, the sisters engaged in a careful and respectful process of discernment about their own governance. They presented their case for a community and Church of greater collaboration to the cardinal. In response, he demanded that they continue to live by traditional monastic discipline with narrow restrictions on what the sisters could wear, when they could pray, and what they could do in their ministries. Rather than engage in dialogue about their points of difference, the cardinal simply told Caspary that her community was wrong and they were to obey him.[44]

In 2012, the Vatican issued a critique of US women religious based on a widespread investigation of their practices and leadership. A particular focus was placed on the LCWR that represents about 80 percent of contemporary US religious women. The report argued that the leadership had challenged Church teachings and promoted "radical feminist themes incompatible with the Catholic faith." Sisters were reprimanded for making public statements that "disagree with or challenge the bishops, who are the Church's authentic teachers of faith and morals."[45] The LCWR leadership argued that sisters had been responding to the real needs of the people they served. Particularly striking has been the public support for sisters that includes recognition of their contributions to American society by Catholics and non-Catholics alike.[46] Sadly, as Barry Sullivan points out in his upcoming chapter in this volume, this conflict between transparency and authority, dialogue and reprimand, was being simultaneously played out in the US Church over the clerical sexual abuse crisis.

Over 250 years after the first Catholic sisters arrived in what would become the United States, women religious are still grappling with the tensions of what it means to be both Roman Catholic and American. Religious orders that had concentrated on guiding waves of immigrants into full participation in a democracy through teaching, social work, and health care had gradually expanded their ministries to include legal aid, immigration reform, support for migrant workers, LGBTQ rights activism, peace advocacy, efforts to curb domestic violence, environmental protection, campaigns to end the death penalty, and more. These sisters would say that they have been called both by Catholic values and democratic ideals to do such work, but their critics see them as upsetting the balance. The Catholic American dialogue continues.

NOTES

1. John Fialka, *Sisters: Catholic Nuns and the Making of America* (New York: St. Martin's, 2003), 2, and Jay P. Dolan, *The American Catholic Experience: A History from Colonial Times to the Present* (New York: Doubleday, 1985), 120–21.

2. Fialka, *Sisters*, 2–3.

3. Ibid., 21.

4. See Carol Coburn and Martha Smith, *Spirited Lives: How Nuns Shaped Catholic Culture and American Life, 1836–1920* (Chapel Hill: University of North Carolina Press, 1999), 42–43, and Fialka, *Sisters*, 49–50. The Know Nothing Party was an anti-Catholic political organization in the mid-nineteenth century that held, among other things, that Catholics could not be true Americans because of their loyalty to the pope in Rome.

5. See Patricia Wittenberg, *The Rise and Fall of Catholic Religious Orders: A Social Movement Perspective* (Albany: SUNY Press, 1994), 87–89.

6. Dolan, *The American Catholic Experience*, 136. See also Margaret McGuinness, "A Puzzle with Missing Pieces: Catholic Women and the Social Settlement Movement, 1897–1915," *Cushwa Center for the Study of American Catholicism Working Paper Series* 22, no. 2 (Spring 1990): 1–30.

7. See Charlie Morris, *American Catholic: The Saints and Sinners Who Built America's Most Powerful Church* (New York: Random House, 1997), 54–80.

8. See William T. Cavanaugh, *The Myth of Religious Violence* (Oxford: Oxford University Press, 2009), 114–18.

9. See Julius Drachsler, *Democracy and Assimilation: The Blending of Immigrant Heritages in America* (New York: Macmillan, 1920); John Dewey, *Democracy and Education: An Introduction to the Philosophy of Education* (New York: Free Press, 1944); Robert McNergney, Edward Ducharme, and Mary Ducharme, eds., *Education for Democracy: Case Method, Teaching and Learning* (Mahwah, NJ: L. Erlbaum, 1999).

10. See Morris, *American Catholic*, 73; Dolan, *American Catholic Experience*, 265–66; Coburn and Smith, *Spirited Lives*, 53–55.

11. Paula M. Kane, *Separatism and Subculture: Boston Catholicism, 1900–1920* (Chapel Hill: University of North Carolina Press, 1994), 59–65. See also Mary Ewen, "Removing the Veil: The Liberated American Nun in the Nineteenth Century," *Cushwa Center for the Study of American Catholicism Working Paper Series* 3 (Spring 1978): 7–8.

12. See Fialka, *Sisters*, 9.

13. Mary Denis Maher, *To Bind Up the Wounds: Catholic Sisters in the U.S. Civil War* (New York: Greenwood, 1989), 18.

14. See Morris, *American Catholic*, 38, 199.

15. Suellen Hoy, *Good Hearts: Catholic Sisters in Chicago's Past* (Urbana: University of Illinois Press, 2006), 5.

16. George Stewart Jr., *Marvels of Charity: History of American Sisters and Nuns* (Huntington, IN: Our Sunday Visitor, 1994), 214–15.

17. Coburn and Smith, *Spirited Lives*, 105.

18. Jay P. Dolan, *In Search of an American Catholicism: A History of Religion and Culture in Tension* (Oxford: Oxford University Press, 2002), 135. See also Kane, *Separatism and Subculture*, 59–65, and Coburn and Smith, *Spirited Lives*, 5.

19. See Maher, *To Bind Up the Wounds*, 148–49.

20. Hoy, *Good Hearts*, 5.

21. Kenneth Briggs, *Double Crossed: Uncovering the Catholic Church's Betrayal of American Nuns* (New York: Doubleday, 2006), 42.

22. Marjorie Noteman Beane, *From Framework to Freedom: A History of the Sister Formation Conference* (New York: University Press of America, 1993), 2–3, 16.

23. Ibid., 38.

24. Ibid., 64.

25. See Briggs, *Double Crossed*, 42.

26. Rose Marie Berger, "Sen. Barbara Mikulski on 'Being Educated by the Nuns,'" January 30, 2011, at www.rosemarieberger.com, April 21, 2013.

27. See Philip Gleason, "The Catholic Church in American Public Life in the Twentieth Century," *Logos: A Journal of Catholic Thought and Culture* 3, no. 4 (Fall 2000): 85–99.

28. Lora Ann Quiñonez and Mary Daniel Turner, *The Transformation of American Catholic Sisters* (Philadelphia: Temple University Press, 1992), 64.

29. Amy Koehlinger, *The New Nuns: Racial Justice and Religious Reform in the 1960s* (Cambridge, MA: Harvard University Press, 2007), 68.

30. See Mary Ellen O'Hanlon, *Racial Myths* (River Forest, IL: Rosary College, 1946), and *The Heresy of Race* (River Forest, IL: Rosary College, 1950).

31. Hoy, *Good Hearts*, 82.

32. See Koehlinger, *The New Nuns*, 75. See also Hoy, *Good Hearts*, 125.

33. Fialka, *Sisters*, 196.

34. See Koehlinger, *The New Nuns*, 74.

35. Ibid., 81–91.

36. What is often called the "second wave" of feminism refers to a resurgence of activism during the 1960s and '70s that addressed a wide range of issues that proponents argued made women second-class citizens. These included economic policy, educational and employment opportunities, health matters, athletics, and violence against women. The "first wave" usually refers to the period from 1848 until 1920, when US women won the right to vote.

37. Fialka, *Sisters*, 197.

38. Ibid, 1.

39. Quiñonez and Turner, *The Transformation*, 76–77.

40. In the early 1950s, the Roman Catholic hierarchy asked US women religious leaders what their founders would do if confronted with the needs of the world today and, by 1956, called on them to form a national conference, which became the Conference of Major Superiors of Women (CMSW). It was charged with promoting sisters' spiritual welfare, increasing efficacy in their work, and fostering cooperation among all religious and clergy. The CMSW functioned as such until 1970 when restructuring resulted in a majority vote to emphasize justice issues and rename the group to the Leadership Conference of Women Religious. A splinter group resisted these changes and became Consortium Perfectae Caritatis (CPC)

41. Quiñonez and Turner, *The Transformation*, 76–77.

42. See Joan Chittister, *The Way We Were: A Story of Conversion and Renewal* (Maryknoll, NY: Orbis Books, 2005).

43. Quiñonez and Turner, *The Transformation*, 107.

44. Briggs, *Double Crossed*, 113–16.

45. Congregatio Pro Doctrina Fidei, "Doctrinal Assessment of the Leadership Conference of Women Religious," usccb.org, April 21, 2013.

46. Nicholas Kristof, "We Are All Nuns," *New York Times*, April 28, 2012.

"First Be Reconciled": Restorative Justice and Deliberative Democracy

William R. O'Neill, SJ

For [Jesus] said that a glass of water given to a beggar was given
to Him. He made heaven hinge on the way we act toward Him
in His disguise of commonplace, frail, ordinary humanity. Did you
give Me food when I was hungry? Did you give Me to drink when
I was thirsty? Did you give me clothes when My own were all rags?
Did you come to see Me when I was sick, or in prison or in trouble?
And to those who say, aghast, that they never had a chance to do
such a thing, that they lived two thousand years too late, He will
say again what they had the chance of knowing all their lives,
that if these things are done for the very least of His brethren
they were done to Him.

— DOROTHY DAY, *Selected Writings*

So wrote Dorothy Day, founder of the Catholic Worker Movement, in December 1945. But seeing "these least" remains a hard grace for a society so given to incarcerating its own. As Robert Bolt reminds us in his play, *A Man for All Seasons*, our perceptions invariably betray our "moral squints," our tacit beliefs or prejudices.[1] This chapter first considers the ethical implications of mass incarceration in the United States from the prevailing "moral squint" of retributive justice. It then explores an alternative view from the rich, yet contested perspective of restorative justice in deliberative democracy. The chapter concludes by assessing distinctively religious contributions to restorative practices, with particular attention to modern Roman Catholic social teaching.

The Politics of Retribution

According to recently published figures from the US Bureau of Justice Statistics, the rate of incarceration in the United States nearly quadrupled between 1980 and 2009. Inmates incarcerated in prison or jail number 2.2 million. This is the highest official rate of incarceration in the world (at 731 per 100,000 population). Including those in probation or on parole, the total number of citizens under the aegis of corrections departments now reaches 7.1 million, an increase of almost 300 percent since 1980. Today, one out of every 137 Americans is incarcerated.[2]

Disaggregating for race and ethnicity, one in ten black males aged 30–34 was in prison or jail in 2010. One in twenty-six Hispanic males was incarcerated, compared with one in sixty-one white males in the same age group. Of inmates in state or federal prisons, 38 percent were black, 32 percent were white, and 22 percent were Hispanic in 2010. Black males have a 32 percent likelihood of serving time in prison. Hispanic males have a 17 percent likelihood and white males 6 percent. In 2010, the rate of incarceration for black women was 2.9 times higher than the rate for white women; the rate for Hispanic women was 1.5 times higher.[3] Felony disenfranchisement deprives "1 of every 13 African Americans" of the right to vote.[4] Such systemic inequities, writes Michelle Alexander, perpetuate the "New Jim Crow" of "racial caste" and "racialized social control."[5] In Adam Gopnik's words, "mass incarceration on a scale almost unexampled in human history is a fundamental fact of our country today . . . as slavery was the fundamental fact of 1850. In truth, there are more black men in the grip of the criminal-justice system . . . than were in slavery then."[6]

The dramatic increase in prison populations over the past half-century stands "in sharp contrast to that of the preceding fifty years, during which time there was a gradual increase in the use of incarceration commensurate with the growth in the general population."[7] So too, our current incarceration practices differ markedly from those of other western democracies with comparable crime rates. Amnesty International reports that the "USA stands virtually alone in the world in incarcerating thousands of prisoners in longer-term or indefinite solitary confinement."[8] Punitive attitudes prevail in what William Stuntz calls the "harshest" judicial system "in the history of democratic government,"[9] despite evidence of other mitigating factors underlying decreases in violent crime.[10]

A similar punitive stance favors summary apprehension, detention, and deportation of the some 11.2 million undocumented migrants—"illegal aliens"—in the United States.[11] The Department of Homeland Security (DHS) and Immigration and Customs Enforcement (ICE) "detain up to 33,400 immigrants and asylum seekers each day—an all-time high of 439,247 in fiscal year 2012 alone."[12] Despite promises of reform, the overwhelming majority of "those detained are held in jails or jail-like facilities . . . at a cost of over $2 billion."[13]

We speak of a "global village" but in the accents of strangers. In my ministry at the Federal Women's Prison in Dublin, California, the majority of the women I serve are poor migrants, some of whom will be summarily deported after completing their sentences. Many of the women are forcibly separated from their children for five to fifteen years, their punishment exacerbated terribly by the punishment thus inflicted on their children. It is not surprising to hear a woman pray for her child who is now also incarcerated. Yet, the crimes for which the women stand convicted are typically nonviolent drug offenses. They are the expendable ones and our punitive moral squint renders them, in the words of the liberation theologian, Gustavo Gutiérrez, "nonpersons."[14] They are, to our contemporary society, unimportant failures.

Roman Catholic bishops have joined other religious leaders in opposing such a punitive regime. Yet their words fail to awaken citizens and co-religionists. Why? Rehearsing the complex genealogy of retributive practices in the United States would be a long and complex task. The aim of this chapter is more modest: to trace several related themes figuring into America's retributive moral squint. The analysis begins with crime, for crime and punishment are intimately linked in the context of the United States: what we say of one bears on the other.

In modern liberal polities, constituted through the legal fiction of a social contract, crime typically appears as a voluntaristic legal construction, an offense against the collective will of the body politic in its various liberal denominations. In the Lockean tradition, citizens cede their natural right of punishment to the state. For Thomas Hobbes, crime is principally an offense against the sovereign's rights. So too for Kant, legal punishment is just deserts for violating the social contract.[15] With little latitude for equity, adversarial adjudication of guilt and punishment restores the formal (procedural) rule of abstract right or law but not the thicker bonds of traditional communitarian membership.[16]

Offenses against the state must be remedied, but in our adversarial legal system, repaying the offender's debt to society favors neither reparations for victims (recognizing victims' positive rights) nor reintegration of the offender into community. Indeed, social bonds are further attenuated as punishment is officially privatized. Crime may not pay but punishment increasingly does, creating incentives for higher incarceration rates.[17] In our modern regime of incarceration, whether publically or privately administered, incapacitation and/or deterrence suffice to protect the body politic, reaffirming the coercive prerogatives of the bureaucratic state. If these prerogatives discipline citizens, even more so do they penalize "aliens" whose bodies (and not mere behavior) become "illegal." The economy of exclusion signified by the social contract proceeds apace as "criminals" or "illegal aliens" are denied the very right to have rights. What Hannah Arendt says of forced migrants pertains no less to all those suffering the "loss of home and political status" (e.g., through mass incarceration and felony disenfranchisement). Such loss, says Arendt, is tantamount to "expulsion from humanity altogether." The "alien" is not the exemplar of humanity in general (the generalized other)[18] but, like the criminal, "a frightening symbol of difference as such."[19]

The symbolization of difference, whether of illegal aliens or criminals, likewise blurs the lines between retribution and vengeance or scapegoating (the sublimation of vengeance) in our punitive regime. The will to punish, independent of consequential considerations such as deterrence, remains a potent force in polities where social bonds are already frayed and violence naturalized. Vengeance, especially against "frightening symbols of difference," seems to have its own cathartic rationale even where less punitive measures suffice for deterrence or reparation.

At play here is a perverse dialectic where our punitive regime constructs its own object: the alien becomes "illegal," the young black man, the "criminalblackman."[20] Difference is feared and punished, reproducing (essentializing) the very differences we fear and, consequently, punish. As Alexander argues, our ostensibly impartial, "colorblind" criminal justice system thus rationalizes, and effectively erases, its racial and ethnic partiality or bias.[21]

Restorative Squint

In recent years, restorative justice has emerged as an alternative moral squint in Roman Catholic social teaching. In their pastoral letter, "Responsibility, Rehabilitation, and Restoration: A Catholic Perspective on Crime and Criminal Justice," the US bishops write:

> An increasingly widespread and positive development in many communities is often referred to as restorative justice. Restorative justice focuses first on the victim and the community harmed by the crime, rather than on the dominant state-against-the-perpetrator model. This shift in focus affirms the hurt and loss of the victim, as well as the harm and fear of the community, and insists that offenders come to grips with the consequences of their actions. . . . Restorative justice also reflects our values and tradition. Our faith calls us to hold people accountable, to forgive, and to heal.[22]

One of its leading theorists, the Mennonite theologian Howard Zehr, describes restorative justice in a similar vein as "a process to involve, to the extent possible, those who have a stake in a specific offense and to collectively identify and address harms, needs, and obligations, in order to heal and put things as right as possible."[23] For proponents of restorative justice, victim–offender reconciliation programs (VORPs), sentencing circles, or family group conferences (FGCs) represent an effective alternative to prevailing regimes of retributive justice.[24]

Yet the distinction fails to do full justice to what is entailed by "putting things as right as possible" in restorative practices, programs, and rationales. Neither retributive nor restorative justice is, after all, a rigidly limited conception.[25] Some interpretations of retributive justice include restorative elements, while restorative practices need not exclude retributive sanctions. Indeed, proponents of restorative justice differ as to their proper balance, such as whether restorative practices should replace, complement, or be integrated within criminal justice systems.

Perhaps the crucial question is what is being restored. Advocates of transformative justice seek not only amelioration of correctional practices (victim–offender reconciliation) but also redress of the social structural violence abetting crime. Such structural criticism overlaps with non-Western uses of restorative justice (e.g., the South African Truth and Reconciliation Commission). The massive crimes against humanity of institutionalized racism signified by apartheid in South Africa precluded a strict, juridical adjudication of individual guilt and punishment.

Despite these considerable differences, a family resemblance remains among conceptions of restorative justice. While punitive practice in the United States views crime primarily as a legal offense against the body politic, restorative justice sees crime as a breach of our natural sociality. In the words of Archbishop Desmond Tutu, Chair of the South African Truth and Reconciliation Commission:

> Retributive justice—in which an impersonal state hands down punishment with little consideration for victims and hardly any for the perpetrator—is not the only form of justice. I contend that there is another kind of justice, restorative justice. . . . The central concern is not retribution or punishment but, in the spirit of *ubuntu*, the healing of breaches, the redressing of imbalances, the restoration of broken relationships. This kind of justice seeks to rehabilitate both the victim and the perpetrator, who should be given the opportunity to be reintegrated into the community he or she has injured by his or her offence.[26]

What might such restorative practices entail juridically, ethically, and theologically? How might such non-Western wisdom, as in Tutu's appeal to *ubuntu*, inflect both ethical and theological interpretations within such resources as modern Roman Catholic social teaching? One turn would be from the dialectic of "crime and punishment" to the discourse of "crime and community." For if crime represents primarily a breach of natural social bonds, what must be restored are the broken relationships.

In interpreting such breaches, both Tutu and modern Catholic social teaching invoke the modern concept of human rights. Robert Araujo, in his historical reflection on Francisco de Vitoria at the end of this section, says as much when he turns to the natural law—and its conceptualization, and grounding, of dignity—as the foundation for contemporary human rights discourse. Here, basic human rights are less properties of sovereign selves, abstracted from the ensemble of social relations (as in modern liberalism), than the moral grammar of deliberative-democratic practices. Rights talk is less talk about rights than the talk rights makes possible (e.g., testimony of both victims and offenders in reconciliation programs). Narratively embodied, rights reveal the breach of social bonds (i.e., the systematic distortions of racial and ethnic bias in constructing the "illegal alien," the "criminalblackman," the "nonperson"). This is the critical, or deconstructive, use of rights rhetoric—a moral squint letting us see crime but, no less, the systemic inequities of white privilege and racial caste in society and, tragically, as Bryan Massingale argues, in our Church.[27]

In this richer, communitarian interpretation, moreover, rights imply correlative duties of forbearance and of provision and protection.[28] Rights are not merely a grammar of dissent disclosing systemic racism and ethnic bias; we must also redeem the cri de coeur "never again." We must seek to heal the breaches, to restore or establish a rights regime in which basic human rights, as the sine qua non of democratic deliberation, are suitably redeemed and protected. To the critical, deconstructive use of rights there thus corresponds a constructive or reconstructive use in refiguring public narrative. As in modern Catholic social teaching, basic human rights generate structural imperatives to redress systemic deprivation as in the new "Jim Crow" of mass incarceration—our own domestic apartheid of punitive segregation.[29]

As in the transformative conception of restorative justice, the question of systemic redress of social inequity looms large. What must be restored is not the status quo ante but the bonds of moral community, that is the rights-based common good of mutual respect and recognition necessary, in Alexander's words, for "a thriving, multiracial, multiethnic democracy free from racial hierarchy." For "the failure to acknowledge the humanity and dignity of all persons has lurked at the root of every racial caste system."[30] Our rights talk must be rich enough to name both victim and offender while essentializing neither. Indeed, under the rubrics of the common good, our moral entitlement to indiscriminate respect justifies preferential treatment for those whose basic rights are most imperiled, or, in the words of Albert Camus, our taking "the victim's side."[31] Such a discriminate response finds expression in the graduated moral urgency of differing human rights and in the differing material conditions presumed for their realization.[32] A regime of rights must thus embody a legislative or juridical preference for victims of racial, ethnic, and gendered violence, and differential material entitlements corresponding to the differing prerequisites of agency.[33]

Prevailing social arrangements, including mass incarceration, must be assessed in light of the *telos* of such a regime. A consequentially sensitive note is sounded: What policies and social arrangements best protect the basic rights of the most vulnerable, including liberties of effective deliberative-democratic participation for those so often consigned to the margins of history? As in the South African TRC and Catholic teaching, the restorative turn entails not only consequential (forward-looking) assessments of deterrence and rehabilitation but also structural (legal, juridical) transformation of prevailing inequities, as in racial and ethnic disparities in sentencing and the incarceration that culminate in effectively disenfranchising minorities.

Finally, the deconstructive and (re)constructive uses of rights rhetoric combine in interpersonal redress. For mutual respect enjoins not so much recognizing the generalized other but generalized respect for the concrete other—the victims of systemic racial and ethnic bias. As Alexander reminds us, justice, to be just, cannot be "colorblind." Neither are crimes primarily an offense against abstract right. Crimes against humanity may indeed be legion, but they are always transgressions of the ineluctably unique, concrete other. While our prevailing incarceration system neglects both victim and offender, restorative practices provide a social stage for interpersonal redress, emphasizing effective participation of victim, offender, and the local community affected by crime. Those who suffer rights violations through state-sponsored violence or criminal behavior acquire ancillary positive rights: of legal/juridical recognition (that harm has indeed been done), of provision (e.g., health care, counseling), and of reparation (including restitution, where feasible). Still, Primo Levi reminds us that even legal punishment cannot exact a just " 'price' for pain."[34] Offenders, conversely, acquire ancillary positive duties: of confessing to the harm done, of rehabilitation, and of reparation through, for example, victim-offender reconciliation programs, sentencing circles, or family group conferences.[35]

In integrating interpersonal and systemic redress, restorative justice looks beyond the rubrics of commutative justice, to which it is often assimilated on the analogy of retributive justice.[36] Indeed, in identifying systemic distortions of racism, ethnic bias, and white privilege, and redressing both interpersonal and systemic inequities, such justice "restores" the social bonds presumed in democratic deliberation. Yet neither interpersonal nor systemic redress dictates a univocal practice. Rather, differing notions of restorative justice turn, in part, on the respective emphases placed upon systemic and interpersonal redress and the nature of the harm or crime itself. Informal victim-offender programs may be unsuitable for crimes of sexual or spousal abuse. Neither, as in the example of the Federal Women's Prison, can we always assume a simple demarcation of victim and offender. Systemic and interpersonal redress must be taken together, in a dynamic and fluid deliberative praxis.

In a similar vein, the systemic aims of deterrence are qualified by the ethical exigencies of personal redress, such as victims' rights and offenders' duties. Moreover, since persons never cease to matter, the basic rights of offenders retain their moral force: cruelty is never permissible, vengeance never justified. Assessments of deterrence must themselves be rights-based, integrating both forward- and backward-looking considerations. Where less coercive measures than protracted incarceration (e.g., VORPs, FGCs) serve the purposes of deterrence and reparation, they would necessarily be preferred. "Here," as Tutu reminds us once again, "the central concern is not retribution or punishment but, in the spirit of *ubuntu* [and, we may say, Catholic social teaching on social solidarity], the healing of breaches, the redressing of imbalances, the restoration of broken relationships."[37]

A Concluding Religious Postscript

The preceding section argued that the varieties of restorative justice make up a distinctive moral squint. Crime is conceived as a breach of social relationship, while restoration implies both systemic redress of broken relations and interpersonal redress of victim and offender. Underwriting this threefold schema is the rhetorical use, deconstructive and (re)constructive, of basic human rights in democratic deliberation. The moral ideal of a rights regime provides the effective template for legal reform. Yet what can be legally codified will always fall short of the moral ideal. Reconciliation presumes, in a moral sense, not only legal recognition of offense (as in the Amnesty proceedings of the South African TRC) but also remorse, repentance, reparation, and restitution. These can only be approximated in the legal realm. Just as there is a moral surplus in democratic deliberation, so too there is a religious surplus. For the distinctively religious beliefs of both *ubuntu* and Catholic social teaching support a common morality of rights, even as they sublate or transcend it in enjoining compassion or forgiveness.[38]

By way of example, one can look to the Christian tradition, while fully recognizing that other religious traditions may move in the same spirit. Believers must tread carefully here; religion has its own intimate betrayals of legitimating violence. Yet, amid the many tragedies of modernity, religious talk of reconciliation can be, in Levinas's words, a form of "prophetism" and hence of "revelation."[39] As in Luke's parable of the Good Samaritan, disciples must "see and have compassion" (Lk 10:33), even as compassion itself becomes a way of seeing the stranger in all his or her truth. The stranger, says Simone Weil, is "exactly like me," albeit "stamped with a special mark by affliction."[40] To "go and do likewise" is to "suffer-with," to "[cross] over" to the world of the *anawîm*.[41] In the words of martyred Archbishop Oscar Romero, "becoming incarnate in their world . . . proclaiming the good news to them," even to the point of "sharing their fate."[42]

To the lawyer's question in the parable, "Who is my neighbor?," Jesus replies with a question of his own: "Who is it that proved himself neighbor?"[43] The lawyer's reply that "the Samaritan" was the neighbor is richly ironic. The Samaritan, a despised schismatic, proves himself neighbor and exemplifies neighborliness as the fulfillment of the law. He is the one the lawyer must imitate. The lawyer must "Go and do likewise!" (Lk. 10:37). For the question posed in Jesus's reading of the law is not finally "Whom shall I love?" but "Who shall I become in loving?" In Kierkegaard's words, "Christ does not speak about recognizing one's neighbor but about being a neighbor oneself, about proving oneself to be a neighbor, something the Samaritan showed by his compassion."[44] This makes all the difference.

In salvific irony, Jesus answers the lawyer's first question, "What must I do to inherit eternal life?," by reversing the second. For the command to "love the Lord, your God, with all your heart, with all your being, with all your strength, and with all your mind, and your neighbor as yourself" (Lk. 10:27) is fulfilled not in this or that particular deed of love[45] but in one's "selving as neighbor."[46] If the disciple is to live, she must enter the world of the *anawîm*, of the half-dead stranger. In Christ, such anamnestic solidarity implies not merely taking "the victim's side" but taking the victim's side as our own.[47] The distinctively Christian virtue of solidarity with the *anawîm*, with those "broken and oppressed in spirit," defines discipleship. "To be a Christian," says Gustavo Gutiérrez, "is to draw near, to make oneself a neighbor, not the one I encounter in my journey but the one in whose journey I place myself."[48] And so, for example, it is: "The prior lament of the victims," writes Massingale, "enables the privileged to engage in lament as well," as "a form of truth-telling and contrition" for complicity in racism.[49]

Compassion thus defines the disciple's way of anamnestic solidarity, a solidarity perfected in forgiveness.[50] If in "going and doing likewise" we come to see Christ as *our* Good Samaritan, so in forgiving, says Augustine, *we* experience God's reconciling love in Christ (2 Cor. 5:18–19).[51] Authentic reconciliation presumes a primordial responsibility to the victims and, a fortiori, systemic redress of injustice, such as systemic racism and ethnic bias. Yet victims may still forgo their particular claims of just retribution in memory of Jesus who "reconciled us with God" (Rom. 5:10). Such forgiveness, as a form of self-sacrificial *agapē*, transcends the exacting rhetoric of rights. For forgiveness cannot be less than just; there is no "teleological suspension of the ethical" of systemic critique.[52] Neither can forgiving reinscribe victimhood. The mother who forgives her child's murderer acts in utter gratuity. Although morally, she too must recognize the divine command upon her enemy's face ("Thou shalt not kill"). Still, the dictates of morality do not entail the further command "Thou shalt love thy enemy." Here the "thou" uttered is utterly particular, the face divine. Only she can forgive and her forgiveness is unexactable: the executioner has no moral claim to her forgiveness, nor can the legacy of suffering deprive the victim her "right to forgive."[53] And yet what is morally supererogatory may be religiously mandated by our narratives. As one mother said to her son's executioner in the South African TRC, "it is my Christian duty to forgive you."[54]

Such grace may be politically efficacious. In Tutu's words, there is "no future without forgiveness."[55] The United States is given to punitive recrimination; here, forgiveness may be the key to freeing victim and offender alike.[56] It is, let us hope, the grace of imagining otherwise.

NOTES

1. Robert Bolt, *A Man for All Seasons* (New York: Random House, 1990), 19. As Hans-Georg Gadamer argues, prejudgments or prejudices set both the

limits and the possibilities of interpretation. For a non-pejorative interpretation of prejudice (*praejudicium*), see Hans-Georg Gadamer, *Truth and Method*, 2nd. ed., trans. Joel Weinsheimer and Donald G. Marshall (New York: Crossroad, 1991), 265–307.

2. Bureau of Justice Statistics, summarized by the Sentencing Project, "Facts about Prisons and Prisoners," January 2012, www.sentencingproject .org.

3. Ibid.

4. The Sentencing Project, "Felony Disenfranchisement," July 2012, www.sentencingproject.org. The Sentencing Project reports that there were an estimated 1.17 million people disenfranchised in 1976, 3.34 million in 1996, and over 5.85 million in 2010. The rate of felony disenfranchisement for African Americans of voting age is more than four times greater than non-African Americans. Christopher Uggen, Sarah Shannon, and Jeff Manza, "State-Level Estimates of Felon Disenfranchisement in the United States, 2010," Sentencing Project, July 2012, www.sentencingproject.org/doc/ publications/fd_State_Level_Estimates_of_Felon_Disen_2010.

5. Michelle Alexander, *The New Jim Crow: Mass Incarceration in the Age of Colorblindness*, rev. ed. (New York: The New Press, 2012), 258. See Laurie M. Cassidy and Alex Mikulich, eds., *Interrupting White Privilege* (Maryknoll, NY: Orbis Books, 2007).

6. Adam Gopnik, "The Caging of America," *New Yorker*, January 39, 2012, 73. Gopnik notes that in the last two decades "the money that states spend on prisons has risen at six times the rate of spending on higher education" (73).

7. Ryan S. King, Marc Mauer, and Malcolm C. Young, "Incarceration and Crime: A Complex Relationship," Sentencing Project, 2005, www.sentencing project.org.

8. Amnesty International, "Entombed: Isolation in the US Federal Prison System," Report published by Amnesty International (London: Amnesty International, 2014), 2.

9. William J. Stuntz, *The Collapse of American Criminal Justice* (Cambridge, MA: Harvard University Press, 2011), 3.

10. The Justice Department itself acknowledges the failure of reintegration. Half of all former state convicts will be incarcerated again within three years of their release. See Stephen J. Pope, "From Condemnation to Conversion: Seeking Restorative Justice in the Prison System," *America*, November 21, 2001, 13.

11. Jeffrey S. Passel, Senior Demographer, Pew Hispanic Center, "Unauthorized Immigrants," December 6, 2012, www.pewhispanic.org/2012/12/06/ unauthorized-immigrants-11-1-million-in-2011.

12. Human Rights First, "Statement for the Record of Eleanor Acer," submitted to the House of Representatives Judiciary Committee (February 5,

2013), www.humanrightsfirst.org/wp-content/uploads/HRF-Statement
-House-Judiciary-Committee.

13. Ruthie Epstein and Eleanor Acer, "Jails and Jumpsuits: Transforming
the U.S. Immigration Detention System—a Two-Year Review," report by
Human Rights First (New York: Human Rights First, 2011), i.

14. Gustavo Gutiérrez, *The Power of the Poor in History: Selected Readings*
(London: SCM, 1983), 193.

15. In his analysis of Kant's views on crime and punishment, Roger Sullivan writes that "justice may be mitigated by benevolence, but the criminal still
owes *society* a strict debt to restore the reciprocal contractual relationship
between obedience to the law and benefits received form living under the
law." Roger J. Sullivan, *Immanuel Kant's Moral Theory* (Cambridge: Cambridge
University Press, 1989), 243.

16. In his critique of the US criminal justice system, Stuntz argues that
"the formal rule of law yields the functional rule of official discretion"—
often racially and ethnically biased. Stuntz, *The Collapse of American Criminal
Justice*, 3.

17. "In 2012, private prisons held 128,195 of the 1.6 million state and federal prisoners, representing 8 percent of the total population. From 1999 to
2010, the number of inmates in private prisons grew by 80 percent, compared
to 18 percent for the overall prison population." Cody Mason, "Too Good to
Be True: Private Prisons in America," Sentencing Project, August 2012,
www.sentencingproject.org.

18. See Seyla Benhabib, "The Generalized and the Concrete Other: The
Kohlberg-Gilligan Controversy and Feminist Theory," in *Feminism as Cri-
tique*, ed. Seyla Benhabib and Drucilla Cornell (Minneapolis: University of
Minnesota Press, 1987), 87.

19. Hannah Arendt, *The Origins of Totalitarianism* (New York: Harcourt,
Brace & World, 1966), 297, 299, 301.

20. Kathryn Russell, *The Color of Crime* (New York: New York University,
1988), cited in Alexander, *The New Jim Crow*, 107.

21. *Alexander*, The New Jim Crow, 236–44. In *Enfleshing Freedom: Body,
Race, and Being*, M. Shawn Copeland writes from a womanist perspective:
"A white, racially bias-induced horizon defines, censors, controls and segre-
gates different, other, non-white bodies." M. Shawn Copeland, *Enfleshing
Freedom: Body, Race, and Being* (Minneapolis, MN: Fortress Press, 2010), 15.
See also, Ada Maria Isasi-Diaz analogous *mujerista* critique in *En la Lucha /
In the Struggle: A Hispanic Women's Liberation Theology* (Minneapolis, MN:
Fortress Press, 1993).

22. United States Conference of Catholic Bishops, "Responsibility, Rehabilitation, and Restoration: A Catholic Perspective on Crime and Criminal
Justice" (Washington, DC: USCCB, 2000), 11.

23. Howard Zehr, *The Little Book of Restorative Justice* (Intercourse, PA: Good Books, 2007), 37.

24. See Gerry Johnstone and Daniel W. Van Ness, eds., *Handbook of Restorative Justice* (Devonshire, UK: Willan Publishing, 2007); Andrew von Hirsch, Julian Roberts, Anthony E. Bottoms, Kent Roach, and Mara Schiff, eds., *Restorative Justice and Criminal Justice: Competing or Reconcilable Paradigms?* (Oxford: Hart Publishing, 2003); Gerry Johnstone, ed., *A Restorative Justice Reader* (Devonshire, UK: Willan Publishing, 2003); Daniel W. Van Ness and Karen Heetderks Strong, *Restoring Justice*, 2nd ed. (Cincinnati, OH: Anderson Publishing, 2002); Howard Zehr, *Changing Lenses: A New Focus for Crime and Justice*, 3rd ed. (Harrisonburg, VA: MennoMedia, 2012).

25. For differing rationales, processes, and programs, see Gerry Johnstone, *Restorative Justice: Ideas, Values, Debates* (Portland, OR: Willan Publishing, 2002), 10–35, 161–71.

26. Desmond Tutu, *No Future without Forgiveness* (London: Rider, 1999), 51. "Ubuntu," says Tutu, "speaks of the very essence of being human." It "means my humanity is caught up, is inextricably bound up" in that of others. "We say, 'a person is a person through other people.' It is not 'I think therefore I am.' It says rather: 'I am human because I belong.' I participate, I share" (34–35).

27. See Bryan Massingale's eloquent *Racial Justice and the Catholic Church* (Maryknoll, NY: Orbis Books, 2010). It is important to note here, as Barry Sullivan does in the following chapter, that Catholic social teaching itself must also make an inward turn in order to reflect upon the structures within the Catholic Church itself that call out for this kind of critical attention. Sullivan identifies the sexual abuse crisis of the Church as a moment where the discourse of restorative vs. retributive justice must be attended to, along with an analysis of human rights discourse today.

28. *Pacem in terris*, nos. 28–38, 53–66, 132–41, in *Catholic Social Thought: The Documentary Heritage*, ed. David J. O'Brien and Thomas A. Shannon (Maryknoll, NY: Orbis Books, 2010), 141–43, 146–49, 159–61; *Gaudium et spes*, nos. 25–30, in *Catholic Social Thought*, 189–92; *Dignitatis humanae*, nos. 6–7, in *Vatican Council II: The Conciliar and Post Conciliar Documents*, vol. 1, ed. Austin Flannery, OP (Northport, NY: Costello Publishing, 1987), 803–5; *Populorum progressio*, nos. 22–24, 43–75, in *Catholic Social Thought*, 258–59; *Sollicitudo rei socialis*, nos. 38–40, in *Catholic Social Thought*, 451–55. See David Hollenbach, *The Common Good and Christian Ethics* (Cambridge: Cambridge University Press, 2002); Charles Curran, *Catholic Social Teaching: A Historical, Theological, and Ethical Analysis* (Washington, DC: Georgetown University Press, 2002); Kenneth R. Himes, ed., *Modern Catholic Social Teaching: Commentaries and Interpretations* (Washington, DC: Georgetown University Press, 2004).

29. See Walter H. Moberly, *The Ethics of Punishment* (London: Faber and Faber, 1968), 97–98, cited in Johnstone, *Restorative Justice*, 13.

30. Alexander, *The New Jim Crow*, 259. See James Bohman and William Rehg, eds., *Deliberative Democracy: Essays on Reason and Politics* (Cambridge, MA: MIT Press, 1997).

31. Albert Camus, *The Plague* (New York: Alfred A. Knopf, 1960), 230. In the present context, the term "victim" is an evaluative moral description referring to those suffering deprivation of their basic rights; as such, it is reducible neither to class membership nor to a particular psychological state. See William R. O'Neill, "No Amnesty for Sorrow: The Privilege of the Poor in Christian Social Ethics," *Theological Studies* 55, no. 4 (December 1994): 638–56.

32. See Gene Outka, *Agape* (New Haven, CT: Yale University Press, 1972), 20. See also, Ronald Dworkin, *Taking Rights Seriously* (Cambridge, MA: Harvard University Press, 1978), 227, and Aquinas, *Summae Theologiae* II-II, Ques. 31, art. 2.

33. See Jean Drèze and Amartya Sen, *Hunger and Public Action* (Oxford: Clarendon, 1989), 37–42.

34. Primo Levi, "The Symposium: Primo Levi," in *The Sunflower: On the Possibilities and Limits of Forgiveness*, ed., Simon Wiesenthal (New York: Schocken Books, 1998), 191.

35. See Zehr, *Changing Lenses*, 197.

36. Commutative justice rectifies the transactions of legal individuals, whether voluntary (e.g., contracts) or involuntary (e.g., crime).

37. Desmond Tutu, *No Future without Forgiveness* (London: Rider, 1999), 51.

38. As I have argued elsewhere, religious belief supplies not only ultimate grounding for ascribing dignity (creation in the *imago dei*) but also motivation and interpretative resources (e.g., the parable of the Good Samaritan). See William R. O'Neill, *The Ethics of Our Climate: Ethics and Hermeneutical Theory* (Washington, DC: Georgetown University Press, 1994), chap. 7.

39. Emmanuel Levinas, *Ethics and Infinity* (Pittsburgh, PA: Duquesne University Press, 1985), 113. For Levinas, "the Infinite comes in the signifyingness of the face. The face signifies the Infinite" (105).

40. Simone Weil, "Reflections on the Right Use of School Studies with a View to the Love of God," *Waiting for God*, trans. Emma Craufurd (New York: G. P. Putnam's Sons, 1951), 115.

41. In Scripture, the anawîm signify the "humble and lowly." See John Donahue, "The Bible and Catholic Social Teaching: Will this Engagement Lead to Marriage?," in Himes, *Modern Catholic Social Teaching*, 21–22.

42. Oscar Romero, "The Political Dimension of the Faith from the Perspective of the Option for the Poor," in *Liberation Theology: A Documentary*

History, ed. Alfred T. Hennelly, 292–303 (Maryknoll, NY: Orbis Books, 1990), 298.

43. See John Donahue, "'Who Is My Enemy?' The Parable of the Good Samaritan and the Love of Enemies," in *The Love of Enemy and Nonretaliation in the New Testament*, ed. Willard M. Swartley, 137–56 (Louisville, KY: Westminster/John Knox Press, 1992).

44. Søren Kierkegaard, *Works of Love*, trans. Howard and Edna Hong (New York: Harper and Row, 1962), 38.

45. See Karl Rahner, "The 'Commandment of Love in Relation to the Other Commandments,'" in Karl Rahner, *Theological Investigations* 5, trans. Karl H. Kruger (New York: Seabury, 1966), 453. See also, Karl Rahner, "The Theology of Freedom," in *Theological Investigations* 6, trans. Karl H. and Boniface Kruger (New York: Seabury, 1974), 178–96; and Karl Rahner, "Reflections on the Unity of the Love of Neighbour and the Love of God," in *Theological Investigations* 6, 240.

46. See Gerard Manley Hopkins, "As Kingfishers Catch Fire," in *The Poems of Gerard Manley Hopkins*, 4th ed., ed. W. H. Gardner and H. M. MacKenzie (Oxford: Oxford University Press, 1970), 90.

47. Karl Rahner, "On the Question of a Formal Existential Ethics," in *Theological Investigations* 2, trans. Karl H. Kruger (Baltimore, MD: Helicon, 1963), 217–34. See also, Gustavo Gutiérrez, *We Drink from Our Own Wells: The Spiritual Journey of a People*, trans. Matthew J. O'Connell (New York: Orbis, 1984), 125–26.

48. Gustavo Gutiérrez, "Toward a Theology of Liberation," trans. Alfred T. Hennelly, in *Liberation Theology: A Documentary History*, 74.

49. Massingale, *Racial Justice and the Catholic Church*, 111.

50. See Walter Benjamin, *Illuminations*, ed. H. Arendt (New York: Harcourt, Brace, & World, 1968), 253. See also, Thomas McCarthy, *Ideals and Illusions: On Reconstruction and Deconstruction in Contemporary Critical Theory* (Cambridge, MA: MIT Press, 1991), 205–10.

51. Augustine, *Quaestiones Evangeliorum* 2:19, *Corpus Christianorum, Series Latina*, XLIV B (Turnhout, Belgium: Brepols, 1980), 62–3; *De Natura et Gratia*, 43, 50, *Patrologia Series Latina*, ed. Jacques-Paul Migne (Paris, 1844), 247–90, at 271–72. See *Nature and Grace*, trans. Roland Teske, SJ, in Augustine, *Selected Writings on Grace and Pelagianism* (New York: New City Press, 2011), 295–379, at 352–53.

52. See Søren Kierkegaard, *Fear and Trembling*, trans. Walter Lowrie (Princeton, NJ: Princeton University Press, 1954), 64–77.

53. Albie Sachs, "Reparations: Political and Psychological Considerations," *Psychoanalytic Psychotherapy in South Africa* 16, no. 25 (Summer 1993): 2.

54. Testimony in the Amnesty Hearings of the TRC, author recollection.

55. Tutu, *No Future without Forgiveness*, 255–82.

56. Hannah Arendt writes that forgiving "is the only reaction which does not merely re-act but acts anew and unexpectedly, unconditioned by the act which provoked it and therefore freeing from its consequences both the one who forgives and the one who is forgiven." Hannah Arendt, *The Human Condition* (Chicago: University of Chicago Press, 1958), 241.

Access to Information:
Citizenship, Representative Democracy, and Catholic Social Thought

Barry Sullivan

For, Freedom comes from God's right hand.

—THOMAS DAVIS, *A Nation Once Again*

No government can operate entirely in the round. Some amount of secrecy is both necessary and inevitable.[1] But secrecy is fundamentally an affront to representative democracy, and it always exacts a cost. Secrecy engenders distrust, frustrates accountability, encourages arbitrary action, compromises the value of citizen participation, and disrespects human dignity. Secrecy also adds to the sense that government is distant and unresponsive. Institutions practice secrecy at their peril, yet many yield to its siren song. Institutions practice secrecy to various degrees and for various reasons: sometimes leaders or others have something terrible to hide, but often it simply seems easier to hide facts than to explain them.

Access to information has emerged as a central problem for the theory and practice of representative democracy. Proponents of transparency believe that secrecy devalues the consent of the governed, impedes the fulfillment of their responsibilities as citizens, and disrespects their dignity as human persons. Many officials, however, contend that they cannot do their work without large measures of secrecy. How one resolves these competing claims is important. In practical terms, much depends on whether government acts on the principle that information should be disclosed unless there is a compelling need to withhold, or, alternatively, adopts the view that information should be withheld unless there is a compelling need to disclose. In theoretical terms, those alternatives reflect divergent understandings of core values: human dignity, conscience and authority, and the nature of citizenship.

The first section of this chapter reviews the new attitudes about transparency that took hold in the period after the Second World War. The second section considers arguments from political theory concerning the citizen's need for information in a representative government. The third section addresses the connection between informed political participation and the concept of human dignity in contemporary Catholic social thought. The fourth concludes that democratic theory and Catholic social thought both support a strong presumption in favor of transparency but suggests that the Church's own lack of transparency necessarily limits the effectiveness of its advocacy in this area.

New Attitudes about Transparency

Almost fifty years ago, Donald C. Rowat, a Canadian political scientist, sounded the alarm. He urged everyone to "face the fact that any large measure of government secrecy is incompatible with democracy." Rowat thought that excessive secrecy engendered fear, eroded trust, and denied citizens the knowledge necessary to hold government accountable. However, Rowat also recognized that secrecy was dominant: "The principle followed almost everywhere [has been] that all administrative documents and activities shall be secret unless and until the Government chooses to reveal them. The public has no right to know the manner in which the government is carrying out its trust." Rowat attributed the continued dominance of secrecy to an unquestioning acceptance of practices previously followed by absolute monarchies. The theoretical basis for government changed, but important government practices endured.[2]

In the years following the Second World War, new attitudes came to the fore. The Universal Declaration of Human Rights recognized access to information as a human right: "Everyone has the right to freedom of opinion and expression [including the] freedom . . . to seek, receive, and impart information and ideas through any media and regardless of frontiers."[3] New national and supranational rights instruments followed suit, and some courts eventually interpreted such provisions as not merely protecting the citizens' right to seek information without government interference but as sometimes imposing on governments an affirmative obligation to provide information to citizens.[4]

The goal of these twentieth-century initiatives was not to establish an absolute right to government information; it was to replace a presumption of secrecy with one favoring transparency. The proponents of such initiatives thought that representative democracy required a different default rule, namely, that information should be presumed available unless and until the government decided otherwise. They also thought that government should not withhold information unless it had a compelling reason to do so.

But opposing forces were also at work. The perceived needs of the Atomic Age and the Cold War challenged transparency in long-lasting ways. In 1953, for example, John Gorham Palfrey observed that the secrecy surrounding the American atomic energy program was so excessive, and information "so tightly 'compartmentalized,' that even top officials in the government, military and civilian alike, had no knowledge of it."[5] More recently, Gary Wills has argued that the American constitutional order was itself transformed by the development of the bomb and the awesome, unreviewable discretion that the president was given with respect to its deployment. Furthermore, "World War II faded into the Cold War, and the Cold War into the War on Terror, giving us over two-thirds of a century of war in peace, with growing security measures, increased governmental secrecy, [and] broad classification of information. . . . Normality never returned."[6] The George W. Bush administration made a cult of secrecy. The Obama administration, while proclaiming its intention to be the most transparent in history, has prosecuted more whistleblowers under the 1917 Espionage Act than all previous administrations combined.[7] The administration has classified the legal memoranda that purportedly justify the president's authority to assassinate citizens abroad,[8] and it even invoked executive privilege to protect the White House social secretary from testifying about "party-crashers" at a state dinner.[9]

"Particularly in the field of national security," Rowat argued, "the public needs to be more fully informed if it is to judge intelligently a Government's policy decisions."[10] Ironically, that is the field in which the most extravagant claims of secrecy are typically made. Governments deny access to information and often assert that national security considerations prevent them from even confirming or denying its existence. They also regularly assert that their decisions are not judicially reviewable; merely being required to explain their decisions would threaten national security. Those who speak for government insist on secrecy when it suits their purposes; they favor disclosure when that serves their interests. Sometimes the information they provide is true; sometimes it is false; sometimes it is partial or incomplete. In this respect, representative democracies are no different from other institutions.[11]

Deciding questions of access to information often requires a complicated balancing of competing goods. With threats to national security, for example, probability as well as magnitude must be considered. Neither is easily calculated, and questions of acceptable risk necessarily involve normative judgments. Balancing also implicates more fundamental concerns, such as the value of political participation and its relationship to human dignity.[12] What is the proper role of citizens? Should they actively audit their government or be content simply to elect representatives they think trustworthy? If one believes, with James Madison, that the people should be "consulted between elections, continually," and treated as "partners in government," the need for information is clear.[13] There is no point in consulting citizens who are uninformed. But what if citizens are not to be "consulted continually" and government is to be left mainly to "leaders"? Citizens might seem to have less need for information in those circumstances. If the fundamental purpose of government is to serve the interests of its citizens, however, those who are not to be "consulted continually" (or at all) may have an especially compelling need for information. For them, transparency may be the only means of ensuring the accountability of those who rule.

Active Citizenship: Arguments from Political Theory

"To secure all the advantages of [a representative republic]," James Madison wrote in 1792, "every good citizen will be at once a [s]entinel over the rights of the people; over the authorities of the confederal government; and over both the rights and the authorities of the intermediate governments."[14] In 1819, Benjamin Constant, the French political theorist, likewise expressed the view that "the people . . . must exercise an active and constant surveillance over their representatives . . . reserv[ing] . . . the right to discard them if they betray their trust." Constant warned that, "the danger of modern liberty is that [the people], absorbed in the enjoyment of [their] private independence . . . [may] surrender [their] right to share in political power too easily." According to Constant, "the holders of authority are only too anxious to encourage us to do so. They are so ready to spare us all sorts of troubles, except those of obeying and paying!"[15]

Max Weber, the great German sociologist, described a different model of citizenship. The citizen's role is "to obey law and perhaps, in periodic elections, to confirm the choice of leaders whose election gives them the power to enact into law whatever policies they see fit . . . guided only by expediency, personal vision, and the legal restraints of the constitution which, if adhered to, confer unchallenged legitimacy on their acts."[16] Weber's model aptly describes the modern state. While it does not reflect the views of Madison or Constant, it is not wholly inconsistent with an older view of representation—one that emphasized the representative's independence, his obligation to the nation, rather than to a particular constituency, and the legitimacy of representation unconnected to popular election.[17] According to Edmund Burke, the representative owed the country his "unbiased opinion, his mature judgment, [and] his enlightened conscience, [which] he ought not to sacrifice to [anyone, including his electors]."[18]

Alexander Meiklejohn, an American philosopher and constitutional scholar of the postwar period, echoed Madison and Constant. For Meiklejohn, robust public debate was not only essential to self-government but also the central purpose of the First Amendment. In Meiklejohn's account, freedom of speech is based not on "a sentimental vagary about the 'natural rights' of individuals" but on "a reasoned and sober judgment" about the practical requirements of government. It is essential that "every voting member . . . [achieve] the fullest possible . . . understanding of the problems with which . . . citizens . . . must deal." Meiklejohn therefore believed that the First Amendment implicitly includes a "right to know." "What would be the value of giving to American citizens freedom to speak," Meiklejohn asked, "if they had nothing worth saying to say?"[19]

Meiklejohn's claim did not go unchallenged. For example, legal scholar Lillian BeVier took issue with what she took to be Meiklejohn's premise that the Constitution requires "public issues [to] be decided by universal suffrage," noting "the democratic processes embodied in the Constitution prescribe a considerably more attenuated role for citizens." BeVier wrote: "It is surely more accurate to [say] that public issues shall be decided by *representatives of the people* who shall be elected by universal suffrage." Citizens "do not directly . . . make or implement public decisions" but direct policy only by voting for candidates. In BeVier's view, citizens act principally through representatives, have few decisions to make, and therefore have a limited need for information. According to BeVier, the people might be entitled to speak but not necessarily to engage in informed speech.[20]

To assert that citizens have the right to speak, but not to engage in well-informed speech, trivializes speech and misunderstands representative democracy. The people's representatives may do much of the work of government, but it does not follow that citizens have little need for information or informed debate. Democratic theory teaches that the people are sovereign, and, as Thomas I. Emerson, another First Amendment scholar of the period, argued, "the public, as sovereign, must have all information available in order to instruct its servants."[21] Certainly, the public must have all the information necessary to instruct its servants. Even if the responsibilities of citizenship were limited to periodic voting, how could citizens vote intelligently without being continuously informed? Madison's view of citizenship is more compelling today than ever.

But there is a more fundamental problem with BeVier's approach. The legitimacy of any modern government is generally thought to depend, at a minimum, on its attentiveness to the needs and interests of its people.[22] If that is the case, the government (whatever its form) must be accountable in some sense to the people, and accountability requires information.

Political Participation and Human Dignity

What does Catholic social thought have to contribute? One might respond that the Catholic Church has had little good to say about democracy, which was true for long enough. Some Catholic thinkers, particularly in France and the United States, supported democracy at an early point.[23] But the popes long preferred the rule of princes. Temporal as well as spiritual leaders, they were concerned with navigating the shoals of European politics and safeguarding the Church's temporal interests. But Church authorities also opposed democracy because they equated it with individualism, autonomy, moral relativism, popular excess, instability, and anti-clericalism.[24] Democracy was not consistent with their static, hierarchical view of human society.[25] In 1832, the year of the English Reform Act, Gregory XIV sided with the Russian tsar against the nationalist aspirations of Catholic Poland and compared those who aspired to democratic rule in the Papal States to "bilge water in a ship's hold, a congealed mass of all filth."[26]

Notwithstanding Pius IX's famous dictum, the popes eventually would have to "come to terms with . . . progress, liberalism, and modern civilization."[27] They also would have to come to terms with democracy.[28] But it was a long, slow, and painful process, ultimately stretching into the twentieth century and beyond and demanding a richer understanding of individual conscience and human dignity. Even in the twentieth century, for example, some Catholic theologians continued to hold that slavery was not "intrinsically wrong," and, as late as 1943, Monsignor John A. Ryan, America's "foremost Catholic liberal," declined to support African American voting rights, saying that "the only moral right possessed by the citizen in the political field is to have a government that promotes the common good," which "can be obtained without universal suffrage."[29]

It was a different conception of human dignity that caused the French philosopher Jacques Maritain to oppose fascism and affirmatively embrace democracy as "an advance towards justice and law and towards the liberation of the human being."[30] Maritain recognized the strong temptation "to renounce active participation in political life" and "pass over to their leaders all the care of the management of their community," but that course, in Maritain's view, betrayed human dignity.[31] As Paul Sigmund observed, "Maritain was responsible for a new development in Catholic political thought . . . the argument that democracy was not simply one of several forms of government, all of which were acceptable provided that they promoted the 'common good,' but . . . the one . . . most in keeping with the nature of man and with Christian values."[32] The influence of Maritain's innovation was profound and far-reaching. As Arūnas Streikus noted in the chapter opening this volume, Maritain's thought was crucial for Lithuanian Catholics living under the harsh oppression of communism.

Maritain sought to reconcile democracy and Catholic thought by providing a fuller account of the individual and his relationship to community. Civic life had come to be dominated by individualism or totalitarianism, which understood the human person as either a self-interested individual or a being whose whole meaning depends on the collectivity. Neither gave human dignity its due, and neither acknowledged the human person as a whole, integrated being necessarily existing in community.[33] For Maritain, as David Hollenbach has noted, "personal existence is existence in relationship with other persons."[34] Moreover, "the dignity of persons can be realized only in community, and genuine community can exist only where the dignity of persons is secured. Personhood and community are mutually implicating realities."[35]

By focusing on "the person," Maritain hoped to convey an understanding of human dignity that included a respect for autonomy, but one that was richer and better grounded than that associated with "the individual." Thus, "Maritain's discussion of the common good leads immediately to a theological warrant for many liberal values and institutions." As Hollenbach observes, "rights are not simply claims to pursue private interests or to be left alone. Rather, they are claims to share in the common good of civil society." They are "positive" rights because they empower the person to act in society. 36 Significantly, Maritain considered the right to "freedom of investigation and discussion" as a "fundamental natural right, for man's very nature is to seek the truth."[37]

Maritain helped draft the Universal Declaration of Human Rights, and his influence on the documents of the Second Vatican Council is manifest. For example, the conciliar document *Dignitatis humanae* observes:

> A sense of the dignity of the human person has been impressing itself more and more deeply on the consciousness of contemporary man, and the demand is increasingly made that men should act on their own judgment, enjoying and making use of a responsible freedom, not driven by coercion but motivated by a sense of duty. The demand is likewise made that constitutional limits should be set to the powers of government, in order that there may be no encroachment on the rightful freedom of the person and of associations. This demand for freedom in human society chiefly regards the quest for the values proper to the human spirit.[38]

The council further observed that "all men are bound to seek the truth, especially in what concerns God and His Church, and to embrace the truth they come to know, and to hold fast to it." The council thus affirmed the centrality of conscience, professing that, "the truth cannot impose itself except by virtue of its own truth, as it makes its entrance into the mind at once quietly and with power." Finally, the council stated its intention "to develop the doctrine of recent popes on the inviolable rights of the human person and the constitutional order of society."[39]

In *Gaudium et spes*, the council noted the connection between "the present keener sense of human dignity" and efforts to create "a politico-juridical order" that will protect "the rights of the person in public life," ensuring that "citizens, individually or collectively, can take an active part in the life and government of the state." Normatively, the council proclaimed that governments "should . . . afford all their citizens the chance to participate freely and actively in establishing the constitutional bases of a political community, governing the state, determining the scope and purpose of various institutions, and choosing leaders."[40] The critical importance of these Church statements for mobilizing and legitimating social action in the name of human rights is discussed in Oscar Espinosa's earlier chapter regarding the crisis facing indigenous people in the Peruvian Amazon.

The Church today expresses a keen interest in democracy in the sense of encouraging governments to follow the forms of democracy as well as in the more important sense of encouraging "authentic democracy." The Church proclaims that, "representative bodies must be subjected to effective social control," and those who govern must be answerable to the governed. The Church also recognizes that "information is among the principal instruments of democratic participation" and that "society has a right to information based on truth, freedom, justice and solidarity." Meaningful political participation requires an understanding of "the situation of the political community, the facts, and proposed solutions to problems," which necessarily requires access to information.[41]

The Challenge of Transparency

It is tempting to conclude that democratic theory and Catholic social thought have now made their peace. Such congruence would not be surprising, particularly given the common influence of Jacques Maritain and the fact that some conception of human dignity animates both. Democratic theory recognizes the need to protect human rights as well as democratic processes. Authentic democracy respects human dignity by recognizing that citizens are entitled to participate in government in an informed way and to be governed by sound decisions; informed debate makes sound decisions more likely. But the claims of human dignity extend beyond the processes of government. Human dignity speaks to the person in community, to her connections with the institutions of civil society, to her place in the cosmos. It was in that spirit that the bishops observed in *Justitia in Mundo* "that anyone who ventures to speak to people about justice must first be just in their eyes."[42]

Catholic social thought can make an important contribution to our understanding of human dignity, civil government, and the people's right to know. But the Church's attitude concerning its own governance necessarily diminishes the power of its advocacy. In 2002, John Paul II proclaimed that "the Church is not a democracy, and no one from below can decide on the truth."[43] Such enthusiasm for top-down structures bears scrutiny. Cardinal Newman and others have taught that truth can indeed come "from below."[44] Bren Ortega Murphy provides a vivid illustration of that point in an earlier chapter in this volume, where she describes the resistance encountered by women religious in the United States as they sought to speak truth to power. Moreover, as one commentator has suggested, to say that " 'the Church is not a democracy' obscures more than it illuminates."[45] In purely factual terms, of course, John Paul's statement is true. The Church bears no resemblance to a democracy, or to any similarly accountable form of government; it has chosen to organize itself as an absolute monarchy, cloaking its operations in secrecy, disdaining even the most rudimentary means of accountability, and acknowledging little responsibility for providing information about its operations to the People of God.

Clearly, the Church does not operate on the principle that information should be disclosed unless there is a compelling reason for secrecy. Rather, the presumption of secrecy is virtually irrefutable. But are these qualities essential to the nature of the Church? Are they anything to boast about? Are they even compatible with the values of the Gospels? Should the Church be less concerned than civil institutions with designing structures that respect human dignity?[46] These vital issues have been raised in previous chapters, by Gonzalo Gamio in connection with the Church's responses to the Peruvian Truth and Reconciliation Report and by Bren Ortega Murphy in connection with the organization of women religious in the United States.

The sexual abuse scandal is another instructive case. When its full history is written, one suspects that the narrative will be more about the effects of institutional secrecy, lack of accountability, and hierarchical hubris than about concupiscence, or even abuse of power, within the presbytery. It comes as no surprise to Christians that "the evils of sin, pride, and domination can be found among those who make up the Church."[47] Nor is it surprising that power corrupts or that the flesh is weak. What does surprise—no, shock—is to know that allegedly responsible Church leaders put children in danger, not once or twice but on occasions beyond counting, in an ultimately futile effort to avoid "scandal." It is the Church leadership, not a relatively few priests, who have eroded the faith of the faithful and caused Church members as well as former friends of the Church, men and women of good will from every background and belief, to perceive only inexplicable perversity in a Church they previously admired.

The Catholic Church could speak prophetically on the subject of transparency and its relationship to human dignity. But its words will not be heard unless it adjusts its own attitudes and conforms its own ways to those it recommends. To depend on secrecy and an ill-informed communion of the faithful to conceal corruption and preserve an illusion of sanctity is not a strategy that can succeed in the long term. Nor is it a worthy example for the Church to provide to the world.

NOTES

1. The author thanks Alessandro Ferrari, David Ingram, Michael Schuck, and Winnifred Fallers Sullivan for thoughtful comments on an earlier draft and Courtney Clark and Abigail Ledman for excellent research assistance.

2. Donald C. Rowat, "The Problem of Administrative Secrecy," *International Review of Administrative Sciences* 32, no. 2 (1966): 100–1. See also Donald C. Rowat, "How Much Administrative Secrecy?" *Canadian Journal of Economics & Political Science* 31, no. 4 (1965): 479, 491; and Donald C. Rowat, "The Right to Government Information in Democracies," *International Review of Administrative Sciences* 48, no. 1 (1982): 59.

3. UN General Assembly, *Universal Declaration of Human Rights*, December 10, 1948, art. 19.

4. Barry Sullivan, "FOIA and the First Amendment: Representative Democracy and the People's Elusive 'Right to Know,'" *Maryland Law Review* 72, no. 1 (2012): 1.

5. John Gorham Palfrey, "The Problem of Secrecy," *Annals of the American Academy of Political and Social Science* 290, no. 1 (1953): 94.

6. Gary Wills, *Bomb Power: The Modern Presidency and the National Security State* (New York: Penguin, 2010), 2.

7. Joshua Keating, "Is the Obama Administration Abusing the Espionage Act?," *Foreign Policy Blog*, February 27, 2012, http://blog.foreignpolicy.com/posts/2012/02/27/is_the_obama_administration_abusing_the_espionage_act#.T71igj_h2uk.email.

8. Scott Horton, "The Drone Secrecy Farce," *Harper's Magazine*, March 13, 2012, http://harpers.org/archive/2012/03/hbc-90008485.

9. Michael Scherer, "No Testifying for Obama's Social Secretary?," *Time Magazine*, December 3, 2009, http://www.time.com/time/politics/article/0,8599,1945192,00.html.

10. Rowat, "The Problem of Administrative Secrecy," 497.

11. See John J. Mearsheimer, *Why Leaders Lie: The Truth about Lying in International Politics* (Oxford: Oxford University Press, 2011).

12. See, for example, Jeremy Waldron, "The Core of the Case against Judicial Review," *Yale Law Journal* 115, no. 6 (2006): 1346; and Aileen Kavanagh, "Participation and Judicial Review: A Reply to Jeremy Waldron," *Law and Philosophy* 22, no. 5 (2003): 451.

13. See Richard Brookhiser, *James Madison* (New York: Basic Books, 2011), 107.

14. James Madison, "Government," in *James Madison: Writings*, ed. Jack N. Rakove (New York: Library of America, 1999), 502.

15. Benjamin Constant, "The Liberty of the Ancients Compared with That of the Moderns," in *Constant: Political Writings*, ed. Biancamaria Fontana (Cambridge: Cambridge University Press, 1988), 307, 310–12, 325–26. Tocqueville likewise argued that citizens who only participate in periodic elections will "gradually los[e] the faculty of thinking, feeling, and acting for themselves." Alexis de Tocqueville, *Democracy in America*, trans. and ed. Harvey C. Mansfield Jr. and Delba Winthrop (Chicago: University of Chicago Press, 2000), 665. See also Jacques Maritain, *Man and the State* (Chicago: University of Chicago Press, 1951), 67 (quoting Tocqueville).

16. Roger Cotterrell, *Law's Community: Legal Theory in Sociological Perspective* (Oxford: Oxford University Press, 1995), 149.

17. See Gordon S. Wood, *Representation in the American Revolution*, rev. ed. (Charlottesville: University of Virginia Press, 2008), 3–13.

18. Edmund Burke, Speech to the Electors of Bristol, November 3, 1774, http://press-pubs.uchicago.edu/founders/documents/v1ch13s7.html. The people's role in a representative government has long been contested. See, for example, Richard Gwyn, *The Man Who Made Us: The Life and Times of John A. Macdonald* (Toronto: Random House Canada, 2007) (noting Macdonald's view that even the decision on Canadian confederation did not require a popular vote); Carlos Closa, "Why Convene Referendums? Explaining Choices in EU Constitutional Politics," *Journal of European Public Policy* 14, no. 8 (2007): 1311 (discussing the choice between plebiscite and parliamentary action in EU treaty ratification); and Gavin Barrett, "A Rough Passage: Lessons from the Experience of the Ratification of the Lisbon Treaty in Ireland," in *The Making of the EU's Lisbon Treaty: The Role of the Member States*, ed. Finn Laursen (Brussels: Interuniversity Press, 2012), 273 (same).

19. Alexander Meiklejohn, *Free Speech and Its Relation to Self-Government* (Clark, NJ: Lawbook Exchange, 2011), 65, 102. Meiklejohn's contemporary, Thomas I. Emerson, expressed a similar view. Thomas I. Emerson, "Legal Foundations of the Right to Know," *Washington University Law Quarterly* 1 (1976): 16.

20. Lillian BeVier, "An Informed Public, an Informing Press: The Search for a Constitutional Principle," *California Law Review* 68, no. 3 (1980): 484–85, 505–6.

21. Emerson, "Legal Foundations of the Right to Know," 16. BeVier's narrative gives scant attention to the historical development of constitutional government in the United States, which, by virtue of formal amendment, case law development, quasi-constitutional legislation (including the nineteenth and twentieth civil rights acts), and evolving governmental practice,

has produced a more democratic regime and a greater role for citizens at the national level. See Sullivan, "FOIA and the First Amendment," 35.

22. See J. R. Pole, *The Gift of Government: Political Responsibility from the English Restoration to American Independence* (Athens: University of Georgia Press, 1983), 38. "Over the period that begins with the Restoration and ends with the American Revolution, we can discern a transition from a theory of government sustained by some form of divine right to a theory which makes the very authority of government depend on the utilitarian test of its ability to protect and promote interests."

23. Félix Dupanloup, Félicité de Lamennais, Charles de Montalembert, and Frédéric Ozanam come to mind, along with John Ireland and John B. Purcell, among others. See generally, Jay P. Corrin, *Catholic Intellectuals and the Challenge of Democracy* (South Bend, IN: University of Notre Dame Press, 2002); and John T. McGreevy, *Catholicism and American Freedom: A History* (New York: W. W. Norton, 2003).

24. As Jonathan Israel has noted, some Enlightenment thinkers, such as Voltaire, did not favor democracy. It was only the "Radical Enlightenment" that insisted "on full freedom of thought, expression, and the press" and "identif[ied] democracy as the best form of government." Jonathan Israel, *A Revolution of the Mind: Radical Enlightenment and the Intellectual Origins of Modern Democracy* (Princeton, NJ: Princeton University Press, 2010), 21.

25. According to Michael Rosen, the popes traditionally held that "all members of society have dignity, but their dignity consists in their playing the role that is appropriate to their station within a hierarchical social order, one in which 'some are nobler than others.' Instead of sharing in equal dignity, the orders of society should differ in 'dignity, rights and power.'" Michael Rosen, *Dignity: Its History and Meaning* (Cambridge, MA: Harvard University Press, 2012), 49. See also Rosen, *Dignity*, 91–92 (arguing that this understanding of dignity was used in opposition to the idea of human rights in the nineteenth century). Samuel Moyn has argued that *Mit brennender Sorge* (1937) marked an important shift in the Church's understanding of dignity. See Samuel Moyn, *The Last Utopia: Human Rights in History* (Cambridge, MA: Harvard University Press, 2010), 50. See also Samuel Moyn, "The Secret History of Constitutional Dignity," *Yale Human Rights and Development Law Journal*, 17, no. 1 (2014): 39 (exploring the Catholic background of the human dignity provision in the Irish Constitution of 1937); and John T. Pawlikowski, OSM, "Liberal Democracy, Human Rights, and the Holocaust," *Catholic International* 9 (1998): 454, 455–56 (exploring the ideological background of Vatican response to the Holocaust).

26. Gregory XIV, *Mirari vos*, Encyclical letter, 5. *Mirari vos* was the second of two extraordinary encyclicals that Gregory published in 1832. It is a

screed against modernity and pluralism, liberty of conscience, freedom of the press, separation of church and state, and, in general, the democratic aspirations of modern man, as we understand them. It also predicts "the destruction of public order, the fall of principalities, and the overturning of all legitimate power." His earlier encyclical, *Cum primum* (1832), addressed the situation in Poland. In 1831, Gregory had suppressed a liberal revolution in the Papal States. See Richard P. McBrien, *Lives of the Popes: The Pontiffs from St. Peter to John Paul II* (New York: Harper Collins, 1997), 337.

27. Pius IX, *Syllabus Errorem*, 80 (1864).

28. Compare Pius IX, *Non expedit* (1874) (forbidding Italian Catholics from voting or holding public office) with Pius XII, *Christmas Address: The Problem of Democracy* (1944) (cautious, and somewhat ambiguous, endorsement of "authentic" democracy). See also Leo XIII, *Libertas* (1888) (holding that "it is not of itself wrong to prefer a democratic form of government" but admonishing that "it is quite unlawful to . . . grant unconditional freedom of thought, of speech or writing, or of worship, as if these were" natural rights).

29. McGreevy, *Catholicism and American Freedom*, 67, 56, 298.

30. See Mortimer J. Adler with Walter Farrell, OP, "Democracy: The Best and Only Just Form of Government," *Proceedings of the American Catholic Philosophical Association* XX (December 27–28, 1945): 31. Maritain, like other Catholic opponents of fascism, was ostracized by those co-religionists who saw the Spanish Civil War as a "Holy War." Corrin, *Catholic Intellectuals*, 346.

31. Jacques Maritain, *The Rights of Man and Natural Law* (London: Centenary Press, 1944), 47.

32. Paul Sigmund, "The Catholic Tradition and Modern Democracy," in *Religion and Politics in the American Milieu*, ed. Leslie Griffin (Notre Dame, IN: University of Notre Dame Review of Politics and the Office of Policy Studies, 1986), 13.

33. Jacques Maritain, *The Person and the Common Good* (New York: Scribners, 1947), 2–3.

34. David Hollenbach, SJ, "The Common Good Revisited," *Theological Studies* 50, no. 1 (1989): 86.

35. Ibid.

36. Ibid., 88.

37. Maritain, *The Rights of Man*, 49.

38. Walter M. Abbott, SJ, ed., *The Documents of Vatican II* (New York: America Press, 1966), 675.

39. Second Vatican Council, Dignitatis humanae, December 7, 1965. See also Winnifred Fallers Sullivan, "'The Conscience of Contemporary Man': Reflections on U.S. v. Seeger and Dignitatis Humanae," *U.S. Catholic Historian* 24, no. 1 (Winter 2006): 107. In *Pacem in Terris*, for example, John XXIII noted that "in our time the common good is chiefly guaranteed when personal rights and duties are maintained." Likewise, "a natural consequence of men's dignity is unquestionably their right to take an active part in government" and to be "accurately informed about public events." *Pacem in Terris*, 46, 51, 52, 60 73, 44, 12.

40. Second Vatican Council, *Gaudium et spes*, 73, 75, 31. The council also emphasized the need for dialogue and sincere cooperation among all persons of good will and noted that "God alone is the judge and searcher of hearts, for that reason He forbids us to make judgments about the internal guilt of anyone." Ibid., 28. See also Paul VI, *Populorum progressio* (1967).

41. Pontifical Council for Justice and Peace, *Compendium of the Social Doctrine of the Church*, §408, 414, 415. Of course, elected officials must be free to engage in "that function of synthesis and mediation that serve the common good, one of the essential and indispensable goals of political authority." Ibid., 408. But it is preeminently the role of democratic leaders to persuade citizens as to the justice of the outcomes they choose.

42. World Synod of Bishops, *Justicia in Mundo* (1971), 40.

43. Bruce Russett, "Monarchy, Democracy, or 'Decent Consultation Hierarchy?,'" in *Governance, Accountability, and the Future of the Catholic Church*, ed. Francis Oakley and Bruce Russett (New York: Continuum, 2004), 196. See also Pius X, *Vehementer Nos*, para. 8 (1906): "The Church is essentially an *unequal* society . . . comprising two categories of persons, the Pastors and the flock. . . . With the pastoral body only rests the necessary right and authority for promoting the end of the society and directing all its members towards that end; the one duty of the multitude is to allow themselves to be led, and, like a docile flock, to follow the Pastors."

44. See generally John Henry Newman, *On Consulting the Faithful in Matters of Doctrine* (New York: Sheed & Ward, 1961).

45. Paul Lakeland, "Book Review," *Theological Studies* 65, no. 4 (2004): 886.

46. Only recently, Cardinal Burke chastised the Catholic press for not doing a better job of explaining the Church's need for secrecy, particularly with respect to such matters as the child sexual abuse scandal. Carol Glatz, "Catholic Communicators Must Obey Church Teaching, US Cardinal Says," *Catholic Sun*, April 19, 2012, http://www.catholicsun.org/2012/04/19/catholic-communicators-must-obey-church-teaching-us-cardinal-says/.

47. Hollenbach, "The Common Good," 84.

Foundations of Human Rights: The Work of Francisco de Vitoria, OP

Robert John Araujo, SJ

In this note on the US Voices, Robert John Araujo offers a reflection on one of the most formidable contributions of the Catholic Church to the public discourses on culture, politics, and religion in the United States: the tradition of the natural law. While this discourse certainly carries with it a long, and highly debated, history, it nevertheless constitutes one of the major contributions of Roman Catholicism to everything from human rights, to the relationship between church and state, to the freedom of religion. This tradition stretches far back into Roman Catholicism, but the contemporary instantiations of it in public discourse—particularly in the contemporary discourse on human rights— go back to the sixteenth century and, according to Araujo, the writings of the philosopher, legal theorist, and Dominican friar Francisco de Vitoria.

De Vitoria, suggests Araujo, ought to be understood as a seminal figure in the development of the natural law tradition, as well as the contemporary discourse on human rights. Seen most clearly in his De Indis, *de Vitoria offers an argument in favor of the inherent dignity and inviolable rights of the inhabitants of the New World—the native people whose existence was just being discovered from the European perspective. De Vitoria argues that these "others" in the New World are, in fact, human persons, with equal dignity and rights to those of their European counterparts. This argument put de Vitoria at odds with many of his contemporaries, yet, according to Araujo, remained influential for a line of natural law thinking in the Catholic Church that found its way into our contemporary discourses on human rights and the United Nations' Universal Declaration of Human Rights. De Vitoria's influence stretches far beyond the borders of the United States, but insofar as Roman Catholicism has made a formidable contribution to the discourses on human rights, the separation of church and state, and religious freedom in the United States, we owe a debt of gratitude to Francisco de Vitoria.*

To the extent that our modern understanding of democracy includes respect for human rights, a debt is owed to Francisco de Vitoria, OP, a sixteenth-century Dominican priest who made an important but often unrecognized contribution to the advancement of human rights. This chapter examines de Vitoria's contribution and, by extension, the importance of the Catholic intellectual tradition to human rights theory then and now. Underlying this chapter is a question raised by the Second Vatican Council's Pastoral Constitution on the Church in the Modern World (*Gaudium et spes*): *quid est homo*? What is man? What is the human person?[1] The council fathers understood well that the human person possesses an inherent dignity that is protected by the concept of human rights. This dignity is not a gift of the state or of society; rather, it is an endowment of the Creator, God. Still, the human person and human societies have a role to protect this dignity by legal concepts such as human rights.

De Vitoria (1480–1546) lived during the age of the conquistadors and the Reformation. He was a Dominican friar and professor of theology at the University of Salamanca who worked legal concepts into his lectures about the New World. The source of his legal principles was the natural law, a method of legal reasoning that helped lead him to the important notion of popular sovereignty.[2]

In de Vitoria's view, sovereignty was not just for some people but for all, including the native peoples of the New World. His justification for being concerned about all persons highlighted the relevance of the *suum cuique* (to each person his or her due), particularly as he contemplated the consequences of European expansion into the Western Hemisphere and its impact on the rights of native peoples. On this point, a rich comparison could be made to Montaigne's less principled and more pragmatic endorsement of the "Other" in political society, as explored in David Posner's earlier chapter.

De Vitoria's principle of *suum cuique* is found in ancient legal precepts. For example, there is *juris praecepta sunt haec—noseste vivere; alterum non laedere; suum cuique tribuere*—these are the precepts of the law: to live honorably; to hurt nobody; to render everyone his due. Another is a traditional definition of justice: *Justitia est constans et perpetua voluntas jus suum cuique tribuendi*—justice is a steady and unceasing disposition to render everyone his due. The essential concept underlying these various formulations may be summed up in the following manner: Justice—an issue of vital importance to most understandings of natural law—is a critical element of legal systems and international order, particularly those concerned with the rights and obligations of people. In the natural law tradition with which de Vitoria was familiar, justice is considered to exist in the context of the *suum cuique*.

Since the adoption of the Universal Declaration of Human Rights (UDHR) by the United Nations General Assembly in December of 1948, many people have become familiar with the phrase "human rights" as both an abstract concept and a concrete reality applicable to their own lives. Indeed, chapters in this volume by Oscar Espinosa and Barry Sullivan give witness to this fact. Though it was not until the post–World War II era that discussion of international human rights laws and protections fully emerged, de Vitoria recognized the moral power needed for protecting those who were considered expendable by other human beings.

Comparing Francisco de Vitoria and the UDHR

One of de Vitoria's most influential works regarding the natural law and its application to human rights discourse is *De Indis* (1531).[3] A side-by-side comparison of sections from *De Indis* with related discussions in the UDHR shows how far ahead of his time de Vitoria was in identifying and defending principles that eventually found their way into the UDHR.

Table 1 indicates how intellectually linked the modern idea of human rights is to the thought of de Vitoria. To explore this claim further, more needs to be said about the UDHR. The methodology used first lists the principle presented and developed by de Vitoria in *De Indis* and then identifies it with the same or similar concept found in the UDHR. This table illustrates the similarities between the sections of *De Indis* and the corresponding principles found in the specific UDHR articles.

The Emergence of the UDHR

The UDHR begins with an important claim: "All human beings are born free and equal in dignity and rights. They are endowed with reason and conscience and should act towards one another in a spirit of brotherhood."[4] Questions immediately arise about the meanings of the terms "dignity" and "rights." De Vitoria provided a foundation for considering the meaning of these two terms. Regarding the term "dignity," its significance cannot be restricted to the concepts of self-respect, self-esteem, or pride. Those definitions would undermine the term's significance insofar as they are self-relational, subjective, and focused on the individual person vis-à-vis the individual himself or herself. If the term is to mean something substantive in the context of universal human rights, it must refer to a relationship one has with others: to each his or her due (i.e., the *suum cuique*). What is claimed by one must be the sort of thing that can be rightfully claimed by others. In this context, Jacques Maritain, who chaired the

TABLE 1. Comparing Francisco de Vitoria's De Indis and the United Nations' Universal Declaration of Human Rights on the Moral Defense of Human Beings

De Indis (Francisco de Vitoria)	*Universal Declaration of Human Rights*
Question 1, Article 1 argues that the native peoples were the true masters prior to the arrival of the Spaniards; if this is so, then their status did not change with the arrival of the Spaniards, so they must, in this respect, be the equals of the Spaniards.	Article 1: "All human beings are born free and equal in dignity and rights."
Question 1, Article 6 argues for a type of equality with others, including Europeans, on the grounds of judgment and reason which enable them to establish civil society based on their own culture.	Article 2: "Everyone is entitled to all the rights and freedoms set forth in this Declaration, without distinction of any kind, such as race, colour, sex, language, religion . . . "
Question 1, Article 2 argues that while humans bear the image of God, those who sin do not, and, therefore, they cannot have dominion; but the native peoples do have proper dominion; therefore, they must have the image of God within them and, therefore, have the right to live and to exist Article 3: "Everyone has the right to life . . . "	Article 3: "Everyone has the right to life . . . "
Question 1, Article 1, and Question 1, Conclusion argue that slaves cannot exercise dominion; but the native peoples can; therefore, the native peoples cannot be slaves.	Article 4: "No one shall be held in slavery or servitude . . ."
Question 1, Article 6 argues in favor of the "proper marriages" of the native peoples.	Article 12: "No one shall be subjected to arbitrary interference with . . . privacy, family, home . . ."
Question 3, Article 1 argues for the ability of the Spaniards to move peacefully into the territories of the native peoples, but they must not harm them; moreover, they are free to engage the natives in trade that will be of mutual benefit to both groups of peoples, but again no harm must result.	Article 13: "Everyone has the right to freedom of movement and residence within the borders or each state."
Question 3, Article 1 asserts that children born of a Spanish father are entitled to citizenship in the community of native peoples; in de Vitoria's natural law theory, this would imply a right to nationality.	Article 15: "(1) Everyone has the right to a nationality. (2) No one shall be arbitrarily deprived of his nationality nor denied the right to change his nationality."

(continued)

TABLE I. *(continued)*

De Indis (Francisco de Vitoria)	Universal Declaration of Human Rights
Question 1, Article 6 argues that the native peoples have "proper marriages" that should be free from the impositions of the Europeans.	Article 16: "Men and women of full age, without any limitation due to race, nationality or religion, have the right to marry and to found a family."
Question 1 asserts the right of the native peoples to their territory and the further right not to be denied this possession and dominion by the Europeans without consent.	Article 17: "(1) Everyone has the right to own property alone as well as in association with others. (2) No one shall be arbitrarily deprived of his property."
Question 1, Article 6 argues that the native peoples have their own form of religion, and Question 2, Article 4 confirms that they cannot have Christianity or any other faith imposed on them. Question 3, Article 2 permits the possibility of religious conversion but prohibits the imposition of a foreign faith.	Article 18: "Everyone has the right to freedom of thought, conscience and religion; this right includes freedom to change his religion or belief . . ."
Question 3, Article 2 acknowledges the right of Christians to preach and announce the Gospels; however, the right does not extend to forcing religion or ideas on the native peoples; they are free to accept what is proposed, but it cannot be imposed upon them.	Article 19: "Everyone has the right to freedom of opinion and expression . . ."
Question 3, Article 1 argues, via the parable of the Good Samaritan in Luke 10:29–37, that the Europeans and native peoples are "neighbors," and are required to love each other as themselves.	Article 29: "(2) In the exercise of his rights and freedoms, everyone shall be subject only to such limitations as are determined by law solely for the purpose of securing due recognition and respect for the rights and freedoms of others and of meeting the just requirements of morality, public order and the general welfare in a democratic society."

UNESCO committee that advised the drafting committee of the UDHR, had this to say in 1943:

> The human person possesses rights because of the very fact that it is a person, a whole, master of itself and of its acts, and which consequently is not merely a means to an end, but an end, an end that must be treated as such. The dignity of the human person? The expression means nothing if it does not signify that by virtue of natural law, the

human person has the right to be respected, is the subject of rights, possesses rights. *There are things which are owed to man because of the very fact that he is man.* The notion of right and the notion of moral obligation are correlative. They are both founded on the freedom proper to spiritual agents. If man is morally bound to the things which are necessary to the fulfillment of his destiny, obviously, then, he has the right to fulfill his destiny; and if he has the right to fulfill his destiny he has the right to the things necessary for this purpose.[5]

With this understanding of dignity in mind (i.e., what is owed the human person because of the very fact that he or she is a human person), the term "rights" comes into better focus. "Right" or "rights" are familiar words today; they are used frequently in everyday discourse. Yet, when placed in the phrase "human rights," the notion of rights requires careful consideration. Does the possession of a right mean that a person can claim anything he or she desires? Alternatively, is the possession of a right contingent upon one's relation to the rights—the due—of others? As understood in the UDHR, rights involve the qualities of the human person that relate to that which is proper, correct, and consistent with what is just rather than unjust (if "justice" is viewed as right relationship among all people). The UDHR emerges from the Charter of the United Nations (Preamble and Article 1), which calls for peace and security in the world premised on the concepts of justice, faith in fundamental human rights, and reliance on principles of justice.

The notion of reason thus has much to do with defining rights of persons and the justification of claims made about them. Rights deal with the moral dimension of human nature and existence and with the contexts of individual persons who live in societies with other persons.

The rights claimed by a person are legitimate and morally proper when justice, objective reason, and facts either fortify or deny the legitimacy of the claim. In short, rights have to do with the essence of what is due the individual person because he or she is an individual person to whom something is due (the *suum cuique*). In addition, what is due a person exists not because persons, organizations, societies, or civil authorities determine what is due; rather, what is due is determined by the fact that the claimant is a person for whom something determined by objective reality is due. The claim must be sustained because of the inherent nature and essence of the person, qualities he or she shares with all other persons.

If the notion of rights addresses claims, it must take stock of duties, obligations, and responsibilities. This facet of human rights claims was well-understood by de Vitoria and acknowledged as essential to the discussion.

Moral obligation exists as a guarantor of all legitimate rights claims. It ensures that rights are reciprocal, perhaps not in all their precise details but reciprocal nonetheless. Reciprocity aids in distinguishing well-ordered rights claims from disordered ones. As de Vitoria explained, rights claims must be inextricably connected to obligations and responsibilities.

The concepts of liberty and equality are integral to human rights, but these are not solely or firstly the work of English and French Enlightenment thinkers. They have deep roots that go back to earlier thinkers, especially those in the Catholic neo-Scholastic tradition such as de Vitoria. The neo-Scholastic tradition was the revival and reliance on the philosophical method of Thomas Aquinas upon which de Vitoria, Francis Suarez, and other sixteenth-century philosopher-theologians relied. The works of these authors had a great impact on the development of public international law and the man who is often considered its founder, Hugo Grotius.

James Brown Scott often noted that de Vitoria was ahead of his time in advancing the ideal of universal rights principles based on the natural law.[6] However, how did de Vitoria's work provide a foundational basis from which the contemporary identification and understanding of universal human rights could emerge in the twentieth century? Some answers are found in the background of the UDHR.

An important illustration of the solidarity and rights articulated in the UDHR that established the realm of contemporary international human rights law is antecedently found in the Charter of the United Nations.[7] As the Charter notes, one major purpose for the United Nations Organization is to "achieve international co-operation in solving international problems of an economic, social, cultural or humanitarian character, and in promoting and encouraging respect for *human rights* and for fundamental freedoms for all without distinction as to race, sex, language, or religion."[8]

It follows that in the advancement of universal human rights, "friendly relations between nations" is essential and states "in co-operation with the United Nations" must pledge themselves to "universal respect for and observance of human rights and fundamental freedoms."[9] These are principles quickly identifiable in de Vitoria's work, as the table suggests.

After identifying the nature of human rights, other questions follow: Who or what confers them? What is their source? These questions can be answered by considering the natural law jurisprudence that informed de Vitoria's thinking.

The Natural Law Foundation of Human Rights

In the Roman Catholic intellectual tradition, the natural law is not so much a body of substantive law as it is a means by which the human mind formulates legal principles that can then be applied to govern a specific matter. In essence, the natural law is planted within the objective reasoning process innate to the human person. This process enables one to develop the positive law with essential substantive principles that are desirable for the just governing of society. Such just governing means that rights and responsibilities coexist side by side in order to bring order to the appetites of any and all persons. The natural law assists individuals and societies in recognizing the private and public good: individuals living together in peace and prosperity where virtue is sought and vice is eschewed. As understood by de Vitoria, the natural law is a moral system wherein principles are always in relation to practical applications.

While legal theorists may disagree as to the relationship between morality and law (Oliver Wendell Holmes's classic discussion comes to mind), there is little dispute about the role of reason in the development of law.[10] Reason and cognitive function have played a crucial role in the evolution of law and they have been prominent participants in natural law philosophy. Aquinas acknowledged that law might be understood as "an ordinance of reason for the common good, made by him who has care of the community."[11] The exercise of reason was of crucial concern to de Vitoria and continues to play an important theoretical and practical role in international law today. De Vitoria understood that the use of reason necessarily leads the legal thinker to the notion of the common good, a key moral principle that supports and reinforces the existence of international law.[12]

International law, too, has a strong foundation in the natural law tradition that is very much at the core of international human rights law.[13] Pope Pius XII, for example, was both a seasoned diplomat and juridically trained in the natural law as it applied to international law. From this experience, he wrote in his first encyclical *Summi pontificatus* (1939) that "the new order of the world, of national and international life, must rest no longer on the quicksands of changeable and ephemeral standards that depend only on the selfish interests of groups and individuals. No, they must rest on the unshakable foundation, on the solid rock of natural law and Divine Revelation."[14] De Vitoria was no stranger to this idea of the law of nations as defined by Pius XII and relied upon it in his construction of the rights and responsibilities of the native peoples of the Americas and the Europeans in *De Indis*.

De Vitoria's training embraced the spirit of Saint Matthew's Gospel: "Go forth and teach all nations, baptizing them in the name of the Father, and of the Son, and of the Holy Spirit."[15] Writing at a time of European exploration into previously unknown lands and the subsequent encountering of other peoples, de Vitoria did not see this scriptural exhortation as a threat to an ordered relationship between the European explorers and the newly encountered native people. De Vitoria likely asked himself: Are the native peoples willing to accept the Christian faith? This question would surely have led him to ponder the status of native people and what their moral rights and responsibilities might be.

Some of de Vitoria's contemporaries concluded that native peoples were not morally due anything. Native people were not Europeans. Based on this prejudiced belief, some thought native people could be subjugated, enslaved, and have their wealth confiscated. De Vitoria saw things differently. Grounded intellectually in the method of objective natural law reasoning and in the belief that human dignity belonged to native peoples, de Vitoria astonished many of his contemporaries with his views. Almost half a millennium later, his ideas still make an extraordinary and necessary contribution to human rights discourse.

One principal claim de Vitoria makes in *De Indis* is that native peoples were not, as was widely assumed at the time, a savage or subhuman race but rather were individuals and human persons created, like Europeans, in the divine image of God. As such, they had the right to make the same claims based on human dignity as did their European contemporaries. This principle led de Vitoria to other important conclusions about human rights that would eventually find their way into the UDHR and other human rights instruments of the twentieth century.

De Vitoria, the United Nations, and the UDHR

The preamble of the United Nations Charter suggests the relevance of the *suum cuique* to human rights discourse when it states that the peoples of the United Nations "are determined . . . to reaffirm faith . . . in the equal rights of men and women and of nations large and small." This assertion of equality regarding rights echoes de Vitoria and suggests that rights can be claimed by any member of the human family, which, in turn, implies that each member of the human family is entitled to one's respective due. The preamble of the Charter additionally states that these ends shall be furthered by employing "international machinery for the promotion of economic and social advancement of *all* peoples."[16] These are moral perspectives that de Vitoria acknowledged many years earlier.

The UDHR notices these Charter points when it states that a common standard of achievement "for *all* peoples and *all* nations" shall apply. The UDHR further acknowledges the universality of rights when it states that "*all* human beings are born free and equal in dignity and rights." Moreover, it declares that each person is "endowed with reason and conscience and should act towards one another in a spirit of brotherhood."[17] Thus, the UDHR speaks not just for some but for all members of the human family. Here again, de Vitoria thought along these lines centuries before.

In relying on natural law reasoning, de Vitoria paved the way for recognizing the universality of rights. Of course, the natural law was not the only source de Vitoria used for arriving at the universality of rights. He also relied on the scriptural account of Jesus telling the lawyer the parable of the Good Samaritan. As de Vitoria noted, Jesus's intended response to the lawyer's question "Who is my neighbor?" was that everyone is the neighbor, including the native peoples of *De Indis*.[18]

Formed in both natural law and scripture, de Vitoria's intellectual spirit animates both the principles of the UDHR and the human rights doctrine that later get codified in so many juridical instruments worldwide. At the same time, de Vitoria's perspective remains remarkably invigorating for human rights discourse today because it does not portray any particular individual or group as being solely victim or victimizer by nature of their humanity. This is a truth about human nature that is often lost in today's discourse on rights. De Vitoria always balanced the rights of both native peoples and Europeans by acknowledging their mutual responsibilities. For de Vitoria, the concepts that bridged the respective rights and duties of both parties were self-determination and subsidiarity. Although the doctrine of subsidiarity did not find its way into Catholic social teaching until Pope Pius XI's encyclical letter *Quadragesimo anno* (1931), de Vitoria acknowledged that the native people's self-determination enabled them to promulgate norms for their own culture. In this context, de Vitoria asserted by way of example that the Indians' understanding of matrimony and family life should not be disturbed by the authorities in Spain. Spanish authorities should rightfully issue norms directing the activities of the Spaniards in the Americas. However, they should not issue European norms for the native peoples; these people had the right to live by their own law.

De Vitoria understood native peoples as rational human beings capable of exercising their own self-determination.[19] Because of this, native peoples are masters of their dominions and owners of their property. Europeans could come as bearers of Christianity, western education, and commerce, but the native peoples' right of election over these goods was to be respected. Europeans were not to impose these goods on the native people as conquerors or enslavers. It is important to note that de Vitoria's thinking on native peoples surfaces in later papal writings down to the twentieth century.[20]

In de Vitoria's view, while it would be permissible for Europeans to claim uninhabited territories for the sovereign back home, they could not deprive the natives of their land, their culture, and their way of life in the name of an alleged superior civilization. The spirit of de Vitoria's thinking would resurface in later Church teaching. Four hundred years later, for example, Pius XII would write in his encyclical *Summi Pontificatus* that "it is indispensable for the existence of harmonious and lasting contacts and of fruitful relations, that the peoples recognize and observe these principles of international natural law which regulate their normal development and activity. Such principles demand respect for corresponding rights to independence, to life and to the possibility of continuous development in the paths of civilization."[21]

A further crucial point advanced by de Vitoria focuses on concerns around the relationship between the native and the alien.[22] If people are peace-loving, they are entitled to call some place of their choosing home. Within this discussion, de Vitoria offered his views on the freedom of movement of one person into the territory of another. Assuming that the traveler (the alien) has no ill purpose in mind, the ability of the traveler to enter and meet and deal with the local peoples was a right supported by natural reason. Once again, de Vitoria clearly articulated notions about a right to migrate that are widely acknowledged today.

Conclusion

The Catholic voice of Francisco de Vitoria undergirds a large part of legal discourse today concerning authentic human rights. In that sense, de Vitoria's spirit animates the struggles for democratic governance that extend from Peru to Indonesia and from Lithuania to the United States. But his spirit is challenged today by views on human rights that do not go beyond the self, views that never consider the author of the self's very existence. De Vitoria recognized that human culture can be riddled with errors that deny the rights that belong to every person created in God's image. That which is of purely human origin can be flawed. However, an alternative perspective that offers moral resources for a better world remains within our grasp—especially when we ponder the wisdom of individuals like Francis de Vitoria.

NOTES

1. Vatican II, *Gaudium et spes*, art. 10 and 12.

2. The concept of the natural law is vital to this project, and I offer further explication of its meaning and relevance throughout this paper. But for assistance to the reader at this point, I suggest that this term's meaning is founded on these three points: (1) the human person is intelligent and possesses the capacity to exercise objective reasoning capability that transcends the particulars of the person's own circumstances; (2) the human person is surrounded by intelligible reality; and, (3) the combination of these first two points enables the individual person and all persons to identify universal norms that assist in the development of human law.

3. Francis de Vitoria, *De Indis*, in *Vitoria: Political Writings*, ed. Anthony Pagden and Jeremy Lawrance (Cambridge: Cambridge University Press, 1991). This text was based on a series of lectures he delivered at the University of Salamanca addressing the rights of the Indians in the New World. Acquaintances of his collected notes of the lectures and then had them published after his death.

4. United Nations General Assembly, *Universal Declaration of Human Rights*, December 10, 1948, 217 A (III), art.1.

5. Jacques Maritain, *The Rights of Man and Natural Law* (New York: Charles Scribner's Sons, 1943), 65. Emphasis added.

6. See James Brown Scott, *The Spanish Origin of International Law* (London: Clarendon Press, 1934), and *The Spanish Origin of International Law: Lectures on Francisco de Vitoria [1480–1546]* and *Francisco Suàrez [1548–1617]* (Washington, DC: School of Foreign Service, Georgetown University, 1928). See also John P. Doyle, "Francisco Suàrez: On Preaching the Gospel to People like the American Indians," *Fordham International Law Journal* 15 (1991–1992): 879, and Ramon Hernandez, OP, "The Internationalization of Francisco de Vitoria and Domingo de Soto," *Fordham International Law Journal* 15 (1991–1992). For an extremely helpful explanation of the role of natural law in international law, see James V. Schall, SJ, "Natural Law and the Law of Nations: Some Theoretical Considerations," *Fordham International Law Journal* 15 (1991–1992). In particular, Schall states, "the law of nations itself was a necessary derivative from natural law. It was based on the principle that human beings throughout time and space were the same in their essential structure, in that they each possessed reason, and that reason could be formulated, communicated, understood, and debated

wherever men sought understanding. The theories and actions of anyone, even rules, could and should be tested by reason. This testing would result in an agreed upon law if the reasonable solution could be found. It would result in violence, disagreement, and even war if it could not." Schall, "Natural Law," 1017.

7. The concept of solidarity is one that is central to Catholic social thought and therefore relevant to the confluence of democracy, culture, and Catholicism in the context of human rights. By solidarity I mean: "the intrinsic social nature of the human person, the equality of all in dignity and rights and the common path of individuals and peoples towards an ever more committed unity." Pontificium Consililium de Iustitia et Pace, *Compendium of the Social Doctrine of the Church* (Vatican City: Libreria Editrice Vaticana, 2004), n192. In essence, solidarity acknowledges the interdependence of everyone; moreover, it undergirds the notion of the common good as the simultaneous flourishing of each person and all persons. The writings of de Vitoria recognize this concept as he talks about the right relations between the Europeans and the native peoples and the advancement of their mutual welfare.

8. United Nations, *Charter of the United Nations*, October 24, 1945, art. 1.3. Emphasis added.

9. Universal Declaration of Human Rights, preamble.

10. Oliver Wendell Holmes, "The Natural Law," *Harvard Law Review* 32 (1918): 40. Holmes, the well-known American jurist, had a dim view of natural law and universal principles having juridical application. He was a strong positivist who was comfortable with the law being whatever the law-maker said was the law. He was skeptical about any possible intersection between law and moral considerations. He is often considered a founder of the legal school of thought known as legal realism.

11. Thomas Aquinas, *Summa Theologiae* I-II, q. 90, a. 4.

12. A review of classical and contemporary writings on natural law will demonstrate a connection between natural law and the common good. One major example is the 1787 Constitution in the United States and John Locke's *Second Treatise on Government*, sec. 131.

13. James Leslie (J. L.) Brierly, *The Law of Nations: An Introduction to the International Law of Peace* (Oxford: Oxford University Press, 1963), 16–25.

14. Pius XII, *Summi pontificatus*, art. 82.

15. Matthew 27:19.

16. Universal Declaration of Human Rights, art. 1. Emphasis added.

17. Ibid.

18. *De Indis*, q. 3, a. 1, in *Vitoria: Political Writings*, 278–279. See also Luke 10:25–37.

19. *De Indis*, q. 1, conclusion in *Vitoria: Political Writings*, 250–51, and *De Indis*, q. 3, a. 6, in *Vitoria: Political Writings*, 288–89.

20. Paul III, *Sublimus dei*, May 29, 1537.While noting that Christians were encouraged by Jesus to "Go ye and teach all nations," he stated that in any missionary activities, Christians must acknowledge that "the Indians are truly men and that they are not only capable of understanding the Catholic Faith but, according to our information, they desire exceedingly to receive it." The pope hastened to add that "the said Indians and all other people who may later be discovered by Christians, are by no means to be deprived of their liberty or the possession of their property . . . that they may and should, freely and legitimately enjoy their liberty and the possession of their property; nor should they be in any way enslaved; should the contrary happen, it shall be null and void and have no effect." Other popes reiterated the concerns of Paul III during their pontificates. For example, in 1435, Eugene IV condemned the slave trade occurring in the Canary Islands; subsequent popes such as Urban VIII (*Bull of April 22, 1639*), Benedict XIV (*Bull of December 20, 1741*), and Gregory XVI (*Constitution against the Slave Trade, November 3, 1839*) did the same. See John Eppstein, *The Catholic Tradition of the Law of Nations* (Washington, DC: Catholic Association for International Peace, 1935), 418–26.

21. *Summi Pontificatus*, art. 74.

22. *De Indis*, note, q. 3, a. 1, in *Vitoria: Political Writings*, 278–79.

Global Interpretations

Any foray into the relationship between democracy, culture, and Catholicism calls for critical reflection on two interrelated questions: first, what exactly do we mean by the terms "democracy," "culture," and "Catholicism," and, second, what foundation(s) can we provide for their alleged relationality. The final section of this volume attempts a response to these questions by turning to the notion of praxis. A praxis-oriented approach is one that combines the theoretical and the practical, so that they may mutually inform and correct each other in the dialectical process of deliberation. Theory without practice is ineffective; practice without theory is irresponsible. The chapters in this section invite us, as readers, to reflect upon how we conceptualize the terms in question, how we understand their relationality, and, finally, how we can/ought to enact them in our day-to-day lives.

Peter Schraeder analyzes whether or not Catholicism is compatible with democracy by evaluating the levels of democratization within predominantly Catholic nations. Schraeder argues that Catholicism is compatible with democracy and that Catholicism was one of the engines of Samuel Huntington's "third wave" of democratization. While at the end of the day, certain political positions, which are adopted as the result of the democratic process, may not be entirely in line with Catholic positions, this reality of democratic deliberation is not enough to diminish the contemporary Catholic Church's commitment to the democratic form of political engagement.

David Ingram argues that, if we are to arrive at genuine consensus on, and recognition of, the rights of fellow citizens with regard to religious commitment, we must, from both ends of the spectrum, move beyond the liberal principle of toleration and toward the republican principle of non-domination. This is a challenging move, given the strength of the commitments religious individuals make via their faith claims. If this is to be achieved, and if religion is to remain, for Ingram, "a legitimate political force in democracy," then religion must recognize that its truth claims may have to be compromised in public discourse—and this is the price it must pay to participate in democratic processes. Likewise, the more secular forces in democratic communities must more robustly adopt the principle of non-domination. The religious voice must be offered a genuine place at the table and must be allowed to speak authentically—this is the price the secular voices must pay to participate in democratic processes. Thus non-domination, rather than toleration, becomes imperative for this interaction and, for Ingram, any future interaction between democracy, culture, and Catholicism.

In his epilogue, Michael Schuck offers a compelling narrative to bring together the many voices, contexts, and perspectives articulated in this volume as a whole. He does this by offering the following hermeneutic: democracy is a response to suffering. Schuck traces this line of thinking throughout many of the contributions to this volume. Democracy, as equality more fundamentally than as freedom, is a response to the suffering of those who feel themselves to be seen as, or more often treated as, less than human in both their local and more global communities. Both culture and religion help form the topography of this democratic impulse and give voice, each in their own way, to the suffering and inequality that call out for a democratic response. Schuck's analysis proves to be a compelling conclusion to the scholarly endeavors undertaken in this volume as well as to the encounters and experiences that emerged out of the Democracy, Culture, and Catholicism International Research Project—the three-year international initiative that has resulted, at least in part, in the present volume.

Rendering unto Caesar?
State Regulation of Religion
and the Role of Catholicism in
Democratic Transitions and Consolidation
in Predominantly Catholic Countries

Peter J. Schraeder

Observers of the complex relationship between church and state have noted throughout history that religious activity seems greater where religion is more free from state regulation.[1] Yet it is only recently that social scientists began systematically working out the mechanisms by which varying levels of church-state separation have contributed to enhanced religious vitality and religiously based political activism, most notably in support for transitions toward democracy. Indeed, the last quarter century has been marked by an increase in scholarship exploring the role and compatibility of various religious traditions with the spread and consolidation of democratic practices. Such research has included studies of democracy and Buddhism, Christianity (Catholicism, Eastern Orthodox, and Protestantism), Hinduism, Islam (Sunni and Shia), and Judaism.[2]

Not surprisingly, in the aftermath of the terrorist attacks of September 11, 2001, research in this realm turned to the Islamic world and the question as to whether Islam is compatible with democracy.[3] Less attention has been given within the discipline of political science and the social sciences in general to the relationship between Catholicism and democracy. A comprehensive analysis of the Catholic Church's impact on democratic transitions, and its continuing involvement in post-transition democratic arrangements, has not been done.

The primary purpose of this chapter is twofold. First, the chapter explores the role of Catholicism in contributing to democratic transition and democratic consolidation in fifty-five predominantly Catholic countries in which Catholics make up more than 50 percent of the national population. This is unlike earlier studies that have focused on the role of the Catholic Church in specific countries, such as Poland,[4] or specific regions, such as Africa,[5] Eastern Europe,[6] or Latin America.[7] The second purpose of this chapter is to promote an interdisciplinary understanding of the above phenomenon by drawing on research from the disciplines of economics, international relations, political science, sociology, and theology.

Catholicism and the Third Wave of Democratization

Democracy and its global promotion emerged at the end of the twentieth century as two of the most important norms of international relations. Samuel Huntington captured this new trend in international politics in his seminal 1991 book, *The Third Wave: Democratization in the Late Twentieth Century*. The "third wave" refers to the dramatic surge in the number of democracies in the world during the last quarter of the twentieth century. Since the appearance of Huntington's book, the "third wave of democratization" has become one of the most cited metaphors in the field of political science.

This wave of democratization began in 1974 with the downfall of dictatorships in southern Europe, such as Portugal, Spain, and Greece. The wave spread to Latin America, the African continent, and to Eastern Europe where communist regimes collapsed after the fall of the Berlin Wall in 1989 and the downfall of the Soviet Union in 1991. The 2011 "Arab Spring" that began in Tunisia went on to influence the downfall of dictatorships in Egypt, Yemen, and Libya, representing the most recent manifestation of the trend to democracy in a region once thought impervious to such change.[8]

An important outcome of this global trend is that scholars and policy-makers are increasingly prone to speak of democracy as a universal value that is shared throughout all regions of the world. This is a shift in discourse within the academic world and the world of policymaking. Earlier, the Cold War kept the discussion focused on whether democracy is the best form of governance. In the post-Cold War period, however, the discussion has turned to the degree to which the international community should be actively involved in promoting democracy and what forms of intervention are appropriate to that end. Such forms range from standard interventionist tools like diplomacy and foreign aid, to the imposition of political conditions and economic sanctions, to directly coercive forms of intervention, such as military force.[9]

In both of these Cold War and post-Cold War discussions, the religious dimensions of democracy promotion have been either missed or misunderstood. This was true of early studies in the 1950s and the 1960s, as exemplified in Seymour Martin Lipset's landmark book, *Political Man: The Social Bases of Politics*. Lipset, like many of his colleagues, made three errors as concerns the relationship between religion and politics. First, he ignored the role of religious groups in promoting democratic practices. An excellent example of this is discussed in Bren Ortega Murphy's earlier chapter in this volume on the role Catholic religious women played in teaching democratic citizenship to immigrants. Second, he mistakenly assumed that the religiosity of a country's population would naturally fade as that country became increasingly democratic. Third, he incorrectly assumed that certain religious faiths prevent the spread of democracy.[10] Lipset noted in 2004, for example, that he and other scholars harbored serious doubts during the 1950s and the 1960s as to whether predominantly Catholic countries were compatible with democracy. This doubt is analogous to recent debates over the relationship between Islam and democracy. As argued by Huntington, however, history has demonstrated that Catholicism is compatible with democracy and also served as one of the engines of the third wave of democratization. Indeed, Huntington refers to the third wave as an "overwhelmingly a Catholic wave," one that initially unfolded in predominantly Catholic countries.[11]

The emergence and spread of this Catholic wave is shown in the democracy rankings that Freedom House puts together on an annual basis for every country of the world and publishes as part of its annual *Survey on Freedom*.[12] Countries are annually ranked from the best score of 2 (high level of protection of civil liberties and political rights; therefore, a high level of democracy) to the worst score of 14 (low level of protection of civil liberties and political rights; therefore, a high level of authoritarianism). Focusing on the subset of fifty-five predominantly Catholic countries in which the populations are at least 50 percent Catholic (see Table 1), the Freedom House statistics are impressive. Whereas only fifteen Catholic countries could be classified as democratic in 1973 (the year immediately preceding the third wave of democratization), by 2013 an extraordinary thirty-five Catholic countries had emerged as democracies.

TABLE 1. Predominantly Catholic countries (population that is at least 50 percent Catholic).

Country	Total Population	Percent Catholic
Argentina	39,537,943	92
Austria	8,265,926	74
Belgium	10,364,388	75
Belize	279,457	50
Bolivia	8,857,870	95
Brazil	186,112,794	74
Burundi	6,370,609	62
Cape Verde	429,474	95
Chile	16,267,278	70
Colombia	42,954,279	90
Congo-Kinshasa	60,085,004	50
Costa Rica	4,016,173	76
Croatia	4,495,904	88
Dominican Rep.	9,105,034	95
East Timor	1,040,880	90
Ecuador	13,363,593	95
El Salvador	6,704,932	79
France	60,656,178	83
Gabon	1,389,201	50
Grenada	89,502	53
Guatemala	14,655,189	55
Haiti	8,521,622	80
Honduras	7,335,204	97
Hungary	10,006,835	77
Ireland	4,234,925	88
Italy	59,102,112	90
Lesotho	1,867,035	70
Liechtenstein	33,863	76
Lithuania	3,596,617	79
Luxembourg	468,571	87
Malta	400,214	95
Mexico	108,700,000	77
Monaco	32,543	90
Nicaragua	5,142,098	59
Panama	3,339,150	85
Paraguay	6,347,884	90
Peru	27,925,628	81
Philippines	87,857,473	81
Poland	38,635,144	90
Portugal	10,566,212	85
San Marino	29,251	95
Seychelles	81,188	82
Slovakia	5,431,363	69
Spain	44,708,462	94
Uruguay	3,415,920	58
Vatican City	921	100
Venezuela	25,375,281	95

There are three explanations for the success of democratic transitions in predominantly Catholic countries during the third wave of democratization. One explanation cites the impact of change in Catholic Church teaching toward recognizing democracy as the preferred form of political governance.[13] This point has been made by John Langan, SJ, Cardinal Bernardin Chair in Catholic Social Thought at Georgetown University. He explains that because of a shift in teaching, the Church changed "from being a vehement, conservative force in opposition to democracy, to a sturdy and reliable supporter of liberal democratic regimes during the second half of the 20th century."[14]

As discussed in Barry Sullivan's earlier chapter in this volume, key texts that communicated the new teaching were Pope John XXIII's 1963 encyclical *Pacem in terris* and the 1965 Second Vatican Council document *Gaudium et spes*. These texts influenced a change in thinking that filtered down to Catholic dioceses around the world and served as a basis for concrete action by Catholics against authoritarian regimes. Arūnas Streikus's chapter at the beginning of this volume emphasized this last point by noting how Church teaching uplifted and mobilized Catholics living in Soviet-dominated Lithuania.

Although this shift in Church teaching is important, it does not answer the following question: Why did the Church in some predominantly Catholic countries oppose authoritarian states and contribute to transitions to democracy, while the Church in other predominantly Catholic countries remained indifferent to or allied with authoritarian regimes? The answer to this question suggests a second explanation for the success of democratic transitions in predominantly Catholic countries during the third wave of democratization. Daniel Philpott persuasively demonstrates that when the Catholic Church in predominantly Catholic countries has a high degree of autonomy from state control, it is more likely to embrace the pro-democracy teachings of Vatican II and therefore pressure authoritarian states to democratize.[15] This was the case in Spain where the Catholic Church's decision to withdraw its support from the military dictatorship of Francisco Franco played an important role in Spain's transition to democracy. By contrast, the lack of such autonomy from state control in Rwanda meant that the Catholic Church there failed to condemn the 1994 state-sponsored genocide against the Tutsi ethnic group and also participated in it in certain cases.[16]

It should also be noted that autonomous Catholic Churches in predominantly Catholic countries were especially successful in supporting democracy when they coordinated their support with other organizations in society.

This was the case in Poland, where the Catholic Church effectively coordinated its opposition to communism with the actions of the Solidarity trade union to overturn the pro-Soviet communist regime. It is also important to underscore the role of individual Catholic bishops in this process. Philippine Cardinal Jaime Sin, for example, emerged as one of the most influential leaders of a pro-democracy movement that led to the 1986 overthrow of the pro-Western dictatorship of Ferdinand Marcos. At a key moment in the "yellow revolution," Cardinal Sin called on Catholics to "surround the police and military headquarters in the nation's capital." More than one million Catholics took to the streets, "clutching bibles and uttering prayers, in an outpouring that shielded anti-government rebels from attack."[17]

A third explanation for the success of democratic transitions in predominantly Catholic countries involves the degree to which religious competition exists within a society. Drawing on the discipline of economics and rational-choice theory, sociologists have developed a supply-side theory of religious behavior.[18] This theory argues that religious "markets" function like economic markets. Religious participation should be higher in "free-market" systems in which there is low state regulation of religion and therefore greater possibility for religious competition. Religious participation should be lower in "closed-market" systems where certain religious institutions are granted monopolistic or oligopolistic privileges by the state.

Supporters of this supply-side theory have tested whether a state's direct financial aid to a religious institution promotes or inhibits the Catholic Church in states where Catholics are a majority. Mark Chaves and David Cann developed a measure based on answers to each of the following six questions:

1. Is there a single state church?
2. Is there official state recognition of some denominations but not others?
3. Does the state appoint or approve the appointment of church leaders?
4. Does the state pay church personnel salaries?
5. Is there a system of ecclesiastical tax collection?
6. Does the state directly subsidize, beyond mere tax breaks, the operating, maintenance, or capital expenses of churches?[19]

Anthony Gill also adopted the supply-side theory to explore why the Catholic Church was either willing or unwilling to confront authoritarian states in twelve Latin American countries. He found that Catholic Churches in states where competitive religious markets exist are more likely to pressure authoritarian states to democratize. Conversely, Catholic Churches in non-competitive religious markets with a high degree of state regulation of religion are less likely to pressure authoritarian states to democratize.[20]

Catholicism and Democratic Consolidation

Less research has been conducted on the position of the Catholic Church in post-transition democracies. On this topic, the experiences of predominantly Catholic countries during the third wave of democratization raise an interesting question: What happens after the Catholic Church in a predominantly Catholic country has successfully pressured an authoritarian state to democratize? Does the Church subsequently retreat from politics or does it remain engaged in the post-transition political system? Looking at it from the side of government, does the state retreat from regulating the Church after the transition to democracy, or does it remain engaged in oversight of religious institutions? Many questions remain unanswered about the nature of church-state relationships in post-transition political environments where the Catholic Church played an important role in the transition.

Non-Catholic and Catholic Americans approach these questions from the standpoint of their own historical and cultural experiences. According to these experiences, American Catholics overwhelmingly reject theocratic models of governance where either the Church or the state claim hegemonic authority over the other. Non-Catholic and Catholic Americans overwhelmingly support the separation of church and state. These positions grew out of a historical clash between at least three different visions of social authority:

1. The anti-clerical Jacobin model of secularism that emerged out of the French Revolution of 1789 and led to the persecution of the Catholic Church.
2. The anti-clerical Bolshevik or communist model of secularism that emerged out of the Russian Revolution of 1914 and sought the extermination of the Catholic Church.
3. The Anglo-Saxon model of secularism, in which the state separates itself from the religious activity of the Christian churches but does so without engaging in anti-clericalism or rejecting religion outright.

American Catholics largely support the Anglo-Saxon model of secularism and assume that transitions to democracy will result in polities with a strong separation of church and state.

The reality of the new democracies within predominantly Catholic countries during the third wave of democratization offers a more complex picture of church-state relationships than the American experience might disclose. In fact, a number of possibilities exist between the two extremes of theocratic governance (where church and state are one) and secularist governance (where the state is not only separate from but also indifferent toward the church).

One way of sorting out this complex picture is to look again at the data provided by Freedom House (recalling that countries with high levels of democracy score 2 and countries with low levels of democracy score of 14). One would expect that transitioning democracies in predominantly Catholic countries would have lower levels of politically inspired restrictions on religious institutions. A dataset established by Jonathon Fox in 2004 is also helpful in this regard.[21] Fox ranked countries from 1990 to 2002, according to each of the following questions:

Are there restrictions on religious political parties?
Is there arrest, continued detention, or severe official harassment of religious figures, officials, and/or members of religious parties?
Are there restrictions on formal religious organizations other than political parties?
Are there restrictions on the public observance of religious practices, including religious holidays and the Sabbath?
Are there restrictions on public religious speech, including sermons by clergy?
Are there restrictions on access to places of worship?
Are there restrictions on the publication or dissemination of written religious material?
Are people arrested for engaging in religious activities?
Are there restrictions on religious public gatherings that are not placed on other types of public gathering?
Are there restrictions on the public display by private persons or organizations of religious symbols, including religious dress, nativity scenes, and icons?
Are there other religious restrictions?

The yes or no answers to these questions were subsequently collated for each country into a "religious restriction" score that ranged from a high positive score of 0 (no religious restrictions by political authorities) to a low negative score of 33 (extensive religious restrictions by political authorities). The data showed that political restriction on religious authorities in predominantly Catholic countries is inversely related to levels of democratization in post-transition countries (i.e., the higher the level of democratization, the lower the level of political restrictions on religion).

Additionally, Fox has data pointing to the fact that the processes of democratization in predominantly Catholic countries have resulted in greater levels of state *involvement* in the religious sphere. Fox ranked countries annually from 1990 to 2002 according to their responses to each of the following questions:

> Does the state support dietary laws (restrictions on the production, import, selling, or consumption of specific foods)?
>
> Does the state restrict or prohibit the sale of alcoholic beverages?
>
> Is the personal status of citizens defined by clergy (i.e., can marriage, divorce, and/or burial only occur under religious auspices)?
>
> Are laws of inheritance defined by religion?
>
> Are there restrictions on conversions away from the dominant religion?
>
> Are there restrictions on interfaith marriages?
>
> Are there restrictions on public dress?
>
> Are there blasphemy laws, or any other restriction on speech about religion or religious figures?
>
> Are the press or other publications censored on grounds of being antireligious?
>
> Is there mandatory closing of some or all businesses during religious holidays, including the Sabbath or its equivalent?
>
> Are there restrictions on activities during religious holidays, including the Sabbath or its equivalent?
>
> Is religious education standard in public schools; is it possible to opt out of this portion of the education?
>
> Is religious education mandatory in public schools?
>
> Is there government funding of religious schools or religious educational programs in secular schools?
>
> Is there government funding of religious charitable organizations?
>
> Does the government collect taxes on behalf of religious organizations (religious taxes)?
>
> Do clergy occupy official government positions, receiving government salaries or other government funding?
>
> Is there funding for religious organizations or activities other than those listed above?
>
> Do religious speeches in public or in places of worship require government approval?

Are some official clerical positions made by government appointment?

Is there an official government ministry or department dealing with religious affairs?

Are certain government officials given an official position in the state church by virtue of their political office?

Do certain religious officials become government officials by virtue of their religious position?

Are some or all government officials required to meet certain religious requirements in order to hold office?

Do religious courts have jurisdiction over some matters of public law?

Are seats in the legislative branch and/or government cabinet made by laws or customs granted, at least in part, along religious lines?

Are there prohibitive restrictions on abortion?

Are there religious symbols on the state's flag?

Is a citizen's religion listed on their state identity card?

Must religious organizations register with the government in order to obtain official status?

Is there an official government body that monitors "sects" or minority religions?

Are there restrictions on women other than those listed above (i.e., restrictions on education, jobs that they can hold, or on appearing in public without a chaperone)?

Are there other religious prohibitions or practices that are mandatory according to the government?

The yes or no answers to these questions were collated for each country into a "religious legislation" score that ranged from a low religious legislation score of 0 (no religious legislation by the state) to a high religious legislation score of 32 (extensive religious legislation by the state). It is fascinating to note that state adoption of religious legislation in predominantly Catholic countries is positively related to higher levels of democratization in post-transition countries (i.e., the higher the level of democratization, the greater the level of state involvement in the religious sphere).

Full Catholic Embrace of Democracy?

An overarching theme of this chapter is that Catholicism is compatible with democracy and has served as one of the engines of the third wave of democratization. On the matter of Catholicism in post-transition democracies, data suggests that while post-transition states are legislatively involved with religion, the nature of this involvement is not predominantly restrictive in the majority of cases. It would appear that most post-transition states with historic ties to Catholicism legislatively seek to protect, not delimit, the freedom of religious expression in the public sphere.

At the same time, one cannot expect Catholicism to embrace every result of the democratic process in newly created democratic states. This point has been made by Thomas Michel, SJ, former secretary for interreligious dialogue for the Society of Jesus. "Although there are a variety of reasons for this," explained Michel, "one in particular stands out: the skepticism associated with the fact that the democratic process often leads to political outcomes that run counter to Catholic moral norms in the areas of sexual morality and family law."[22] According to Michel, this will not lead to a per se rejection of democratic procedures and values by the Catholic Church, but it will lead Church leaders to look at the consequences of democracy with a critical eye when these include such things as the legalization of abortion and the recognition of same sex marriage. Nerija Putinaitė's chapter in this volume on the situation in Lithuania gives evidence to this point.

Catholic support for democracy as a political principle and a political practice emerged in the twentieth century. This support has been given concrete manifestation in the third wave of democratization and in post-transition contexts. The future test for this mutuality between democratic states and the Catholic Church will be its maintenance during periods when fundamental principles dear to both institutions are debated in government and in the public square.

NOTES

1. See Adam Smith, *An Inquiry into the Nature and Causes of the Wealth of Nations* (New York: Modern Library, 1965), 740–41, and Alexis de Tocqueville, *Democracy in America* (Garden City, NY: Doubleday, 1965), 297. This chapter is based on extensive field research in transitioning countries in Africa and Europe, especially in Eastern Europe in summer 2011.

2. See the April and July 2004 issues of the *Journal of Democracy*.

3. See Saad Eddin Ibrahim, "Toward Muslim Democracies," *Journal of Democracy* 18, no. 2 (2007), 5–13.

4. Irena Borowik, "The Roman Catholic Church in the Process of Democratic Transformation: The Case of Poland," *Social Compass* 49, no. 2 (2002): 239–52, and Mirella W. Eberts, "The Roman Catholic Church and Democracy in Poland," *Europe-Asia Studies* 50, no. 5 (July 1998): 817–42.

5. See Paul Gifford, *The Christian Churches and the Democratization of Africa* (Leiden, Netherlands: Brill, 1995), and Isaac Phiri, *Proclaiming Political Pluralism: Churches and Political Transitions in Africa* (London: Praeger, 2001).

6. See Timothy A. Byrnes, *Transnational Catholicism in Postcommunist Europe* (Lanham, MD: Rowman and Littlefield, 2001).

7. See Jeffrey Klaiber, *The Church, Dictatorship, and Democracy in Latin America* (Maryknoll, NY: Orbis Books, 1998), and Frances Hagopian, *Religious Pluralism, Democracy, and the Catholic Church in Latin America* (Notre Dame, IN: Notre Dame University Press, 2009).

8. See Peter J. Schraeder and Hamadi Redissi, "Ben Ali's Fall," *Journal of Democracy* (July 2011): 5–19.

9. Peter J. Schraeder, "Tunisia's Jasmine Revolution and the Arab Spring: Implications for International Intervention," *Orbis* (Fall 2012): 662–75.

10. Jean Bethke Elshtain, "Religion and Democracy," *Journal of Democracy* 20, no. 2 (2004): 5–17.

11. See Samuel P. Huntington, *The Third Wave: Democratization in the Late Twentieth Century* (Norman: University of Oklahoma Press, 1991).

12. See www.freedomhouse.org; see also John Anderson, "Religion, Politics and International Relations: The Catholic Contribution to Democratization's 'Third Wave': Altruism, Hegemony or Self-Interest?," *Cambridge Review of International Affairs* 20, no. 3 (2007): 383–99; and Daniel Philpott, "The Catholic Wave," *Journal of Democracy* 15, no. 2 (2004): 32–46.

13. Paul E. Sigmund, "The Catholic Tradition and Modern Democracy," *Review of Politics* 49, no. 4 (1987): 530–48.

14. John P. Langan, "Theological Perspectives on the Evolving Role of International Democracy Promotion and the Rule of Law in Catholicism" (paper presented at The Cross, the Crescent and the Ballot Box: Catholic and Islamic Perspectives on Promoting Democracy and the Rule of Law, conference organized by Loyola University Chicago and the John Felice Rome Center, Rome, Italy, March 1–2, 2008).

15. Daniel Philpott, "Explaining the Political Ambivalence of Religion," *American Political Science Review* 101, no. 3 (2007): 505–25. See also Daniel Philpott, *Revolutions in Sovereignty: How Ideas Shaped Modern International Relations* (Princeton, NJ: Princeton University Press, 2001).

16. Carol Rittner, John K. Roth, and Wendy Whitworth, eds., *Genocide in Rwanda: Complicity of the Churches?* (St. Paul, MN: Paragon House, 2004).

17. Qtd. in Martin Weil, "Philippine Cardinal Jaime L. Sin Dies at 76," *Washington Post*, June 21, 2005. See also Antonio Moreno, *Church, State and Civil Society in Postauthoritarian Philippines: Narratives of Engaged Citizenship* (Quezon City, Philippines: Ateneo de Manila University Press, 2006); and Aloysius Lopez Cartagenas, "Religion and Politics in the Philippines: The Public Role of the Roman Catholic Church in the Democratization of the Filipino Polity," *Political Theology* 11, no. 6 (2010): 846–72.

18. Laurence R. Iannacone, "The Consequences of Religious Market Structure: Adam Smith and the Economics of Religion," *Rationality and Society* 3 (1991): 156–77.

19. Mark Chaves and David E. Cann, "Regulation, Pluralism, and Religious Market Structure: Explaining Religion's Vitality," *Rationality and Society* 4 (1992): 272–90.

20. Anthony Gill, "Rendering unto Caesar? Religious Competition and Catholic Political Strategy in Latin America, 1962–1979," *American Journal of Political Science* 38, no. 2 (1994): 403–25.

21. Jonathan Fox, "World Separation of Religion and State into the 21st Century," *Comparative Political Studies* 39, no. 5 (2006): 537–69, and Jonathan Fox and Samuel Sandler, "Separation of Religion and State in the Twenty-First Century: Comparing the Middle East and Western Democracies," *Comparative Politics* 37 (2005): 317–35.

22. Thomas Michel, discussant comments made at a panel on Theological Perspectives, at The Cross, the Crescent and the Ballot Box: Catholic and Islamic Perspectives on Promoting Democracy and the Rule of Law, a conference organized by Loyola University Chicago and the John Felice Rome Center, Rome, Italy, March 1–2, 2008.

Civil Discourse and Religion in Transitional Democracies: The Cases of Lithuania, Peru, and Indonesia

David Ingram

On January 19, 2004, world-renowned German political theorist Jürgen Habermas met with Cardinal Joseph Ratzinger (later Pope Benedict XVI) to discuss religion as one of the cultural foundations of the democratic state.[1] Two points of convergence emerged from their discussion. First, both agreed that reason alone cannot sustain respect for individual dignity and the common good without more substantive faith commitments. Second, they agreed that these values, however complementary they might be philosophically, are difficult to harmonize in practice. Agreeing on policies that respect the right of each to pursue his or her own conception of the good appears all but impossible in light of incommensurable belief commitments and especially so whenever these commitments are viewed as divine commands whose truth cannot be doubted and whose prescriptive meaning cannot be compromised.

This chapter focuses on the duty of citizens living in democracies to wrestle with this dilemma in a civil manner. Recent events surrounding the Arab Spring confirm that religion can be a powerful weapon in furthering the transition to democracy, now recognized as crucial to the realization of peaceful coexistence and respect for human rights. Democracy sustains a stable and enduring respect for the rule of law because citizens recognize its legitimacy as a fair procedure. This chapter argues that the capacity of religion to promote democratic reform in a way that respects this procedure must extend beyond its recognition of the liberal principle of human rights and toleration. It must also extend to recognizing the republican principle of non-domination.

Non-domination goes beyond guaranteeing individual freedom from government encroachment and the freedom to elect government officers. Such liberal freedoms still permit majorities to impose unilaterally their interpretation of rights and public welfare on minorities. To avoid this tyranny, republicanism recommends constitutional checks and balances that divide power, including provisions guaranteeing effective political representation of minorities and other vulnerable groups, such as women. Beyond these institutional arrangements, republicanism urges the cultivation of free and inclusive political deliberation aimed at the common good, but in a manner that respects, rather than suppresses, basic religious differences.

The question here is whether such deliberation requires citizens to refrain from imposing policies that restrict basic constitutional liberties whenever the rationales underlying these policies are based exclusively on premises whose authority cannot in principle be universally accepted. The argument here is that it cannot, for the simple reason that what counts as publicly reasonable in any given polity will reflect shifting value commitments that ultimately rest on particular authoritative traditions and comprehensive beliefs.

Deliberative civility will often (but not always) require framing political arguments in terms of this substantive public reason. Rules of civility will depend on the degree of ideological pluralism as well as on the establishment (or lack thereof) of democracy out of transitional process. Following discussions of Lithuania, Peru, and Indonesia, this chapter holds that the very dynamics of democratic deliberation offer strategic incentives to religious parties for becoming increasingly more respectful of difference and less sectarian by arguing for social justice positions that have broad appeal across groups. Such moderation of religious discourse can lead, in turn, to forging a more inclusive and balanced public reason for morally principled (not merely strategic) reasons. That said, republican embrace of political pluralism, even when morally principled, need not incorporate respect for individual rights unless institutional guarantees (above all, independent judges) protect this liberal value against communitarian domination.

First, a clarification is needed of what is meant here by civil deliberation grounded in public reason. A citizen's feeling morally obligated to voluntarily abide by a law she opposed is dependent on her belief that those backing the law tried to convince her of its rightness by appeal to evidence she could recognize as authoritative, even if she did not judge the evidence to be compelling. However, expecting religiously motivated citizens to provide generally acceptable reasoning cannot be construed in such a way as to restrict their freedom of religious expression. Believers should not have to subordinate their faith to secular reason. To demand that persons who are guided by divine revelation abstain from political life because they cannot yet formulate reasons based on more commonly accepted authorities, the natural sciences, for example, imposes a burden on them that their more secularly minded consociates do not carry. For this reason, some proviso to the effect that such reasons be given in due course (as Rawls recommends) or that nonbelievers equalize the burden by taking it upon themselves to reformulate religious arguments in more secular language (as Habermas recommends), seems eminently reasonable.[2] Indeed, everyone (nonbelievers included) should try to translate their dogmatic, comprehensive core commitments into language that others find acceptable.

The antagonism of liberals toward Catholicism in Europe and Latin America was linked to fear of religion intruding into politics.[3] Well into the twentieth century, the Roman Catholic Church opposed liberalism and democracy. These ideas and their accompanying social movements threatened the authority of the pope as guide to all things moral and spiritual.[4] Yet it was precisely the Catholic Church's decision to participate in democratic politics that eventually restrained its hegemonic demands and enabled it to support political frameworks of public reasoning congenial to its values.

As discussed by Marcia Hermansen and Peter Schraeder in this volume, Samuel Huntington observes that the "third wave" of democratization from 1974 to 1990 was "overwhelmingly a Catholic wave," with roughly three-quarters of the thirty countries transitioning to democracy being predominantly Catholic.[5] Among the beneficiaries of this wave were Peru and Lithuania. In Peru, the Catholic Church took an active role in organizing the urban and rural poor in accordance with liberation theological precepts while condemning guerrilla- and government-sponsored violence. Meanwhile, in Lithuania, with a Catholic majority of 81 percent, the Church opposed the communist regime by strongly advocating on behalf of liberal constitutional principles and human rights.

What made the Church's role as a promoter of liberal democratic reform possible in these countries? In both Peru and Lithuania, Catholicism was part of the national identity while it simultaneously stood apart from the state proper. The separation of the Church from the state in these countries enabled the Church to become more accepting of liberal democracy and vice versa. Hence, it is not surprising that the Church's authority in pushing authoritarian regimes toward democracy was strongest in situations where it refused state accommodation (e.g., Poland) and weakest where it accepted it (e.g., Spain).[6]

The Lithuanian Catholic Church's leading role in resisting communist "Russification" reflects a third outcome midway between that of Spain and Poland. The reasons for the diminished prestige of the Church today are complex, ranging from the peculiar nature of the Lithuanian reform movement prior to post-Soviet independence, to what many scholars perceive to be the incursion of secular attitudes among a population that remains highly distrustful of any institutional authority. The chapter by Nerija Putinaitė in this volume goes far in explaining this phenomenon. Lithuanian perestroika was headed by the 1988 Lithuanian Reform Movement Sąjūdis and supported by the Lithuanian Communist Party. Hence, it was divided between factions that sought only national autonomy from the USSR and factions that sought full liberal democracy within a multiparty system.[7] The Catholic Church saw itself (and was seen by most Lithuanians) as primarily a defender of national religious and linguistic identity, rather than an advocate of liberal democratic reform. Economic liberalization has since trumped the social agenda proposed by the Church, with most of the significant political parties and organizations within civil society representing labor and business interests.[8]

Lithuania's fragmented political environment seems to call for a recommitment to the republican ideal of democratic solidarity, but it is uncertain whether the Catholic Church can lead in this area. Some critics defend a secular morality based on Kantian notions of individual freedom and responsibility, seeing that as more in keeping with modern notions of liberalism.[9] Others argue that the moral skepticism generated by fifty years of Communist dictatorship "in the name of the common good" instilled in Lithuanians a shallow version of liberal toleration. This shallow toleration eliminated commitment to fraternity, the civic virtue that prevents liberal democracy from degenerating into a winner-take-all contest.[10] With this in mind, it would seem that greater Church involvement in Lithuanian political life will require an expansion of its agenda to address social justice issues and refocus its commitment to defending republican solidarity. This move would require bridging Church doctrine and secular economic theory.

If the Peruvian Catholic Church has had more success in reaching out to the broader public, it is because its strong commitment to the poor has found greater appeal among a population that is less willing to embrace neoliberal economic policies. Again, the Church's defense of human rights against predations by both revolutionary movements and government forces, as well as its promotion of reconciliation based on a full disclosure of the truth concerning war atrocities, has enabled it to appear as the chief defender of republican civility, public reason, and the common good.

Although the Church has had a long history of defending the rights of indigenous people, at least conceptually, dating back to the colonial era, its advocacy on behalf of the poor and disadvantaged in Latin America achieved unprecedented political impact with the emergence of the Liberation Theology Movement in the late 1960s. In 1976, the Episcopal Commission for Social Action established its own department of human rights and became a major force for raising popular consciousness regarding human rights abuses during the second phase of the military government. Given its singular responsibility for organizing poor rural and urban communities (not to mention its vital role in being the primary conduit for almost all donations, voluntary services, and international aid targeting the disadvantaged), the Church today is regarded as the one public institution that Peruvians trust most in administering resources for human development.

Thanks to its unrivaled prestige among all sectors of civil society, the Church has maintained its high profile by branching out to other sectors. As described in Soledad Escalante's contribution to this volume, having lost its status as the official state religion in 1980, the Catholic Church remains officially recognized (see Article 86 of the 1979 Peruvian Constitution) as "an important element in the historical, cultural, and moral formation of Peru" with which the state offers its cooperation, in conjunction with collaborating with other confessions. Despite its privileged status, the Church had also endured a tense relationship with the state antedating the Constitution and the subsequent concordat with the Holy See (1980).[11] At times, this has placed the Church in the uncomfortable and unpopular position of having to defend its particular vision of public morality against both state and public opinion. The Peruvian Catholic Church opposed liberalization of abortion and divorce by the Fujimori government, yet it had earlier supported the distribution of birth control pills for purposes of family planning and poverty reduction.[12] The Church later aligned with public opinion and the growing woman's movement (itself a major force in the advancement of human rights) in opposition to forced government sterilization of poor women. Today, the gender studies program of the Catholic University of Peru is regarded as one of the strongest in the Andean region.

In recent years, Church involvement in the political life of the country has been subdued due to internal political divisions between conservatives and progressives. During the "dirty war" of the 1990s, the Church hierarchy was split in its criticism of the Fujimori government. While the Council of Bishops sided with most local priests in criticizing the government for its human rights abuses, the archbishop of Lima adopted a more forgiving attitude toward the government's brutal counterinsurgency policy. Since the departure of Fujimori in 2000, the Church base (if not its hierarchy) remains united in promoting social justice and human rights. Catalina Romero, Dean of the School of Social Sciences at Peru's Catholic University, notes that the Peruvian Catholic Church continues to enjoy so much public prestige as a political force today precisely because of its ability to pluralize without fragmenting.[13]

The Peruvian and Lithuanian cases illustrate different outcomes for the Roman Catholic Church in negotiating the separation of church and state. The privileged place enjoyed by the Peruvian Catholic Church above all other religions and public institutions is partly a function of its independence from the state (not to mention the internal independence of its own public spheres) and partly a function of its official status as a quasi-governmental institution responsible for dispensing health, welfare, and education. In playing a predominant role in Peru's democratic civil society, it has had to present both a public face, as defender of human rights and the common good, and a private face as promoter of an orthodox creed that increasingly finds less support among Peruvians, who are more open to alternative lifestyles. The less favored position enjoyed by the Lithuanian Catholic Church reflects, by contrast, its relative inability to break out of a narrow sectarian standpoint and diversify its message so as to embrace broader struggles for social justice.

The case of the Catholic Church in Indonesia presents a fascinating comparison in relation to the Lithuanian and Peruvian situations. There, Catholics represent a small minority of the majority Muslim population. Yet, the debate over whether Islam is compatible with democracy reflects, in some measure, the same concerns expressed over Catholicism, though with several striking differences. To begin with, although both Islam and Catholicism have had to confront the threat of modern secularization, they have experienced this threat differently. Muslim countries, unlike majority Catholic ones, experienced this threat as a foreign export imposed by Western colonial powers, retained by domestic rulers bent on suppressing traditional religious sects as rivals to their power. For instance, coercively imposed religious privatization and pluralization in Iran under the Pahlavi dynasty (1925–1979) provoked an Islamist backlash. This backlash adopted the revolutionary hegemonic aims of rival Marxist dissidents without their Western humanist ideology.

Not all Islamic fundamentalists who reacted against religious pluralization and privatization, the roots of which are in Western modernity, sought to impose their hegemonic aims by a centralized state apparatus. Although fundamentalist Muslim scholars have entered into tactical alliances with Islamist ruling elites in exchange for maintaining or increasing their local pedagogical and juridical authority, they have also used this expanded authority to challenge the Islamist state for not being Islamic enough. It is from certain of these scholarly traditions that many contemporary Muslim reformers draw their commitment to democracy and religious pluralization.[14]

Indonesia's young constitutional government arguably approximates liberal and republican ideals more closely than any other Muslim majority country in the world.[15] Indonesia's democracy followed upon the resignation of General Suharto and his often-brutal "New Order" regime that ruled from 1965 to 1998. Baskara Wardaya's chapter in this volume clearly outlines these developments. Like the Islamic democracy that emerged in the wake of the 1979 Iranian Revolution, the 1999 reform was a response to the corruption, ineptitude, and oppression (economic as well as religious and regional) of authoritarian government. Although the government it replaced was not consistently secular (the Suharto regime increasingly advanced Islamic policies to divide the opposition and gather popular support), it was still condemned by many pious Muslims. This condemnation was for siphoning off vast amounts of wealth for its own privileged elites and ignoring the spiritual and material needs of its poorest citizens.[16] Indonesians thus supported democratic reform in direct opposition to a corrupt and brutal dictatorship that often masqueraded as Islamist.

Not surprisingly, Islamic organizations were at the forefront of the 1999 reform. Abdurrahman Wahid, a senior Islamic cleric, headed Indonesia's largest Muslim organization, the Awakening of Religious Scholars, or Nahdlatul Ulama. Amien Rais, who joined Wahid in the struggle against Suharto, led the second largest Muslim organization, Muhammadiyah, and helped focus student demands on democracy. While Rais went on to create a new non-Islamist political party with leadership shared with non-Muslims (the National Mandate Party), Wahid formed his own Islamic political party, the National Awakening Party, which expressly rejected the idea of an Islamic state in favor of a religiously pluralistic one. In keeping with the pluralistic tenor of his party, Wahid joined in an alliance with the secular nationalist party of Megawati Sukarnoputri, the Indonesian Democratic Party—Struggle, which included secular Muslims, Christians, and non-Muslim minorities.[17] Wahid was subsequently elected the fourth president of the nation and the second president in post-Suharto Indonesia.

Toleration of political Islamist organizations within civil society induces a corresponding paradox, whereby these organizations both moderate and broaden their political platforms and arguments. Importantly, these organizations have managed to combine strategies for partially fulfilling strictly religious aims, such as the passage of blasphemy laws, with commitment to republican ideals of civil discourse. To cite the authors of an important study on Indonesian democracy and the transformation of political Islam:

> The transformation of political Islam has been one of *normalization of Islamist party politics*, whereby single-issue Islamist parties have become ever more similar to Indonesia's larger mass-based parties in terms of their broad campaign messages and inclusive political strategies. At the same time, however, we observe the transformation of Indonesian democracy through what we term *insider Islamization*, through which Islamists mobilize political support for individual Islamist policies on a case-by-case basis with the goal of influencing the substantive outcomes of the policymaking process. This is a strategy through which Islamists change the substantive policies enacted under Indonesia's democratic government so as to fulfill Islamists' political demands without requiring them to prevail in competitive elections.[18]

While liberals have criticized Indonesia's Islamist anti-blasphemy statute, no standard of public reasonableness is neutral vis-à-vis secular and religious values. Recall that debates over the humanity of non-European descended peoples (today extended to the unborn) were resolved by religion before they were resolved by science. The fact that anti-blasphemy statutes descend from religion makes them no less reasonable than anti-obscenity laws. Failure to demonstrate the harmfulness of such incivilities will not compel those offended to desist from suppressing them unless it can be shown that suppression is more harmful than toleration. However, Indonesia's blasphemy law may eventually be moderated by the republican doctrine of *Pancasila*, which emphasizes deliberative democracy as well as social justice and the dignity of the individual.[19]

Deliberative democracy was on full display during the transition to the new regime in 1999. Following Suharto's resignation, groups representing almost all sectors of society pushed for elections to legitimate whatever new political order would come into existence. In the 1999 elections, it became apparent that Islamic parties that did not focus on single-issue messages based on political Islam fared better than those (such as the Crescent Star Party) that did. The message was clear: Pious Muslims who constituted a large segment of the population were also interested in issues revolving around their emerging market economy, such as health, welfare, security, jobs, and basic subsistence. Political Islamist parties, such as the Prosperous Justice Party, which abandoned single-issue politics in order to broaden their appeal to moderate and liberal Muslims, saw dramatic improvements in their popularity in the elections of 2004 and 2009. Another step forward occurred in 2009, when the Prosperous Justice Party and the United Development Party joined with the nonpolitical Islamic National Mandate Party and the National Awakening Party to re-elect the government of former army general and corruption fighter, Susilo Bambang Yudhoyono, himself a member of the secular Democratic Party.[20]

The mainstreaming of political Islamist parties has had a reciprocal impact on substantive legislation in Indonesia. Policies that permit local shari'a ordinances and ban blasphemy are moderated by the fact that they are often enacted with the support of many secularists. For instance, in 2009 the legislator of Aceh, a special region of Indonesia on the island of Sumatra, passed a "stoning law" based on shari'a that expressly punished adulterers and other religious offenders. Less publicized was the fact that that the passage of this law was intended as a parting shot by a legislative majority that had just been voted out of office. The law was vetoed by Aceh's democratically elected governor, Irwandi Yusuf, himself a pious Muslim, and has not been taken up by the new legislature. Yusuf himself worked to reign in Aceh's Islamic "police" in his pursuit of social policies revolving around increased spending on education and welfare and restrictions on logging. Although Yusuf was voted out of office in 2012 for allowing palm oil concessions in protected habitats, Aceh's legislature continues to demonstrate a commitment to democratic accountability that exhibits a considerable degree of republican civility on the part of moderate Muslims and all who are principally concerned with environmental protection and other pressing universal issues that transcend religion.[21]

In the absence of a strong constitutional separation of powers with independent courts that are empowered to intervene forcefully in the protection of minority rights, Indonesia's *Pancasila*-based efforts at instituting non-domination will remain incomplete.[22] Furthermore, without the cultivation of liberal toleration and republican civility in the public sphere (again, secured by government-sponsored consciousness-raising campaigns and educational reforms) the exercise of public reason will remain equally partial. Since willingness to entertain viewpoints that clash with one's own is essential to deliberative democracy, Islamic reform movements must learn to relinquish some of their power and platform for the sake of furthering liberal and republican ideals.

Indeed, Islam can be a legitimate force within democracy only if it actively promotes both republican and liberal values. Russell Powell makes a convincing case for this point in his discussion of Turkey in this volume. As with Catholicism, this outcome favors polities wherein multiple religions compete for political influence through embracing social justice concerns, political cultures encourage deliberative compromise and constitutional power sharing, and judges aggressively defend freedom of speech and minority rights.

It would be premature to conclude that religion can embrace these values without relinquishing at least some of its power to secular authority. Nevertheless, the question remains: How can religion embrace liberal democracy when it claims to be the sole proprietor of divine truth? As this chapter argues, a paradox exists in enlisting this truth in service to a merely mundane end whose realization would entail its partial denial. Born out of an uncompromising dual commitment to social justice and the dignity of the individual, only a faith that moves mountains can risk life itself for the sake of ending oppression and realizing on this earth that always-imperfect semblance of God's Kingdom.

Today there is mounting evidence that democracies, which incorporate both liberal and civic republican values, are the best worldly approximations of that Kingdom. That the dignity of the individual instantiated in the liberal defense of human rights can degenerate into a destructive worship of unrestrained individual self-assertion unless coupled with a civic republican devotion to the common good has been a mainstay of democratic theory for over three hundred years. A democracy that does nothing more than protect against tyrants and aggregate selfish preferences still permits the tyranny of the dominant preference to reign supreme. Conversely, a democracy premised on a common good that stifles individual freedom and suppresses diversity of belief and lifestyle permits an even worse tyranny: totalitarianism.

Authentic democracy, a democracy premised on the principle of nondomination, must somehow fuse the dignity of the individual with an orientation to the common good. The ideal of civic deliberation is one way to accomplish this aim. In upholding the possibility of achieving consensus on a common good, this ideal retains a belief in something transcendent and unconditional that it shares with religion in resisting the subjectivism of unexamined individual preferences. In upholding the superiority of dialogue over personal revelation as a method for discovering this truth, the ideal invokes the fallibility and open-endedness of mutual criticism. It thus leaves open the possibility that consensus may not be reached, that something like an agreement to disagree, coupled with an agreement to compromise on some issues and tolerate individual differences of opinion on others, may be inevitable.

The risking of one's faith in civic deliberation, in a form of Socratic dialogue, explains part of the ambivalence religion has toward democracy. Indeed, if what has been argued in this chapter is true, then the moderation of religious conviction in civic discourse, coupled with its "contamination" by more mundane concerns, is a price religion must pay for remaining a legitimate political force within democracy, as opposed to surviving solely as a matter of private conscience. By contrast, those philosophers who invoke the language of public reason as a touchstone for civil political engagement have something different in mind. Public reason for them must consist of rational disputation in which all premises descend from commonly accepted authorities whose presumed neutrality extrudes any reference to religion.

The motivation behind this suggestion—to avoid the totalitarian imposition of religion—is entirely laudable, but the strategy of avoiding religious language ignores the fact that our public reason is not an abstract universal devoid of historical tradition. Even when it assumes the outward form of secular common sense, what is reasonable always reflects but the temporarily settled history of an evolving ideological struggle for recognition. The historical confrontation of Catholicism and democracy in the twentieth century and the parallel confrontation of Islam and democracy in the twenty-first century might suggest that this struggle invariably resolves itself in the form of a strategic *modus vivendi*. Here, toleration of the other is suffered out of necessity rather than embraced for its own sake. Such may be the case initially, but the stories told here offer hope for a more civil resolution wherein "the other" is not just tolerated outwardly but internalized dialogically.

NOTES

1. Their dialogue was published under the title *The Dialectics of Secularization: On Reason and Religion*, trans. B. McNeil (San Francisco: Ignatius Press, 2006).

2. John Rawls, "The Idea of Public Reason Revisited," in *The Law of Peoples* (Cambridge, MA: Harvard University Press, 1999), 144; Jürgen Habermas, *Between Naturalism and Religion* (Malden, MA: Polity Press, 2008), 131.

3. Anthony Mansueto, "Religion, Pluralism, and Democracy: A Natural Law Approach," and Edward Bell, "Catholicism and Democracy: A Reconsideration," both articles included in *Journal of Religion and Society* 10 (2008); Paul Sigmund, "The Catholic Tradition and Modern Democracy," *Review of Politics* 49, no. 4 (Autumn 1987): 530–48.

4. In his encyclical, *Mirari vos*, Gregory XVI (1831–1846) strongly condemned liberty of conscience and freedom of speech. Although his successor Pius IX (1846–1878) began his pontificate expressing more sympathy for liberalism, *The Syllabus of Errors* that accompanied his encyclical *Quanta cura* (1864) retracted this sentiment. Leo XIII (1878–1903) reaffirmed Gregory's attack in *Liberates humana* (1888), defending toleration only in non-Catholic nations as a necessary expedient (a view that later gave rise to the thesis/hypothesis distinction in Church policy), although earlier (1885) in *Immortale Dei* he allowed that non-monarchical government might be acceptable. Leo's successor, Pius X (1903–1914), continued to lash out against modernism, liberalism, and democracy following passage of France's secularism law (1905), while Pius XI (1922–1939) reconciled Catholicism with Italian and German Fascist dictatorships (1929 and 1933) before changing his mind (1937). There were still restrictions on the rights of Protestants to proselytize in Spain and Colombia when Pius XII issued his 1944 Christmas message defending "liberty and equality" and "true democracy."

5. Samuel P. Huntington, *The Third Wave: Democratization in the Late Twentieth Century* (Norman: University of Oklahoma Press, 1991), 91. See also Daniel Philpott, "The Catholic Wave," *Journal of Democracy* 15, no. 2 (2004): 32–46.

6. Alfred Stepan, "Religion, Democracy, and the 'Twin Tolerations,'" *Journal of Democracy* 11 (October 2000): 37–57.

7. Nerija Putinaitė, "The Good vs. 'The Own': Moral Identity of the (Post-) Soviet Lithuania," *Studies in Eastern European Thought* 60 (2008): 261–78.

8. Aneta Piasecka, *2009 Freedom House Report: Nations in Transition: Lithuania*, http://www.unhcr.org/refworld/publisher,FREEHOU,,LTU,4a5 5bb40c,0.html.

9. Ibid., n30.

10. John F. X. Knasas, "A Fulbrighter Observes Lithuania Going West," *Lituanus* 53, no. 1 (Spring 2007): 54–64, http://www.lituanus.org/2007/07 _1_06%20Knasas.htm.

11. The Peruvian Constitution recognizes freedom of religion and state-church separation. However, in accordance with the agreement between the Peruvian government and the Holy See of 1980, the Catholic Church enjoys special privileges in areas of education, taxation, government funding, immigration of clerical personnel from abroad, and in military ministry. All public

schools are required to teach the Catholic religion, an exemption from religious instruction is provided to non-Catholics and nonbelievers.

12. The Movimiento Familiar Cristiano began to distribute birth control pills in the late '60s with the aim of providing poor women with up to two years of "ovarian relief." Raúl Necochea López, "Priests and Pills: Catholic Family Planning in Peru, 1967–1976," *Latin American Research Review* 43, no. 2 (2008): 34–56.

13. Cited by the Woodrow Wilson International Center for Scholars, Latin American Program: Religion and Values in the Formation of a Democratic Public Space in Latin America, March 22, 2010.

14. Günes Tezcür, *Muslim Reformers in Iran and Turkey: The Paradox of Moderation* (Austin: University of Texas Press, 2010), 64–76.

15. Elections in Iran, Iraq, Afghanistan, Pakistan, and Bangladesh are all marked by corruption and instability; Malaysia is a multiethnic and multireligious nation whose democratic monarchy is founded on the structural dominance of a coalition uniting three ethnic parties (Chinese, Indian, and Malay), with the last having a Muslim presence.

16. Robert Hefner, *His Civil Islam* (Princeton, NJ: Princeton University Press, 2000), esp. chaps. 6 and 7.

17. Stepan, "Religion, Democracy, and the 'Twin Tolerations,'" 49–50.

18. Thomas B. Pepinsky, R. William Liddle, and Saiful Mujani, "Indonesian Democracy and the Transformation of Political Islam," March 21, 2010, http://www.lsi.or.id/riset/385/Indonesian%20Democracy.

19. Pancasila combines two Sanskrit words: *Panca* (five) and *sila* (principle). The five principles it incorporates are a belief in (1) the one and only God; (2) just and civilized humanity; (3) the unity of Indonesia; (4) democracy guided by the inner wisdom in the unanimity arising out of deliberations among representatives; and (5) social justice for the whole of the people of Indonesia. These principles were fashioned by later president Sukarno in 1945 as a synthesis of monotheism, socialism, and nationalism and incorporated into the Constitution. While the first principle has been criticized for excluding polytheism, atheism, and agnosticism, its major thrust is support for a transcendent foundation for respecting the inherent dignity of the individual and humanity.

20. In his first election to the presidency Yudhoyono ran on a platform of prosperity, peace, justice, and democracy and had the support of several political Islamist parties, the National Awakening Party, the Crescent Star Party, and the Reform Star Party.

21. Damien Kingsbury, "Islam and Democracy Can Happily Co-exist," *Sydney Morning Herald*, January 4, 2010.

22. Günes Mural Tezcür, "Constitutionalism, Judiciary, and Democracy in Islamic Societies," *Polity* 39, no. 4 (October 2007): 479–501.

Epilogue on Democracy, Culture, Catholicism

Michael J. Schuck

In the *Nichomachean Ethics*, Aristotle famously defined the human being as a *zoon politikon*, a political animal. Small wonder, then, that group endeavors often reap rewards. For scholars, such rewards include the satisfaction of exploring ideas with new colleagues. Again, from Aristotle: "The whole is more than the sum of its parts."[1] As a collection of chapters by new acquaintances from very different cultures, this volume's emergent whole presents an intriguing montage. Like any montage, there are pieces present and pieces absent. This epilogue considers both.

Democracy

One piece present within many chapters of this volume is social suffering. This is the suffering of being treated in society as less than human, as an object of social ridicule, disempowerment, prejudice, marginalization, exclusion, discrimination, silencing, or torture. The methods used to inflict this "positional suffering" are as limitless as the dark side of human imagination.[2] Danutė Gailienė's chapter on Lithuania's social trauma under Soviet rule makes this point. She, like others in this volume, has personally experienced social suffering. The interest these scholars have in democracy is allied with the frankness by which they name the suffering woven into their national histories.

As a response to positional suffering, democracy comes from the luminous side of imagination, the place where humans yearn for social respect, for a chance to have a say, to have standing. Robert Dahl identifies this democratic desire as the "logic of equality."[3] It lives in tension with another human desire, the desire Ivone Gebara aptly calls the "pathology of superiority."[4] The historical play of these desires on the social level are richly observed in Baskara Wardaya's study of Indonesia and Arūnas Streikus's portrait of Lithuania.

Societies honor the human desire to be treated as an equal by building social processes that enable it. "Entrance into democracy," writes Michel Schooyans, "is *first of all a moral event* which . . . entails primordial recognition of the equal dignity of all men."[5] From such recognition flows "the requirement that all members are equally entitled to participate."[6]

The processes of participation range from open civic debate, to free and fair elections, popular representation, rule of law, government accountability, and protection of human rights. Cultural distinctions shaped by unique national histories, ethnographies, and geographies inevitably give rise to different styles of democracy. Over centuries, this has birthed an array of democratic theories, such as direct, representative, liberal, deliberative, and polyarchic.[7] The impact of culture on the theory and practice of democracy surfaces in several chapters of this volume, including Paulus Wiryono Priyotamtama's description of traditional Indonesian *musyawarah* and Marcia Hermansen's discussion of reserved electoral seats for religious minorities in Jordan, Lebanon, and Pakistan.

The value of equality and the social processes that protect it pose a perennial question in every democratic society: What is the relationship between equality and freedom? One response, going back to ancient Greece, is that recognition of human equality is the precondition for the expression of individual freedom. Thomas Jefferson may have been closer to this sentiment in his American Declaration of Independence than many contemporary Americans are willing to admit: "We hold these truths to be self-evident, that all men are created equal, that they are endowed by their Creator with unalienable Rights, that among these are Life, Liberty and the pursuit of Happiness." This response survives in the contemporary view that before democracy is a political arrangement in service of human freedom, it is a method of reinforcing human equality.[8]

This is why the celebration of freedom is deeply divisive in democracies where significant numbers of people experience inequality. True freedom does not exist in circumstances where certain citizens suffer in this way. There are classes of citizens in Indonesia, Lithuania, Peru, and the United States who know this suffering. Oscar Espinosa's chapter on the situation of the indigenous people of the Peruvian Amazon identifies this evil. So too, William O'Neill references the structures of racism at the root of the United States's mass incarceration rate. Though not an absent piece, racism and discrimination are social acids that require greater attention than is given in the volume overall.

When people truly see one another as equals, they see each other—and society—in a new way. "Democracy allows people to see certain issues," remark Maria Paula Saffon and Nadia Urbinati, "which for a long time they might have considered natural or unchangeable."[9] Seeing society as a community of equals gives encouragement and moral legitimacy to free speech.

Equal regard and free speech allow for social disagreements. The freedom that flows from the social assurance of equal regard means that communication in the public forum will be as contentious as it is collusive. Claudio Orrego remarks:

> The highest virtue of all democratic societies is to recognize the existence of conflict and to accept it as legitimate. There is only one condition: *that no difference of interests can endanger the common destiny and express itself in terms that destroy the social peace.*[10]

In a democracy, one expects that no matter how contentious a disagreement may be, resolution comes by way of argumentation, not force of arms. As John Courtney Murray stated, the climate of democracy "is not feral or familial but forensic." "Society is civil," he said, "when it is formed by men locked together in argument."[11] These arguments are products of civil procedures delicately fashioned, as David Ingram superbly points out in his chapter on civic discourse in transitional democracies.

Culture

To be a determining characteristic of society, democracy must grow from the "first nature" desire of a citizen into the "second nature" practice of civic culture. Democracy must become, as Ronald Inglehart and Christian Welzel note, a "deep rooted orientation among the people themselves."[12]

Such growth occurs when the value of equality moves from a resonance in the heart of a person or group to a tone within and across the larger culture's symbolic media. When reinforced by language, storytelling, customs, art, education, and religion, democracy can become "a state of mind . . . a second nature which is first the product of culture"[13]

This social state of mind is hard won and fragile. New democracies struggle to build supportive civic cultures and old democracies struggle to retain them. This is difficult because all cultures have histories of inequality and suffering and what counts as inequality and suffering is constantly under cultural negotiation. In a given culture, distinctions of race, gender, sexual orientation, ethnicity, disability, class, and age may or may not prompt systemic discrimination. If one or more does, the depth and breadth of such cultural "entrapment" will vary within and between societies.[14]

A cultural "anthropology of suffering" must include these humiliations of social inequality, exclusion, and suppression.[15] Paul Farmer analyzes such abuses in his "anthropology of structural violence," unveiling the many ways a society's structures and processes can erode the equality, participation, and argumentation necessary for a democratic culture.[16]

One way democracy can be eroded is by the actions of an unregulated, competition-driven economy where human beings are free to succeed or fail at the game of life in an open market.[17] Consistent with Farmer's analysis, David Held argues that "one of the main threats to liberty in the contemporary world" is "the liberty to accumulate unlimited economic resources [which] . . . poses a challenge to the extent to which political liberty can be enjoyed by all citizens, i.e. the extent to which citizens can act as equals in the political process."[18] Missing from the accounts of free market neoliberal economics are the system's externality costs of human poverty, socially encouraged greed, and environmental destruction. Over time, the inequitable distribution of these costs to the poor and the shrinking middle class destroys everyone's freedom, a freedom only made possible in a culture where, in principle, no person is treated as less than human. As mentioned earlier, Oscar Espinosa's chapter on the struggle of native people against the deforestation of the Peruvian Amazon is a gripping example of this point. More than with the topic of racism, however, the acidic effects of free market neoliberal economics on democratic culture is an important piece absent from the volume overall.

Another social process that threatens democratic culture is bureaucratization. Nearly every institution of modern society is organized so that legally recognized, impersonal, and equitably applied procedural rules replace inequitable (and inefficient) procedures based on personal privilege, group favoritism, and public patronage. It is ironic that bureaucratic systems created to treat people equitably so often calcify into non-participatory systems of depersonalized power and authority. Max Weber already observed this phenomenon in the early twentieth century:

> [In bureaucratic organizations] . . . the gain in formal equality [has] equivocal results from the standpoint of democratic values. . . . The very measures that ensure a bureaucracy against the abuse of authority and the encroachment of privilege—the certified qualification of appointees, regular promotions, pension provisions, and regulated supervision and appeals procedures—can give rise to new status privileges buttressed by monopolistic practices.[19]

When structured and legitimated over time, these new inequities narrow the range of participation necessary for a healthy democratic culture. This kind of bureaucratization is one aspect of the problem Barry Sullivan explores in his fascinating chapter on the deteriorating level of access to government information in the United States.

Most national cultures possess more collective memory than any one person or group can narrate at any given time. Yet, as Emile Durkheim has pointed out, social solidarity requires a shared cultural story from which to build a "collective conscience."[20] No less than a person, a society needs "the unity of a narrative" that links past founding events to present challenges and visions of the future.[21] Selecting and regulating the central cultural narrative is an important leadership function in society. The challenge of leadership in a democratic society is to resist turning this selection and regulation into an exercise of erasure.

A society's history of inequality can too easily be forgotten, especially if the victims are gone and their survivors are ignored. "Erasing history," says Farmer, "is perhaps the most common explanatory sleight-of-hand relied upon by the architects of structural violence."[22] Recalling, again, the United States's legacy of racism, one finds James Baldwin's comment from a half century ago still apropos: "The brutality with which Negroes are treated in this country simply cannot be overstated, however unwilling white men may be to hear it."[23]

In a democracy, past and present social injustices, as well as past and present social virtues, must remain open for argumentation and inclusion in the society's ongoing narrative of identity. Writing in the 1950s, John Courtney Murray presciently noted the importance of this fact for American society:

> The complete loss of one's identity is, with all propriety of theological definition, hell. In diminished forms it is insanity. And it would not be well for the American giant to go lumbering about the world today, lost and mad.[24]

Gonzalo Gamio's provocative chapter on the manipulation and protection of memory in response to the Final Report of the Peruvian Truth and Reconciliation Commission is a riveting exposé that engages this very issue of erasing history and losing memory.

Catholicism

With its fundamental identity in the story of Jesus Christ, the whole of the Roman Catholic Church—its laity, ministers and clergy, orders of religious women and men, episcopal authorities from local dioceses to Rome—has struggled in the modern world to understand the relationship between its faith and democracy. The story of this struggle is well known.[25]

The democratic movement unleashed by the French Revolution expropriated Church property, closed Church schools, imposed state loyalty oaths, deported and killed thousands of priests and bishops, and created laws eliminating centuries-old traditions such as Sunday religious observance, Church marriage regulations, and almsgiving. Between 1789 and 1848, democrats of varying sorts abducted Pope Pius VI and imprisoned him in Valence, France, where he died, captured Pope Pius VII and incarcerated him in Savona, Italy, for six years, and besieged Pope Pius IX in the Quirinal while murdering the bishop of Parma in his presence.

From these violent origins evolved French *laïcité*—the secularist form of Church-state separation that went beyond removing Church control from the political functions of the state to excluding religious expression from political discourse itself. With religion confined to private life, public policies were expected to be argued on purely secular grounds and the state was to refrain from supporting religion in society. In Europe (and, later, Latin America), a state system of "aggressive neutrality" against religion developed, distinct from the American model of "benevolent neutrality" toward religion.[26] Russell Powell's chapter offers a very helpful discussion of these two forms of secularism. He applies them to the circumstances of Turkish democracy and Islam, which makes for a fascinating comparison to early European democracy and Catholicism.

Aggressive neutrality in the European context blocked Church leaders from perceiving the true suffering of inequality at the core of the democratic political movement. However, another source of suffering from inequity did reach them: the misery of industrial workers caused by grave economic inequality. Energized by grassroots Catholic social movements and the writings of Catholic scholars and activists, a lively intra-Church debate ensued over the "worker question."

In the 1891 encyclical *Rerum novarum*, Pope Leo XIII's support for a worker's right to a just wage, safe working conditions, Sunday rest, private property, and labor associations secured a measure of respect for democratic equality within the Church's official teaching on economic justice. This measure increased forty years later when Pope Pius XI's encyclical *Quadragesimo anno* suggested that worker participation be enhanced by contracts of partnership with employers, "for thus workers and executives become sharers in the ownership or management."[27] Even the role of democratic argumentation in the process of negotiating for economic justice was eventually validated in Pope John XXIII's 1961 commemoration of *Rerum novarum*:

> Catholics often come in contact with men who do not share their view of life. . . . in their conduct they should weigh the opinions of others with fitting courtesy and not measure everything in the light of their own interests. They should be prepared to join sincerely in doing whatever is naturally good or conducive to good.[28]

By this time, says Drew Christiansen, "correction of inequality becomes the key to the social strategy of the Church."[29]

Given the history of negative encounters between European Church leaders and democratic politics, an appreciation of the values and processes of political democracy would take more time. Though the American Church had flourished within the context of a democratic state, it took Europe's fascist nightmare and the tragedy of the Second World War for official Church teaching to begin a positive overture toward political democracy.

Grassroots Catholic movements and writings by Catholic intellectuals would pave the way. In this case, the rise of Christian Democratic parties and the work of scholars like Jacques Maritain were crucial. Pope Pius XII's 1944 Christmas message on "True and False Democracy" was an important step toward an official endorsement of political democracy, as was Pope John XXIII's encyclical *Pacem in terris*. These built toward the "epiphany of Vatican II" where, says Emile Perreau-Saussine, "a novel fusion between the Church and democracy" was born.[30]

From *Gaudium et spes*'s location of the Church in all people's "joys and hopes . . . griefs and anxieties," to the endorsement of religious freedom and the separation of Church and state in *Dignitatus humanae*, it was evident that the official Church finally perceived the suffering of political inequity and the dignity democracy recognizes. By the middle of the twentieth century, Church teaching endorsed not only the principles of religious freedom and the separation of Church and state but also free and fair elections, popular representation, rule of law, government accountability, and human rights to political participation, juridical protection, internal and external migration, assembly and association, freedom of information, and freedom of expression. These developments in Church teaching played an important part in the third wave of democratization, the world event that Peter Schraeder so ably analyzes in his chapter on democratic transitions and consolidation.

Since the Second Vatican Council, support for democracy in economics and politics has been secure in Catholic teaching. As Pope John Paul II stated in his 1991 encyclical *Centesimus annus*:

> The Church values the democratic system inasmuch as it ensures the participation of citizens in making political choices, guarantees to the governed the possibility of both electing and holding accountable those who govern them, and of replacing them through peaceful means when appropriate.[31]

At the same time, a concern surfaced in the writings of Pope John Paul II and Pope Benedict XVI over interpretations of democracy that view it as simply a technique for equal participation and not, in itself, the carrier of moral values central to human dignity. In Pope John Paul II's words, "nowadays there is a tendency to claim that agnosticism and skeptical relativism are the philosophy and the basic attitude which correspond to democratic forms of political life."[32] The offenders here seem to be procedural minimalists, political theorists claiming a "strong neutrality thesis" for democracy with respect to any moral values beyond procedural equity.[33] In her chapter on contemporary democracy in Lithuania, Nerija Putinaitė calls this phenomenon of moral relativism and antagonism a "national danger." Rather more optimistic on this issue, Brian Hehir remarks: "It would be a strange version of Catholicism that did not pursue a critical conversation with the culture of democracy."[34] In either case, this is a critical conversation within Catholicism over the interpretation of democracy, not over its intrinsic value. That question has been settled.

Dorothee Soelle once observed that "only those who themselves are suffering will work for the abolition of . . . suffering."[35] Frédéric Ozanam, founder of the Society of St. Vincent de Paul in 1833, understood this when he required that his volunteers go beyond simple almsgiving and build friendships with the poor through regular direct contact. This wisdom surfaced again in the concept of the "preferential option for the poor," called forth by the Latin American Church and the liberation theology movement and first adopted by official Catholic social teaching in Pope John Paul II's 1988 encyclical *Sollicitudo rei socialis*. The history of Catholicism and democracy validates this option. In addition to the impact of

Catholic movements and Catholic scholarship, official Church teaching now challenges Church leaders to make genuine efforts at placing themselves alongside the suffering and the poor in order to feel the experience of being treated as less than human in the economic and political structures of social life.

Nevertheless, the full implementation of this challenge remains unrealized. One can consider, again, the issue of racism in the United States. Official documents from the Vatican Pontifical Council for Justice and Peace and the United States Catholic Conference of Bishops have been issued that unequivocally declare: "racism is a sin." However, as Bryan Massingale points out with respect to the strongest of these statements (the US Catholic Conference statement of 1979, *Brothers and Sisters to Us*), "the publicity given this document was very limited."[36] Massingale also notes that the predominant approach in these documents is to address racism as a sinful action of individuals and not as a social-structural issue. "The church's teaching on racism," says Massingale, "is uninformed by current social science."[37] In short, Church social teaching on race suffers from a "pervasive paternalism," insufficient attention to "the nexus of race and cultural power," and "*lack of passion*."[38] In terms of the argument here, too few Church leaders have literally situated themselves alongside those suffering racial discrimination and prejudice.

A shared experience of suffering among Church leaders is likewise insufficiently in evidence when it comes to unjust treatment caused by the Church itself. The command model of Church organization can too easily accommodate actions of discrimination, non-participation, and suppression of human beings. In the 1980s, a detrimental, non-consultative Vatican intervention in the drafting of an American pastoral letter on women put an end to this much-needed discussion within the Catholic Church. In the 2000s, a non-disclosive, obstructionist response by Church officials to the clergy sexual abuse crisis permanently alienated thousands of people from the Catholic Church. Among the chapters in this volume, no one articulates the problem of non-consultation in the Church as clearly as Bren Ortega Murphy in her discussion of religious women in the United States. These and other examples call for a transition in the Church from a command hierarchy to what Terrence Nichols calls a "participatory hierarchy," a hierarchy containing democratic elements of "participation, inclusion, integration, and subsidiarity."[39]

Saffon and Urbinati note that democracy is "expansive by nature."[40] When people experience being treated equitably, they naturally seek a replication of the experience in all the structures and processes within which they live and work. A slow but erratic appreciation for this natural process is discernable within the Catholic Church. Paul Sigmund remarks that while "the Church itself has not become a democracy . . . it has, however, moved away from the nineteenth-century monarchical model to a mixture of forms of authority."[41] Hehir makes a similar observation: "It is clear that democracy is not the polity of Catholicism. . . . At the same time there is a spectrum of methods and modalities about how authority is to be exercised."[42] Schooyans goes a step further:

> Although the Church is not a democracy in the political sense of the term, it is a community of persons of equal dignity, sons and daughters of the same Father; and although the Church has a hierarchical structure, it can be accepted that people should participate in the choice of the person to be the repository of authority, and also provide input for his [*sic*] decisions.[43]

The organization of the Catholic Church will adopt democratic features when, as in economic and political life, a critical mass of official Church leaders come to perceive and feel the suffering a person experiences when treated as less than human within the Church. Of course, the affective experience of equality and inequality is necessary for people working in all institutions that function within democratic societies. Here is an area requiring more attention than is given in the volume overall—the importance of an *affective* appreciation for equality among citizens in a democracy and the Church's role in facilitating it.

The rich comparisons and contrasts given in the experiences of Lithuania, Indonesia, Peru, and the United States with democracy, culture, and Catholicism reveal a whole greater than the sum of each particular chapter. The whole that is sounded is the hope placed in democracy as a response to social suffering and the significance of equality to that hope. Certain pieces absent or too lightly broached are also significant to note, such as racism and discrimination, the effects of neoliberal economics, and the affectivity necessary for democratic equality. Yet the montage of pieces present and pieces absent is a rich one, making *Democracy, Culture, Catholicism: Voices from Four Continents* a truly instructive volume. The scholars who gave themselves to this group endeavor have reaped a rich reward.

NOTES

1. Aristotle, *The Metaphysics* (New York: Penguin Books, 1998), 248.
2. On "positional suffering," see Pierre Bourdieu, et al., *The Weight of the World: Social Suffering in Contemporary Society*, trans. Priscilla Parkhurst Ferguson, et al. (Stanford, CA: Stanford University Press, 1993), 4.

3. Robert A. Dahl, *On Democracy* (New Haven, CT: Yale University Press, 1998), 10.

4. Ivone Gebara, *Out of the Depths: Women's Experience of Evil and Salvation* (Minneapolis, MN: Fortress Press, 2002), 39.

5. Michel Schooyans, "Democracy in the Teaching of the Popes," in *Democracy in Debate: The Contribution of the Pontifical Academy of Social Sciences*, ed. Hans. F. Zacher (Vatican City: Pontifical Academy of the Social Sciences, 2005), 35.

6. Dahl, *On Democracy*, 37.

7. These and other forms of democracy are masterfully outlined in David Held's *Models of Democracy*, 3rd ed. (Stanford, CA: Stanford University Press, 2006).

8. For further discussion of equality as the basis of democracy, see Robert Dahl, *Polyarchy: Participation and Opposition* (New Haven, CT: Yale University Press, 1989). As Maria Paula Saffon and Nadia Urbinati have more recently argued, "liberty is made possible through equality in political rights." See Maria Paula Saffon and Nadia Urbinati, "Procedural Democracy: the Bulwark of Equal Liberty," *Political Theory* 41, no. 3 (2013): 444.

9. Saffon and Urbinati, "Procedural Democracy," 458.

10. Quoted in Hugo Villela G., "The Church and the Process of Democratization in Latin America," *Social Compass* 26, nos. 2–3 (1979): 274.

11. John Courtney Murray, SJ, *We Hold These Truths: Catholic Reflections on the American Proposition* (New York: Sheed and Ward, 1969), 7, 8. Maria Paula Saffon and Nadia Urbinati identify "conflict channeled through political institutions as a basic trait of democracy." See Saffon and Urbinati, "Procedural Democracy," 442. On the capacity of democracy to replace violence, see Adam Przeworski, "Minimalist Conception of Democracy: A Defense," in *Democracy's Value*, ed. Ian Schapiro and Casiano Hacker-Cordón (Cambridge: Cambridge University Press, 1999), 23.

12. Ronald Inglehart and Christian Welzel, *Modernization, Cultural Change, and Democracy: The Human Development Sequence* (Cambridge: Cambridge University Press, 2005), 2.

13. Franz-Xavier Kaufman, "Democracy Versus Values?," in *Democracy: Some Acute Questions*, Proceedings of the Fourth Plenary Session of the Pontifical Academy of Social Sciences, April 22–25, 1998 (Vatican City: Pontifical Academy of the Social Science, 1998), 120.

14. Mark Eggerman and Catherine Panter-Brick, "Suffering, Hope, and Entrapment: Resilience and Cultural Values in Afghanistan," *Social Science & Medicine* 71 (2010): 79.

15. John Davis, "The Anthropology of Suffering," *Journal of Refugee Studies* 5, no. 2 (1992): 155.

16. Paul Farmer, "An Anthropology of Structural Violence," *Current Anthropology* 45, no. 3 (2004): 305.

17. Ibid., 313.

18. Held, *Models of Democracy*, 223. According to Adam Przeworski, "political equality is effectively undermined by economic inequality." See Adam Przeworski, *Democracy and the Limits of Self-Government* (Cambridge: Cambridge University Press, 2010), 13.

19. Reinhard Bendix, *Max Weber: An Intellectual Portrait* (Garden City, NY: Doubleday, 1960), 437.

20. Anthony Giddons, *Emile Durkheim: Selected Writings* (Cambridge: Cambridge University Press, 1972), 123–40.

21. Alasdair MacIntyre, *After Virtue: A Study in Moral Theory* (Notre Dame, IN: University of Notre Dame Press, 1981), 191.

22. Farmer, "An Anthropology of Structural Violence," 308.

23. James Baldwin, "Down at the Cross: Letter from a Region of My Mind," in *James Baldwin* (Garden City, NY: Doubleday, 1988), 82.

24. Murray, *We Hold These Truths*, 6.

25. See, for example, Mary Jo Bane, "Democracy and Catholic Christianity in America," in *Christianity and American Democracy*, by Hugh Heclo, 147–65 (Cambridge, MA: Harvard University Press, 2007); Thomas Bokkenkotter, *Church and Revolution: Catholics in the Struggle for Democracy and Social Justice* (New York: Doubleday, 1998); Jay P. Corrin, *Catholic Intellectuals and the Challenge of Democracy* (Notre Dame, IN: University of Notre Dame Press, 2002); J. Bryan Hehir, "Catholicism and Democracy: Conflict, Change, and Collaboration," in *Christianity and Democracy in Global Context*, ed. John Witte, 15–30 (Boulder, CO: Westview Press, 1993); John Langan, SJ, "The Christmas Messages of Pius XII," in *Modern Catholic Social Teaching: Commentaries and Interpretations*, ed. Kenneth R. Himes, OFM, 175–90 (Washington, DC: Georgetown University Press, 2005); Marvin L. Krier Mich, *Catholic Social Teaching and Movements* (Mystic, CT: Twenty-Third Publications, 1998); Paul Misner, *Social Catholicism in Europe from the Onset of Industrialization to the First World War* (New York: Crossroad, 1991); Emile Perreau-Saussine, *Catholicism and Democracy: An Essay in the History of Political Thought*, trans. Richard Rex (Princeton, NJ: Princeton University Press, 2012); Michel Schooyans, "Democracy in the Teaching of the Popes,"; Paul E. Sigmund, "The Catholic Tradition and Modern Democracy," *Review of Politics* 49, no. 4 (1987): 530–48.

26. Ted G. Yelen and Clyde Wilcox, *Public Attitudes toward Church and State* (Armonk, NY: M. E. Sharpe, 1995), 3.

27. Pius XI, *Quadragesimo anno*, 65.

28. John XXIII, *Mater et magistra*, 239.

29. Drew Christiansen, SJ, "On Relative Equality: Catholic Egalitarianism after Vatican II," *Theological Studies* 45 (1984): 655.

30. Perreau-Saussine, *Catholicism and Democracy*, 140.

31. John Paul II, *Centesimus annus*, 46.

32. Ibid., 46, 47.

33. Robert Audi, "Moral Foundations of Liberal Democracy, Secular Reasons, and Liberal Neutrality toward the Good," *Notre Dame Journal of Law, Ethics & Public Policy* 19, no. 197 (2005): 210. Democratic theorists who took a procedural minimalist approach at different points in their careers include Joseph Schumpeter, John Rawls, and Jürgen Habermas. See Joseph A. Schumpeter, *Capitalism, Socialism and Democracy*, 3rd ed. (New York: Harper & Row, 1950), 242; John Rawls, *Political Liberalism* (New York: Columbia University Press, 1995); and Jürgen Habermas, *Between Facts and Norms: Contributions to a Discourse Theory of Law and Democracy*, trans. William Rehg (Cambridge, MA: MIT Press, 1996), chap. 7. On the Catholic debate over value and procedure in democracy, see Perreau-Saussine, *Catholicism and Democracy*, 132–46.

34. Hehir, "Catholicism and Democracy," 30.

35. Dorothee Soelle, *Suffering*, trans. Everett R. Kalin (Philadelphia: Fortress Press, 1975), 3.

36. Bryan N. Massingale, *Racial Justice and the Catholic Church* (Maryknoll, NY: Orbis Books, 2010), 67.

37. Ibid., 74.

38. Ibid., 75–77.

39. Terence L. Nichols, *That All May Be One: Hierarchy and Participation in the Church* (Collegeville, MN: Liturgical Press, 1997), 8.

40. Saffon and Urbinati, "Procedural Democracy," 458.

41. Sigmund, "The Catholic Tradition and Modern Democracy."

42. J. Bryan Hehir, "Catholicism and Democracy," 30.

43. Michel Schooyans, "Democracy in the Teaching of the Popes," 32.

ACKNOWLEDGMENTS

This book is the product of the three-year Democracy, Culture, and Catholicism International Research Project spearheaded by the Joan and Bill Hank Center for the Catholic Intellectual Heritage at Loyola University Chicago. The project received sustained encouragement and support from Loyola University Chicago's president, Reverend Michael J. Garanzini, SJ. Also vital to the development of the project was Patrick Boyle, Vice Provost of Academic Centers and Global Initiatives at Loyola University Chicago. We extend our deep thanks to Father Garanzini, Dr. Boyle, and their staff.

The thirty-one scholars who collaborated on this project from 2010 to 2013 met during a workshop at Loyola University Chicago in 2010. The next year, the scholars gathered for regional colloquia at Universitas Sanata Dharma in Yogyakarta, Indonesia; Vilnius University in Vilnius, Lithuania; and Universidad Antonio Ruiz de Montoya in Lima, Peru. The scholars met for a final time, in 2013, for a conference at the Pontificia Università Gregoriana in Rome, Italy. We offer our sincere gratitude to each of these wonderful scholars, all of whom stayed with the project from beginning to end. This book presents the work of twenty-two project members, each of whom benefited from the impressive scholarship of the entire group.

We express our gratitude to the presidents of each university, who offered warm welcomes and hospitality at our project's Chicago workshop, regional colloquia, and Rome conference. We also offer our sincere gratitude to the support staffs at each university, without whom this project would never have come to fruition: Katie O'Donnell (Loyola University Chicago), Dixta Menavia (Universitas Sanata Dharma), Father Vidmantas Šimkunas, SJ (Vilnius University), Isabel Lavado (Universidad Antonio Ruiz de Montoya), Monica Fucci (Pontificia Università Gregoriana), and Stefano del Bove, SJ, from the Society of Jesus.

We also wish to thank our benefactors, whose generosity enabled the project's success: Loyola University Chicago's Office of the President, Joan and Bill Hank, and the Helen V. Brach Foundation.

Finally, we thank Fredric Nachbaur and his staff at Fordham University Press for their interest in our unique project and their patient and professional assistance in the creation of this book.

JORGE ARAGÓN TRELLES is a research professor in the Political Science and Government, Faculty of Social Services, at the Pontificia Universidad Catolica del Peru.

ROBERT JOHN ARAUJO, SJ, is the John Courtney Murray, SJ, University Professor Emeritus, at the School of Law at Loyola University Chicago in Chicago, Illinois.

JOHN CROWLEY-BUCK is a Ph.D. candidate in the Department of Theology at Loyola University Chicago in Chicago, Illinois.

MARÍA SOLEDAD ESCALANTE BELTRÁN is the Director of Philosophy at the Universidad Antonio Ruiz de Montoya in Lima, Peru.

OSCAR A. ESPINOSA is a professor in the Department of Social Science, Anthropology Section, at the Pontificia Universidad Catolica del Peru.

DANUTĖ GAILIENĖ is a professor in the Department of Psychology at Vilnius University in Vilnius, Lithuania.

GONZALO GAMIO GEHRI is a professor in the Department of Philosophy at the Universidad Antonio Ruiz de Montoya in Lima, Peru.

MARCIA HERMANSEN is a professor in the Department of Theology at Loyola University Chicago in Chicago, Illinois.

DAVID INGRAM is a professor in the Department of Philosophy at Loyola University Chicago in Chicago, Illinois.

JEFFREY KLAIBER, SJ, was a professor in the Department of Education at the Universidad Antonio Ruiz de Montoya in Lima, Peru.

BREN ORTEGA MURPHY is a professor of women's studies and gender studies in the School of Communication at Loyola University Chicago in Chicago, Illinois.

WILLIAM R. O'NEILL, SJ, as an associate professor at the Jesuit School of Theology of Santa Clara University in Berkeley, California.

DAVID M. POSNER is an associate professor in the Department of Modern Language and Literature at Loyola University Chicago in Chicago, Illinois.

RUSSELL POWELL is a professor in the School of Law at Seattle University in Seattle, Washington.

PAULUS WIRYONO PRIYOTAMTAMA, SJ, is a professor at the Universitas Sanata Dharma in Yogyakarta, Indonesia.

NERIJA PUTINAITĖ is an associate professor in the Institute of International Relations and Political Science at Vilnius University in Vilnius, Lithuania.

PETER J. SCHRAEDER is the chair of the Department of Political Science at Loyola University Chicago in Chicago, Illinois.

MICHAEL J. SCHUCK is the codirector of the International Jesuit Ecology Project and an associate professor in the Department of Theology at Loyola University Chicago in Chicago, Illinois.

VIDMANTAS ŠAKIMKUNAS, SJ, is the director of the Pastoral Center of Academic Study at the Archdiocese of Vilnius in Vilnius, Lithuania.

ARŪNAS STREIKUS is an associate professor in the Department of History at Vilnius University in Vilnius, Lithuania.

BARRY SULLIVAN holds the Cooney & Conway Chair in Advocacy at the School of Law at Loyola University Chicago in Chicago, Illinois.

ALBERTUS BUDI SUSANTO, SJ, is the director of the Realino Institute of Studies at the Universitas Sanata Dharma in Yogyakarta, Indonesia.

BASKARA WARDAYA, SJ, is a professor at the Center for History and Political Ethics at the Universitas Sanata Dharma in Yogyakarta, Indonesia.

FRANCISCA NINIK YUDIANTI is the university vice-rector at Universitas Sanata Dharma in Yogyakarta, Indonesia.

Project Contributors

NOVITA DEWI is a professor in the graduate program in English language studies at the Universitas Sanata Dharma in Yogyakarta, Indonesia.

JUAN CARLOS DÍAZ LARA is an instructor in the Department of Humanities at the Institute of Faith and Culture at the Universidad Antonio Ruiz de Montoya in Lima, Peru.

JAMES GARBARINO holds the Maude C. Clarke Chair in Humanistic Psychology in the Department of Psychology at Loyola University Chicago in Chicago, Illinois.

CHRISTINA SIWI HANDAYANI was a professor of psychology at the Universitas Sanata Dharma in Yogyakarta, Indonesia.

ELIZABETH JONES HEMENWAY is a senior lecturer in the Department of History and is the director of the women's studies and gender studies program at Loyola University Chicago in Chicago, Illinois.

CHRISTINE FIRER HINZE is the director of the Curran Center for American Catholic Studies and professor in the Department of Theology at Fordham University in Bronx, New York.

KĘSTUTIS KĖVALAS is the vice dean of the Department of Catholic Theology at Vytautas Magnus University in Kaunas, Lithuania.

JULIA PRYCE is an assistant professor in the School of Social Work at Loyola University Chicago in Chicago, Illinois.

GÜNEŞ MURAT TEZCÜR is an associate professor in the Department of Political Science at Loyola University Chicago in Chicago, Illinois.

INDEX